DEFENDER OF THE FAITH

DEFENDER OF THE FAITH

William Jennings Bryan:
The Last Decade,

1915–1925

LAWRENCE W. LEVINE

Harvard University Press
Cambridge, Massachusetts
London, England
1987

Copyright © 1965 by Lawrence W. Levine
All rights reserved
Printed in the United States of America.
10 9 8 7 6 5 4 3 2 1

LIBRARY OF CONGRESS CATALOGING IN PUBLICATION DATA

Levine, Lawrence W.
  Defender of the faith.

  Reprint. Originally published: New York : Oxford University
Press, 1965.
  Bibliography: p.
  Includes index.
  1. Bryan, William Jennings, 1860–1925. 2. Statesmen — United
States — Biography. 3. Presidential candidates — United
States — Biography. 4. Populism — United States — History.
5. United States — Politics and government — 1865–1933. I. Title.
E664.B87L4 1987   973.91'092'4   86-25679
ISBN 0-674-19542-6

For my parents

ABRAHAM AND ANNE LEVINE

Acknowledgments

I AM GRATEFUL to the staffs of the libraries in which this study was researched for the many kindnesses they extended to me. I particularly want to thank the personnel of the Manuscripts Division of the Library of Congress where the Bryan Papers are housed. Grants from Princeton University and the Institute of Social Sciences of the University of California aided in the financing of travel and typing costs.

The necessary loneliness of historical research and writing was broken by the aid and encouragement of a number of friends and colleagues who can receive only the barest acknowledgment here. Richard Abrams, Robert Dallek, Betty Glad, and Yonathan Shapiro read various versions of this manuscript and contributed many helpful criticisms and suggestions. Robert Middlekauff took time from his own research to give the final draft a meticulous reading and searching criticism from which it has profited in every way. Sheldon Meyer of Oxford University Press guided this manuscript into print with great patience and critical understanding. I am especially indebted to two of my teachers. William E. Leuchtenburg read a very early version of the manuscript and suggested several important improvements, but the intellectual stimulation and warm support he has provided at every stage of my career go far beyond this specific project. Richard Hofstadter, who first suggested that I explore Bryan's final years, has been an unending source of wise counsel and friendly encouragement. I have benefited more than I can say from the example of his scholarship and his willingness to see his students go their own way. Finally, the nature and depth of my gratitude to my wife Cornelia are best understood by her alone.

Preface

IT IS DOUBTFUL that William Jennings Bryan, who always maintained that a man must be judged by his life as a whole and not by any one part of it, would have approved of a study which concentrated exclusively upon the years between his resignation from Woodrow Wilson's Cabinet in June 1915 and his death in Dayton, Tennessee, in July 1925. Yet such a study has long been needed, for the fact is that Bryan *has* been judged by just these years. The image of Bryan which has prevailed since his death was fashioned by Clarence Darrow in the Dayton courtroom and given voice by H. L. Mencken in his famous eulogy: "He came into life a hero, a Galahad, in bright and shining armor. He was passing out a poor mountebank." "A radical all his life," wrote one of Bryan's biographers, following Mencken's lead, "William Jennings Bryan was to end his days an ultra conservative." It was this very image that first led me to undertake this inquiry in the hope of discovering what had transformed Bryan from a crusader for social and economic reform to a champion of anachronistic rural evangelism, cheap moralistic panaceas, and Florida real estate.

As is perhaps too often the case in modern historical research, I have ended by turning a basically simple picture into a far more complex one; by finding indeed that the very transformation I had set out to understand never really took place. In William Jennings Bryan, reform and reaction lived happily, if somewhat incongruously, side by side. The Bryan of the 1920's was essentially the Bryan of the 1890's: older in years but no less vigorous, no less optimistic, no less certain.

vii

His goals remained the same, and if he added a new dimension to his methods they too failed to undergo any radical alteration. The problem, then, becomes one of understanding not why Bryan did change, but why he did not—why he was incapable of change in a world which demanded it, why he was able to continue his fight for social and economic betterment, even while he closed his eyes to the evils of the Ku Klux Klan and conducted a crusade to banish the theory of evolution from the classroom, and why he was able to retain his hold upon many of those who had followed him throughout the Progressive Era.

One or two friends who have read this study in manuscript have been a bit troubled by my failure to inject a sense of moral outrage into my writing, to take Bryan to task more frequently for his violations of what they—and I—consider to be the tenets of liberalism. I have not done so for a number of reasons. Many of the biographies and studies of Bryan have been written in just such a tone; have been written, in fact, almost in the form of a dialogue between Bryan and his contemporary critic, with Bryan, of course, invariably coming out second best. This is a tempting way to write history but not a particularly enlightening one. Bryan, especially in the latter stages of his career, has been too often judged and too little understood. The desire to understand him and those he spoke for is the spirit that I hope informs every page of this volume. This is not to maintain that there are no judgments in this work; there are. I am not naïve enough to think that I could divest myself completely of my own age and my own beliefs, and these come through again and again. But I have striven to keep them subordinate to the basic purpose of this study which, to repeat myself, is not judgment but comprehension.

I should say something more about my approach. I have written what amounts to a public life of Bryan. I have been forced to do so both because of the nature of the materials at my disposal and the nature of the man about whom I was writing. There is very little of a personal nature relating to Bryan in his own papers or in the papers of his closest contemporaries. This is so not because Bryan was especially secretive. Even had the Bryan Papers been preserved in their entirety, I doubt that they would have revealed much of a personal nature. Bryan almost totally lacked any introspective quality; he never questioned his own actions, he never sought to know his deepest motives, he never agonized about the "real" meaning of things. The public Bryan, I am convinced, was the only Bryan there was. "The wonderful thing about Mr. Bryan," his secretary has written, "was that what he said in the intimacy of his household was the same as his expressions of belief to the public. There was no difference between his public and private utterances." There was no difference because Bryan was psychologically incapable of having a private life in any meaningful sense. "My obligation," Bryan wrote in 1920, "is to the mass, not to individuals." This sense of obligation conditioned almost all of his actions; actions which no individual, not even his wife, was capable of altering.

Although this is primarily a biographical work it is also something more. When one individual has the influence upon others that Bryan had, his life has more than a purely biographical significance. As the debate over the fate of progressivism in post-World War I America continues, detailed studies of the later careers of American progressives become all the more important. If Bryan remained as accurate a spokesman for the fears and aspirations of his rural followers as I believe he did, then a sharper understanding of the forces operating upon him and the nature of his response to them should be a step forward in unraveling the enigma of the rural West and South in the years after 1918.

L. W. L.

Berkeley, Calif.
September 1964

Contents

DEFENDER OF THE FAITH

I: The Armor of a Righteous Cause

*When God tells a man to speak he cannot stop to count those
who stand with him. He must speak even though he cries in the
wilderness; he must stand up even if he has to stand alone.*
— WJB

(1)

ON TUESDAY MORNING, June 8, 1915, Secretary of State William Jennings Bryan attended his last Cabinet meeting. The day before, after weeks of anxiety, Bryan had submitted his resignation to the President rather than sign the second *Lusitania* note to Germany.[1] The distress which the 55-year-old Nebraskan had experienced in arriving at his decision was apparent to his colleagues. Secretary of Agriculture David F. Houston recalled that Bryan, "looking exhausted and appearing to be under a great emotional strain, leaned back in his chair with his eyes closed" until the meeting had terminated.[2] Bryan then rose and invited his fellow Cabinet members to join him for lunch.

Seated in the dining room of the University Club, Bryan turned to the six officials who had accepted his invitation [3] and

1. WJB to Woodrow Wilson, June 8, 1915, Woodrow Wilson Papers (Library of Congress, Washington, D.C.), File II, Box 82. Cited hereafter as Wilson Papers. Bryan had actually composed and submitted his letter of resignation on June 7, but dated it to take effect the following day. See Grace Bryan Hargreaves MSS., William Jennings Bryan Papers (Library of Congress, Washington, D.C.). Cited hereafter as Bryan Papers.

2. David F. Houston, *Eight Years with Wilson's Cabinet* (Garden City, New York, 1926), II, 141.

3. The Cabinet officers who attended the luncheon were Secretary of the Navy Josephus Daniels, Secretary of the Interior Franklin K.

attempted to explain his resignation. Reviewing his differences
with the President, Bryan said emphatically:

> I have had to take the course I have chosen. . . . I cannot go
> along with him [Wilson] in this note. I think it makes for war.
> I believe that I can do more on the outside to prevent war than
> I can do on the inside. I can work to control popular opinion
> so that it will not exert pressure for extreme action which the
> President does not want. We both want the same thing, Peace.[4]

Bryan's desire to aid in bringing about an era of permanent,
universal peace was one of the things which had made Wilson's offer of the secretaryship of State so attractive. Bryan
had never looked upon his appointment to the most important
position in Wilson's cabinet as a mere reward for his past
services to the Democracy and a recognition of his continuing
political power, though, in fact, these had been the primary
reasons.[5] Rather, he viewed his new post as a vehicle for the
implementation of his ideals on an international plane. Two
days before assuming office Bryan told an audience at Ra-
leigh, North Carolina, that it was "the imperative duty of the
United States . . . to set a shining example of disarmament."
After his speech, he turned to his old friend Josephus Daniels,
who was to sit beside him in the Cabinet as Secretary of the
Navy, and told him: "There will be no war while I am Secretary of State." [6]

Lane, Postmaster General Albert S. Burleson, Secretary of War
Lindley M. Garrison, Secretary of Labor William B. Wilson, and
Secretary of Agriculture David F. Houston. Ibid.

4. Ibid. II, 146.

5. On this point see Albert S. Burleson to David F. Houston, February 6, 1926, Ray Stannard Baker Papers (Library of Congress, Washington, D.C.), Box 3. Cited hereafter as R. S. Baker Papers. See also
Arthur S. Link, *Woodrow Wilson and the Progressive Era, 1910–
1917* (New York, 1954), p. 26.

6. Jonathan Daniels, *The End of Innocence* (New York, 1954), p.
49; Josephus Daniels, *The Wilson Era: Years of Peace, 1910–1917*
(Chapel Hill, 1944), p. 428.

(2)

The dreams of peace enunciated by Bryan in 1913 were no new thing with him. When still a boy of nineteen, he had written his cousin Thomas Marshall of Salem, Illinois:

> The sound of glittering steel and the gory field of battle have no claims for me! . . . Tom, do you know that the time is swiftly passing by when armies rule? The dawn of a better day is at hand. Right is beginning to rule in the place of might. I rejoice that in a few years it will not be necessary to shoot a man to convince him that you are right and to blot out a nation to prove to them that their principles are false.[7]

The dawn of that "better day," however, was still not at hand in 1898 when the United States took up arms against Spain, and a now nationally prominent William Jennings Bryan did not as yet see fit to raise his voice in behalf of peace. Rather, he supported his country's every move, even to the point of eagerly serving in its army as a colonel. His service took him no farther than the malarial coast of northeastern Florida, and at best he proved to have little aptitude for military life.[8]

His brief military career and his subsequent campaign against imperialism, however, seem to have solidified and strengthened his early pacific sentiments, for in his speech accepting the Democratic Presidential nomination in 1900 he spoke of the United States as "a republic standing erect while empires all around are bowed beneath the weight of their own armaments . . . a republic gradually but surely becoming the supreme moral factor in the world's progress and the

7. WJB to Thomas Marshall, December 8, 1879, WJB and Mary Baird Bryan, *The Memoirs of William Jennings Bryan* (Philadelphia, 1925), p. 383. Cited hereafter as *Memoirs*.
8. J. R. Johnson, "William Jennings Bryan, The Soldier," *Nebraska History*, XXXI (June 1950), 100 ff.

accepted arbiter of the world's disputes." [9] In 1905, during the Russo-Japanese War, these words received concrete formulation in Bryan's proposed peace treaty plan which provided for the submission of *all* international disputes of *every* kind and character to a permanent tribunal for investigation; for a year's time for the investigation to take place "during which time there should be no resort to hostilities"; and for the right of the parties involved to take independent action once the investigation was concluded.[10] For the next six years Bryan championed this treaty plan both in America and in Europe, and the plan was approved by the Interparliamentary Union in London in 1906, by the International Peace Conference in New York in 1908, by Prime Minister Sir Henry Campbell-Bannerman of Great Britain, and by President Taft, who incorporated part of it in his treaties with Great Britain and France which died in Congress.[11]

When President-elect Wilson called Bryan to Trenton to offer him the secretaryship of State, the latter spoke of his desire to make his peace plan a reality and received Wilson's "hearty approval." [12] Thus it was that Bryan knew exactly where he was going when he took over the reins of the State Department in March 1913. His treaty plan had received the blessings of both the President and the Senate Committee on Foreign Relations, and he soon began to secure the approval of one foreign nation after another. The outbreak of war in Europe only served to deepen his belief in the need for his treaties and he became even more enthusiastic in his efforts to secure the endorsement of all nations. On September 15, 1914, more than a month after the war began, his treaties were

9. *Memoirs*, p. 501.
10. *The Commoner*, February 17, 1905, p. 1, February 24, 1905, p. 1.
11. *Memoirs*, p. 385.
12. WJB to Harry Walker, January 20, 1915, Bryan Papers; *Memoirs*, p. 386.

signed by Great Britain, France, Spain, and China. By 1915, Bryan had negotiated thirty treaties. Every major nation had signed with the exceptions of Germany, Austria-Hungary, and Japan.[13]

"None of his work gave him more pleasure than his peace treaties which he regarded as his greatest constructive effort," wrote Mrs. Bryan in later years.[14] Had there not been a war raging in Europe, these would have been happy and fruitful years for Bryan. While the war may have diminished the joy Bryan experienced in witnessing the favorable reception accorded his peace treaties, it did not kill his vision of inaugurating an era of peace and brotherhood. No event, regardless of its nature, was capable of casting Bryan into anything more serious than a momentary mood of despair. His own brand of fundamentalist religiosity, his imperishable faith in the reason and goodness of his fellow man, and his belief in the divinely ordained nature of his own and his nation's destiny, combined to make him almost compulsively optimistic, a characteristic which is extremely important in understanding his final years.

It is true that to Bryan the war always remained a "cosmic nightmare," a relic of the pre-Christian era which civilized men should shun. Nevertheless, he was also able to convert it into a supreme opportunity, for if men had looked favorably upon his work for peace before they were suffering the agonies of a prolonged war, how much more amenable they would be now, and how much more essential his efforts for peace had become. While the complexities of working for peace in the midst of international carnage often depressed his colleagues, Bryan remained resolutely sanguine. Like Mr.

13. Ibid.; James Brown Scott, "Treaties for the Advancement of Peace," *The Commoner*, August 1919, p. 7.

14. *Memoirs*, p. 383. Toward the close of his life, Bryan wrote: "I think it is possible my treaty plan may prove to be the most important thing I have contributed." WJB to Mrs. Etta Root Edwards, July 21, 1923, Bryan Papers.

Dooley's constitutional lawyer, Bryan had the knack of seeing a triumphal archway where others could see only a stone wall. Perhaps no other Secretary of State has worked more diligently and more devotedly for peace than this ex-colonel of the Third Nebraska Volunteer Infantry. Certainly none of his predecessors were more cruelly disappointed or bitterly thwarted in their aims.

(3)

From the moment the war began, Bryan wrote note after note to the President, his fellow Cabinet members, Ambassador Walter Page in London, Colonel Edward House, and to the heads of the belligerent powers themselves, proposing schemes, offering solutions, asking, pleading, cajoling, all in the name of peace. He devised plan after plan and received rebuff after rebuff. Yet constant defeat only seemed to feed his enthusiasm and determination. The war was still young when Bryan wrote the President:

The European war distresses me. . . . I cannot but feel that this nation, being the nation on friendly terms with all, should urge mediation, since none of the nations engaged are willing to take the initiative. The responsibility for continuing the war is just as grave as the responsibility for beginning it, and this responsibility, if pressed upon the consideration of the belligerent nations might lead them to consent to mediation — no nation can afford to refuse. . . . The world looks to us to lead the way. . . . It is not likely that either side can win so complete a victory as to dictate terms, and if either side does win such a victory it will probably mean preparation for another war. It would seem better to look for a more rational basis of peace. . . . my suggestion is that you earnestly appeal to them to meet together and exchange views as to terms upon which permanent peace can be insured . . . there is reason to believe that such an offer would not be refused. . . . Even if it fails — and that cannot be known until the offer is made —

you would have the consciousness of having made the attempt.[15]

Despite Wilson's refusal to act, Bryan persisted in his pleas for mediation.[16] Shortly before his resignation he was still urging Wilson to make an "appeal to the nations at war to consider terms of peace." In a tone which suggests that he was now even more firmly convinced of the righteousness of his proposals than he had been seven months earlier, he wrote:

I submit that it is this nation's duty to make, not a secret but a public appeal for the acceptance of mediation. . . . Our own interests justify it — we may be drawn into the conflict if it continues. Our obligation to the neutral nations demands it. Our friendship to the nations at war requires it. . . . As the well-wisher of all we should act; as the leader in peace propaganda we should act; as the greatest Christian nation we should act — we cannot avoid the responsibility. . . . You have such an opportunity as has not come to any man before. I most earnestly urge you to make the appeal.[17]

Wilson responded by assuring Bryan that he had studied his proposal carefully, but that the moment simply was not propitious. "To insist now would be futile and would probably be offensive. We would lose such influence as we have for peace." [18]

(4)

Although Bryan was disappointed at Wilson's reluctance to breathe life into his arbitration proposals, his resignation from the Wilson Administration came not over this issue so much

15. WJB to Wilson, September 9, 1914, *Memoirs*, pp. 388–92.
16. See WJB to Wilson, December 1, 1914, Bryan-Wilson Correspondence (National Archives, Washington, D.C.), Vol. II; WJB to Wilson, April 19, 1915, April 23, 1915, Bryan Papers.
17. WJB to Wilson, April 23, 1915, ibid.
18. Wilson to WJB, April 28, 1915, R. S. Baker Papers, Box 3.

as over the question of neutrality — a question made more complex by Germany's use of the submarine.

From the very onset of the war Bryan was determined that the United States would take an absolutely neutral stand no matter how great the difficulties. He persuaded Wilson to place a ban on loans by American bankers to the belligerent governments, a step which outraged the Allies until it was revoked; and he refused to support an embargo on the export of American munitions, a step which, he insisted, would have favored the Central Powers.[19] When American vessels were stopped and searched, their cargoes seized and their mail tampered with by the British Navy, Bryan and Wilson protested; but their protests, which at no time were as strong as Bryan would have liked, were largely negated by the pro-British sentiments of our ambassador to Great Britain, Walter Hines Page. On one occasion Page went to the British Foreign Office to deliver a long dispatch from Washington protesting British interference with contraband going to neutral ports. After reading the communication to the Foreign Secretary, Sir Edward Grey, Page said: "I have now read the dispatch but I do not agree with it; let us consider how it should be answered." [20] Page's pro-Allied sentiments were not unique; they extended to many members of official Washington including Colonel House, Counselor Robert Lansing — Bryan's chief adviser in the State Department — most of the members of Wilson's Cabinet, and, to a lesser extent, the President himself.[21] By the spring of 1915, Bryan was one of the few

19. Ray Stannard Baker, *Woodrow Wilson, Life and Letters* (Garden City, New York, 1927–39), V, 175, 187; WJB to William J. Stone, January 20, 1915, quoted in Robert Lansing, *War Memoirs of Robert Lansing* (Indianapolis, 1935), p. 54.

20. Edward Grey, *Twenty-five Years, 1892–1916* (New York, 1925), II, 110.

21. Ibid. II, 124–5; Robert Lansing Diaries (Library of Congress, Washington, D.C.), see entries for 1915. Cited hereafter as Lansing

members of the Administration who still adhered to Wilson's original request that Americans remain impartial "in thought as well as in action." [22]

Although the nation as a whole was to maintain its determination to stay out of the war until the very eve of America's entry, the inception of the submarine controversy with Germany served the purpose not only of turning many Americans into supporters of the Allied cause, but also of revealing where the sympathies of many Americans had been all along. On March 28, 1915, the British liner *Falaba* was torpedoed, causing the death of 104 passengers, including one American. "Piracy," "Barbarism run mad," "Shocking bloodthirstiness," "A crime against humanity," were merely a few of the epithets with which an outraged Northeastern press assailed the Imperial German Government.[23] For Bryan this incident inaugurated a period of anguish and uncertainty which was not to end until his resignation. The torpedoing of the *Lusitania* on May 7, 1915, with the loss of more than a hundred American lives, deepened the country's horror and made the thin line between peace and war thinner still.

Bryan was quick to direct Wilson's attention to the fact that both vessels had carried munitions as well as passengers, and thus the Americans on board had been taking unnecessary risks. "Germany has a right to prevent contraband going to the Allies," he wrote Wilson, "and a ship carrying contraband should not rely upon passengers to protect herself from attack

Diaries. Ray Stannard Baker interview with William B. Wilson, January 12–13, 1928, in which Secretary Wilson said that with the exception of Bryan, all the members of the Cabinet sympathized with the Allies. R. S. Baker Papers, Box 58; Arthur S. Link, *Wilson the Diplomatist* (Baltimore, 1957), p. 35.

22. Wilson had made this request on August 18, 1914. See Arthur S. Link, *Wilson: The Struggle for Neutrality, 1914–1915* (Princeton, 1960), pp. 65–6.

23. Walter Millis, *Road to War, America: 1914–1917* (Boston, 1935), p. 146.

—it would be like putting women and children in front of an army." In addition, he reminded his chief of the many violations of American neutrality which England had committed in her attempt to cut Germany off from all outside supplies. "Why be shocked at the drowning of a few people," he asked Wilson after the *Falaba* tragedy, "if there is no objection to the starving of a nation?" [24]

The Chief Executive's position was clearly not an enviable one. On one side he was being assailed by ex-President Roosevelt and his small but vocal band of interventionists as "the popular pacifist hero" who had the support of the "professional pacifists, the flubdubs and the mollycoddles." Wilson's supporters, Roosevelt raged, included "Every soft creature, every coward and weakling, every man who can't look more than six inches ahead, every man whose god is money, or pleasure, or ease . . ." [25] On the other side, he was being urged by his Secretary of State, by a number of newspapers, especially in the West, and by such influential citizens as William Allen White, to exercise caution and moderation, to be patient and understanding. [26] In the end he determined upon following a middle course; a course that still veered too much to one side, in Bryan's opinion.

The first *Lusitania* note, composed by Wilson, was far from a warlike message, yet it had an air of finality about it which troubled Bryan. The note, he complained to Wilson, might be misconstrued by Germany as an unfriendly act since it was

24. WJB to Wilson, May 9, 1915, April 19, 1915, Bryan Papers.

25. Mark Sullivan, *Our Times* (New York, 1926-35), V, 206; Theodore Roosevelt to Archibald Bulloch Roosevelt, May 19, 1915, Elting E. Morison, ed., *The Letters of Theodore Roosevelt* (Cambridge, 1954), VIII, 922.

26. See, for example, the *Nebraska State Journal*, May 8, 1915; see also William Allen White to Woodrow Wilson, May 1915, Walter Johnson, ed., *Selected Letters of William Allen White, 1899-1943* (New York, 1947), p. 161.

not accompanied by a simultaneous protest to England against her flagrant and numerous violations of American neutrality, and also because it failed to conclude with a reiteration of our friendship. "I cannot bring myself to the belief," he wrote, "that it is wise to relinquish the hope of playing the part of a friend to both sides in the role of peacemaker and this note will, I fear, result in such relinquishment." Still Bryan signed it, but "with a heavy heart," and only because he convinced himself that it was merely "the opening statement of our position and simply called for a similar statement on the part of Germany." [27]

These were hard days for Bryan. It seemed to him that he was carrying the whole burden of peace on his own shoulders. The tension within the inner circles of the Administration increased so markedly that at one point he openly accused his fellow Cabinet members of being pro-Ally. After one such meeting, he came home "with bloodshot eyes and weary steps," and exclaimed to his wife: "Mary, what does the President mean! *Why* can't he see that by keeping open the way for mediation and arbitration, he has the opportunity to do the greatest work man can do! I cannot understand his attitude." [28]

When Germany's reply to the first American note proved to be equivocal, Wilson and his advisers, after lengthy deliberations, decided to send a second note along the same lines. Bryan, tired but still hopeful, tried for the last time to dissuade them. Again he pleaded for arbitration; again he asked that Americans be prevented from traveling on belligerent vessels carrying contraband; again he urged sending a simulta-

27. WJB to Wilson, May 12, 1915, Bryan Papers; WJB to Wilson, May 13, 1915, Bryan–Wilson Correspondence (National Archives), Vol. IV; *Memoirs*, p. 421.
28. Houston, *Eight Years with Wilson's Cabinet*, I, 137; *Memoirs*, pp. 420–21.

neous protest to Great Britain for her infractions of our neutrality; and again he was rebuffed.[29] On June 5, Wilson wrote his Secretary of State: "I hope that you realize how hard it goes with me to differ with you in judgment about such grave matters as we are now handling. You always have such a weight of reason, as well as such high motives, behind what you urge that it is with deep misgiving that I turn from what you press upon me." [30]

The day before, Bryan had informed Wilson of an interview he had with Congressional leaders who assured him that both houses of Congress were vehemently opposed to war, and he now warned the President that "the sober judgment of the people will not sustain any word or act that provokes war . . . they will do all in their power to prevent war, and I fully share their desire and purpose in this respect." [31] His path was still to be one of strict neutrality and peace, and rather than abandon it he was prepared to leave the Cabinet.

(5)

Although Bryan had more than once intimated to the President that he would resign rather than sign the second *Lusitania* note, his final decision was first made known to Wilson's son-in-law, Secretary of the Treasury William G. McAdoo, on June 5. Appalled at what such a step would mean to the country as well as to the Democratic party, McAdoo tried to alter Bryan's determination, but succeeded only in helping Mrs. Bryan persuade her husband to go away for a few days to give the

29. WJB to Wilson, June 2, 1915, June 3, 1915, Bryan-Wilson Correspondence (National Archives), Vol. IV; WJB to Wilson, June 5, 1915, Bryan Papers.
30. Wilson to WJB, June 5, 1915, ibid.
31. WJB to Wilson, June 4, 1915, Bryan-Wilson Correspondence (National Archives), Vol. IV; WJB to Wilson, June 5, 1915, Bryan Papers.

matter more careful thought.[32] After a sleepless weekend at the home of Senator Blair Lee in the suburb of Silver Spring, Bryan returned to Washington with his decision unaltered. Again McAdoo appealed to him, saying that if the second *Lusitania* note did not lead to war, as he maintained, it would put him in a ridiculous position; it would, in fact, ruin him. "I don't want you to destroy yourself," he said with feeling. After a moment of reflection, Bryan answered fatalistically: "I believe you are right; I think this will destroy me; but whether it does or not, I must do my duty according to my conscience."[33]

That same day, Monday, June 7, at noon, Bryan went to the White House and made one last attempt to convince Wilson that the course he was pursuing would lead to war. "It will be Germany's turn to make the next move," he had told his wife a day or two before. "If it were our turn, I could trust the President to find a way out. It is virtually placing the power to declare war in the hands of another nation." Wilson, though he did try to persuade Bryan to remain in the Cabinet, proved adamant on the question of the note to Germany.[34] When Bryan returned home, his daughter reports that he was on the verge of a complete physical collapse: "His face was flushed as in a high fever, his eyes clearly showed the great emotional agony he was enduring, and his gait was that of a person suffering from a great weakness." Lying on a sofa, he told his wife and daughter: "We have come to the parting of the ways. The President does not seem to realize that a great part of America lies on the other side of the Allegheny Mountains. These people have a right to be considered. I would not be true to the trust that thousands of Americans have imposed in me if I joined in any action that might lead to

32. *Memoirs*, pp. 422–3.
33. William G. McAdoo, *Crowded Years* (Boston, 1931), pp. 335–6.
34. *Memoirs*, pp. 422–4; Baker, *Woodrow Wilson*, V, 356.

the loss of life and property. . . . By resigning I will be free to assist them in their struggle against entering this heart-breaking conflict on either side." [35]

That afternoon, in a note remarkably free of rancor or bitterness, Bryan informed the President, "with sincere regret," of his decision to sever "the intimate and pleasant relations which have existed between us during the past two years."

> Obedient to your sense of duty and actuated by the highest motives, you have prepared for transmission to the German Government a note in which I cannot join without violating what I deem to be an obligation to my country, and the issue involved is of such moment that to remain a member of the Cabinet would be as unfair to you as it would be to the cause which is nearest my heart, namely, the prevention of war. . . .[36]

Wilson replied in kind:

> I accept your resignation only because you insist upon its acceptance; and I accept it with much more than deep regret, with a feeling of personal sorrow.
> . . . I yield to your desire only because I must and wish to bid you Godspeed in the parting. We shall continue to work for the same causes even when we do not work in the same way.[37]

35. Grace Bryan Hargreaves MSS., Bryan Papers. According to Bryan's daughter, his decision to resign deeply affected Mrs. Bryan. "Anticipating the storm of abuse which was sure to follow the announcement of father's resignation, together with the loss of position as hostess of the diplomatic corps, which had meant so much to her, completely destroyed my mother's composure. Quietly leaving the dinner table she went to her room and locking herself in she refused admittance to everyone. For the only time in her life she gave way to loud hysterical sobbing."
36. WJB to Wilson, June 8, 1915, Wilson Papers, File II, Box 82.
37. Wilson to WJB, June 8, 1915, ibid. Box 491.

Josephus Daniels visited Bryan on the morning of June 8, the day his resignation went into effect, and found him "gray with sleepless worry." "Although I have known him as a brother for nearly forty years," Daniels has recorded, "I have never seen him as deeply moved over anything as he was over his resignation." [38] As we have seen, Bryan's emotional strain persisted during the Cabinet meeting and luncheon that followed. When he had finished explaining the reasons for his resignation to the six Cabinet members who had attended the University Club luncheon, Bryan's eyes — and the eyes of several of his associates — were "dimmed with tears." [39] After a pause, Secretary Lane turned to Bryan and said with emotion: "You are the most real Christian I know." To which Bryan, now visibly struggling to retain his composure, responded: "I go out into the dark. The President has the Prestige and the Power on his side." Then, breaking down completely, he added: "I have many friends who would die for me." [40]

(6)

"The wilderness is becoming populated," gloated Walter Hines Page two days after Bryan's departure from the State Department. Bryan, the rejoicing Ambassador wrote, had now taken his place "in the Bad Lands of dead men who don't know they are dead. They talked themselves into greatness and, not knowing when to stop, also talked themselves out of it." [41]

Bryan's staunchest supporters would have found it difficult to curb Page's joy in those first days after the resignation. Even Secretary McAdoo, who had strongly cautioned Bryan

38. "Behind the Scenes with William Jennings Bryan," Daniels Papers.

39. Josephus Daniels, *The Wilson Era: Years of Peace*, p. 432.

40. Houston, *Eight Years with Wilson's Cabinet*, I, 146.

41. Page to Edward House, June 10, 1915, Charles Seymour, ed., *The Intimate Papers of Colonel House* (Boston, 1926–28), II, 9.

against taking the step, was surprised at "the hurricane of abuse" that howled around the ex-Secretary. "Unspeakable treachery, not only to the President, but to the nation," cried the *New York World*,[42] and this cry was taken up by newspapers throughout the country. The *New York Sun* predicted that Americans would not soon forgive the man "who skulked and ran away when honor and patriotism should have kept him at his post."[43] Bryan's note, asserted the *Philadelphia Inquirer*, "will be read in Berlin with great pleasure. . . . It will be applauded uproariously by every sympathizer with red-handed murder on the high seas." In a moment of national crisis, the *Inquirer* charged, "Mr. Bryan thrusts his personal views to the front, throws himself into the public arena and stabs — yes, let it be said — stabs the United States in the back."[44] Under the caption "Treachery Unspeakable," one of the nation's best known editors, Henry Watterson of the *Louisville Courier Journal*, ominously warned that "men have been shot and beheaded, even hanged, drawn and quartered, for treason less heinous."[45] Watterson and his fellow editor, George Harvey of the *North American Review*, questioned not only Bryan's vision but his personal motives. He was, they raged, "unfeeling," "disloyal," "inordinately selfish," "avaricious," "egotistical," "a repudiator," "a betrayer," "a self-seeking marplot."[46] Bryan, announced the *Providence Journal* happily, "has bowed himself into oblivion."[47]

Ironically, Bryan's resignation was misinterpreted by a

42. Quoted in McAdoo, *Crowded Years*, p. 336.
43. *New York Sun*, June 9, 1915.
44. Reprinted in the *Literary Digest*, L (June 19, 1915), 1450.
45. Reprinted in *New York Herald*, June 12, 1915.
46. Ibid., and George Harvey, "The Revolt of Bryan," *North American Review*, CCII (July 1915), 3–4.
47. Reprinted in *New York Times*, June 14, 1915.

good many papers in Germany itself. The *Berliner Zeitung am Mittag* assumed that he left the Cabinet because he "wanted a sharper note"; the *Berliner Morgenpost* felt that with his departure "the most dangerous anti-German in America has passed off the scene"; and the *Berliner Vossische Zeitung* hoped that "perhaps from now on America's foreign policy will be less English." [48]

Though it would be difficult to exaggerate the amount of vilification and condemnation to which Bryan was subjected during and after the summer of 1915, it would be a mistake to ignore the ground swell of approval and support that soon made itself felt. The *Literary Digest*, after conducting a survey of the initial reactions to Bryan's defection, announced: "it is evident from Western and Southern comment that a considerable portion of the country today retains its confidence in the motives and purposes of William Jennings Bryan." [49] Many small — and several large — newspapers in the West and South rushed to Bryan's defense. In Brookneal, Virginia, the *Union Star* spoke for these when it predicted that "many will file in behind him in defence of the doctrine that national and international murder shall cease." [50] "His name," echoed the *Los Angles Tribune*, "will be honored and revered by all the peoples of the earth . . . as that follower of the Prince of Peace who wrote the Sermon on the Mount into the Statutes of the world." [51] In the East, too, there were still a few papers that could speak Bryan's name without foaming at the mouth. The *New York American* called him "the only diplomat and the only statesman who has been associated with the Wilson Administration," and the *Pittsburgh*

48. Quoted in the *Literary Digest*, L (June 26, 1915), 1527.
49. Ibid. p. 1517.
50. *Union Star*, June 18, 1915, clipping in Bryan Papers.
51. Reprinted in the *Literary Digest*, L (June 26, 1915), 1519.

Leader announced that "Mr. Bryan may not be America's greatest man, but he is greater today than before he resigned." [52]

The German-American press generally echoed these sentiments, as did the organs of numerous pacifist societies throughout the nation, although the latter had some doubts as to the wisdom of Bryan's resignation. The editor of the Socialist *New York Call* voiced these reservations when he wrote that Bryan's departure removed from Wilson's Cabinet "the last piece of timber that resolutely barred the door against war." [53]

In addition to the far from insignificant segment of the press that vindicated him, Bryan could find comfort in the numerous letters and telegrams that poured into Lincoln, Nebraska, most of them supporting him, and many evincing an almost blind loyalty and devotion. "I have just learned of your resignation," wrote an inhabitant of Indiana, "and don't know just what the trouble is, but whatever it is I know you are right and I am with you." [54] From Minneapolis a supporter wrote: "For twenty years asked what I thot [*sic*] of anything you have done my reply has always been, The King can do no wrong, you are my King and no matter what you do I am at all times with you . . ." [55] "The reason we have given him allegiance," an old time supporter wrote Mrs. Bryan, "the reason we have followed him, is because we believed in him always. . . . And today . . . we love him, if it

52. *New York American*, July 25, 1915, clipping in Albert Burleson Papers (Library of Congress, Washington, D.C.), Vol. 15. Cited hereafter as Burleson Papers; *Pittsburgh Leader*, June 10, 1915, clipping in Bryan Papers.

53. Reprinted in the *Literary Digest*, L (June 19, 1915), 1451. For examples of the sentiment of the German-American press, see *The Outlook*, CX (June 16, 1915), 345.

54. Printed in *The Commoner*, July 1915, p. 25.

55. T. J. Hickey to WJB, June 12, 1915, Bryan Papers.

is possible, the more, because among the few great ones of the world he still puts principle above self." [56]

Even in the wilderness the "Peerless Leader" had his followers, though just how far they would go remained to be seen.

(7)

Aside from his two terms of service in the House of Representatives during the last decade of the nineteenth century, the secretaryship of State was the only official position Bryan was to hold. By resigning when he did, Bryan had cast away a unique opportunity to continue his fight for peace among the very men whose decisions would finally determine the course the country would take. It was this factor that made many pacifists doubt whether their cause would reap any substantial benefits from Bryan's resignation. Still, Bryan himself never doubted the wisdom of his decision. "I resigned only when I became convinced that the opportunities for service were larger outside the Cabinet," he told audience after audience.[57] In a democracy, he reasoned, the people were the fountainhead of all power, and if their representatives spurned his arguments in behalf of peace, the only remaining course was to take his cause directly to the people themselves. If Bryan had voluntarily vacated the seat of authority and power, he expected to return before very long, not in an official capacity perhaps, but at the head of a vast army of mankind, flying the banner of universal peace and brotherhood. He had cast aside the garb of the statesman and once again assumed the role for which he was so well fitted, that of the evangelical crusader.

Though the jibes of the press probably troubled him more than he was willing to admit, he characteristically armed himself against them by relegating most hostile newspapers to the

56. Printed in *The Commoner*, June 1915, p. 25.
57. Ibid. November 1915, p. 7.

status of the hirelings of selfish Eastern interests. For Bryan the peace issue, and every other issue with which he concerned himself throughout his career, was in large part a sectional one with the West and the South on the side of the angels. "I have been in politics for a quarter of a century," he told a New York peace rally, "and I have never known the New York Press to take the side of the American people on any question." Similarly, upon returning to Lincoln, Nebraska, he congratulated its inhabitants for being a "thirty-six hours journey from the New York newspapers," and he hailed the Allegheny Mountains as a "godsend" to the Mississippi Valley, for "they serve as a sort of dyke; they protect it from being inundated by the prejudice and intolerance of that portion of the eastern press which affects a foreign accent." [58]

Nevertheless, Bryan never embarked upon the hopeless task of changing newspaper opinion. It was the people — not the press — that he sought to convince. To accomplish this end he still had several effective means at his disposal. One, of course, was his "silver tongue" which continued to make its possessor one of the most formidable orators in the country: a fact which newspaper after newspaper, friendly and hostile alike, testified to throughout his final years. Physically, Bryan was no longer the commanding figure of 1896. His once trim physique was now paunchy; his famous head of hair, still worn long in the back, was rapidly thinning into an almost invisible wisp on the top of his head; his once sharply-etched features were becoming heavy and lined with the first traces of age; and his long-standing indifference to clothes seemed to become even more accentuated as he grew older. Yet, according to William Allen White, with whom Bryan visited during the summer of 1915, "his voice was fresh and his eyes were keen," [59] and, more important, he still retained the indefatiga-

58. Ibid. pp. 9, 11.
59. *The Autobiography of William Allen White* (New York, 1946), p. 508.

ble energy and zeal which he had first displayed during the dramatic campaign of 1896, and which was to continue to amaze his friends and exasperate his opponents during the years following his resignation. In addition, Bryan had his newspaper, *The Commoner*, which brought his message into tens of thousands of homes, especially in the West and South.[60]

Bryan frequently expressed the conviction that his resignation would not be misinterpreted in any circles other than those from which he could expect condemnation regardless of what he might do. He told Daniels that while it had been difficult to break with his former associates, "It would have been unbearable if I had been compelled to sever the ties of friendship which bind me to them and to none so strongly as to you." [61] These feelings seemed to be confirmed by a number of letters of regret and praise from members of the Administration containing expressions of friendship which could not fail to touch a man of Bryan's temperament.[62] It is possible that these letters were purely *pro forma*, but it is more likely that they indicate the magnetic effect of Bryan's personality upon even those who disagreed with his views.

Even more dramatic confirmation came on June 25, when employees of the State Department gathered in the diplomatic reception room to present Bryan with an engraved watch. The chief clerk spoke briefly and without emotion and Bryan

60. Bryan had begun publication of *The Commoner* as a weekly in 1901. Upon becoming Secretary of State in 1913 he changed the paper into a monthly and, in spite of the protests of many of its readers, it remained a monthly even after his resignation. The average monthly circulation of *The Commoner* in 1915 was 100,000. N. W. Ayer and Son's, *American Newspaper Annual and Directory* (Philadelphia, 1915), p. 570. Unfortunately, 1915 was the last year for which circulation figures are available, so that we have no indication of what effect, if any, Bryan's resignation had upon the periodical's popularity.

61. WJB to Daniels, June 20, 1915, Daniels Papers, Box 37.

62. See, for example, Robert Lansing to WJB, June 9, 1915, Lansing Papers; Joseph P. Tumulty to WJB, June 9, 1915, Wilson Papers, File VI, Box 491.

responded in an equally short speech. Then, according to
William Phillips, Third Assistant Secretary of State, "an extraordinary thing happened. As the men and women came
forward in line to shake his hand, I noticed to my amazement
that many were weeping; some with handkerchiefs to their
eyes, others with tears streaming down their faces. . . .
These several hundred clerks jammed into the diplomatic
reception room were not his friends; presumably they were
relieved that no longer need they fear his preference for deserving Democrats. But the mere presence of the man before
them, standing up for his principles, right or wrong, created a
wave of emotion beyond control." [63]

As interesting and, to Bryan, as pleasing was the continuance of his cordial relations with the President. The day after
he resigned, Bryan formally took leave of the President at the
White House. A Washington correspondent who was present
reported that the faces of both men were "grave and sad, each
showed that they were deeply sorry over this official parting." As they clasped hands before Bryan left, each murmured: "God bless you." Nine days later, on the eve of
Bryan's departure from the Capital, the President called on
him at his home to say goodbye once more.[64] During the
next five years the two men were driven further apart by a
combination of factors, not the least of which was Wilson's
doubts as to Bryan's ability; doubts which had never been
fully dispelled by his growing admiration for Bryan's "high
motives and constant thought of the public interest." [65]

63. William Phillips, *Ventures in Diplomacy* (Boston, 1952), p. 72;
New York Times, June 26, 1915.

64. *Washington Star*, June 9, 1915; *New York World*, June 10,
1915; *Nebraska State Journal*, June 19, 1915; WJB to Josephus Daniels,
February 13, 1924, Bryan Papers.

65. Phrases used by Wilson in a birthday message to Bryan on
March 18, 1915, in which he also wrote: "I have learned not only to
value you as a friend and counsellor but if you will let me say so, I

Bryan had been so loyal to the President during their more than two years of association that although Wilson later claimed that his resignation had probably been inevitable, he also admitted that he viewed it with a "certain degree of amazement." [66] But if Bryan's resignation and his subsequent activity in behalf of peace were matters of concern to the President, he never doubted his former Secretary's motives. When Stockton Axson, Wilson's brother-in-law, told him of a discussion he had had with several Cabinet members concerning Bryan's sincerity, the President replied: "He is *absolutely* sincere." Then, after a pause, he added grimly: "That is what makes him dangerous." [67]

Similarly, Bryan refrained from questioning the intensity of Wilson's desire for peace. "The President," he told 2000 peace enthusiasts in Chicago, "has not been given full credit always for the efforts he has made and is making to preserve peace." [68] In the period following his resignation he took pains to point out that he and the President were both sincerely working for peace and that the only difference between them was the method by which peace might be assured.[69] A major part of Bryan's time and energy in the weeks and months that followed was devoted to his attempt to explain the "irreconcilable" differences between the methods advocated by Wilson and himself. A study of these explanations makes it evident that in his crusade for international peace and understanding Bryan was proceeding upon the identical assumptions and was guided by the identical values that had shaped — and would continue to shape —

have found a very strong affection growing for you in my heart." Wilson Papers, File VI, Box 491.

66. Wilson to Cleveland H. Dodge, June 14, 1915, ibid. Box 82.
67. Baker, *Woodrow Wilson*, V, 360.
68. *New York Times*, September 7, 1915.
69. See Bryan's statements in *The Outlook*, CX (June 16, 1915), 341, and *The Commoner*, June and July 1915.

every one of his domestic crusades: a belief in the existence of a Divine Law, which might be found in the teachings and precepts of the Bible, which men were obliged to consult and obey; a belief in the operation of a harmony of interests among nations as well as among individuals; the conviction that the United States, the most fortunate nation in the world in material things, was also more heavily endowed with morality and Christian ethics than any other nation, and was therefore compelled by its destiny to spread its moral code throughout the world by precept and example; and, finally, a persistent faith in the essential goodness of Man who would respond immediately and wholeheartedly to truth once he was made to see and understand it.

(8)

Bryan lost no time in assuring the public that his disagreement with the President had not been personal. If it had been, Bryan admitted, he would have no right to appeal to the people over Wilson's head for all the "presumptions" were on Wilson's side. "He is your President. I am a private citizen without office or title . . ." "But the real issue," he quickly added, "is not between persons; it is between systems." The standards followed by Wilson in drafting the second note to Germany were those of the "old system" of force "whose precedents were written in characters of blood upon almost every page of human history." The "new system" advocated by Bryan conformed to the standards of persuasion, of love, of brotherhood; it was the system laid down by the Prince of Peace more than nineteen hundred years before. If Christianity had successfully guided the conduct of individuals for so long, why should it not be equally successful in guiding the conduct of nations? "It is time," he told his neighbors in Lincoln, Nebraska, "for the world to turn to the teachings of the Nazarene and to learn that there is a greater power than force." "Christianity," he asserted confidently, "presents not only a solution but the Best solution of international problems." [70]

Where previously many had seen only a question of policy, Bryan was characteristically endeavoring to substitute a question of morality; what had been formally a choice between peace or war, was to become a choice between good or evil. These were the terms in which Bryan thought and they were the terms with which he invested every issue he championed. There was to be no room for personalities, for the issue was not one of personal opinions, but one of immutable principles. "There is no limitation to a moral law," he maintained in an argument suggestive of those set forth by the sociologist E. A. Ross earlier in the century. "The attempt to limit the law against stealing to petty thefts has given us the reign of the pirate and the plunderbund, and so the attempt to limit the commandment against killing to individual murder has led to the riot of war." [71] To Bryan, then, the question of peace presented a unique opportunity not only to reassert the wisdom of Christ's teachings, but to broaden their application as well, and he wrote: "I could not shirk the responsibility which accompanied that opportunity." [72]

But the crusade for a peace based upon Christian precepts and example was more than an opportunity; it was a necessity. On this issue, as on so many others, Bryan revealed an inability to entertain, or even to ignore, any ideas whose implications might attack his basic faith. "To say that the war must necessarily continue any length of time, even for a day," he told reporters in Washington, "is equivalent to saying there are questions which can be settled only by the sword and to

70. Ibid. June 1915, p. 3, July 1915, p. 2; *Nebraska State Journal*, June 30, 1915.
71. *The Commoner*, November 1915, p. 6.
72. Ibid. July 1915, p. 2.

say that is to deny the coming of the day when war will be no more. To deny the possibility of an era of peace, based upon love and brotherhood, is to challenge Christian civilization — a return to savagery . . ." [73] Fundamentalism was a part of Bryan's intellectual equipment long before Darwinian evolution held the center of his attention.

If Bryan's dreams of a halcyon world derived much from Christianity, they were also indebted to his nationalism; a fact which undoubtedly disturbed many interventionists since the latter was one of their own favorite weapons. In the preface to his memoirs, a nostalgic Bryan listed the manifold blessings bestowed upon him throughout his lifetime, not the least of which was the land of his birth: "It was a gift of priceless value to see the light in beloved America, and to live under the greatest of republics in history." [74] His trip around the world in 1905 and 1906 merely reaffirmed this conviction, and he never tired of telling audiences in later years that he returned to America "with an even firmer conviction than when I left it that our Government was superior to all others." [75]

This belief in the superiority and destiny of his country played an important role in every campaign Bryan undertook, from free silver to anti-evolution, but never more so than in his crusade for peace. As early as 1900 Bryan called upon the United States to become "the supreme moral factor in the world's progress and the accepted arbiter of the world's disputes." Following his resignation he was to dwell upon this theme tenaciously. Christianity and national destiny became inextricably linked together in his mind; the former provided the principles upon which an everlasting peace could be con-

73. *New York Times*, December 6, 1915.
74. *Memoirs*, p. 10.
75. John Reed, "Bryan on Tour," *Collier's*, LVII (May 20, 1916), 46.

structed, and his own nation was to be the instrument which would make those principles a reality. "Some nation," he wrote with recurring frequency, "must lead the world out of the black night of war into the light of that day when 'swords shall be beaten into ploughshares.' Why not make that honor ours? Someday — why not now?" [76]

A careful reading of Bryan's speeches during this period reveals that although the specter of war's desolation and chaos was never far from his mind, his primary objection to our entry was not merely that it would mean the loss of life and property, for man could create new life and labor could produce new wealth; rather it was that we could not join in the battles of Europe "without surrendering an opportunity that never before came to any nation and may never come again! That is the worst thing about a war now." [77] The difficulties attendant upon building a new standard of international ethics in the midst of the worst war the world had known were never fully clear to the former Secretary of State; they were obscured by his vision of America and Christianity marching forward hand in hand.

(9)

On June 19, 1915, Bryan spoke on "Labor's Interest in Peace" before a capacity audience at Carnegie Hall in New York City. This address was a portent of the type of appeal he was to make throughout the country. He stressed the fact that throughout its history the United States had "sought to aid the world by example. . . . We have been the friend of all nations and the counsellor of many," and to depart from this role to enter the power politics of Europe "would not be an ascent to a higher plane; it would be a descent and would impair our influence and jeopardize our moral prestige." At

76. *The Commoner*, June 1915, p. 3.
77. Ibid. July 1915, p. 10; *Nebraska State Journal*, June 30, 1915.

another point he cried: ". . . we cannot afford to exchange the moral influence which we now have for the military glory of all the empires that have risen and fallen since time began." "Our appeal," he said feelingly, "is not to the fears of men, but to their hearts and consciences. Our mission is to implant hope in the breast of humanity and substitute higher ideals for the ideals which have led nations into armed conflicts." Bryan, however, was too experienced a politician to base his arguments solely upon moral principles and a roseate picture of national destiny; he also appealed to self-interest. No other group in the country, he assured his listeners, had a deeper interest in the preservation of peace than did labor. War deranges business "and that is apt to subject the laboring man to idleness"; war increases taxes "and the poor man pays more than his share of the taxes"; war calls for vast armies and navies and the workers "always fight the nation's battles." [78]

Bryan's attempt to win the support of organized labor received a severe setback when Samuel Gompers declared that labor was squarely behind Wilson and that the meeting addressed by Bryan "in no way" represented American labor. If Gompers was reluctant to give Bryan his blessings, a number of his associates were not, and many union men actively participated in the meeting.[79]

Five days later, 70,000 people tried in vain to crowd into Madison Square Garden to hear Bryan speak on "National Honor." The 15,000 who finally gained admittance heard Bryan explain in detail the reasons for his belief that neutrality was the only course consistent with national honor. The

78. "Labor's Interest in Peace," *The Commoner*, July 1915, pp. 8–9.
79. "Mr. Bryan and Organized Labor," *The Outlook*, CX (June 30, 1915), 482. Among the labor officials who addressed the gathering were Ernest Bohm of the Central Federated Union, Joseph P. Holland of the International Brotherhood of Firemen, and Joseph Cannon of the Western Federation of Labor.

United States, he asserted, was in a unique position in that it was more closely tied to all of the belligerent powers than any other neutral nation. "They poured the wealth of their blood into the United States; they helped to develop our country; they are a part of citizenship; they have shared in establishing our greatness and in shaping our destiny. Ties, stretching from the old world to the new, unite our hearts to all of them; not a soldier dies on any battlefield anywhere in Europe but his death makes us sad." "Tonight," he said, "I plead with the American people against war with Germany; tomorrow, if a similar condition arises and we are brought near to war with England or France or Russia, I shall come here and plead as earnestly against war with any of these nations." Bryan's address was as well received as almost any he had delivered. "Applause came in roars, deep-chested and sincere," wrote one of the newspapermen present, and Bryan responded with "the flashing eye, the passionate gesture, the ringing voice of fifteen years ago." [80]

The meeting was a great triumph, yet it had unfortunate repercussions. Henry Weissman, the president of the United German–American Alliance of Greater New York, had introduced Bryan, and many of those on the platform, as well as in the audience, were obviously friendly to Germany. This, added to the fact that when he spoke at Carnegie Hall Bryan had shared the platform with several representatives of the Central Powers, including Captains Boy-Ed and von Papen — both of whom were ordered out of the country several months later because of their activities on behalf of their government — convinced many that Bryan was not as impartial an observer of the war as he claimed.[81] He had, after all, re-

80. *New York World*, June 25, 1915; for Bryan's address see *The Commoner*, July 1915, pp. 9–11.

81. Merle Curti, *Bryan and World Peace* (Northampton, Mass., 1931), pp. 229–30; Millis, *Road to War*, pp. 203–4.

signed his post rather than sign a stern note to Germany, and the German-American press had lavishly bestowed its blessings upon his action (the condemnation of the German press itself was conveniently forgotten). The New York press, at least, needed no more evidence. The *World* openly accused him of being pro-German; the *Times* labeled him "A Standard Bearer of the Hyphen"; and the *Sun* called him the "Boy-Orator-of-the-Platte-Deutsch." [82]

Though he was to exercise more discretion in the future, Bryan refused to refute these charges. He justly felt that his past record vindicated him ably enough. Bryan was, in fact, no more pro-German than pro-British. As Secretary of State he had steadfastly opposed an embargo on the sale of war supplies to belligerents on the ground that such an act would aid Germany and therefore would be "an unjustifiable departure from the principle of strict neutrality." [83] His views on the subject did not change after his resignation, and he refused to speak at several peace rallies when their sponsors urged the passage of an arms embargo. [84] The criticism which his position brought him from many of his allies in the peace movement failed to alter his resolution. [85] An embargo, he wrote, is "so obviously intended to help Germany as against the Allies that it gives the pro-Ally press an excuse for discrediting the entire peace movement." [86] Bryan summed up

82. *New York World*, June 26, 1915; *New York Times*, June 26, 1915; *New York Sun*, June 26, 1915, clippings in Bryan Papers.

83. Lansing, *War Memoirs*, p. 227.

84. *New York Times*, June 29, July 8, 1915; *New York Sun*, September 7, 1915; WJB to Henry Weissman, August 27, 1915, Bryan Papers.

85. The *New York American*, for example, said of Bryan: "When he advocates the exportation and sale of arms to nations which are using those arms to make war and murder each other's people he cannot be considered a consistent or wholly sincere advocate of peace." June 26, 1915.

86. WJB to [Harry] Walker, August 28, 1915, Bryan Papers.

his feelings in a letter to Henry Weissman: "My sole interest is in keeping this country out of war with any belligerent and I am just as much opposed to helping one side as I am of [sic] helping the other." [87]

It was this attitude that had prevented Bryan from sharing the growing pro-British sentiment of his associates in the Cabinet. He was never able to read meaning into those lines of Kipling:

> Who stands if freedom fall?
> Who dies if England live?

Nor would he have understood what Wilson meant when he told Joseph Tumulty in the fall of 1914 that "England is fighting our fight . . . she is fighting for her life and the life of the world." [88] To Bryan the hope of the world was not England but America. He could not clothe the European war in idealistic raiment; if there was a noble cause to be supported it was not that of either England or Germany, but the cause of Christ, the cause of peace.

On June 29, Bryan returned to Lincoln, Nebraska, where a friendly crowd greeted him enthusiastically. The *Nebraska State Journal* commented: "The people took particul..r pains on this visit to show that in spite of all that has happened their hearts are still true to William." Six thousand cheering Lincolnians lined the street in front of the Lindell Hotel when Bryan, who was introduced by Governor Morehead, stepped out on the south balcony to speak to them of "The Farmer's Interest in Peace." [89] Except for the shift in emphasis, the speech very much resembled his New York labor address. "Those who are demanding war," he declared, "do not repre-

87. WJB to Weissman, August 27, 1915, ibid.
88. Joseph P. Tumulty, *Woodrow Wilson as I Know Him* (Garden City, New York, 1924), pp. 229–31.
89. *Nebraska State Journal*, June 30, 1915.

sent the farmers . . . they do not represent the laboring men . . . and they do not represent the business men who buy from, and sell to, the farmers and laborers, or those engaged in transporting the products of the country." Eighty per cent of the American people do not want war, he assured his listeners, for its burdens and its grief would fall upon their shoulders. Nor was there any reason "to go to war to avenge the death of less than 250 Americans whom Germany had no desire to kill . . ." [90]

The last point made by Bryan in his Lincoln speech was one that he was especially anxious to expound. English and German interferences with American rights, he explained, were merely incidental; they were not intended and did not indicate unfriendliness. There was, after all, a vast difference between *intended* and *accidental* injuries. "It would be bad enough to go to war with people who were enemies and want to fight us — God forbid that we should compel any nation to engage in war against us AGAINST ITS WILL." [91]

From Lincoln, Bryan journeyed to the Pacific Coast where he had been invited to participate in the International Exposition being held in San Francisco. It was an ideal opportunity and he took full advantage of it in speeches before more than 100,000 people on every aspect of the peace issue.[92] "We have had an exceedingly busy time in California," he wrote to Louis Post, "and I am sure you will be interested to know that my series of speeches met with larger crowds and a more enthusiastic response than on any previous visit out here." [93]

While he was on the Coast Bryan toured Oregon and

90. "The Farmer's Interest in Peace," *The Commoner*, July 1915, pp. 11–12.

91. Ibid. August 1915, p. 3.

92. Ibid. July 1915, pp. 3–4, 15; *Memoirs*, pp. 429–31; *New York Times*, July 6, 7, 1915.

93. WJB to Post, August 11, 1915, Louis F. Post Papers (Library of Congress, Washington, D.C.). Cited hereafter as Post Papers.

Washington in behalf of peace and found the people there "fully as cordial as those of California." [94] He returned to Nebraska on August 3, after a leisurely trip home during which he made many short speeches from the rear platform of his train. He stayed in Lincoln only long enough to complete arrangements for an extended tour which was to take him through the Midwest and South. Bryan was unable to remain still for a moment. Although he had never been as inept or as unhappy a Secretary of State as many of his contemporaries had believed, he now seemed almost ecstatic over being able to discard the ill-fitting bit of official reticence. To Bryan the lure of the platform was always stronger than the lure of the desk, and never more so than during the months following his resignation. Mrs. Bryan, who accompanied her husband on part of his tour, noted in her diary at the time: "These days are full of trains and changing cars and small hotels and crowds and shouts and rain and wind and auto rides across country. He has been making two speeches daily. It is hard work." [95] But it was also rewarding work. While at first the audiences he addressed were often small and hostile, they gradually began to grow in size and enthusiasm.[96] By October Mrs. Bryan was able to write triumphantly: "The effort of the press to brand him as a traitor has evidently failed. He seems not only to have kept his old friends but to have added new ones." [97]

It was, in many respects, 1896 all over again. What one of

94. *Memoirs*, p. 431.
95. Ibid. p. 432.
96. Recollections of Louis J. Alber, who managed many of Bryan's tours, in *Cleveland Plain Dealer*, March 14, 1937, clipping in Daniels Papers, Box 761; *Dallas News*, October 3, 1915, reprinted in *The Commoner*, October 1915, pp. 22–3; *Nashville Tennessean and Nashville American*, September 29, 1915, clipping in Bryan Papers; *Memoirs*, pp. 432–3.
97. Ibid. p. 434.

his biographers has called "the eternal crusading urge in his temperament" [98] was again being satisfied. Once more he was to traverse the country speaking in cities and "whistle stops" alike. Once more he was to hear the cheers of the multitudes; to speak to them and often for them. Once more he felt himself "clad in the armor of a righteous cause," and in no role was he happier.

98. J. C. Long, *Bryan: The Great Commoner* (New York, 1928), p. 284.

II: Crusade for Peace

*If others desire that our flag be feared, let us prefer that it shall
be loved; if others would have the world tremble in awe at the
sight of it, let us pray that the plain people everywhere may
turn their faces toward it and thank God that it is the emblem
of justice and the hope of peace. I desire that my country shall
maintain the national honor which such a flag represents.* — WJB

(1)

FOR SOME TIME after his resignation there was speculation in
many quarters that Bryan would carry his peace crusade to
the shores of Europe itself. Bryan had often contemplated
such a mission when he was Secretary of State but each time
he found his plan balked by Colonel House.[1] Bryan's resignation increased House's anxiety and he was soon writing
Ambassador Page in England: "X writes me that Bryan told
him that he intended to go to Europe soon and try peace
negotiations . . . I anticipated this when he resigned. I knew
it was just a matter of time before he would take this step." [2]
Page, who had worked as diligently as House to keep Bryan
out of Europe when the latter was Secretary of State, now
appeared unconcerned:

> Never mind about Bryan. Send him over here if you wish to
> get rid of him. He'll cut no more figure than a tar-baby at a

1. As early as August 1, 1914, House urged Wilson to prevent
Bryan from personally contacting the European belligerents. "They
look upon him as absolutely visionary," he assured the President.
Seymour, ed., *Intimate Papers of Colonel House*, I, 279.
2. House to Page, August 12, 1915, Burton J. Hendrick, *The Life
and Letters of Walter Hines Page* (New York, 1923), II, 12–13.

Negro campmeeting. If he had come while he was Secretary I
would have jumped off London Bridge . . . But I shall enjoy
him now. . . . It'll be fun to watch Bryan perform and never
suspect that anybody is lying to him or laughing at him. . . .
He can do no harm on this side of the world. It's only your side
that's in any possible danger . . .[3]

Bryan himself evidently felt that for the time being at least
he could work for peace more effectively in America than in
Europe. However, there continued to be strong pressure put
upon him to lead a peace movement to Europe. In September
a group of representatives of foreign language newspapers
printed in the United States urged him to go abroad. In October this appeal was seconded by the Federal Council of
Churches of Christ in America and by ex-Congressman
Richard Bartholdt, the founder of the American branch of
the Interparliamentary Union, who assured Bryan that the
President could not possibly decline to support a European
peace mission headed by him.[4]

A month later Bryan was invited to accompany the Ford
Peace Ship on its journey. He immediately assured Ford that
he was "in hearty sympathy with your proposed peace plan.
It is worthy of all praise and will I trust accomplish much
good." After "earnest consideration," however, he decided he
could render a greater service at home "opposing the plan to
commit this country to a large and indefinite increase in expenditures for army and navy." [5] Although it is true that by
this time Bryan was fully engaged in the growing clash over
preparedness, his subsequent actions indicate that an even
more important reason for his decision was his fear of lending

3. Page to House, undated, ibid., pp. 13–14.
4. *New York Times*, September 18, 1915; Shailer Matthews to
WJB, October 11, 1915, Richard Bartholdt to WJB, October 9, 1915,
Bryan Papers.
5. *New York Times*, November 26, 1915; WJB to Henry Ford,
December 1915, Bryan Papers.

his name to an enterprise which was rapidly taking on many of the characteristics of a comic opera. Months of vilification in the nation's press seem to have made Bryan wary not so much of failing as of not being taken seriously. Nevertheless, Bryan did not completely cut himself off from the undertaking. On December 4, when Ford and his party sailed from Hoboken, Bryan was there to see them off. He announced that he expected to join them at the Hague before long. Bryan apparently intended to watch the progress of Ford's peace party closely. Should the American group be taken seriously in Europe, Bryan had every intention of allying himself with it. He even went so far as to book reservations for himself and his wife on the S.S. *Rotterdam* which was due to sail for Europe on December 28.[6] The futility of the peace expedition, however, became apparent as soon as it landed in Europe. When a disillusioned Henry Ford deserted his own party prematurely to return to the United States, Bryan canceled his reservations.[7] Although he continued to nurture the dream of personally carrying the message of universal peace and brotherhood to Europe, he found much to keep him occupied in his own country.

(2)

From the time of the sinking of the *Falaba* in March 1915, Bryan had become convinced of the necessity of prohibiting American citizens from traveling on belligerent vessels. Indeed, his failure to win the President's support in this matter helped to bring about his resignation. In the months that followed, Bryan carried his fight to the people and to the halls of Congress itself. He advocated the passage of an act forbidding

6. WJB to Seely, December 7, 1915, ibid.
7. *New York Times*, December 28, 1915; WJB to "Ford Party, Stockholm," December 1915, Mary B. Bryan to Daniel Bride, January 7, 1916, Bryan Papers.

belligerent ships to sail from American ports with American passengers aboard, and a supplementary act making it unlawful for American ships to carry both passengers and munitions on the same voyage.[8]

In almost every speech and every issue of *The Commoner* during this period he championed the passage of such legislation. In one of his most popular lectures, "The Causeless War," which he delivered from Chautauqua platforms throughout the country, he first solemnly described the horrors of war and then asked his audience if they were willing to send thousands of young men to destruction "to avenge the death of a few Americans who went on ships which they should not have taken into zones which they knew to be dangerous." [9] It was a line of reasoning which appealed to a great many simply because there was a great deal of logic to it; and its appeal was enhanced by the manner of Bryan's delivery. ". . . he did not bluster, gesture, act," John Reed, who accompanied Bryan on a trip through the South, has recorded, "he spoke slowly as if appealing to our reason, not our emotions. And yet the rising and falling of that extraordinary voice, the way he played upon the sentimental prejudices of common men, were what got them most of all." [10]

The specter of the submarine continued to plague Bryan long after it had driven him from the State Department; he was haunted by the fear that the combined irresponsibility of an over-eager U-boat commander and of American citizens who insisted on traveling upon belligerent vessels would plunge the nation into war. The sinking of the British steamer *Arabic* on August 19, 1915, with the loss of two Americans, increased his anxiety. He hurriedly explained that the ques-

8. *The Commoner*, November 1915, p. 6.
9. "The Causeless War," ibid. September 1915, p. 7.
10. Reed, *Collier's*, LVII (May 20, 1916), 12.

tion was not whether American citizens have the right to travel on belligerent vessels, "that is admitted. The question just now is whether an American citizen should put his convenience or even his rights above his nation's welfare." If they persisted in doing so then a second question arose, "namely, whether the Government should permit a few persons to drag their country into this unparalleled war." [11] When, on September 1, the German Ambassador pledged that his government would refrain from sinking liners without warning, Bryan telegraphed the Administration his "hearty congratulations," [12] but continued to urge it to accept legislation that would effectively prevent a recurrence of the *Arabic* crisis.

Though Bryan's extended campaign for prohibitory legislation did not produce immediate results, it did have the effect of keeping the question before the country. The entire issue came to a head when, on December 30, the British liner *Persia* was sunk with the loss of more than three hundred lives including two Americans. This disaster, the worst since the *Lusitania*, led the newly married President to hurry back to Washington from his Virginia honeymoon retreat and caused a reaction in the nation's press which was reminiscent of the earlier tragedy.[13] The fact that only two Americans had perished prevented the issue from ever reaching the proportions of the *Lusitania* crisis. In addition, more than a few Americans now attributed the incident to the lack of adequate travel restrictions as well as to German malevolence. Bryan immediately rushed into print with an editorial underlining the need

11. *New York Times*, August 23, 1915.
12. WJB to Robert Lansing, September 1, 1915, Robert Lansing Papers (Library of Congress, Washington, D.C.), Vol. 12. Cited hereafter as Lansing Papers.
13. Baker, *Woodrow Wilson*, VI, 156–7; Millis, *Road to War*, p. 255.

for the United States to take steps which would prevent Great Britain from using American citizens as shields for contraband cargoes. "This country cannot be neutral and unneutral at the same time," he asserted. "If it is to be neutral it cannot undertake to help one side against the other." [14]

On January 5, Senator Gore of Oklahoma, who had been in close touch with Bryan during the preceding weeks and had, in fact, conferred with him just a day or two before, introduced a bill "to prohibit the issuance of passports for use on the vessels of a belligerent country," and another one prohibiting American and neutral vessels from transporting American citizens and contraband "at one and the same time." [15] Although the Senate refused to take action on either of these measures, resolutions embodying their essence were introduced in Congress a month later by Representative Jeff McLemore of Texas in the House and by Gore himself in the Senate. Bryan was elated. Not only was Congress finally going to consider resolutions incorporating the position which he had been advocating for nearly a year, but there were unmistakable signs that both Houses would pass them. On February 25, several prominent Democrats informed the President that adoption of the resolutions was inevitable. Speaker Champ Clark went so far as to predict that should the McLemore Resolution come up for a vote in the House of Representatives, it would be adopted by a two to one majority.[16]

Wilson was understandably alarmed. The revolt brewing in Congress had emanated from within the ranks of his own

14. *The Commoner*, January 1916, p. 2.
15. *New York Times*, February 26, 1916; Baker, *Woodrow Wilson*, VI, 157.
16. *New York Times*, February 26, 1916. See also Robert Woolley Memoirs, p. 3a, MSS. in Robert Woolley Papers (Library of Congress, Washington, D.C.). Cited hereafter as Woolley Papers.

party and was being led by such Democratic stalwarts as House Majority Leader Claude Kitchin.[17] Following the introduction of the McLemore Resolution in the House, Wilson roused Postmaster General Albert Burleson out of bed to seek his opinion. Without hesitation, Burleson warned the Chief Executive that should the McLemore Resolution be adopted the "scepter of control" would pass from his hands to Bryan's. A week later, during a conference on the Gore Resolution, Burleson repeated his warning with Secretaries Gregory and McAdoo in agreement.[18] The New York press also held Bryan responsible for the Congressional revolt. The *Herald* claimed that it was the work of a conspiracy headed by German Ambassador von Bernstorff and "sub-officered by William J. Bryan," and a *Times* editorial stated that "the pro-German insurrection in Congress is largely the fruit of Mr. Bryan's work and he is openly in charge." [19]

Wilson immediately threw his considerable power and prestige into a concerted drive to defeat both resolutions. In a widely circulated letter to Senator Stone, the chairman of the Senate Committee on Foreign Relations, Wilson reaffirmed his desire to keep the nation out of the war but added that there was one price he would not pay: "the loss of honor." He refused to consent to any abridgement of the rights of American citizens: "Once accept a single abridgement of right and many other humiliations would follow." [20] Wilson also held

17. For Kitchin's role in this affair see Alex Mathews Arnett, *Claude Kitchin and the Wilson War Policies* (Boston, 1937), pp. 159–82.

18. Albert Burleson to Ray Stannard Baker, February 25, 1931, R. S. Baker Papers, Box 22.

19. *New York Herald*, March 3, 1916, quoted in Arnett, *Claude Kitchin*, p. 164; *New York Times*, February 26, 1916.

20. Wilson to William J. Stone, February 24, 1916, *New York Times*, February 25, 1916.

several conferences with Congressional leaders in which he warned that an open breach between President and Congress might possibly cost the Democratic party the forthcoming election and would certainly encourage Germany to greater acts of defiance. In at least one newspaper the President was reported to have threatened to refuse to run for re-election unless Congress upheld his policy.[21]

With Wilson actively and openly pulling the strings, the opponents of the Gore-McLemore Resolutions had one supremely important factor operating in their favor which their adversaries lacked — organization. Despite the newspaper's shrill warnings of a tightly knit conspiracy, the advocates of the resolutions seem to have been badly disorganized, divided, and confused.[22] Bryan, utilizing all of his influence, attempted to maintain the initial advantage which the supporters of the resolutions had. On the same day that Wilson wrote his decisive letter to Senator Stone, Bryan telegraphed a number of Congressmen urging their support of the measures. If Congress has the right to declare war, he argued, it must also have the right to promote peace: "A Mayor keeps the people of his city out of the danger zone during a riot. Can our Government afford to do less when the world is in riot?"[23]

On March 3, the Senate, by a series of intricate and confusing parliamentary maneuvers, scuttled the Gore Resolution.[24]

21. Arnett, *Claude Kitchin*, p. 163; *New York Evening Sun*, March 1, 1916, quoted in Ibid. p. 166.

22. On the subject of the lack of organization among the peace faction in Congress, see Warren Worth Bailey to Clyde H. Tavenner, October 9, 1915, November 10, 1915, George Huddleston to Bailey, April 11, 1917, Warren Worth Bailey Papers (Princeton University Library), Boxes 8, 10. Cited hereafter as Bailey Papers.

23. WJB to Warren Worth Bailey, February 24, 1916, *New York Times*, February 26, 1916.

24. For a discussion of these maneuvers, see Arnett, *Claude Kitchin*, pp. 171–80; see also *New York Times*, March 4, 1916.

The next day Bryan arrived in Washington in a vain attempt
to counter Wilson's influence in the House. He conferred
with Representative Warren Worth Bailey — his chief
spokesman in Congress during the peace crusade — and other
Democratic Congressmen, he spoke before a luncheon gathering of undecided Democratic Representatives, and he help-
lessly watched the McLemore Resolution go down to defeat
on March 7.[25] Wilson's influence had effectively dissipated
Champ Clark's predicted two to one majority. Claude Kitchin
had proven the more able prophet when he warned that if
Wilson applied the full force of his political power and skill
the majority of Democrats in Congress would "fling away
their convictions and vote to please the President." [26] Representative Bailey, who was convinced that seven out of eight
Democrats in the House had favored the resolutions, complained: "I have never seen a more humiliating spectacle than
that presented the other day when Democrats by the score
voted with the administration in direct violation of their own
inmost convictions. I was among the lonely ones . . ." [27]

The defeat of the Gore-McLemore Resolutions was another in the long, almost unbroken chain of disappointments
which Bryan suffered during these years. Still he refused to
admit that the issue was dead. A majority of Representatives
and Senators, he claimed, favored travel restrictions but were
prevented from expressing their beliefs by the confused

25. Ibid. March 5, 6, 7, 8, 1916.
26. Arnett, *Claude Kitchin*, p. 163.
27. Bailey to A. C. Daniels, March 11, 1916, Bailey to George Fred
Williams, March 8, 1916, Bailey Papers, Box 5. Although Bailey's
figures were probably exaggerated, a number of Democrats openly
admitted that they had voted against their own convictions. Representative Henry D. Flood, chairman of the House Foreign Affairs
Committee, for example, stated that he personally favored the resolutions but declared that all patriotic Americans should stand by the
President. *New York Evening Telegram*, March 7, 1916.

and meaningless manner in which the issue was finally presented to Congress.[28] "Nine-tenths of the voters of the
United States," he maintained, "believe that AMERICANS
SHOULD BE KEPT OFF OF BELLIGERENT SHIPS."
What would history say of us, he asked almost endlessly, "if
we went into such a war as this to vindicate the right of an
American citizen to safeguard a contraband cargo on a belligerent ship — a war which we can easily avoid by keeping
our citizens off such ships." [29]

The torpedoing of the unarmed French channel steamer
Sussex on March 24, with the loss of more than eighty lives
and the injury of several Americans, brought dramatic ur-
gency to Bryan's fears that the defeat of the resolutions had
placed American neutrality in an increasingly precarious position. Secretary of State Lansing angrily informed the President that the time for writing notes had passed, and Colonel
House urged him to sever relations with Germany.[30] In his
final action Wilson indicated only a partial acceptance of the
counsel of his two closest advisers. He sent another note to
Germany in which he warned that unless that government
immediately abandoned its "present method of submarine warfare against passenger and freight-carrying vessels," the
United States "in behalf of humanity and the rights of neutral
nations" would be forced to sever diplomatic relations. On

28. *New York Times*, March 8, 1916. Interestingly, Secretary of
State Lansing, who was of course an unqualified opponent of the
resolutions, has written: "Mr. Bryan . . . declared that the affirmative
votes on these two resolutions did not represent the full voice of the
American people in favor of the restrictions which they contained. I
think that he was right. I thought so at the time." Lansing, *War
Memoirs*, p. 117.

29. *The Commoner*, March 1916, p. 3, May 1916, p. 3.

30. Robert Lansing to Woodrow Wilson, March 27, 1916, Lansing,
War Memoirs, pp. 133–4; Seymour, ed., *Intimate Papers of Colonel
House*, II, 227–30.

April 19, Wilson appeared before Congress to explain his course and secure its approval and support.[31]

Bryan was on his way to New Orleans to deliver an address when news of the President's actions reached him. He immediately canceled his engagements and journeyed to Washington where Bailey and Representative Calloway of Texas met him at the station and hurried him off to a series of conferences with Democratic leaders. Exactly what Bryan hoped to accomplish is not clear; he himself admitted that he had no definite plan and stated: "I do not know of anything that I can say or do, but as a citizen of this country I want to do what I can on the side of peace." While his conferences with "prominent Democrats" were kept secret, in his public statements Bryan voiced the hope that Germany would accede to the wishes of the United States, but, even if she did not, diplomatic relations must continue until an amicable settlement was reached. "The responsibility for declaring war is on Congress, not upon the President," he said pointedly.[32]

Although Bryan had planned to remain in the Capital for at least three days he departed after only thirty hours.[33] The *New York Times*, which seemed to delight in alternately seeing in Bryan a Machiavellian superman and a pitiful, impotent country politician, now crowed: "The Capital was cold to him. . . . Nobody cared a rap about his views. He came. He failed. He went." [34] Germany's decision to restrict its submarine warfare within the limits which Wilson insisted upon took a great deal of the sting out of Bryan's defeat. The nation would remain at peace for the time being at least, and time was what

31. Baker, *Woodrow Wilson*, VI, 188–90; Lansing, *War Memoirs*, pp. 135–40.
32. *New York Times*, April 21, 1916; *Nebraska State Journal*, April 21, 1916.
33. Ibid.; *New York Times*, April 22, 1916.
34. Ibid. April 23, 1916.

Bryan desired above anything else. The people, he was convinced, responded to nothing so surely as to the truth, and he asked only for an opportunity to help bring the truth to them.

(3)

At the height of the conflict over the problem of the submarine and America's response to it — a conflict that brought the nation to the verge of war and almost disrupted the Democratic party in the process — the nation's leaders, its press, and the people themselves were simultaneously engaged in another distinct though related struggle over an even more divisive issue — preparedness.

The course followed by Woodrow Wilson on this issue was uncertain. His correspondence and conversations with Colonel House and Secretary of War Garrison indicate that his initial attitude toward preparedness was one of cautious hostility.[35] In his annual message to Congress on December 8, 1914, he made this attitude public by declaring that those who were advocating the extension of the nation's military arm were urging no less than "a reversal of the whole history and character of our polity." "We never have had, and while we retain our present principles and ideals we never shall have, a large standing army," he declared, while both Houses cheered enthusiastically.[36] Nor did the President *publicly* alter his position during the months that followed.

Throughout his tenure in the State Department, Bryan adamantly opposed any plan to increase the armed forces,[37] and,

35. Seymour, ed., *Intimate Papers of Colonel House*, I, 298–300; R. S. Baker interview with Lindley M. Garrison, November 30, 1928, Lindley M. Garrison to Ray Stannard Baker, November 12, 1928, R. S. Baker Papers, Box 34.

36. Baker, *Woodrow Wilson*, VI, 4–5.

37. Colonel House, who sought out Bryan's views on preparedness only three months after the war began, noted in his diary at the time: "I found him in violent opposition to any kind of increase by the

for a change, he found himself in agreement with the President, most of his fellow Cabinet members, and the majority of Congressmen. Nevertheless, he hardly could have been oblivious to the existence of a highly vocal group of prominent citizens who were demanding immediate and extensive additions to the army and navy. If Bryan's official position prevented him from taking open issue with these men, his resignation presented him with a unique opportunity to do so, and he allowed little time to elapse before entering the fray.

In his Carnegie Hall labor address he first publicly attacked the policies advocated by Theodore Roosevelt as those designed to turn the United States into "a vast armory with skull and crossbones above the door." His policies, Bryan charged, would involve the nation in a financially and morally ruinous competition with the countries of the Old World. And, worst of all, the preparedness advocated by Roosevelt "would provoke war instead of preventing it." [38] "If preparation prevents war," he asserted, "there would have been no war in Europe. They spent twenty years preparing for it." [39] This latter observation, which was not wholly without its historical foundations, was one of the factors conditioning the ex-Secretary's whole attitude toward preparedness. Equally important was his devotion to Christian ideals. "The preparedness demanded by the jingoes," he wrote in August, "is a challenge to Christian civilization — it is a plea for a return to barbarism." [40] What particularly incensed Bryan was Roose-

reserve plan. He did not believe there was the slightest danger to this country from foreign invasion, even if the Germans were successful. He thought *after war was declared* there would be plenty of time to make any preparations necessary. . . . He spoke with great feeling, and I fear he may give trouble." Seymour, ed., *Intimate Papers of Colonel House*, I, 300.

38. "Labor's Interest in Peace," *The Commoner*, July 1915, pp. 8–9.
39. *New York Sun*, September 7, 1915.
40. *The Commoner*, August 1915, p. 4.

velt's intimation that war often acted as a moral stimulant. "If the Lord so made us that bloodletting is necessary to keep us from becoming degenerates, why not repeal all laws against murder," he asked. "If any philosophy can rot a soul it is the Roosevelt philosophy that puts man on a level with the brute." [41]

As important as these factors were in shaping Bryan's outlook on preparedness, they were soon eclipsed by a line of reasoning that was equally characteristic. Preparedness was not an honest issue to be discussed in a reasonable way by rational men; it was a selfish and calculated conspiracy put forth by those who had only their own interests at heart. He first hinted at the existence of this "conspiracy" in July when he wrote that "the builders of battleships and the manufacturers of munitions grow fat on the policy that prepares for war, and they will grow fatter still if they carry preparedness to the point of provoking an international conflict." [42] A few months later he was proclaiming:

> Now a new power has arisen in the land and demands control of the taxing power. It is the preparers of preparedness — the battleship builders and the manufacturers of munitions. They have been making enormous profits supplying the belligerent nations with war materials. There is only one way to insure their continued prosperity — they must lash this country into a chronic state of fear, and then coin this fear into dollars. They already have their subsidized organs setting up a false standard of national honor — the duelist's standard; they are glorifying brute force. They are transplanting upon American soil the European tree of hatred which is bearing its bloody fruit across the Atlantic. [43]

In his own mind, Bryan identified the advocates of preparedness with the selfish interests which the hosts of progressiv-

41. Ibid. May 1916, p. 2.
42. Ibid. July 1915, p. 3.
43. "The People Vs. the Special Interests," ibid. October 1915, p. 1.

ism had been fighting for more than twenty years.[44] The Republicans, he charged, wanted a larger army for use in labor troubles and a larger navy to carry on trade wars.[45] When a reporter asked him to outline his plans for the future, he replied militantly: "I shall continue to exert whatever influence I have for the protection of the public from exploitation whether that exploitation is attempted by the tariff barons, the trust magnates, the money power, or this new bunch of exploiters, the manufacturers of munitions of war and the preparers of preparedness." [46]

But even while Bryan was enjoining the Democratic party to oppose the demands of the advocates of preparedness, Wilson was preparing to make major concessions to them. On November 4, 1915, in an address before the Manhattan Club at the Biltmore Hotel in New York, the President substantially endorsed the plans of the General Board of the Navy and Secretary of War Garrison by calling for an increase in the navy and the regular army and a reserve of 400,000 men. On the whole the President's program was too ineffectual for such avid militarists as Theodore Roosevelt, who characterized it as a "shadow program" of "half preparedness" which was as dangerous as the schemes of Bryan and Henry Ford.[47]

Bryan, however, could find no solace in Roosevelt's chagrin. To him the President's speech was a matter of "sorrow and concern," for the plan it proposed was "not only a depar-

44. This identification was common to many of the foes of preparedness. At the outset of the struggle, Representative Bailey wrote that if the preparedness program succeeded "every forward-looking movement in which we are interested must be halted and turned back. Militarism is absolutely fatal to progress. It has been so in all time and it must be so in our time." Bailey to Daniel Kiefer, November 13, 1915, Bailey Papers, Box 9. For many examples of this kind of reasoning among the peace advocates see the correspondence in the Bailey Papers, Boxes 1, 5, 8, 9.
45. *The Commoner*, November 1915, p. 6.
46. *Richmond Times*, October 10, 1915, reprinted in ibid. p. 29.
47. Baker, *Woodrow Wilson*, VI, 17–18.

ture from our traditions, but a reversal of our national policy . . . not only a menace to our peace and safety but a challenge to the spirit of Christianity . . ." "The spirit which makes the individual carry a revolver leads him not only to use it on slight provocation," Bryan argued, "but to use language which will provoke." The United States, he maintained, had won its position in the world "without resorting to the habit of toting a pistol or carrying a club," and he could not understand why the President had chosen this critical moment to "revolutionize" our national policy. "Why abandon the hope that we have so long entertained of setting an example to Europe? Why encourage the nations of Europe in their folly by imitating them?" [48] But although he challenged the President's plan he would not attack the President himself, saying in a press interview: "He is doing what he believes to be his duty and so long as a man follows his conscience and judgment, we cannot criticize his motives but we may be compelled to differ from his conclusions." [49] Wilson, too, refused to let the new breach between himself and Bryan become personal. "I can't help being disturbed that Mr. Bryan should see things as he does," he wrote to the editor of the *Birmingham News.* "My own feeling towards him remains of the most cordial sort." [50]

Bryan never made any real distinction between Wilson's advocacy of a relatively mild form of preparedness and the

48. *New York Sun,* November 6, 1915.

49. *The Commoner,* November 1915, p. 4. A month earlier, he had written Secretary Daniels: "If my opposition to the policy of preparedness embarrasses you in any way, my dear Daniels, I hope you will not hesitate to say so, for while I feel it my duty to pursue the course I am pursuing, I shall do it without any dimunition [*sic*] of my affection and regards for you and for others from whom I am differing." WJB to Josephus Daniels, October 16, 1915, Daniels Papers, Box 37.

50. Woodrow Wilson to Frank P. Glass, November 10, 1915, Wilson Papers, File VI, Box 491.

more ambitious dreams of Roosevelt and his followers. A wrong policy was a wrong policy whether it was administered in large or small doses. Wilson's new position only caused Bryan to become more militant in his opposition. Shortly after the President's speech, Bryan called upon Congress to "Investigate the activities of the business group particularly interested in increased appropriations for army and navy . . . TURN ON THE LIGHT and let the country see the fraudulent character of a pretended patriotism which is now being paraded before the country by men who claim a superior attachment to the nation, but are in fact nothing but leeches and parasites." [51]

Bryan's anti-preparedness campaign caused the usual reaction in the nation's press. Even if we discount the more vindictive and abusive journals, there still remained many newspapers that were sorely troubled over Bryan's stand. The *Sioux Falls Press* spoke for these when it confessed its inability to understand Bryan's position: "He thinks we are brainy enough to settle all disputes by arbitration, and yet we are subject to rabies if there is a weapon in sight! Some of Mr. Bryan's utterances fail miserably to dovetail with his oft-professed faith in human nature." [52] This apparent dichotomy in Bryan's outlook, which so troubled the editor of the *Press*, has remained to plague many historians and biographers as well. Although Bryan's "oft-professed" faith in human nature was both real and sincere, his early and prolonged religious training, his prodigious study of the Bible, and the strain of

51. "Investigate," *The Commoner*, November 1915, p. 1. A few weeks later, Representative Augustus P. Gardner of Massachusetts attempted to turn the tables on Bryan by asking the House of Representatives to investigate his peace propaganda to determine whether he was making any money out of it. *New York Times*, December 18, 1915.

52. "Pacifism and Preparedness: a Poll of the Press," *The Outlook*, CX (June 30, 1915), 496.

evangelism which was as much a part of him as his faith in his fellow man, made him aware of many of the weaknesses of those for whom he was fighting, and lent a somewhat exaggerated importance to the temptations which beset man. In addition to his own weaknesses, the average man was also subject to the influences of the "selfish interests" who stood to gain if they could lure him into the path of temptation. Throughout his lifetime, then, Bryan fought not only for the economic and political rights of his fellow citizens but also — and to him this fight was equally important — to free his fellow men from the perils which temptation set in their path, whether that temptation be lodged in munitions, alcohol, or the iconoclastic preachments of intellectuals. The irony implicit in this double crusade, however, was not to become fully apparent until his declining years.

Bryan's fight against preparedness was merely one element in his many-faceted attempt to keep the country out of war. He opposed going to war in the interests of agriculture as well as in the interests of the munitions manufacturers. When, in the fall of 1915, the Allies announced their decision to declare cotton contraband, the South, which had been protesting against English interference with cotton shipments for some time, intensified its protests and demanded a firmer stand against England.[53] Bryan, who was extremely sensitive to the needs of the South, immediately agreed that the cotton farmers were being punished mercilessly and unnecessarily by the belligerents, but "to go to war to relieve them would simply increase the sacrifice called for. There is an easier way." The "easier way" was for the government to fix a price for cotton which was based upon normal prices, and either purchase and hold the cotton which producers would be forced to sell below that price, or issue loans upon it. When the war ended,

53. Many letters to this effect from Southern Congressmen may be found in the Burleson Papers, Vol. 15.

the United States could present the Allies with a claim for damages.[54]

The phrase "when the war ends," became an increasingly important one in Bryan's crusade. Even if the government came to the conclusion that American rights were being openly and shamefully flouted, it should not resort to force "DURING THE PRESENT WAR." "If it is necessary to resort to force at all it should be AFTER this war is over when we can have a war of our own." To enter into the European conflict would be to take part in a war that belonged to everybody; it would mean being drawn into the settlement of disputes with which we had no possible connection. If we had to have war, let it be our own war, fought at the proper time, for reasons that were meaningful to us.[55]

Nor should the government even contemplate war until the people were consulted and their will was made known. When Wilson, in his Manhattan Club address, said: "I think the whole nation is convinced that we ought to be prepared . . . for defense," Bryan responded: "The real question is not what the President THINKS the people want, but WHAT THE PEOPLE ACTUALLY WANT." [56] Shortly after he resigned Bryan first proposed that a popular referendum be held before war could be declared, except in case of invasion.[57] This proposal constituted one of the most consistent planks in his peace platform. "The people who do the dying," he maintained again and again, "should also do the deciding about whether the United States should enter a war." "The masses," he complained, "are never consulted by the special interests. The plain people are expected to give their money in time of peace and their lives in time of war — while the

54. *The Commoner*, September 1915, p. 5.
55. Ibid. November 1915, p. 7.
56. Ibid. p. 3.
57. Ibid. August 1915, p. 5.

profits go to the few." [58] When Senator Owen of Oklahoma proposed a referendum on war early in 1916, Bryan proved to be one of its most enthusiastic supporters. "Let the people rule," he demanded in an editorial defending Owen's proposal. "Nowhere is their rule more needed than in deciding upon war policies — nowhere would their influence be more salutary." [59] Bryan was perfectly sincere when he promised to follow the wishes of the people without hesitation. "I so believe in the right of the people to have what they want," he told John Reed, "that I admit the right of the people to go to war if they really want it." [60] Bryan, of course, was more than reasonably certain of the outcome of such a referendum, especially in the Western portions of the country where his peace program was more readily accepted.[61]

Bryan's ardent desire to perpetuate the peace sentiment of the West, as well as his opposition to preparedness, led him to denounce Wilson's tour of the Midwest on behalf of preparedness in January and February 1916. Bryan had been only one of a surprisingly large number of Democratic leaders, both in and out of Congress, who had opposed the President's plea for preparedness in the fall of 1915. Although House Majority Leader Kitchin informed Bryan in October that the President had been caught by the "war goblins and jingoes," and unhappily predicted that he could see no reason to hope that his program would be defeated,[62] Wilson soon found himself engaged in a battle which was to make the struggle

58. Ibid. October 1915, p. 4, January 1916, p. 3.
59. Ibid. February 1916, p. 6.
60. Reed, *Collier's*, LVII (May 20, 1916), 12.
61. For a discussion of the reception accorded Bryan's crusade in the West, see William Hard, "What About Bryan," *Everybody's*, XXIV (April 1916), 456–66.
62. Claude Kitchin to WJB, October 20, 1915, Arnett, *Claude Kitchin*, p. 68; see also Kitchin to Warren Worth Bailey, October 8, 1915, Bailey Papers, Box 9.

over the Gore-McLemore Resolutions seem almost insignificant. Such Democrats as James Hay, Chairman of the House
Military Affairs Committee, and, of course, Kitchin himself
opposed Garrison's plan.[63] Nor were they leaders without an
army. A large number of Democrats in both Houses either
opposed any degree of preparedness at all, or at least favored
a much more limited program than that advocated by Secretary Garrison.[64]

Faced with this intransigence among members of his own
party, Wilson decided to take his case directly to the American people. In a speaking tour which began in New York
City on January 27, and proceeded as far west as Topeka,
Kansas, the President reiterated his determination to keep the
nation out of the war, stressed the dangers of the world situation, and pleaded for a military force large enough to allow
him to protect the nation's honor. The tour ended in St. Louis
on February 3, where Wilson caused an uproar by asking for
"incomparably the greatest navy in the world." [65]

Bryan, of course, was outraged at the sight of the President
taking the stump on behalf of a cause which he felt to be so
dangerous. He immediately challenged Wilson to produce a
detailed explanation of his change of heart in regard to military preparation, and, when the President ignored the challenge,
Bryan undertook a speaking tour of his own which followed
closely upon the heels of the Presidential party, and in which

63. Lindley M. Garrison to Ray Stannard Baker, November 12,
1928, R. S. Baker Papers, Box 34. See also Link, *Woodrow Wilson and
the Progressive Era,* pp. 181–4.

64. Newton D. Baker, who replaced Garrison as Secretary of War
in March 1916, has written of "the existence in both Houses of Congress of a very strong and active body of men who were opposed to
our going into the war, who felt that we never would go into the war
and that any increase in our military preparation was provocative and
dangerous." Newton D. Baker to Charles Seymour, September 26,
1921, R. S. Baker Papers, Box 20.

65. Baker, *Woodrow Wilson,* VI, 26–30.

he called Wilson's plan "revolutionary," "an abandonment of the historic policy of his party and the traditions of the country," a departure "from the safe path of experience," and an unfortunate acquiescence in "the dubious ways pointed out by the big papers which voice the wishes of the manufacturers of munitions." It was on this tour that Bryan made his most forthright attack upon the President, accusing him of "joyriding with the jingoes" and of being applauded "by grandstanders whose voices are unfamiliar to Democratic ears." What caused his change of attitude, he asked. "Is he diplomatically so close to the European war that its uproars prevent his hearing 'the still, small voice' of the people? Has he gazed upon the floor of the trans-atlantic slaughterhouse until the soil of his country looks red?" Still, the irrevocable split between Wilson and himself, which now seemed imminent, was not yet to take place, and by the end of February Bryan was quoted as saying once more: "The President is doing his duty as he sees it . . . I am doing my duty as I see it." [66]

Instead of waging a negative war of criticism aimed at the President, Bryan devised an appeal calculated to impress those sections of the country — the West and South — whose support Wilson desperately needed if he was to win national backing for his program. By adroitly, if somewhat unfairly, comparing the value of the farm crop of 1915 with the military budget proposed by arms experts, he was able to demonstrate to his rural audiences that in one year alone the government would spend "MORE THAN ONE-FOURTH OF THE CORN CROP, or MORE THAN ONE-HALF OF THE HAY CROP, or NEARLY ALL OF THE COTTON CROP, or MORE THAN TWICE THE POTATO CROP, *GETTING READY FOR WAR*." And even more

66. *The Commoner*, February 1916, pp. 1, 3–6; *New York Times*, February 19, 1916.

appalling, if one estimated the farmer's net profit at 8 per cent of the gross value of his crop, it could be seen that the country was being asked to spend on the army "MORE THAN THE ENTIRE NET CROP INCOME OF ALL THE FARMERS OF THE UNITED STATES." [67]

Bryan turned this argument upon the politicians as well, and asked them what action the voters would take when they sat in judgment upon "the insolent extravagance of these worshippers of the scimitar who would absorb in preparations for imaginary wars more than the net income of all the farmers of the United States." [68] It was one of the questions which many farmbelt Congressmen may well have been asking themselves, for, though his tour had been a triumphant one, Wilson returned to find Congress as obstinate as ever. Five days after Wilson's stumping expedition had ended, Kitchin informed Bryan that he saw "no real change" in the attitude of Congress.[69] In the end, Wilson had to abandon the Continental Army plan set forth by Secretary Garrison and adopt the more moderate plan of Representative Hay. Garrison resigned in indignation, and the more temperate anti-preparationists rejoiced at their success in forcing the Administration to accept what Representative Bailey called "reasonable preparedness." [70]

Bryan, however, could find no cause for rejoicing. The most moderate preparedness was too extreme for him. Throughout the remainder of 1916, as Congress gradually increased military appropriations, Bryan continued to strike out against preparedness, calling it an "international conspiracy" to drag us into the war; a plot by Wall Street to raise

67. "Shall Militarism Devour the Farm," ibid. January 1916, p. 3.
68. Ibid. February 1916, p. 9.
69. Claude Kitchin to WJB, February 9, 1916, quoted in Link, *Woodrow Wilson and the Progressive Era*, p. 186.
70. Ibid. p. 189; Bailey to F. P. Dawson, February 29, 1916, Bailey Papers, Box 5.

troops in order to put down strikes; pointing out the absurdity of spending as much on the army as on education; pleading with the nation not to abandon its true honor, its real mission, its supreme opportunity. Again Bryan demonstrated his remarkable optimism and his inability to give up a cause even when it was lost. He was to continue his fight against preparedness until the issue itself expired with the coming of war.

(4)

While there had been a gradual erosion of the traditional Progressive credo even before 1914, the World War was a traumatic event for Americans of the Progressive Era. It challenged many of the basic tenets of their credo: their belief in inevitable progress, their faith in the essential goodness of man, their conviction that social Christianity would shortly transform the earth into a haven of peace and brotherhood. For many it became necessary to find some way to explain and cope with the problems created by the war. Some, like Bryan, chose to regard the war as an aberration, an anachronism which Christian men must repudiate. For many others, however, the dilemma was not so easily solved.

For John Dewey the solution came through the medium of his discovery that there was a difference between force and violence. Force *per se* was morally neutral; it was the energy behind every action man undertook from speaking to walking: "No ends are accomplished without the use of force." Violence, on the other hand, was a waste of force, it was force used "idly or destructively." "Squeamishness about force," he observed, "is the mark not of idealistic but of moonstruck morals." The criterion was not the mere use of force but the way in which it was used and the ends to which it was devoted. Thus if war could be shown to be the most direct and efficient mode of accomplishing a constructive purpose, it was no more morally reprehensible because it utilized force than were driving in a nail or pushing a baby carriage.[71]

On June 17, 1915, a group of more than one hundred men under the leadership of ex-President Taft, President A. Lawrence Lowell of Harvard University, Theodore Marburg, the former Ambassador to Belgium, and Hamilton Holt, editor of *The Independent*, met in Philadelphia, and while they refrained from indulging in the tortured semantic arguments of Dewey, they, like the latter, recognized the existence and even the necessity of force and sought to find a means of using it constructively. Although throughout history force had been used to wage war, they concluded it might also be used to preserve peace. Their deliberations led to the establishment of a new organization, the League to Enforce Peace, which was based upon the conviction that it was desirable for the United States to join a "league of nations" whose members would agree to submit all disputes not settled by negotiation to a tribunal for arbitration and would pledge to use "both their economic and military forces" against any one of their number that refused to do so.[72]

The founders of the League openly acknowledged their indebtedness to the Bryan Treaties.[73] Their one major inno-

71. For an excellent discussion of Dewey's distinction between force and violence, see Morton White, *Social Thought in America* (Boston, Beacon Press Edition, 1957), pp. 161–72.

72. *Enforced Peace: Proceedings of the First Annual National Assemblage of the League to Enforce Peace, Washington, May 26–27, 1916* (New York, 1916), pp. 7–8. For more detailed discussions of the origins and principles of the League, see Ruhl F. Bartlett, *The League to Enforce Peace* (Chapel Hill, 1944), Chapter II, and Theodore Marburg, *League of Nations* (New York, 1917), I, *passim*.

73. Theodore Marburg, one of the founders of the League, has written: "What the League to Enforce Peace proposes is to take the present Bryan Treaties of obligatory inquiry, made in pairs, and make them common to all members of the League. It proposed further to add to the obligation which alone attaches to them now the element of compulsion in order to force a resort to inquiry before a nation is

vation was to add to those treaties the element of force which would be used to compel a reluctant member to arbitrate before it resorted to war. It was this addition that troubled Bryan and formed the basis of his initial hostility toward the new organization. The rapid endorsement of the League by such interventionists as Roosevelt and Henry Cabot Lodge merely confirmed his suspicions and deepened his hostility. The League was only two days old when Bryan first spoke out against it in his Carnegie Hall address, denouncing it as an attempt to fight "militarism with militarism." [74] From that time forward he neglected no opportunity to strike out against the League. Such performances as his widely reported address at the Lake Mohonk Conference on International Arbitration in May 1916, and his written debate with the League's president, William Howard Taft, which filled an entire volume, soon made Bryan "the most influential opponent" of the League in the United States.[75]

Bryan's primary objection to the League was that it was committing the same error as the preparationists: it was attempting to build peace upon a foundation of force when it was clear that "Love and the spirit of brotherhood are the only foundation upon which a permanent peace can be built." [76] "Peace is not a thing that can be enforced," he wrote the German Ambassador. "It is a result that follows from the establishment of friendship and co-operation." [77] Taft objected to Bryan's emphasis upon the coercive aspects of the

allowed to precipitate war. It is on the fairness and usefulness of this principle that the League program is mainly based." Ibid. I, 65.

74. "Labor's Interest in Peace," *The Commoner*, July 1915, p. 9.
75. *Report of the Twenty-Second Annual Lake Mohonk Conference on International Arbitration, May 17, 18, and 19, 1916*, pp. 144–7; *World Peace: A Written Debate Between William Howard Taft and William Jennings Bryan* (New York, 1917); Bartlett, *The League to Enforce Peace*, p. 70.
76. *The Commoner*, February 1916, p. 3.
77. WJB to Count von Bernstorff, December 15, 1916, Bryan Papers.

League. No one, the ex-President pointed out, contemplated using force to uphold the decisions of the League's tribunals but only to insure that all members would lay their disputes before the courts; after that they were free to act as they pleased. Bryan characteristically refused to see the difference. Force was force, and force was wrong. "Do not reason and experience combine to prove that it provokes rather than prevents war?" he asked. Throughout his youth Bryan had been taught the Christian principle that truths should be propagated by example. It seemed self-evident, then, that if a nation wished to be loved and not merely feared, it must "conquer with its ideals rather than with its arms." [78]

Bryan's early objections to the League as a futile and outmoded attempt to fight fire with fire were soon reinforced by arguments which were as badly warped by historical fundamentalism as his later views on science were by Scriptural fundamentalism. The plan advocated by the proponents of the League, he charged, was a repudiation of the teachings of Washington and Jefferson. To participate in such an organization would necessitate a "revolutionary" change in our international policy and an abandonment of the "priceless advantage of isolation"; it would mean scrapping the Monroe Doctrine and delegating the Congressional power to declare war to "a council controlled by European nations." [79] Using phrases which he later came to regret, Bryan cried: "America first! . . . Beware of Entangling Alliances." He would give "millions for defense" against any nation that ever attacked us, "but not one American boy to march under the banner of a foreign monarch or sacrifice his life in the settlement of European disputes." [80]

Bryan frequently appeared to be more of an isolationist

78. WJB and Taft, *World Peace*, pp. 19, 27, 139.
79. Ibid. pp. 98, 101–2, 138.
80. *The Commoner*, May 1916, pp. 1–2, 4.

than he actually was. He comprehended the growing interdependence of the international community as clearly as did the advocates of the League, but he sought to deal with it by a series of treaties in which moral compulsion would constitute the chief deterrent to war rather than by an alliance in which physical compulsion was contemplated. His vision of the moral superiority of the United States prevented him from engendering any degree of enthusiasm for an alliance which he felt would force his country to take part in the amoral power politics of the European nations and drag it down to their "lower level." [81] America's destiny was not to join hands with other nations as an equal, but to maintain an example toward which they could strive: to stand as a beacon to the older nations who finally would come to be inspired and would emulate the Christian purity of the American republic. The curious combination of faith and fear which so colored his attitude toward the people, was an equally potent factor in determining his attitude toward his country's role in the world.

When the *New Republic* called Bryan's policy of disarmament on the one hand and opposition to any kind of international organization on the other "the perfect example of how do-nothingism may go hand in hand with immense pretensions," [82] it was not being entirely just, for Bryan's program was far from one of "do-nothingism." His opposition to the League was by no means purely negative. On the contrary, he proposed a series of alternatives to it, the most important of which was his own peace treaty plan. [83]

81. One of Bryan's favorite ways of illustrating this fear was by telling the story of the man who, when he was asked for help by a drunken companion lying in the gutter, replied: "I can't help you up; but I will lie down with you." WJB and Taft, *World Peace*, p. 40.

82. *New Republic*, III (June 26, 1915), 187.

83. These alternatives may be found in WJB and Taft, *World Peace*, pp. 141-2.

Throughout his long struggle for peace, the treaties that he himself had negotiated were never far from Bryan's mind. Again and again he brought them forth and pleaded for their implementation. "I have such faith in these treaties," he wrote frequently during these years, "that I believe that a thousand years from now the name of Woodrow Wilson and my name will be linked together in these treaties, in the capitols [sic] of the world, and that these treaties, by furnishing machinery by which peace can be preserved with honor, will still be preserving the peace of our nations." [84]

Bryan's plea for the utilization of his treaties went unheeded. The world had undergone many changes since his proposals were first introduced, and while to Bryan these changes constituted additional evidence of the need for his treaties, to others they revealed the inadequacies of the method he proposed. William Allen White, who shared Bryan's enthusiasm for the treaties, was to write of them in later years:

> Of course I now know that the world was not ready for them. . . . Why did we not see? Why did he [Bryan] and I talking about peace, run on and on, without ever realizing that treaties alone cannot maintain peace? [85]

This realization, which came to White only belatedly, was never really to dawn upon Bryan despite his later advocacy of the League of Nations. Bryan had a greater understanding of world affairs than many have given him credit for, and a number of his specific proposals were more realistic than those of his contemporaries and might well have succeeded in keeping the nation out of the war. Nevertheless, he was so positive that the interest of all nations was virtually identical and that ideas in themselves could compel action if they con-

84. *The Commoner*, October 1916, p. 14.
85. *The Autobiography of William Allen White*, p. 509.

formed to the mandates of God, that he was led to devote
his time and energy more to the formulation of ends than
of means. His proposals were too often ridden through with
inconsistencies and conflicting desires. He called upon the
United States to lead the nations of the world upon the road
of brotherhood and peace but seemed convinced that should
it extend its hand in fellowship it would not only fail to elevate its sister nations but would be dragged down to their
level. He ignored the need for law enforcement agencies in
international politics and advocated a complete reliance upon
moral precepts: a course of action which he never would have
supported domestically. He called for the introduction of
Christian principles into international relations and yet placed
his hopes in a plan which assumed that those very principles
were already operative. And, like so many Americans of his
generation, he tended to equate American accomplishments
with morality and to brand the actions and institutions of the
rest of the world, insofar as they differed from those of the
United States, as anachronistic and unworthy. If Bryan's foreign policy failed it was not because he was too dense to
perceive the world's needs but because the assumptions upon
which he operated led him to unrealistic or inadequate solutions to very real problems. Too often he equated good intentions with carefully planned action, and he never really
learned that treaties alone, regardless of their importance, cannot establish permanent peace, any more than prohibition can
establish sobriety, or anti-evolution laws, orthodoxy.

(5)

The Presidential elections scheduled for November 1916
formed a backdrop against which the fight over such issues as
preparedness and American entry into an international alliance must be viewed. In committing themselves to one course
or another, the leaders of the Democracy never quite lost sight

of the impending contest. The dilemma in which they found themselves was not an enviable one. On the one hand, they must not follow a policy which the Republicans could attack as one of appeasement or cowardice, and, on the other, they must not permanently alienate the Bryanite wing of the party. It was this latter consideration that troubled many members of the Administration, for although Bryan no longer held an official post and although his every action was roundly castigated by a large segment of the press, he still had a following the size and loyalty of which no one could estimate and whose votes no one could disregard.[86]

Wilson, regardless of what he thought privately, publicly refused to criticize any of the actions or statements of his ex-Secretary even when they directly endangered the success of his policies. Still more indicative of the respect which the President and his advisers had for Bryan's political power was their decision to continue to consult with him over appointments. Bryan's long-standing feud with Senator Gilbert M. Hitchcock of Nebraska had complicated and, in some cases, prevented the distribution of patronage in their state.[87] Bryan's departure from the inner circles of the Administration led the Hitchcock forces to believe that they would become the sole dispensers of federal patronage in Nebraska, but their expectations were short-lived. Both Secretary McAdoo and Attorney General Gregory, presumably with Wilson's compliance, refused to make any appointments from Nebraska without Bryan's approval. In addition, they allowed him to select one-half of all the appointments made. Any other

86. The *Nebraska State Journal*, a strongly pro-Administration paper, estimated that Bryan was "the absolute leader of two or three million people." July 1, 1915.
87. WJB to Woodrow Wilson, August 21, 1914, WJB to Hitchcock, August 21, 1914, Bryan Papers; William Gibbs McAdoo to Hitchcock, July 1, 1915, William Gibbs McAdoo Papers (Library of Congress, Washington, D.C.). Cited hereafter as McAdoo Papers.

course of action would create a party schism, McAdoo insisted. "Mr. Bryan," he added, "is one of the great leaders of the party. He has long occupied a distinguished place in its counsels, and even as a private citizen his recommendations are entitled to consideration and to weight."[88]

Many observers, however, felt the Administration's attempts to conciliate Bryan were futile. They reasoned that a man who would risk personal oblivion by resigning his post in the midst of a crisis would have few compunctions about risking the ruin of his party in an attempt to coerce it into following his own convictions. Shortly after Bryan's resignation, Colonel House glumly predicted that the ex-Secretary's differences with the President would soon break out into "open-antagonism," and there were others who went much further in their predictions.[89] Bryan's vehement denunciations of Wilson's preparedness plan, his support of those Congressmen who were attempting to override the President's wishes on several issues, and his statement during the Nebraska primaries that on questions of peace and preparedness he represented the sentiments of the common people better

88. McAdoo to Hitchcock, July 1, 1915, McAdoo to Gregory, July 3, 1915, McAdoo Papers; McAdoo to Hitchcock, July 21, 1915, Gilbert M. Hitchcock Papers (Library of Congress, Washington, D.C.), Vol. I. Cited hereafter as Hitchcock Papers. *Nebraska State Journal,* June 20, 1915.

89. Edward House to Walter Hines Page, August 12, 1915, Hendrick, *Life and Letters of Walter Hines Page,* II, 13. George Harvey, for instance, wrote: "Mr. Bryan means war. He means to torpedo the Democratic party precisely as Mr. Roosevelt shot the fatal bolt into the Republican organization three years ago . . .", Harvey, *North American Review,* CCII (July 1915), 5. Similarly, John Temple Graves wrote in the *New York American:* "the ex-Secretary and his chief will be engaged in the most spectacular and slashing controversy of the decade." *Literary Digest,* L (June 26, 1915), 1517. In addition, many Republicans proclaimed the inevitability of a Democratic split in 1916 which would insure their victory. Ibid. L (June 19, 1915), 1440.

than the President,[90] seemed to substantiate these prophecies. Wilson received numerous letters warning him that Bryan's supporters were actively working in the states to create sentiment against his programs and in some cases were working for Bryan's nomination in 1916.[91]

Could the Administration's supporters have seen Bryan's private correspondence during the spring of 1916, their fears would have deepened. Secretary Daniels, who had adroitly managed to retain the friendship and confidence of both Bryan and Wilson, asked the former to make an announcement regarding Wilson's renomination as soon as possible. Bryan's first reply to this request came at the height of the preparedness controversy and was far from reassuring. He was reluctant to make any statement just yet, he wrote Daniels, for it might not be favorable to Wilson:

I have been amazed at the slush he [Wilson] has been pouring out upon the West. Is he simply imposing upon the public and trying to *scare* the voters into accepting his policy? Or does he really mean that he is writing *notes* only because our unpreparedness prevents a resort to force? If he means the latter then he wants the increase *in order to enter into this war* and if that is his reason what difference is there between him and Roosevelt? It is disturbing to see our Party's chances of success disregarded and the country's peace menaced by one in

90. *Nebraska State Journal*, March 26, 1916.
91. See letters to Wilson from the following: Peter J. Hamilton, November 23, 1915; William T. Sapp, January 21, 1916; E. C. Weber, January 21, 1916; Joseph F. Guffey, March, 10, 1916; Wilson Papers, File VI, Box 491. See also the following letters to Joseph P. Tumulty: John T. Short, July 2, 1915; Senator Atlee Pomerene, August 5, 1915; ibid. Bryan repeatedly denied that he was interested in running for the Presidency. He curtly refused to allow any delegates in California "or anywhere else" to be pledged to him. WJB to Daniel O'Connell, March 17, 1916, Bryan Papers. See also *New York Times*, August 1, September 29, 1915; *The Commoner*, November 1915; John R. Dunlap to Woodrow Wilson, January 16, 1916, Wilson Papers, File VI, Box 491.

whom we had such high hopes. If I find that his purpose is to drag this nation into this war I may feel it is my duty to oppose his nomination. I can conceive no greater calamity than an endorsement by the Democratic party of such a policy.[92]

His subsequent letters to Daniels and others continued in the same vein. In one of them he wrote: "My difference with the President is more religious than political. His course seems to me a repudiation of all that is essential in the Christian religion." [93] Daniels may well have repeated these views to Wilson, for in March the President told House that he feared Bryan would bolt.[94]

It is probable that Bryan intended that the contents of his correspondence with Daniels be revealed to the President in the hope that they might have a restraining influence upon him. In any case, these letters are more revealing as an indication of Bryan's momentary indignation and disappointment than as an accurate portent of his plans. Those who flatly predicted that Bryan would bolt the party disregarded the enduring strength of his partisanship and, even more important, they overlooked the fact that despite any doubts he might have had about the President's foreign policy, he was genuinely pleased with and intensely proud of the reform measures carried out during the past three years. His apprehensions about the possibilities of American involvement in the war failed to blunt the joy he received in seeing so many of the laws he had fought for since the 1890's placed upon the statute books. For the first time in his political career Bryan was able to look forward to a Presidential campaign in which he could direct attention to the concrete accomplishments of

92. WJB to Daniels, February 4, 1916, Daniels Papers, Box 37.

93. Jonathan Daniels, *The End of Innocence*, p. 187. See also WJB to Charles M. Rosser, February 5, 1916, Charles McDaniel Rosser, *The Crusading Commoner* (Dallas, 1937), p. 250; WJB to Albert S. Burleson, March 8, 1916, Burleson Papers, Vol. 17.

94. Link, *Wilson and the Progressive Era*, p. 224n.

a Democratic Administration, rather than merely to uncertain promises of future reforms. He was understandably reluctant to forgo such an opportunity, especially when the President demonstrated that he was not going to carry his preparedness program beyond the limits of moderation.

Months before the Democratic convention met, Bryan gave ample evidence of his decision to refrain from playing a divisive role. In speeches he delivered in March and April, while touring Nebraska during the primary campaign there, he congratulated the Wilson Administration for having enacted into law "more important measures than were passed by any previous administration in our history, in the same length of time," and added somewhat inaccurately, "With the exception of the question of 'Preparedness' which has arisen since I resigned from the Cabinet, on no other question have I differed from the President." [95] Similarly, in a magazine article published in early April, Bryan reviewed the various reforms realized under the Administration, praised them highly, and stated his belief that the Democratic party "has earned the confidence of the public and should therefore receive it." [96] In his own periodical, too, Bryan carried on a campaign of praise for the "remarkable" accomplishments of the Wilson Administration. Using his own brand of logic, he even found it possible to vindicate Wilson partially for his stand on preparedness: "Where the President has conceded more than he should to the scaredness program, the Republican leaders have demanded even more, so that the President is nearer to the people than the Republican leaders." [97]

95. *The Commoner*, April 1916, p. 3. In another speech Bryan said: "If Woodrow Wilson owes me anything he has more than paid it back by giving himself to the nation as President instead of Roosevelt." *Nebraska State Journal*, March 21, 1916.

96. WJB, "The Democrats Should Win," *The Independent*, LXXXVI (April 3, 1916), 14.

97. *The Commoner*, April 1916, p. 3.

Bryan's decision to support Wilson's bid for re-election did not restrain him from continuing his public clamor for an American-initiated peace movement. In May he reminded the Democratic party that Wilson had been elected by virtue of a breach in the Republican party which was now healed. If the President was to be re-elected it was necessary that he appeal to those who did not vote for him in 1912. The most important group in this category, Bryan maintained, was the "peace element" in the Republican party whose support could easily be assured if Wilson appealed to the belligerents to call a peace conference. Should the President thus "give voice to the world's conscience and humanity's hope" he would destroy the advantage the Republicans had and would be able to run on the record of a peacemaker.[98] Although Wilson did not follow Bryan's advice, he did make a number of statements in the weeks that followed which the latter was able to construe as meaning he was not opposed to the idea of mediation. Thus Bryan attended the party's convention in a hopeful frame of mind.[99]

The Democrats who began to gather in St. Louis during the second week in June for the national convention that was to begin on June 14, could hardly have looked forward to a very exciting affair. There was some talk about replacing Vice President Marshall, and there was considerable grumbling over the proposed declaration for woman suffrage, but outside of these there were few interesting issues. Wilson was to be renominated without opposition, the platform had already been written by him in Washington, and word had been received that the keynote of the convention was to be Americanism.[100] Probably the most novel aspect of the convention

98. *New York Times*, May 14, 1916.

99. WJB to Albert S. Burleson, May 24, 1916, Burleson Papers, Vol. 17.

100. Newton Baker to Ray Stannard Baker, April 30, 1932, R. S. Baker Papers, Box 20; *New York Times*, June 12, 14, 1916.

was that it was the first such gathering in twenty years in which William Jennings Bryan was neither a leading candidate nor an important delegate. Bryan had been defeated earlier by the Democrats of Nebraska in his bid for election as delegate-at-large,[101] and although Wilson had expressed the hope that some way might be found to permit his participation in the proceedings and more than a score of delegates had offered to give up their seats to him, Bryan attended as a reporter for a nation-wide syndicate of newspapers.[102] This, however, did not prevent those present at the convention from manifesting "spontaneous and genuine enthusiasm" for him. He occupied a prominent seat in the press gallery and every time he came in the delegates cheered him. He received so consistently warm a reception that even before the proceedings had ended the *New York Times* was calling him "the outstanding figure of the Convention." [103]

The keynote address was delivered by temporary chairman Martin H. Glynn of New York, who had previously discussed his speech with Bryan who found it "most satisfactory." [104] Glynn's desire to justify the foreign policy of Woodrow Wilson led him to attempt to prove, through historical precedent, that "the policy of neutrality is as truly American as the American flag"; that it was, in fact, the policy pursued by every great American President from Washington to Cleveland.[105] Specifically, the former New York Governor pro-

101. This defeat, however, came about over the issue of prohibition and not of peace. See below, pp. 113–16.

102. *Nebraska State Journal*, April 27, 1916. Bryan had attended the Republican and Progressive national conventions in the same role. He called the former a "comedy" and the latter a "tragedy." *The Commoner*, June 1916, p. 14.

103. Harry Howland, "Sounding the Keynote at St. Louis," *The Independent*, LXXXVI (June 26, 1916), 11; *New York Times*, June 15, 16, 1916.

104. *Memoirs*, p. 440.

105. For Glynn's address see *Official Report of the Proceedings of the Democratic National Convention held in Saint Louis, Missouri,*

ceeded to discuss Grant's difficulties with Spain, Harrison's with Chile, and Lincoln's with England and France, showing in each case how these disputes could have led to war had not the Presidents involved insisted upon settling them peacefully. Though he had come prepared with still more precedents, Glynn, who had the orator's fear of tiring his listeners by the recitation of too many facts, attempted to pass on to another matter, but he misjudged the temper of the convention. Cries of "go on, go on," "Hit him again," "Hit him again," "Give it to them," filled the hall. Glynn, who seemed as surprised as anyone else at this burst of enthusiasm, cheerfully complied, citing the actions of Van Buren, John Adams, Washington, and Jefferson. As he described the manner by which each of these Chief Executives had been driven to the verge of war, the delegates would cry: "What did he do?" "What did he do?" and Glynn would respond: "What did he do? . . . He settled our disputes by negotiation just as the President is trying to do. . . . We didn't go to war!" [106]

When the full impact of what was happening reached the Administration leaders they became alarmed. Senator John W. Smith of Maryland rushed to the platform to confer with National Chairman William F. McCombs and both men agreed that if Americanism was to be made the keynote of the convention the effect of Glynn's speech had to be modified. McCombs snatched a sheet of paper, jotted down the words "But we are willing to fight if necessary," signed his name to it and passed it up to Glynn, who glanced at it and called back: "I'll take care of that." [107] But this phrase never found its way into his speech. Instead Glynn roused his audience to even greater heights of frenzy by thundering that while the

June 14, 15 and 16th, 1916, pp. 14–41. Cited hereafter as *Official Proceedings . . . 1916.*

106. Ibid. pp. 22–4.
107. *New York Times,* June 15, 1916.

policy he was describing did not satisfy "those who revel in destruction and find pleasure in despair . . . the fire-eater or the swashbuckler," it did satisfy

> those who worship at the altar of the God of Peace. It does satisfy the mothers of the land (applause) . . . at whose hearth and fireside no jingoistic war has placed an empty chair. It does satisfy the daughters of this land, from whom brag and bluster have sent no husband, no sweetheart and no brother to the smouldering dissolution of the grave. It does satisfy the fathers of this land, and the sons of this land, who will fight for our flag, and die for our flag, when Reason primes the rifle — (long continued applause) . . . when Honor draws the sword, when Justice breathes a blessing on the standards they uphold.

"And, Mr. Speaker," a Texas delegate cried out when the roar of approval began to subside, "don't forget that this policy also satisfies William Jennings Bryan." [108]

Glynn's speech was an amazing performance which illustrated that anti-war sentiment was not necessarily the pariah which the nation's press tried to make of it. If there were delegates who had wondered whether their desire for peace was heroic, their doubts were dissolved by Glynn's oratory. Up in the press gallery, Bryan wept as he listened to the demonstration for peace, though his joy would have been dampened considerably had he been in Washington that very day to see the President, flag draped over one shoulder, leading a preparedness campaign through the streets of the Capital.[109] The remainder of Glynn's long speech dealt with preparedness, Mexico, the Federal Reserve Act, the tariff, prosperity, and Wilson, and though it was often eloquent and was well received, it seemed anticlimatic. The apex of emotion had already been reached; the assembled Democrats had already

108. *Official Proceedings . . . 1916*, p. 26.
109. *New York Times*, June 15, 1916; Millis, *Road to War*, p. 318.

selected their issue, *the* issue that despite Wilson's reluctance
was to pervade the ensuing campaign.

In his speech the next day permanent chairman Ollie James
of Kentucky took up where Glynn had left off, and brought
the great crowd to its feet by declaring that Wilson, without
orphaning a single child, widowing a single mother, firing a
single gun or shedding a single drop of blood, had "wrung
from the most militant spirit that ever brooded above a battlefield an acknowledgment of American rights and an agreement to American demands." After making the speaker repeat
these sentiments verbatim, the frenzied gathering staged a 21-
minute demonstration.[110] The convention that Wilson had
desired to make a demonstration for Americanism had become
a demonstration for peace instead. Even when James was finally allowed to finish his address the appetite of the galleries
and the delegates for oratory was apparently unsatiated, for as
soon as he requested the report of the Committee on Rules
they began to chant, "Bryan, Bryan, Bryan." Not until the
harassed chairman assured the delegates that they would have
"ample opportunity" to hear from Bryan was order restored.[111]

When the Convention reconvened at nine that same evening, Senator Thompson of Kansas moved that "the rules be
suspended and that the Honorable William Jennings Bryan be
invited to address this convention." The resolution passed
unanimously, and while James was introducing him as "one of
the world's great citizens and one of America's greatest Democrats," Bryan made his way to the platform amidst a thun-
derous ovation.[112] As he began to speak there were still those
who viewed the whole proceeding with uneasiness; some

110. *Official Proceedings . . . 1916*, pp. 88–9.
111. Ibid. p. 91.
112. Ibid. p. 94.

feared that despite his promise to support the ticket, Bryan would assail the President and announce that he was going to bolt the party, while others feared that he would limit his endorsement of the Administration to domestic matters.[113] Their fears were soon assuaged, for Bryan's address, like many of his pre-convention utterances, was an elaborate encomium to the Wilson Administration. Despite any differences within the party, Bryan began, Democrats stood united for the coming battle: "The Democratic party is a party that encourages independent thought among its members. If they all thought alike, it would be proof conclusive that they did not think at all." But differences aside, there were ample reasons for all Democrats to go before the nation and defend the Administration's record. The quantity of social welfare legislation enacted under Wilson, he said proudly, was greater than had been enacted in all previous administrations combined. Furthermore, it had been a Democratic President supported by a Democratic Congress that saved the country from the horrors of war. "My friends," he exclaimed, "I have differed with our President on some of the methods employed, but I join with the American people in thanking God that we have a President who does not want this nation plunged into this war." [114]

The 1916 convention was a far more pleasing experience for Bryan than the events of the preceding year would have led him

113. In a speech to the Progressive National Convention on June 10, Victor Murdock predicted that Bryan would not swallow the Democratic party's preparedness plank and would run for President on a prohibition-pacifist ticket with Henry Ford as his running mate. *New York Times*, June 11, 1916. On the very eve of the convention, a former Governor of "a populous Western state" warned that Bryan "would throw the convention into excitement, uproar, turmoil, confusion and alarm." Hard, *Everybody's*, XXXIV (April 1916), 458. See also *New York Times*, June 16, 1916.

114. *Official Proceedings . . . 1916*, pp. 94–100.

to expect.[115] The phrase "He kept us out of war" was taken by Bryan and by most of the delegates to imply: "He will keep us out of war." Wilson and most of his advisers meant no such thing. The President, in fact, never approved of the use of the phrase at all; it was a product of the convention and its use in the campaign was due to the insistence of Burleson.[116] "I can't keep the country out of war," Wilson complained to Daniels. "They talk of me as though I were a god. Any little German lieutenant can put us into the war at any time by some calculated outrage." [117] Considerations such as this, however, did not plague Bryan; he had no inner doubts as to the real sentiments of the delegates and he entered the campaign with an ardor and determination that were reminiscent of 1896. Bryan, indeed, made more speeches for Wilson in the pivotal West in 1916 than he had ever made in his own behalf.[118] He launched his campaign on September 17, and from then until the night before the election he toured twenty states averaging four or five speeches a day.[119] In the speech which, with some modifications, he delivered before one audience after another, Bryan eloquently hailed each of the reform measures passed by the Democrats under Wilson, praised the President's foreign policy, and then warned his listeners:

115. Mrs. Bryan noted in her diary at the time: "I had dreaded these days for him and am glad to record that they were easier than I had supposed possible." *Memoirs*, p. 440.

116. Albert S. Burleson to Ray Stannard Baker, July 14, 1928, R. S. Baker Papers.

117. Ray Stannard Baker interview with Josephus Daniels, March 20, 1929, ibid. Box 28.

118. Josephus Daniels, "Wilson and Bryan," *The Saturday Evening Post*, CXCVIII (September 5, 1925), 54.

119. Bryan campaigned in the following states: New Mexico, Arizona, Nevada, Utah, Wyoming, Montana, North Dakota, Iowa, Kansas, Oklahoma, Colorado, Missouri, Tennessee, Kentucky, Pennsylvania, Ohio, Michigan, Wisconsin, Illinois, and Nebraska. *The Commoner*, November 1916, p. 2.

tion was won, Bryan maintained, "BY THE WEST AND SOUTH WITHOUT THE AID OR CONSENT OF THE EAST. The scepter has passed from New York, and this is sufficient glory for one year." [127] This mood, which was echoed by numerous progressive Democrats throughout the country, is important for an understanding of the difficulties the Democratic party was to face in the Twenties. It had won the election of 1916 but it was far from a united party and already contained the seeds of the schism that was to render it virtually impotent throughout the next decade.

Of the twenty states in which Bryan had personally campaigned, only five went to Hughes. Bryan felt a sense of personal vindication, and this feeling was enhanced by a letter from the President expressing deep appreciation and indebtedness, and by a flood of congratulatory telegrams from almost every important figure in the Administration.[128] In December, influential Democrats in Washington, D.C., held a victory banquet in Bryan's honor, at which Senator Walsh called Bryan's role in the recent victory "the factor most transcendent in importance." [129] Nor were these sentiments limited to friendly voices alone. The *Chicago Tribune*, which expressed the wish that Bryan had been born a "German or a Jap, or even a Canadian or a Mexican," called him "the most powerful single individual in the United States. . . . He has permeated the West. His mood is the mood of the West. He is more responsible for President Wilson now than he was

127. *The Commoner*, November 1916, p. 1.
128. See the letters and telegrams to Bryan from the following: Woodrow Wilson, November 17, 1916, Joseph Tumulty, November 18, 1916, Thomas W. Gregory, November 12, 1916, Robert Lansing, November 24, 1916, Bryan Papers; William G. McAdoo, November 10, 1916, Albert S. Burleson, November 7, 1916, Franklin K. Lane, November 10, 1916, John Skelton Williams, November 13, 1916, *The Commoner*, November 1916, p. 4. For more of the same, see ibid. December 1916, p. 10.
129. Ibid. January 1917, p. 12.

four years ago." And a correspondent for the *New York Evening Post* wrote: "Now you may have your own guess as to which of twenty things it was that elected Wilson; but if you said Bryan it would be as safe as any one of the twenty." [130]

The Nebraskan, it seemed, was finally emerging from the Wilderness.

(6)

Though war was only five months away, the period following the election of 1916 was one of hope and promise for the advocates of peace. The pacific spirit that made itself manifest in the Presidential campaign continued to grow, and relations with Germany were becoming increasingly friendly. The actions of England rather than of Germany began to occupy the attention and tax the patience of the President.[131] The obvious peace sentiments of his fellow countrymen and his growing disillusionment with Great Britain were probably decisive in determining Wilson's decision to attempt to act as a mediator. His proposal met the immediate opposition of his closest advisers. House insisted that the agreement of the Allies should be sought *before* any peace proposal was made.[132] Lansing was even more vehemently opposed to a negotiated peace at that time. In September, the Secretary of State confided to his diary: "I will never sign an ultimatum to Great Britain; I will act in favor of mediation though with great reluctance, but I would not do it if I thought it would amount to anything." And, in December, he was still writing of his "strong objections" to Wilson's venture in peacemaking.[133]

130. Editorials reprinted in ibid. December 1916, pp. 1, 9.

131. Woodrow Wilson to Edward House, July 23, November 24, 1916, R. S. Baker Papers, Box 7; Wilson to Edward House, October 10, 1916, Wilson Papers, File VII, Box 18.

132. Ernest R. May, *The World War and American Isolation* (Cambridge, 1959), p. 364.

133. See entries for September 1916, December 3, 1916, Lansing Diaries.

On December 12, the Kaiser's overtures for peace negotiations undercut the President's own proposed plea for a peace conference. Nevertheless, six days later Wilson sent notes to all the belligerents asking them to state the terms upon which they would agree to an end of hostilities. Bryan, who had asked Wilson to take this step two years earlier, immediately telegraphed his former chief: "You have rendered an invaluable service to a war-stricken world. . . . "[134] Several days earlier he had cabled Lloyd George: "As a friend of all the nations at war, as a Christian and a lover of humanity, I respectfully but most earnestly appeal to you to use your great influence to secure your government's consent to negotiations. . . . Your decision may mean life or death to millions."[135] The British Prime Minister made no reply.

With the desire for peace apparently firmly entrenched in his own country, Bryan felt a renewed desire to journey to Europe in an endeavor to halt the bloodletting there. In the beginning of December, the American ambassador to Germany, James W. Gerard, informed Wilson that Bryan had recently told him of his intention to inaugurate a peace mission and had asked Gerard to obtain permission for him to see the Kaiser and the officials of the Foreign Office. The President instructed Gerard to do "nothing of the kind," and in relating these facts to House he cited Bryan's proposed trip as an additional reason for him to make his own peace proposal shortly. "Evidently a great deal of deliberate mischief is brewing COMMONERwards," he wrote.[136] The proposed mission, however, never got under way.

Instead of traveling to Europe, Bryan journeyed to Washington for the opening of Congress on December 5. There he

134. WJB to Wilson, December 21, 1916, Wilson Papers, File VI, Box 491.
135. WJB to Lloyd George, December 15, 1916, Bryan Papers. See also WJB to Cecil Spring-Rice, December 15, 1916, ibid.
136. Wilson to House, December 3, 1916, R. S. Baker Papers, Box 7.

received an enthusiastic reception on the floor of the House of Representatives and the assurance of several members that the majority of Congressmen favored the maintenance of peace.[137] Encouraged by the course of events, Bryan continued his crusade for peace, speaking to anyone who would listen. His energy remained inexhaustible. On one trip alone, in the beginning of January, he addressed the legislatures of North Carolina, Ohio, Indiana, Missouri, and Tennessee.[138] In his speech before the Senate on January 22, 1917, the President made the prospects of peace seem still more auspicious by calling for a "peace without victory," and proposing a "definite concert of powers" to make future wars impossible. Although Bryan continued to oppose the latter idea, he praised the President's "epoch-making appeal to the conscience of the world." "Your message," he wrote Wilson, ". . . will place you among the Immortals."[139] Just nine days after Wilson's action inspired such hope among the advocates of peace, Germany announced her intention of resuming unrestricted submarine warfare after February 1.

Two days after Germany's announcement shocked the country, Bryan delivered a previously arranged address at Madison Square Garden. More than 5,000 New Yorkers gathered in the Garden to hear what was perhaps the most eloquent and moving appeal of Bryan's entire struggle for peace. Mingling rustic wit with evangelical fervor, Bryan excoriated the principle of preparedness, pleaded for love and brotherhood, and recited anew the horror with which the events in Europe filled him: "They have exhausted human

137. *Washington Post*, December 6, 1916, clipping in Bryan Papers.
138. WJB, *Address of Honorable William Jennings Bryan to the Forty-Ninth General Assembly of the State of Missouri, January twenty-fourth, 1917* (Jefferson City, Missouri, 1917), pp. 5–6.
139. *The Commoner*, March 1917, p. 8; WJB to Wilson, January 26, 1917, Wilson Papers, File VI, Box 491. For Wilson's response, see Wilson to WJB, February 2, 1917, ibid. File VII, Box 21.

ingenuity to find new ways in which man may kill his fellow man. And these are not barbarous nations; they are among the civilized nations of the earth. They are not heathen nations; they are among the Christian nations of the globe. . . . They kneel and offer their prayers to a Common Heavenly Father and then rise up to take each other's lives." ". . . the men who die and the women who weep," he thundered, "have had neither party nor voice in determining whether there should be peace or war." He did not attempt to minimize the importance of the German announcement but he refused to believe that it necessitated direct and immediate action. Once again his vision of the future proved to be his guidepost for present action:

> If Civilization is to advance, the day must come when a nation will feel no more obligated to accept a challenge to war than an American citizen now feels obligated to accept a challenge to fight a duel. . . . If there ever was a time . . . when a nation was justified, aye, compelled to be patient and exercise Christian forbearance, that time is now and our nation is the nation.[140]

The next day, February 3, Bryan arrived in Washington to find that Wilson had already severed diplomatic relations with Germany. He immediately phoned Senator La Follette, and the two sat in Bryan's room at the Hotel Lafayette desperately searching for a plan to prevent the nation from being stampeded into war. Finally they decided to concentrate on Congress: Bryan would call in as many Democrats as possible while La Follette saw the progressive Republicans in an effort to unite the two groups on behalf of peace.[141] That evening

140. WJB, *America and the European War: Address by William Jennings Bryan at Madison Square Garden, February 2, 1917* (New York, 1917), pp. 6, 14.
141. Belle C. La Follette and Fola La Follette, *Robert M. La Follette* (New York, 1953), I, 594.

Bryan issued an "Appeal To The American People" in which
he resurrected every peace proposal he had advocated during
the past two years. He pleaded with the people to consider
these alternatives and make their views known to the President. "A few cents now," he cautioned, "may save many dollars in taxation and possibly a son." [142] Hundreds of such
communications were, in fact, received by the President and
members of Congress,[143] but the mass protest which Bryan
had hoped for never materialized. Bryan spent the next few
days speaking to Congressmen. "We are so near war that I
feel I ought to stay here," he wrote to his wife. ". . . It is
distressing to see so many men afraid to act. I am needed to
give them courage and help and plan. Have already strengthened several. . . . I am awfully disappointed. . . . How little we know of the future. The President's action bears out
my fears expressed when I resigned." [144]

The year that had dawned so hopefully was turning into
one of the bitterest periods of Bryan's life. The nation's press
assailed him with a harshness that often surpassed that following his resignation; [145] his mail contained threats of assassina-
tion; [146] he was denounced on the floor of Congress as a coward and was compared to the Royalists during the Revolution
and the Copperheads during the Civil War; [147] a rumor

142. *The Commoner*, February 1917, p. 2; *New York Times*, February 4, 1917.

143. Ibid. February 7, 1917.

144. WJB to Mary B. Bryan (undated, but probably February 3,
1917), Bryan Papers.

145. The *Philadelphia Inquirer*, for instance, accused him of action
akin to treason. Quoted in Arnett, *Claude Kitchin*, p. 213.

146. R. K. Gratigny to WJB, February 4, 1917, Bryan Papers.

147. These charges were made by two Republican Congressmen:
Clarence Miller of Minnesota and Augustus P. Gardner of Massachusetts. Bryan was defended by Representatives George Huddleston
of Alabama and Warren Worth Bailey of Pennsylvania, both Democrats, and Charles A. Sloane of Nebraska, a Republican. *New York
Times*, February 6, 16, 18, 1917.

spread through Washington that he had pleaded with von Bernstorff, the departing German Ambassador, to remain in Washington and assured him that America would not back the President in a war with Germany; [148] an effort was made to prosecute him under the Logan Act for allegedly drawing up a cable to Germany urging a spirit of conciliation and repeating his belief that America did not want war; [149] Judge Alton B. Parker, the Democratic Presidential candidate in 1904, publicly called him and his followers aspiring Benedict Arnolds and held him responsible for the dangers the country now faced; [150] and a mob in Baltimore toured the streets chanting: "We'll hang Bill Bryan on a sour apple tree." [151]

Though the hopelessness of his cause was becoming apparent even to Bryan he continued to fight for it. The introduction of several resolutions in Congress providing for a referendum on war encouraged him. Representative Huddleston of Alabama, who passed on the good news, wrote hopefully: "On the whole sentiment in Washington seems more pacific than when you were here and I feel encouragement for peace." [152] Bryan had an opportunity to test the validity of Huddleston's appraisal when Wilson went before Congress, toward the end of February, to ask for authority to arm American merchant ships and to "employ any other instrumentalities or methods that may be necessary and adequate to protect our ships and

148. February 7, 1917, Chandler P. Anderson Diaries (Library of Congress, Washington, D.C.), Box 2. Cited hereafter as Anderson Diaries. February 12, 1917, Charles S. Hamlin Diaries (Library of Congress, Washington, D.C.), Vol. 4. Cited hereafter as Hamlin Diaries.

149. *New York Times*, February 13, 14, 1917. Bryan denied any part in writing or sending this cable, and his innocence was testified to by the cable's authors.

150. Alton B. Parker to WJB, March 4, 1917, Bryan Papers.

151. David Starr Jordan, *The Days of a Man* (Yonkers-on-Hudson, New York, 1922), II, 729.

152. George Huddleston to WJB, February 13, 1917, Bryan Papers.

our people." [153] Bryan read of the President's message while in Jacksonville, Florida. He immediately telegraphed his opposition to the President's request to his friends in Congress, canceled five speaking engagements, and caught the next train for Washington. Bryan arrived in the Capital on February 28, along with a number of other advocates of peace, including Jane Addams, Amos Pinchot, Max Eastman, and Lillian Wald, whose intention it was to bring their influence to bear on the President and Congress. He spent the morning conferring with leaders of the Emergency Peace Federation and the rest of that day and the next talking to members of Congress. He opposed all attempts to give Wilson blanket powers and publicly defended the actions of Senators Norris, La Follette, and the rest of that "little band of willful men" who were talking the President's Armed Ship Bill to death.[154]

Bryan was rapidly becoming the hero of peace enthusiasts throughout the country. At a peace rally in Carnegie Hall, the audience staged several demonstrations in his honor, while Congressman Meyer London compared him to Tolstoy.[155] As pleasing as such scenes undoubtedly were to Bryan they could not obscure the fact that the disclosure of the German note to Mexico proposing an alliance in the event of war with America and the torpedoing of American ships by German submarines was gradually causing a shift in public opinion and was beginning to force Wilson's hand. For Secretary of State Lansing "the days of anxiety and uncertainty" were over. The American people, he noted,

> are at last ready to make war on Germany, thank God. I shall openly and no longer secretly exert my influence in favor of a declaration. . . . It may take two or three years. It may even take five years. . . . It may cost a million Americans; it may

153. Link, *Woodrow Wilson and the Progressive Era*, p. 271.
154. *New York Times*, February 28, March 1, March 10, 1917.
155. Louis Lochner to WJB, March 10, 1917, Bryan Papers.

cost five millions. However long it may take, however many men it costs we must go through with it.[156]

Bryan, however, was still not quite ready to give up. On March 29, he sent a long letter to every member of Congress in which he made his final appeal for the maintenance of peace. "To you, and to you only," he began, "is given constitutional authority to declare war — war which in this case may mean the signing of the death warrant of thousands, even millions, of your countrymen, and the laying of grievous burdens upon future generations." Before they took this step, he begged the Congressmen to remember that the wrongs they were asked to punish, "cruel and unjustified as they are," were not directed against the United States but were acts of desperation committed by belligerents against belligerents and that America was not threatened with invasion but rather "we are asked to go three thousand miles for a chance to fight." "I plead with you," he concluded, "to use all honorable means to preserve peace before you take the responsibility of plunging our beloved land into this unprecedented struggle, begun without any sufficient cause and conducted by both sides in utter disregard of the well settled rights of neutrals." [157]

Having made this appeal, Bryan sat back to wait for what even he now recognized was inevitable, but he still did not understand why men felt compelled to resort to force to settle their differences. When a Congressman asked Bryan for advice on how to vote on the Declaration of War, he replied: "In such a crisis as this no one can advise another. Each must decide his duty for himself. . . . If I were a representative and convinced that my constituents desired war, I would resign and leave them to speak through someone in harmony

156. March 19, 1917, Lansing Diaries.
157. WJB "to the Members of the United States Senate and House of Representatives," March 29, 1917, Bryan Papers.

with their views. I would not share responsibility for this Nation entering the War." [158]

Bryan was in Miami when news of Congress's declaration of war reached him. He had already indicated what his reaction to such news would be when he wrote in February: "I shall live up to a patriot's duty if war comes — until that time I shall try to save my county from its horrors," and he later repeated these sentiments almost verbatim in an open letter to Jane Addams and in an interview with the *Miami Herald*.[159] In accordance with his determination to "live up to a patriot's duty," Bryan immediately wired the President:

> Believing it to be the duty of the citizen to bear his part of the burdens of war and his share of its perils, I hereby tender my services to the Government. Please enroll me as a private whenever I am needed and assign me to any work I can do. Until called to the colors I shall, through the Red Cross, contribute to the comfort of soldiers in the hospitals and, through the Y.M.C.A., aid in safeguarding the morals of the men in camp.[160]

(7)

It is not difficult to find in Bryan's ready acceptance of the war an appalling abandonment of principle. C. Hartley Grattan, for instance, has called Bryan's action "The climatic com-

158. WJB to B. C. Hilliard, April 3, 1917, ibid.
159. *The Commoner*, February 1917, p. 3, March 1917, pp. 3, 28. Bryan had emphasized this point consistently from the time of his resignation. As early as June 24, 1915, he said: "If war comes all will stand as one man behind the Government, but until Congress declares war each citizen is at liberty to express his opinion as to whether or not there should be a war." *Two Addresses Delivered by William Jennings Bryan at Peace Meetings held in New York, June 19 and 24, 1915*, p. 8.
160. WJB to Wilson, April 6, 1917, Wilson Papers, File VI, Box 491.

promise in a life of compromises." "The logic of his position," he continues, "was conscientious objection. Instead, he became the pacifist in arms." [161] More crucial than the question of whether conscientious objection was the logical culmination of pacifism is whether Bryan was in fact a pacifist. Bryan himself never used the term; not once in his long struggle for peace did he refer to himself or to his followers as pacifists. Indeed, if we define pacifism as a devotion to peace above all else, as Grattan seems to do, then Bryan never was a pacifist. He earnestly believed in peace and proved himself an untiring and astute crusader in its behalf, but he had other loyalties as well; loyalties which in the end proved to have an even stronger hold upon him.

To Bryan the peace movement was never an end in and of itself. It was not so much a cause to be championed as a course to be followed: a course that logically emanated from his love of nation and of mankind and his devotion to Christian ethics and principles. Yet Bryan was not a non-resistant, as he himself pointed out: he never apologized for his services in the Spanish-American War; as Secretary of State he utilized force in Mexico and the Caribbean; and in his peace crusade itself he justified war as a means of repelling attack and even admitted that not all wars could be prevented.[162] In all this Bryan showed that the central theme of his peace crusade was something more than merely an abhorrence for war. He struggled for peace not only because he hated force, but, even more important, because he was convinced that peace would best preserve and further the honor, destiny, and welfare of his nation and his countrymen. Bryan's vision of peace, as bright as it was, was never strong enough to obscure his personal conception of duty. When, despite his sacrifices and efforts, war finally came, he accepted it as the course his country's

161. Hibben and Grattan, *The Peerless Leader*, p. 350.
162. *New York Times*, July 7, December 1, 1915, February 3, 1917.

leaders and his country's people, speaking through their representatives, chose to follow, even as he had accepted the establishment of the gold standard and the acquisition of the
Philippines. His acceptance, however, did not mean the abandonment of his dream. Just as he had continued to work for
bimetallism and Philippine independence, so his plans for universal peace continued unabated.

Bryan had been brought up to believe that the democratic
process allowed an individual to oppose a course of action
with all the means at his disposal until it was constitutionally
adopted by the majority. Then one was obligated to adhere to
it, though if it was a reversible decision one could work for its
alteration. War, unfortunately, was not such a decision, and
the best Bryan felt he could do was to continue to work for
the day when he could help to institute reforms which would
make the recurrence of war unlikely. Thus he was able to tell
an audience in Albany, Georgia, just a few hours after war
was declared: "Gladly would I have given my life to save my
country from war, but now that my country has gone to war,
gladly will I give my life to aid it." [163]

163. Ibid. April 7, 1917.

III: Years of Victory

We are travelling towards the dawn; the day grows brighter hour by hour. — wjb

(1)

Toward the end of his life Bryan was fond of recalling the fact that the only real peace he had known since he entered politics was during his six months of service in the army in 1898. It was an ironic recollection, yet not an unusual one, for irony had always played a large role in Bryan's life. Never more so than during the period from April 1917 to November 1918, when the war which he had tried so desperately to avoid was upon his country. If the war brought him a sense of disappointment and futility it also brought him great popularity with many who had opposed him since 1896. Throughout the Spanish-American War Bryan had consistently refused to utter any criticisms of the McKinley Administration, saying facetiously that he was suffering from "military lockjaw."[1] America's entry into World War I brought about a recurrence of this malady, and it was this factor that led to his unprecedented popularity. The "Silver Knight of the West" had, for the duration, dropped his lance, dismounted his charger, and was pulling along with the rest of the nation.

Shortly after sending his prompt offer of service to the President, Bryan wrote Daniels: "I do not want any command. I am too old to learn the art of war. I simply want to do my duty wherever I can when I am needed."[2] Neverthe-

1. Hibben and Grattan, *The Peerless Leader*, p. 218.
2. WJB to Daniels, April 8, 1917, Daniels Papers, Box 37.

less, his use of the phrase "please enroll me as a private," in his letter to Wilson, was widely misinterpreted in the press, and for once the misinterpretation was in his favor. "The world's most distinguished out-and-out pacifist has enlisted for war," commented the *Milwaukee News*, "the country breathlessly awaits the grand rush of the jingo editors, war-shouting politicians, ultra-bellicose statesmen and pseudo patriots towards the recruiting stations. Don't crowd, gentlemen!" The influential *Washington Post* echoed this and scores of similar statements by writing appreciatively: "The War Department has received offers of service from other men enjoying national reputations, but these patriots are not so modest as Mr. Bryan. They have offered to serve in any capacity from field marshall to general but none, like Mr. Bryan, as a private." [3]

Thus lauded, Bryan made his way to Washington where, on the morning of April 16, he conferred with the President. Wilson thanked him warmly for his offer of support but did not seem inclined to invite the former Secretary of State into the wartime administration in any official capacity. He did, however, promise to make available to Bryan all such wartime information and data that the government desired to disseminate.[4] Bryan, then, was to be used as an arm of the vast propaganda machine that was rapidly being assembled, a role apparently entirely satisfactory to him. Indeed, he seemed almost relieved. He had tendered his services out of a sense of duty but at no time did he share Roosevelt's anxious desire to take an official part in the bloodletting. In relating the substance of his interview with Wilson to the reporters waiting outside, Bryan set the pattern of his entire wartime behavior by stating: "I do not care to discuss any question before Congress. Whatever the government does is right and I shall sup-

3. Reprinted in *The Commoner*, April 1917, p. 15, May 1917, p. 11.
4. Ibid. April 1917, p. 7. See also Wilson to WJB, April 7, 1917, Bryan Papers.

port it to the uttermost. . . . In war time the President speaks for the country and there should be no division or dissension." [5]

In the first wartime issue of *The Commoner*, Bryan amplified this view by quoting Jefferson's maxim: "Acquiescence in the will of the majority is the first principle of republics." "The nation has entered the war," he added. "Men differed as to the wisdom of going into the war, but the government has acted and there is no longer division. The people are one." [6] He rarely deviated from this principle. When the Selective Conscription Act was before Congress, Bryan refused to discuss its merits, and once it had passed he gave it his vigorous support.[7] When, on August 28, Wilson rejected the peace proposal set forth by Pope Benedict XV, Bryan again declined to comment explaining to a reporter: "My work, as I conceive it, is to help unify the nation in support of the government. If I were to discuss the merits of propositions I would continually arouse and encourage controversy. But when I insist it is the duty of every citizen to support his government in any act the government takes, I am presenting a proposition which is not open to dispute." [8]

The same conformity that Bryan painstakingly exacted of himself he asked of others as well. "This is the best government on earth," he wrote in August, "the one most responsive to the will of the people, but it is a government of the people — not of one or a few men. If a few are permitted to resist a law — any law — because they do not like it, government becomes a farce. The law must be enforced — resistance is anarchy." Bryan refused to sympathize with those arrested

5. *New York Times*, April 17, 1917.
6. "At War," *The Commoner*, April 1917, p. 3.
7. Ibid. May 1917, p. 1.
8. *Chicago Journal*, August 31, 1917, reprinted in ibid. September 1917, p. 3.

for unpatriotic utterances. "They abuse free speech. And this applies to attacks upon the Allies as well as to attacks upon the United States. . . . There are only two sides to a war — every American must be on the side of the United States." Similarly, if a man's conscience prevented him from complying with the government's demands, he must submit, without complaint, to any punishment inflicted, "whether the punishment be imprisonment or death." [9] "Patriotism," he wrote two months later, "requires some to give their lives; it requires some to give their money; it may require some to hold their peace rather than risk creating dissension or discord . . ." [10]

Statements such as these, of course, raised Bryan's popularity to its zenith. Newspapers which since 1896 had seen in Bryan nothing more than a cheap, demagogic rabble-rouser, suddenly discerned in him a virtue and a nobility of the highest order. "If every man in the nation were as good an American as William Jennings Bryan," gushed the *Albany Times-Union*, ". . . this country would be blessed with an impetus toward better things whose results would be beneficial beyond the realms of mere mathematical calculation." And even the bitterly anti-Bryan *New York World* agreed that "There is no better rule of patriotism for the guidance of all pacifists, conscientious objectors and sticklers for the rights of free speech than that laid down by William Jennings Bryan." [11]

Though Bryan's conformity appeared to be a solid wall, there were nonetheless several small but revealing chinks in it, which have, for the most part, been neglected by his biogra-

9. Ibid. August 1917, p. 1.
10. Ibid. October 1917, p. 1.
11. For these and similar editorials see ibid. September 1917, pp. 6, 9, October 1917, p. 9. Wilson, who read Bryan's editorials, commented: "They show a fine spirit and a very high principle, as I should have expected." Wilson to Josephus Daniels, August 27, 1917, Bryan Papers.

phers. He could not bring himself to go along with those who were heaping abuse upon any member of Congress who opposed the Administration.

> Senators and Representatives in Congress are . . . as much a part of the government as the President himself. A Senator or a Representative has as much right to express himself . . . as the President has. . . . To say that a Senator or Representative in Congress must of necessity agree with the recommendations made by the President is equivalent to advocating the substitution of a despotism for a republic — equivalent to advocating the establishment of an autocracy here while we are trying to overthrow autocracy in other lands. The obligation of a Senator or a Representative is to the people whom he represents, not to the executive.[12]

While he continued to caution the populace against public dissent, he persistently urged them to make their views known to the officials in Washington. American citizens should continue to think and they must continue to express themselves as long as they did so in a manner which would aid their own country and not the enemy. "DO NOT PROTEST THROUGH THE PRESS," he advised. "Talk directly to those who are entrusted with the carrying on of the war. Write!"[13]

While Bryan repeatedly warned others against criticizing the actions of either the United States or its allies, he ignored his own advice in the fall of 1917 when Britain and France announced their decision to retaliate against German bombings by dropping explosives on German cities. "The logic with which the Allies attempt to defend this proposed action will not stand the light of history," he wrote in an impassioned editorial. "Future generations will blush to read that

12. *The Commoner*, October 1917, p. 1.
13. Ibid. August 1917, p. 2.

BOTH sides resorted to the deliberate murder of innocent women and children." [14]

And if Bryan found it impossible to acquiesce in every act of the Allies, he found it equally impossible to join in the spirit of hatred which was being manufactured against Germany. While his good friend Billy Sunday began a prayer in the House of Representatives by saying: "Thou knowest, O Lord, that no nation so infamous, vile, greedy, sensuous, bloodthirsty [as Germany] ever disgraced the pages of history," [15] Bryan could do little more than castigate the autocratic nature of the German government. The one time he allowed himself to enter into the spirit of things even partially was during a speech in St. Joseph, Missouri, two months before the signing of the Armistice, when he denounced Germany as "a cruel, barbarous foe," and called the Kaiser "that old criminal." [16] Even war itself could not transform Bryan into a very effective hater.

The one sphere in which Bryan refused to become a mere "yes man" was characteristically that dealing with business and economics. From the very beginning of the war he attempted to convince the government to call a halt to the process which he claimed had turned every preceding war into an instrument which coined the sacrifices of the many into profits for the few. In the same issue of *The Commoner* in which he had invited the government to draft as many men as necessary, he urged it to draft money as well. "If the citizen must give his life to enable his country to carry on war, why should the property owner be dealt with more leniently? Is money more precious than blood?" In the past it had been "a rich man's war and a poor man's fight," this time it would be different; this time all would give equally so that all might

14. Ibid. October 1917, p. 1.
15. Sullivan, *Our Times*, V, 467.
16. *The Commoner*, October 1918, p. 8.

benefit equally.[17] "If it is right for this government to take a young man, . . . and lay its hands upon him and command him to lay his life on the country's altar," he told a wildly cheering audience in Lincoln, Nebraska, "then it is right that it shall take every dollar of any man's money or property. I would be the last to draw a line between life and property, to place the dollar above the man."[18]

When the Chicago *Tribune* warned that "men of affairs" would support a revenue bill amounting to $1,250,000,000, and no more, Bryan's wrath rose. "The trouble with the 'men of affairs,'" he commented bitterly, "is that they are not willing to bear their share of the burden. They want the expenses of the war raised by bond issues so that the debt will extend over generations — the poor finally paying for it. That is what the people do NOT want."[19] The war, he contended, must be paid for primarily by the present generation and, to effect that end, Congress should raise the excess profits tax and the income tax as high as necessary. When, in framing its revenue bill, Congress showed that its ear had been attuned more closely to the "men of affairs" than to the Bryans of the country, Bryan once again ignored his own injunction against criticizing any act of the government. "The last revenue act did not go far enough," he wrote, ". . . the men engaged in the manufacture of implements of war should not be allowed to fatten out of the nation's perils."[20] He continued this plea throughout 1918, asking again and again: "Why should anyone be allowed to grow rich out of war profits while the masses stint themselves to carry on the war," and assuring his listeners and readers that "ALL ABOVE A REASONABLE

17. Ibid. April 1917, p. 3, May 1917, p. 3.
18. *Lincoln Evening News*, October 6, 1917, reprinted in ibid. October 1917, p. 4.
19. Ibid. September 1917, p. 3.
20. Ibid. November 1917, p. 1.

PROFIT would not equal the tax now collected on blood." [21]

Although the government did not see fit to use Bryan in an official capacity it found him an untiring and effective propagandist. Oratory continued to be the one great joy of Bryan's life, and he traveled throughout the country from Maine to California speaking almost endlessly before Chautauqua audiences, political rallies, and religious groups. In every speech he delivered, regardless of its nature, Bryan managed to incorporate an appeal for aiding the war effort, whether it be by urging his listeners to buy Liberty Bonds or warning them of the debilitating effects of venereal diseases. The cause to which he devoted his energies most extensively, however, was food conservation.

Several weeks after the nation's entry into the war, Secretary of Agriculture Houston accepted Bryan's offer to aid in the movement to increase the nation's food supply and inaugurated the practice of periodically sending him information which he might use in his speeches.[22] While the sight of Bryan leaning from the platform to advise his audiences to use less meat and wheat and sugar, or using his still magnificent voice to spread such trite slogans as "Plant what you can and can all you can," [23] may have seemed incongruous to some of his followers, Bryan entered upon the crusade with all his characteristic energy and sincerity. He also toured the country during the various Liberty Loan drives at the personal request of the Secretary of the Treasury.[24] Besides applauding his efforts and quoting from his speeches, the country's

21. Ibid. February 1918, p. 3.
22. David Houston to WJB, April 24, 1917, May 10, 1917, Bryan Papers.
23. *The Commoner*, June 1917, p. 7. For one of Bryan's typical food conservation speeches, see ibid. November 1917, p. 5.
24. William G. McAdoo to WJB, September 12, 15, 17, 18, 26, 1917, Bryan Papers; McAdoo to WJB, September 25, 1917, September 26, 1918, McAdoo Papers, Box 496.

newspapers held him up as a worthy example by pointing to his frequent purchases of Liberty Bonds and his weekly contribution of fifty dollars each to the Red Cross and the Y.M.C.A. Bryan found himself becoming the very epitome of respectability.

Despite his manifold contributions to the war effort, Bryan never became fully reconciled to the fact of war. "War is a last resort," he wrote four months after war had been declared. "It is a reflection upon civilization that it still reddens the earth." [25] Bryan could not accept the war until he converted it, in his own mind at least, into a war for democracy. In this, he differed little from Wilson, and it was comforting for Bryan to see at his country's helm a President who viewed the war as a moral crusade, who could call it "a People's War" which would "make the world safe for the people who live upon it, the German people themselves included," and who could proclaim a fourteen-point program for a just and lasting peace; a program which Bryan vigorously endorsed.[26]

The most interesting aspect of Bryan's support of the war was the manner in which he fused it to his desire for peace. "The more anxiously one desires peace, the more loyally one should back the President and Congress," for it was obvious that "The shortest road to peace is the road straight ahead of us, with no division among our people." The only way out of the war, he told audience after audience, is "through it." [27] A lasting universal peace remained one of Bryan's chief dreams, but where he had hitherto advocated moral suasion as the means of achieving it, the spur of necessity forced him to view the present war with a somewhat less jaundiced eye and

25. *The Commoner*, August 1917, p. 1.
26. Sullivan, *Our Times*, V, 442; WJB to Woodrow Wilson, January 15, 1918, Wilson Papers, File VI, Box 491.
27. *The Commoner*, November 1917, p. 7, February 1918, p. 2, July 1917, p. 9.

to see in it an equally effective, though less desirable means of realizing his ambition.

And if he came to view the war as a means of achieving peace, he soon discovered that it could have a host of additional beneficial effects as well. The war was spreading democracy throughout the world; the Russians had overthrown their Czar and there were similar rumblings in other European countries. The war was spreading brotherhood, for in the joint effort the distinctions between Gentile and Jew, Protestant and Catholic were becoming blurred. The war was increasing the faith of Americans in their government and teaching them the value of making more extensive use of it.[28] But, above all, the most tangible and immediate effect of the war, so far as Bryan was concerned, was the impetus it was giving to two reforms which he had begun to champion not long before — prohibition and woman suffrage.

(2)

Several months after his resignation from Wilson's Cabinet Bryan had declared that the three great reforms of the age were peace, prohibition, and woman suffrage.[29] Although Bryan devoted the greater part of his time and energy to the first of these reforms, at least until April 1917, he managed to find time for the latter two as well.[30] Of the two, Bryan was more devoted to prohibition, since it constituted a far more bitter struggle and had its roots in the political and moral fabric of the nation to a much greater extent than did suffrage.

28. Ibid. April 1917, p. 4, January 1918, p. 10, October 1918, p. 1.
29. "Three Great Reforms," ibid. December 1915, p. 5.
30. At least two students of this period feel that Bryan's fight for prohibition and woman suffrage, during the years following his resignation, appreciably weakened his peace crusade since it necessitated a division of time and zeal. See Arthur Wallace Dunn, *From Harrison to Harding* (New Hork, 1922), II, 297; Curti, *Bryan and World Peace*, p. 228.

In crusading against alcohol, Bryan and many of his fellow prohibitionists thought of themselves as progressives engaged in a reform which would last for all time and eventually engulf the entire world. The inability of the present generation to understand this aspect of the prohibitionists is not surprising, since even Josephus Daniels's son Jonathan, who had a unique opportunity to observe at close range such leading advocates of national temperance as his father and Bryan, was baffled by them.[31] But if our failure to comprehend just what it was that the prohibitionists were trying to do is understandable, it is, nevertheless, unfortunate. Focusing upon the later phase of the movement in the 1920's, we have tended to view prohibition as the austere instrument of a pack of blue-nosed Puritans who found life a joyless thing and were determined that no one else should be allowed to squeeze any pleasure out of it, as an aberration produced by the spirit of intolerance and summary action fostered by World War I, as a manifestation of rural frenzy and fanaticism in the postwar era, as a caricature of reform.[32] Thus we have not merely misread the motives and aims of many of the prohibitionists, but have failed to understand as well as we might the impulses and assumptions basic to a large segment of the progressive movement in this country.

The fact is that the temperance movement was nurtured in the soil of reform and remained a genuine reform movement right down to the 1920's. It came into being as a movement in the first half of the nineteenth century amidst a generation that was increasingly concerned with elevating and improving the individual not only for his own sake but also in order to safeguard the democratic experiment and establish a more perfect social order. It was an age which was finding that man was indeed his brother's keeper; an age which began to con-

31. Jonathan Daniels, *The End of Innocence*, p. 44.
32. A study containing all of these views is Andrew Sinclair, *Prohibition: An Era of Excess* (Boston, 1962), Chapters I–II, and *passim*.

cern itself with the welfare of women and children; an age in which men built causes around the plight of the slave, the pauper, the drunkard, the mentally unbalanced. Prohibition, with its promise of insuring a more responsible, intelligent, and sober electorate and eliminating the root cause of many of man's greatest problems, fit neatly into the wave of humanitarian reform.[33]

The links that bound prohibition to the larger reform movements of the day continued to hold fast with the passing of the years. The prohibition movement was closely allied with the Northern abolitionist crusade and often pointed out that both movements had as their aim the freeing of enslaved men.[34] The Prohibition party, founded in 1869, exhibited a diversity of interests in regard to reform which often makes one feel that its name was a misnomer. In every platform it issued from 1872 to 1924, with but two exceptions, it fused prohibition to many other reforms which at various times included direct election of Senators, the right of labor to organize, the right of all citizens to vote regardless of "color, race, former social condition, sex, or nationality," liberal immigration policies, the settlement of international difficulties by arbitration, anti-trust legislation, initiative, referendum and recall, a graduated income tax, government ownership or control of public utilities, employer's liability laws, the eight-hour day, prohibition of child labor, and government guarantee of bank deposits.[35] While not nearly enough work has been

33. John Allen Krout, *The Origins of Prohibition* (New York, 1925), pp. 297–300.

34. Ibid. pp. 176, 289.

35. For the platforms of the Prohibition party, see Kirk H. Porter and Donald Bruce Johnson, eds., *National Party Platforms, 1840–1956* (Urbana, Illinois, 1956). They may also be found, along with some sympathetic commentary and brief biographies of the party's nominees, in D. Leigh Colvin, *Prohibition in the United States: a History of the Prohibition Party and of the Prohibition Movement* (New York, 1926).

done on the prohibition movements in the states, a recent study of California has shown that almost every reform movement in that state, from anti-slavery to Populism and Progressivism, was closely linked to the anti-liquor movement.[36] And finally, with but one exception, every church in which the social gospel played an important role was also officially committed to prohibition.[37]

An understanding of this affinity between prohibition and American reform movements in general is essential to a re-creation of the atmosphere that prevailed when men like Bryan, Daniels, and many other progressives joined the movement. More than a few progressives, of course, remained indifferent to the cause and some denounced it as an unwarranted violation of individual liberties. A great many more, however, especially in the rural sections of the West and South, regarded it as a necessary and logical reform which differed from other progressive reforms neither in method nor purpose.[38] To Bryan and many of his co-workers and followers, prohibition was just a continuation of the struggle against the selfish interests that put private profit above human welfare and fed upon the helplessness of the masses. Those who labor for prohibition, he wrote, "are helping to create conditions which will bring the highest good to the greatest number, without any injustice to any, for it is not injustice to any man to refuse him permission to enrich himself by injuring his fellowmen." [39] The brewers and distillers, he asserted, located their saloons among the poor "knowing full well when they do so that

36. Gilman M. Ostrander, *The Prohibition Movement in California, 1848–1933* (Berkeley, 1957), pp. 102–19.

37. Paul A. Carter, *The Decline and Revival of the Social Gospel* (Ithaca, New York, 1954), pp. 33–4; James H. Timberlake, *Prohibition and the Progressive Movement, 1900–1920* (Cambridge, 1962), pp. 23–4.

38. For an exposition of this theme, see ibid. Chapters I, IV.

39. WJB, "Why I am for Prohibition," *The Independent*, LXXXVII (July 17, 1916), 89.

their saloon will absorb the money that their patrons ought to spend on wife and children. They . . . impoverish the poor and multiply their sufferings . . ." [40]

The doctrine of the perfectability of man was one of the secular American political principles that was taken over and given religious connotations by the social gospel and, in this form, was adopted both as an assumption and a goal by many progressives. Bryan, who adamantly believed that "A man can be born again; the springs of life can be cleansed instantly so that the heart loves the things that it formerly hated and hates the things it once loved. If this is true of *one*, it can be true of any number," adopted prohibition partly because he saw in it a means of liberating and elevating the people, of giving them a new and more perfect birth, and this he insisted was the duty of every progressive and every Christian. "I claim no right to tell any body else what to do," he told the Presbyterian General Assembly in 1916, "but I believe in the Christian doctrine that brethen should commune with each other and that they should seek to help each other."

> If I understand what a Christian is, it is not that he is a perfect man, but that he desires to be perfect. . . . If I understand the Christian's attitude it is one of openness and willingness, the desire to have his life censured and his conduct scrutinized that he may get rid of his bestial sins.[41]

Finally, Bryan championed prohibition so vigorously because he was convinced that it was a democratic reform. By 1917 he was arguing that a majority of the American people lived in dry territory and a majority of their representatives in Congress opposed the saloon. "The accurst thing exists only

40. WJB, *Prohibition Address . . . Made in Ohio . . . October 25 to 30, 1915*, p. 6.
41. WJB, *Temperance Lecture Delivered Before the 128th General Assembly of the Presbyterian Church, at Atlantic City, New Jersey, Sunday May 21, 1916.*

because the Constitution, by its ultra-conservative provisions, restrains the majority from immediate and decided action." [42] To Bryan this was the chief consideration before which all abstract discussions of liberty and all questions of political expediency paled. Once the majority had spoken he could be concerned with nothing else, for the right of the people to rule was the one indispensable right which never could be tampered with.

These were the factors that drew many progressives into the prohibition movement and they were the factors that kept them there even after the movement itself began to undergo changes in the 1920's.

(3)

Bryan's favorable attitude toward temperance reform was shaped not only by the reform ethos of his age but by his early training and environment. His parents impressed upon him at a tender age the evils of alcohol. "Even before I had any clear understanding of the temperance question," he wrote in later years, "I began signing the pledge." His first recollections of signing a pledge dated back to 1872, when he was twelve, but he assures us that "it had by that time become a habit with me." [43] During the period when he was practicing law in Jacksonville, Illinois, Bryan delivered a temperance address in which he endorsed the theory of prohibition but asserted that a policy of moral suasion and education was superior to one of legislative proscription. "Our great work is the work of education," he announced. "The best, the most effective way to stop the sale of intoxicating liquor is to stop the demand for it." [44]

42. WJB, "Prohibition's Progress," *The Independent*, XC (May 19, 1917), 332.
43. *Memoirs*, p. 187.
44. Bryan delivered this address sometime between 1883 and 1887. Bryan Papers.

Not long after voicing these sentiments, Bryan moved to Lincoln, Nebraska, and while he remained a steadfast abstainer and privately opposed the saloon, he now refrained from speaking against it publicly. Omaha, Nebraska, which was in Bryan's Congressional district, was the home of the third largest distillery in the country, and Bryan was evidently not willing to jeopardize his political future by speaking out on an issue which he felt was more of a private than a public matter. In 1890 the voters of Nebraska went to the polls to decide the wisdom of adopting state-wide prohibition, and Bryan, who was a candidate for his first term in Congress, not only failed to endorse the amendment, but, as he later admitted, he voted against it as well.[45]

During his tour of duty with the Third Nebraska Infantry in 1898, Bryan made some small contribution to the prohibition cause by excluding intoxicating liquor from his camp canteen.[46] Still he was reluctant to join the crusade. When in 1902 Carry Nation toured Nebraska and spent several days in Lincoln brandishing her famous hatchet against saloons, Bryan not only declined to aid her in her fight but even refused to see her, causing the militant prohibitionist to remark: "From that time forth I knew that Bryan was for Bryan and what Bryan could get for Bryan." [47]

Two years after Mrs. Nation's disillusionment, Bryan took his first cautious step along the road he was eventually to travel, by coming out in favor of local option.[48] Six more years were to pass, however, before he joined the prohibitionist ranks in earnest. The metamorphosis that changed Bryan from a private teetotaler to an active, militant prohibitionist, followed in the wake of his third unsuccessful bid for the

45. *The Commoner*, April 1916, p. 4.
46. Ibid. October 1917, p. 2.
47. Herbert Asbury, *Carry Nation* (New York, 1929), pp. 260–61.
48. *Memoirs*, p. 290.

Presidency in 1908. The reasons for the transformation were as personal and political as those which had hitherto kept him on the sidelines. He became convinced that the liquor interests had been instrumental in causing his defeat in Missouri, Indiana, Ohio, Illinois, New York, and had almost defeated him in his own state as well. While he was still fuming over this, the same interests thwarted him in his attempt to induce the legislature of Nebraska to adopt the initiative and referendum.[49] Thus, added to his long-standing personal dislike for alcoholic beverages and his recognition that sentiment for prohibition was slowly building throughout the country, was Bryan's newborn conviction that the defenders of alcohol were enemies of progressive reform.

Still denying that he was a prohibitionist, Bryan, in the spring of 1910, decided to advocate county option and journeyed to Omaha to open his campaign. Unable to find one Democrat of prominence in the entire city who was willing to introduce him or even sit on the platform with him, Bryan hired a small hall, put his coat and hat on a chair, addressed his opening remarks to that same chair and then launched into his first prohibition speech before a very small audience.[50] Several months later he attended the Democratic State Convention at Grand Island, Nebraska, where he introduced a minority report in favor of county option. He knew he was precipitating a schism in the State Democracy and he did so reluctantly: "Never in my life have I performed a duty that I less desired to perform; and never have I felt more sure that I was performing a duty." He apologized to the fathers and mothers of the state for not speaking out earlier and ended his address by closing the door on all future compromise: "We

49. WJB, *Speeches of William Jennings Bryan* (New York, 1913), I, 326, 332-3.
50. WJB to Warren Worth Bailey, September 22, 1910, Bailey Papers, Box 1; *The Commoner*, October 1918, p. 9.

never espoused a more righteous cause than that which now appeals to us; we never faced an enemy more deserving of attack. . . . If a retreat is to be sounded, it must be sounded by another. I shall not do it — never, never, never!" [51]

This dramatic peroration proved more forceful than his subsequent actions. He was not yet ready to champion nation-wide or even state-wide prohibition.[52] But though his position was by no means an advanced one, it enabled him to lend his great prestige and his eloquent voice to the movement. Bryan has been frequently accused of entering the prohibition movement only after its victory was assured, yet his own party in his own state repudiated him for his temperance leanings in 1910, and during his tenure in the State Department the nation's press attempted to use his temperance views as a means of laughing him out of office. In the beginning they ridiculed his substitution of grape juice for alcohol at the various diplomatic gatherings over which he and Mrs. Bryan had to preside. Their jibes turned to bitter scorn when Bryan continued to address temperance meetings even after the European war began. After one such gathering in 1915 in Philadelphia, where 12,000 spectators stood up and joined Bryan in taking the pledge, the *New Republic* commented: "It is easy to laugh at Mr. Bryan for doing things like this in times like these. It is even a little hard not to." [53]

In October 1915, just four months after his resignation, he toured Ohio speaking in forty counties and making sixty

51. WJB, *Speeches*, I, 324, 346–7.
52. When a national prohibition amendment was before Congress in 1914, Bryan advised against its submission on the grounds that it "would divert attention from other issues pressing for consideration without advancing the cause of prohibition." *The Commoner*, December 1914, p. 1. During the next two years, Bryan continued to oppose the submission of a national prohibition amendment. See WJB to Richmond P. Hobson, August 12, 1915, Burleson Papers, Vol. 15.
53. *New Republic*, II (March 20, 1915), 165.

speeches in six days to almost a quarter of a million people. Licensing a man to sell liquor and then fining people for getting drunk, he asserted, made as much sense as "licensing a person to spread the itch through a town and then fining the people for scratching." The saloon, he declared, "has been not only accused but convicted of being an enemy of the race." He dismissed the idea of compensated prohibition as "superlative impudence," and thundered:

> Let the liquor dealer compensate the mother for the son he has taken from her; let him compensate the wife for the husband of whom he has robbed her; let him compensate the children for the father whom he has first transformed into a brute and then driven to suicide. Let him compensate those whom he has wronged by restoring to them the priceless value of homes ruined and lives wrecked, and then society will be glad to compensate him for whatever pecuniary loss he may suffer by the closing of a business which he knew to be harmful — a business which can not thrive save as the community suffers.[54]

Bryan's campaign was well received by the citizens of Ohio, whose cheers helped to ease the memory of the abuse which his resignation had brought him. "The audiences were so attentive and responsive," Mrs. Bryan noted in her diary, "I do not see how he could have failed to convince many. I had some glimpses of what a national campaign on this subject would be — a veritable religious crusade." [55]

Bryan himself could not have failed to perceive the impact that a national prohibition campaign would have, but he was not yet ready to enter upon one. He was willing to admit that there was but one solution to the liquor question "and that is

---

54. *Memoirs*, p. 433; *Prohibition Address by Hon. William Jennings Bryan Presenting in Substance the Line of Argument Followed by him in the Sixty Speeches Made in Ohio During the Week of October 25 to 30, 1915* (Washington, D.C., 1916), pp. 3–7.
55. *Memoirs*, p. 433.

the nation-wide extermination of the traffic in alcohol," but
he was not willing to carry this admission to its logical conclusion. He would not approve the submission of a national prohibition amendment until a sufficient number of states had
expressed themselves favorably upon it. The country, he explained, was not ready for national prohibition and any attempt to secure it at present would jeopardize the Administration's economic reforms and the work of peace.[56]

There was still an element of expediency in Bryan's prohibition views. Though he condemned the saloon as "the fester-
ing source of political and moral pollution," [57] he was in no
hurry to cut it out of the body politic. He failed to give
serious consideration to the assurances of one of the leaders of
the Prohibition party that he could receive the party's Presidential nomination in 1916 if he desired it.[58] The peace issue
still held his immediate interest, and in all likelihood he envisioned the prohibition crusade as one which might constitute
the main issue of the 1920 campaign but not before that. But
whatever Bryan's views on the proper moment for launching
the prohibition crusade in earnest, he soon discovered that
prohibition, like the Paris mobs in the upheaval of 1848, was
not always content to wait for its leaders. Throughout the
first half of 1916 he continued his efforts to keep the prohibition question out of the forthcoming Presidential campaign.
Shortly after the national conventions he wrote: "I hope to
see the campaign this year fought upon economic issues, and
upon such international questions as it may be necessary to
consider.[59]

56. *The Commoner*, August 1915, pp. 4–5, 24, December 1915, p. 5.
57. Ibid. June 1915, p. 6.
58. Clinton H. Howard to WJB, June 10, 1915, Bryan Papers.
59. WJB, "Why I am For Prohibition," *The Independent*,
LXXXVII (July 17, 1916), 89.

Though he was to have his wish in this respect he was less successful in his own state. Here the prohibitionists were agitating for the submission of a state-wide prohibition amendment to the voters in November. Bryan strongly advised against such a move, protesting that it would divert attention from important national issues during the coming Presidential campaign.[60] The more ardent prohibitionists, however, proved victorious and Bryan found himself in a dilemma. His resignation had already impaired his prestige among his fellow Democrats, and he was convinced that a refusal on his part to attempt to secure a place on the Nebraska delegation would be construed as a lack of interest in the campaign and in the Democratic party.[61] He would have preferred to run on a platform endorsing the economic and social reforms of the Administration and stressing his own efforts to keep the country at peace. The prohibition issue was a complication which he felt certain could only diminish his chances of election. Yet it was clear to Bryan that prohibition was to be one of the leading issues in the not too distant future and that if he repeated his performance of 1890 he would eliminate himself from playing a leading role in the coming struggle.

The factors which led Bryan to his eventual decision were, of course, not all quite so carefully reasoned or politically oriented. By this time he had become convinced that the temperance movement was a righteous one being waged against a contemptible and reactionary foe. It was probably this latter factor that tipped the scales, but, whatever the reasons, Bryan threw expediency to the wind and entered the Nebraska primary campaign bearing the incubus of prohibition. Once Bryan had made his decision, nothing could dissuade him, not even an

60. *The Commoner*, May 1916, p. 2.
61. WJB to Albert S. Burleson, March 8, 1916, Burleson Papers, Vol. 17.

offer of $150,000 for a series of lectures, which he turned down because it would have taken him away from Nebraska during the campaign.[62]

Bryan's month-long tour of Nebraska, which began on March 20, was an exciting and gratifying one. He spoke in forty-four counties averaging three speeches a day, and rarely did he have to look at many empty seats. So enthusiastic was the response that after completing his scheduled speech he was often compelled to address an overflow crowd outside the hall.[63] In the face of this reception, even some of Bryan's opponents began to concede that his election was inevitable.[64] The situation, however, was more complex than it seemed. Bryan, essentially, was waging a dual battle in Nebraska; he was determined not only to defeat the anti-prohibition forces but to destroy the Hitchcock faction of the Democratic party as well. The two groups, unfortunately, were not always identical. Thus Bryan found himself in the uncomfortable position of supporting I. J. Dunn, Hitchcock's opponent for the Senatorial nomination, although Dunn himself was a foe of prohibition. Bryan attempted to justify his action by claiming that, while Dunn was opposed to prohibition, he was not a tool of the liquor interests, and would, therefore, follow the wishes of the electorate when prohibition became a national issue.[65] His rather lame explanation

62. Bryan intimated that "interests" which did not want him to re-enter politics actively were behind the offer. *New York Times*, March 22, 1916.

63. For a detailed description of Bryan's primary campaign, see the *Nebraska State Journal* from March 20, 1916 to April 18, 1916. Senator Hitchcock's newspaper, the *Omaha World-Herald*, is valuable for a description of the activities of Bryan's opponents.

64. *Nebraska State Journal*, April 12, 1916.

65. *Omaha World-Herald*, April 14, 1916. Similar circumstances led Bryan to support another opponent of prohibition, Mayor Arthur Dahlman of Omaha, who was running against Hitchcock's candidate, Arthur Mullen, for Democratic National Committeeman. Ibid.

may well have cost him some prohibitionist support without winning over any wet voters.

Aside from this episode, Bryan conducted himself as a good prohibitionist should. "If, after next November, any saloon is ever licensed in Nebraska," he roared at one point. "it will be in spite of all that I can do to prevent it. If any of these young men, who should be the glory of the state, are ever again led into temptation by the open saloon, it will not be my fault." [66] He was completely candid about his past actions in regard to the liquor issue. He admitted that he had voted against prohibition in 1890 but maintained that he had a right to change his mind in twenty-five years. He confessed also that he had advised against the injection of the issue into the present campaign but quickly added: "it is here, and whenever there is a child born in our family, I take care of it." [67]

Although prohibition was the main issue in the campaign, the Hitchcock forces brought up Bryan's resignation and his subsequent differences with Wilson.[68] Bryan's response was immediate. "If you think Woodrow Wilson doesn't want me in the St. Louis Convention as a delegate from Nebraska," he shouted to a crowd of over 1,500 at Auburn, "just write him a letter and ask him about it, and if he says there is a democrat in Nebraska whom he prefers as a delegate, I'll gladly withdraw on the spot." [69] Though the Democrats of Nebraska may not have doubted the validity of Bryan's assertion, they proved indifferent to it. On April 18 they went to the polls and defeated Bryan, his brother Charles, who had campaigned for the gubernatorial nomination, and every other candidate on the Bryan ticket.[70] Bryan appeared to be neither surprised

66. *The Commoner*, April 1916, p. 5.
67. *Nebraska State Journal*, March 21, 1916.
68. See, for example, the *Omaha World-Herald*, April 7, 1916.
69. *Nebraska State Journal*, March 25, 1916.
70. Ibid. April 23, 24, 1916.

nor dismayed at the results. He attributed his defeat to the fact that the Nebraska Democracy was a prisoner of Hitchcock and the liquor machine and to the wet Republicans who crossed party lines to vote against him. He claimed that an analysis of the primary returns of both parties showed that a majority of the Nebraska electorate was dry, and he correctly predicted a victory for the prohibition amendment in November.[71] Breathing what amounted to a sigh of relief, Bryan turned his attention once again to the issues of peace and economic reform.

During the Presidential election Bryan maintained a consistent silence on prohibition, though he did urge the voters of Nebraska to vote for dry candidates to the state legislature "without regard to party differences on other subjects." [72] Once the Wilson Administration was safely elected to a second term, however, all of Bryan's caution departed, and he became as militant and extreme a prohibitionist as was to be found in the country. "The prohibition issue is here, and here to stay until the saloon is driven out of the United States," he wrote in the first post-election issue of *The Commoner*.[73] The election had given Bryan's support of prohibition additional impetus, for of the 23 dry states, almost all of which were in the West and South, 17 had cast their electoral votes for Wilson. It was evident that the Democratic party had captured the dry vote and Bryan was determined to keep things that way; he was going to turn the Democratic party into the party of prohibition. "My work during the next four years," he told a group of reporters a week after the election, "will be to contribute whatever I can toward making the national Democracy dry. . . . The Democratic Party cannot afford to become the champion of the brewery, the distillery and the

71. *The Commoner*, May 1916, p. 2.
72. Ibid. October 1916, p. 5.
73. Ibid. November 1916, p. 1.

saloon. The members of the party will not permit it to be buried in a drunkard's grave." [74]

Traveling to Indianapolis that same month, Bryan launched a movement to force the Democratic National Convention of 1920 to declare in favor of prohibition. "Prohibition is sweeping the country," he declared. "It will be a Presidential campaign issue in 1920 if a Constitutional amendment is not submitted . . . by that time." [75] He soon had his brother Charles send out circular letters giving the details of his proposal to organize a "Dry Democracy" systematically, precinct by precinct.[76] At the Washington banquet given by leading Democrats in Bryan's honor, Bryan pointed out again, as he had been doing since the election, that Wilson owed his victory to the dry West and South and not to the wet East. "Shall we part with those friends who saved us, in order to ally ourselves with those who would have annihilated us?" He appealed to his comrades to enlist their party "on the side of the mother, the child, the home and humanity," and not allow it to be made the champion "of the most mercenary, the most tyrannical group that ever entered politics for the purpose of debauching party and corrupting government." [77] Bryan was clearly burning all his bridges behind him; there was to be no turning back.

(4)

We have already noted that the war which Bryan had fought so hard to avoid was responsible for bringing him unprecedented popularity. No less paradoxical was the fact that this same war was to pave the way for the rapid adoption of

74. *New York World*, November 15, 1916, reprinted in ibid. December 1916, p. 5.
75. *Indianapolis Star*, November 19, 1916, reprinted in *The Commoner*, December 1916, p. 9; *New York Times*, November 20, 1916.
76. Clarence E. Pitts to WJB, February 22, 1917, Bryan Papers.
77. *The Commoner*, January 1917, p. 19.

national prohibition; a cause to which Bryan now devoted himself wholeheartedly.

The war, of course, was by no means solely responsible for the coming of prohibition. The triumph of national temperance was the result of a long and intensive campaign and, judging from the number of dry Congressmen elected in 1916, it would have come had war not occurred.[78] The war, however, did help to expedite the victory by aiding the prohibition movement in a variety of ways: it centralized authority in Washington to a greater degree than had been known since the Civil War; it brought into the movement such non-prohibitionists as Theodore Roosevelt and Herbert Hoover who now advocated prohibition as an emergency war measure; it diverted the attention of the nation from Washington and the state capitals where the battle for prohibition was raging; and, finally, it furnished the temperance forces with an entire battery of new arguments which enabled them to make prohibition and patriotism synonymous.[79]

Bryan was one of the first to make effective use of these new points. One almost suspects that he was so eager to speak in behalf of food conservation primarily because from this vantage point he could deal liquor some devastating blows. There could be no argument against the fact that prohibition was an efficient means of saving grain, and Bryan never tired of reiterating this point. We have had "meatless" days and "wheatless" days, he exclaimed, "Why doesn't someone sug-

78. Wayne Wheeler of the Anti-Saloon League has written of the election of 1916: "Many hours before the country knew whether Hughes or Wilson had triumphed, the dry workers throughout the nation were celebrating our victory. We knew the prohibition amendment would be submitted to the States by the Congress just elected." Quoted in Timberlake, *Prohibition and the Progressive Movement*, p. 172.

79. Charles Merz, *The Dry Decade* (Garden City, New York, 1931), pp. 25–7; Herbert Asbury, *The Great Illusion: an Informal History of Prohibition* (Garden City, New York, 1950), pp. 136–7.

gest a few beerless days? . . . How can we justify the making of any part of our breadstuffs into intoxicating liquor when men are crying for bread?" In addition to wasting food, the use of alcohol impaired efficiency "and in this crisis we cannot afford to allow efficiency to be impaired either among soldiers or producers." "Alcohol," he cried, "is an enemy at home scarcely less deadly than the foe upon the field." [80]

But merely citing the pernicious effects of spirituous beverages was not Bryan's main aim; it was their manufacturers he was after. If alcohol was a deadly enemy, what could be said of the man who persisted in producing it. "The liquor interests," asserted Bryan in one of the most savage attacks he had ever made against any group, "are the most unpatriotic and conscienceless groups . . . [the United States] ever knew." "So much greater is their passion for dollars than their patriotism that they would, if they could, make drunkards of the entire army and leave us defenseless before a foreign foe." [81]

Though such extreme attacks were both unfair and untrue, they were characteristic of Bryan's righteous, evangelistic fervor and necessary to his style of argumentation. It has often been noted that Bryan was one of the nation's chief exploiters of the conspiracy thesis; it should be added that he was also one of its major victims. As long as an issue remained on the periphery of Bryan's interests he was able to view it with some degree of realism, to perceive many of its complexities, and often to deal with it relatively and fairly. But once the issue was joined, once he became convinced that the time for resolving it was at hand, his mind clamped shut and became incapable of perceiving subtle distinctions. This occurred not because Bryan was an opportunist but because his mind and

80. *New York Times,* January 28, 1918; *The Commoner,* May 1917, p. 3, April 1918, p. 7.
81. Ibid. July 1917, p. 7, January 1918, p. 5; *New York Times,* January 28, 1918.

temperament led him to view all important issues in terms of absolutes. In the uncomplicated world in which he thrived, all decency and depravity were quickly separated and placed into easily recognizable compartments. Good was good and bad was bad and they never joined hands in the Nebraskan's simple universe. Thus he could insist that no man could serve two masters, "he must be on the side of the home or the saloon." "There is only one side to a moral issue," he repeated untiringly, "and that is the moral side." [82]

And if the war accomplished nothing else it made Bryan more confident than ever that he was on the moral side. He not only recited the patriotic arguments in behalf of prohibition, he *believed* in them implicitly. "I have never taken part in any fight which was as great in its far-reaching influence as the fight in which we are now engaged and my heart has never been so deeply in a cause as in the cause which now approaches its complete triumph," he told an audience in the fall of 1918. Never before was Bryan so certain that the fight which he was waging would benefit all mankind: "Thousands, tens of thousands, hundreds of thousands of men who will vote against prohibition and who will think we are violating their personal rights will, when they are released from the habit and relieved from temptation, go down on their knees and thank us for having helped them against their will, and their wives and children will not have to wait a year; they will thank us now for saving their husbands and fathers. . . . I say, my friends, we are fighting a battle where even our opponents will be benefited." [83]

Armed with these certainties, Bryan visited more than half of the states in the Union, speaking under the auspices of the Women's Christian Temperance Union, the Anti-Saloon League, and the Democratic Forward League. Everywhere he

82. *The Commoner*, September 1918, p. 2, March 1917, p. 6.
83. Ibid. October 1918, pp. 7, 9.

went he spoke out boldly and decisively, and at no time was he willing to concede one point to his opponents. All justice and all righteousness were on his side. When it was argued that the prohibition crusade was undermining individual rights, he answered that the rights of the individual could not be placed above his duty to society, and that personal liberty must often be curbed for the greater good. "A man does not have to be run over by a drunken chauffeur more than twice before he learns that no man's personal liberty includes the right to injure another one." [84] Nowhere in these arguments did he recognize the vast majority of wets who drank moderately and injured no one. It is by no means improbable that Bryan, carried away by his own rhetoric, forgot that this type of drinker even existed. When it was sensibly suggested that beers and wines be treated more leniently than whisky in any proposed legislation, Bryan refused to listen. "Whiskey and beer will stand or fall together; it is the alcohol in both that makes them a menace. . . . The entire firm of 'Barleycorn, Gambrinus and Bacchus' must retire from business — a dissolution of partnership is not sufficient." [85]

Once again, the most serious charge leveled against Bryan, that his prohibition crusade belied his own professed faith in the people,[86] was one that he did not even bother to answer; indeed, it was a charge that he probably failed to understand. Anyone well versed in the Scriptures should have known that you cannot elevate man unless you first remove temptation from his path. This was not an attack upon man's innate wisdom or goodness; it was merely a realistic admission of his weaknesses. In an article in which he praised the farmer's advanced

84. Ibid. October 1917, p. 3. See also *Memoirs*, p. 292.
85. *The Commoner*, July 1917, p. 1.
86. Journalist William Hard, for example, wrote of Bryan: "He has abandoned the rights of man and is in favor of state interference and paternalism and tyranny." *Everybody's* XXXIV (April 1916), 454.

position in adopting and championing prohibition, Bryan intimated that this precocity stemmed in large part from the fact that the rural population of the country enjoyed the advantage of living "in the absence of many of the temptations which throng about the city." [87] The fault, then, Bryan unconsciously attributed not to man, who could not help his own weaknesses, but to God, who first created a man who was too weak to withstand certain temptations and then placed those temptations directly in his path. "God never made a human being so strong that he could begin the use of intoxicants with the certainty that he would not become a victim of the habit." [88] The remedy was not to attempt to do what God Himself could not do, but simply to remove the temptation. Bryan was going to prevent all the Adams that still roamed the earth from repeating their precursor's mistake, not by making them better or wiser men, but by confiscating all the apples in sight. That these men who were today too weak to resist temptation, might tomorrow begin to cultivate their own illicit apple orchards, was a thought which apparently never troubled him.

With the eyes of the nation and the nation's press riveted upon the battlefields across the Atlantic, the temperance forces concentrated their attention upon Washington. Despite the fact that Bryan continued to raise the specter of a vast liquor conspiracy which was determined to prevent Congress from complying with the people's wishes, it was the prohibitionists and not their foes who were more efficiently organized and more adept at winning public support. The hitherto well-oiled political machines of the brewers and distillers were by this time thoroughly discredited, and the remainder of the wet forces seemed unable to treat prohibition as a serious

87. "Prohibition and the Farmer," *The Commoner*, September 1917, p. 8.
88. Ibid. May 1918, p. 2.

threat.[89] By the time they did it was too late, for on August 1, 1917 the Senate adopted the Eighteenth Amendment and the following December the House followed suit.

Bryan was seated in the press gallery when the House took its decisive vote, and as soon as victory was assured he entered upon the floor and was immediately surrounded by a score of Democratic Representatives. "Bryan Again Party Leader," ran a headline in the next edition of the *New York Sun*: "As a result of the vote in the House today Bryan has made himself a political leader of the Democratic Party and had pushed his new moral issue to the front as a preliminary to the next campaign." [90] The Legislative Committee of the Anti-Saloon League promptly sent Bryan a letter of congratulations in which they assured him that: "Generations yet unborn will rise up to call you blessed. Women and children without number . . . will not cease to thank God that He sent you to help proclaim the day of their deliverance." [91]

During the battle for ratification Bryan was, if anything, even more zealous than before. As far as he was concerned, the majority had already spoken through two-thirds of its representatives in Congress, and the procedures which compelled three-fourths of the states to concur as well was one of the Constitution's "ultra-conservative" provisions which he was to spend much time combating in the coming years. In this frame of mind Bryan was less willing than ever to make concessions or brook interference. Prohibition, he declared, was "the supreme domestic issue" until the amendment was secured. He continued to regard the East as one of the chief

89. Merz, *The Dry Decade*, p. 36; Asbury, *The Great Illusion*, pp. 108 ff.

90. *New York World*, December 17, 1917, *New York Sun*, December 17, 1917, both reprinted in *The Commoner*, January 1918, p. 8.

91. Ibid. p. 3.

obstacles to reform of all kinds. During the winter of 1918, he
was invited to testify before a joint legislative committee of
the New York State Legislature, and in his address which,
according to the *New York Times*, "held the vast audience
spellbound," Bryan thundered: "New York State, I say to
you that it is time you were leading in something good. New
York, it is time that you got into this race. The South is leading." [92]

In March 1918, Bryan was elected president of the National Dry Federation, an organization consisting of twenty-
eight separate national groups including the Federal Council
of Churches, the Prohibition Party, and the Women's Prohibition League.[93] Despite his new organizational affiliation,
Bryan's most important work still was accomplished through
his oratory: in addresses to numerous state legislatures, in testimony before Congressional committees, and especially on
the platform where he appealed directly to the voters. This
was democracy as he understood it — it was what he knew
how to do best. As the fall elections approached, Bryan, in his
eagerness to have the temperance forces control the state legislatures, made one of his rare nonpartisan appeals: "The voters should lay partisanship aside and vote for the DRY legislative candidate against the WET candidate regardless of party.
A Republican legislator who will vote to ratify the national
prohibition amendment is better than a Democratic legislator
who will vote to defeat the amendment and retain the
saloons." [94]

When news of the final ratification of the Eighteenth
Amendment reached Bryan on January 16, 1919, he commented: "Let the world rejoice. . . . The greatest moral re-

92. *New York Times*, February 27, 1918; *New York Evening Post*,
February 27, 1918.
93. *The Commoner*, March 1918, p. 2.
94. Ibid. September 1918, p. 1.

form of the generation has been accomplished." [95] He was especially pleased because he felt that the settlement of the prohibition issue would remove an important source of friction within the ranks of the Democratic party. To Postmaster General Burleson he wrote: "You have certainly been a good fighter and deserve to retain your side arms if not the contents of your hip pockets. The settlement of the liquor question eliminates the only difference between us as the Civil War removed the root of discord between the North and South." [96] Unfortunately, Bryan's analogy proved to be more apt than he knew.

His work, of course, was still not fully completed. Laws, as he well knew from past experience, are not self-enforcing. Accordingly, he inaugurated his long battle for a rigid enforcement statute. His most bitter struggle, however, centered upon the issue of wartime prohibition. The Eighteenth Amendment was not due to go into effect until January 16, 1920, but in September 1918 Congress had passed an emergency act establishing wartime prohibition beginning the following July. With the end of the war, Wilson proved reluctant to enforce the act and recommended its repeal pertaining to wine and beer. Infuriated by the President's recommendation, Bryan now indulged in an act which was even rarer for him than mere nonpartisanship: he appealed to a Republican Congress to override a Democratic President. [97] On most questions, he announced during a Chicago address, the President might be assumed to know more than the average citizen, "but on the question of the saloon a mother with a drunken son knows more than he does." [98] In the end, widespread opposition to Wilson's recommendation, even among mem-

95. Ibid. February 1919, pp. 1, 8.
96. WJB to Burleson, January 22, 1919, Burleson Papers, Vol. 22.
97. *The Commoner*, June 1919, pp. 1–2.
98. *New York Times*, May 26, 1919.

bers of his Cabinet, forced him to back down, and on July 1, 1919 the saloons all over the United States were legally closed. "What a night of sorrow we have passed through," Bryan told a Methodist Conference at Columbus, Ohio, "but the morning is here and joy cometh with it." Nine years before he had not expected to live to see the nation go dry but now, though he was fifty-nine, he was confident that he would see the day "when there will not be an open saloon in any civilized nation on the globe." [99]

Even with the coming of prohibition Bryan's troubles were far from over. He soon found himself under attack by certain newspapers for having accepted payment for some of his prohibition speeches. "William Jennings Bryan worked for humanity for $250 a day and expenses, spot cash," commented the *New York World*.[100] It was true that in 1919 Bryan had received $11,000 for making a series of lectures for the Anti-Saloon League, but, as the records of the League proved and as Bryan and League officials hurriedly pointed out, he had been speaking for the League and other dry organizations for nine years without receiving a penny even for his personal expenses. Only after Congress had approved prohibition did Bryan agree to accept any compensation for his work and, as he himself maintained, had he been the money-grabbing opportunist pictured by the newspapers he could have earned a fortune years before by speaking in behalf of the liquor interests or any number of other interest groups.[101] The newspaper

99. *The Commoner*, July 1919, p. 5. Bryan went so far as to ask Secretary Lansing to forward all available information relating to the liquor question in other countries. WJB to Robert Lansing, January 20, 1919, National Archives, Washington, D.C.

100. Quoted in Peter H. Odegard, *Pressure Politics: the Story of the Anti-Saloon League* (New York, 1928), p. 203.

101. See ibid. Appendix F, p. 274; *The Commoner*, March 1920, p. 5; Wayne B. Wheeler's statement in the *New York Times*, January 9, 1920.

attacks had hurt him, however, and he reverted to his previous policy of accepting no remuneration for making prohibition speeches and even became wary of speaking under the auspices of such organizations as the Anti-Saloon League.[102]

In addition to difficuties with the press, Bryan also found himself embroiled in a senseless dispute with William H. Anderson, the State Superintendent of the Anti-Saloon League of New York, which was precipitated when Bryan accepted the presidency of the National Dry Federation. Anderson, who saw the new organization as a threat to his own, publicly attacked Bryan for his tardiness in joining the dry forces and asserted that "as a LEADER, as a supposed strategist, as a general, . . . Mr. Bryan is frankly a joke so far as the Prohibition movement is concerned."[103] Bryan had no need to defend himself, for leading prohibitionists throughout the country quickly repudiated Anderson's charges and the National Anti-Saloon League itself eventually censured Anderson for "making an attack of a personal nature upon an outstanding friend of prohibition."[104]

Difficulties of this nature, however, could not mar the joy Bryan felt when a few seconds before Constitutional prohibition was due to go into effect, at a minute past midnight on January 17, 1920, he paused in the midst of his speech before a victory celebration to recite the Scriptural lines: "They are dead which sought the young child's life."[105] At the same moment in Norfolk, Virginia, Billy Sunday, with his usual

102. WJB to Josephus Daniels, December 5, 1922, Daniels Papers, Box 566.

103. A copy of Anderson's article, dated April 2, 1918, is in the Bryan Papers. See also *New York Times*, April 14, 1918.

104. See the following letters to Bryan: Howard H. Russell, April 6, 1918, F. L. Crabbe, April 22, 1918, A. C. Bayne, May 9, 1918, Ella A. Boole, April 24, 1918, Bryan Papers. See also the report of the Anti-Saloon League Committee which investigated the entire affair. Ibid.

105. *The Commoner*, February 1920, p. 1.

flair for turning the sublime into the ridiculous, was holding a full-scale funeral service for John Barleycorn. Despite his unfailing hyperbole, Sunday enunciated the hopes and expectations of many prohibitionists when he cried:

> The reign of tears is over. The slums will soon be only a memory. We will turn our prisons into factories and our jails into storehouses and corncribs. Men will walk upright now, women will smile, and the children will laugh. Hell will be forever for rent.[106]

"King Alcohol" was dead; all that remained was the task of burying the corpse; a task that proved far more exacting than Bryan, Sunday, and their fellow executioners anticipated.

(5)

Although when Bryan eventually came to champion prohibition he did so sincerely, his early stand on the issue was highly inconsistent with his later one and his whole temperance crusade was tinged with a note of expediency. His record on woman suffrage is open to no such charges. Though there is no indication that he committed himself on the question before 1914, when, in that year, it became an issue in Nebraska he canvassed the state in its behalf.[107] From that time forth he made the issue his own.

Bryan's campaign for woman suffrage, which took him through nineteen states in the West alone, was grounded to a greater degree upon simple justice and logic than almost any other cause he championed. If man showed his confidence in woman by giving himself to her in marriage, by turning over to her the physical, mental, and moral development of his children, by making her his partner in the management of all the family's affairs, and by sending his children to schools

---

106. Quoted in Asbury, *The Great Illusion*, pp. 144–5.
107. *Memoirs*, p. 467.

taught largely by female teachers, he asked, with what logic or consistency or justice could he deny her an equal voice in his government? Women, he argued, had a right to a voice in determining the environment in which they lived. "Is it just that men only shall determine when the mother must yield up her son to the battlefield, or when the ties that bind the husband to the wife shall be severed by the sword?" Woman suffrage was right, and the undeniable proof of this lay in the fact that no state or country after having adopted the reform had ever been forced to abandon it. "The suffrage revolution never turns backward. There is not only no return, but there is no agitation for a return." [108]

Bryan's interest in the causes of peace and prohibition deepened the intensity with which he fought for female suffrage. Such events as the election of 1916, in which ten of the twelve states where women had the franchise voted for Wilson, and the work of such organizations as the Woman's Christtian Temperance Union and the Woman's Peace Conference, convinced him that "the world needs woman's vote even more than woman needs the ballot; her conscience, added to man's judgment, will hasten the triumph of every righteous cause." [109] Those who were desirous of promoting world peace would be impotent so long as they stubbornly refused to take women into their councils.[110] And if woman's voice was needed to assure peace, it was even more essential in transforming the United States into a dry nation.[111] Tying prohibition to the suffrage cause was also useful in another respect: it provided Bryan with an opportunity to point an accusing finger at a selfish and iniquitous special interest group in an issue which normally did not lend itself to the conspiracy

108. *The Commoner*, March 1916, p. 11, September 1916, p. 6.
109. Ibid. December 1916, pp. 17, 19, July 1918, p. 1.
110. Ibid. June 1915, p. 7, July 1915, p. 15.
111. Ibid. June 1917, p. 5.

thesis. "Yes, of course," he would rail, "the liquor interests . . . are against woman's suffrage. Every man who traffics
in sin is opposed to woman's suffrage. . . . Those making a
profession of wickedness understand that woman's conscience
is AGAINST them." [112]

Bryan enlisted the aid of his wife in the fight, and Mrs.
Bryan made a number of suffrage speeches in various parts of
the country.[113] At no time did Bryan doubt the eventual
triumph of the reform, though the fact that the Southern wing
of his own party opposed it so vehemently concerned him.
During the winter of 1919 he visited the Capital and urged
Southern Senators and Representatives to vote for the amendment. "I hope," he said before leaving, "the Democrats of the
South will not handicap the Democrats of the North by com-
pelling them to spend the next twenty-five years explaining to
the women of the country why their party prevented the submission of the suffrage amendment to the States." [114]

When Congress finally adopted the amendment a few
months later, Bryan channeled his fervor into the fight for
ratification. He had already made the issue one of the cardinal
points of the political program which he formulated in the
opening days of 1919, and he now advocated its inclusion in
the Democratic platform of 1920.[115] Only when the thirty-
sixth state ratified the amendment on August 18, 1920, did his
labors in its behalf come to a halt.

If, at any time during the beginning of 1920, Bryan had
paused to survey the progress made since America's entry into
the war he could not have failed to find in it much that was
comforting. The nation was dry; woman suffrage was on the

112. Ibid. September 1915, p. 4.
113. Mary B. Bryan to WJB, August 29, 1917, Bryan Papers; *New
York Times*, October 14, 1917.
114. Ibid. February 5, 1919.
115. *The Commoner*, January 1919, p. 5, March 1920, p. 6.

verge of triumph; the war had been fought to a victorious conclusion, and the peace movement, in behalf of which he had received such a resounding defeat only three years earlier, appeared to be approaching its zenith. These indeed had been years of victory and there was little reason to believe that the days which lay ahead would be any less glorious.

IV: The Paths of Duty

It is the duty of every human being to believe in the final triumph of every righteous cause and, believing, work to that end . . . the Lord does not require us to win — He simply requests us to do our duty as we see it. . . . If after trying we find we have failed we have nothing to regret. — WJB

(1)

EVEN WHILE he was engaged in serving the war effort, Bryan turned his thoughts to the time when the belligerents would meet to frame the peace treaty. The nation had been in the war only nine months when he wrote the President: "Acting on the theory that I may be honored with a place on the peace commission, am devoting all my time this winter to study of European politics of the past century and the more important treaties . . ." [1] In what appears to have been an attempt to build up support for his appointment to the peace commission, Bryan sent similar notes to prominent politicians, judges, and journalists throughout the country and received a generally enthusiastic response. [2] The ultimate responsibility for the composition of the peace commission, of course, was Wilson's, and he proved to have a number of reservations about Bryan's participation. In transmitting Bryan's note to

1. WJB to Wilson, January 15, 1918, Wilson Papers, File VI, Box 491.
2. See letters from the following to Bryan: Senator Ollie James, January 14, 1918, Senator Henry L. Meyers, January 15, 1918, Senator Joseph T. Robinson, January 15, 1918, Senator Robert T. Owen, January 15, 1918, Representative J. M. Baer, January 16, 1918, Representative Warren Worth Bailey, January 16, 1918, George Fort Milton, January 13, 1918, Justice Walter Clark, January 15, 1918, Bryan Papers.

Tumulty, the President commented: "What *do* you think of this and what possible answer can I make, for, of course, the assumption he is acting on will never be realized." [3] Wilson, in fact, never did find a satisfactory reply and finally had to content himself by writing Bryan a few lines in which he thanked the ex-Secretary for his letter and praised the value of studying the national problems of European countries.[4]

Though the President's response was far from encouraging, Bryan bided his time and refused to lose hope. A month before the Armistice was signed he wrote Secretary Daniels:

Peace prospects improve — a commission may be needed soon. I hope you will not consider me immodest if I say that it is a task for which I am especially qualified. If I understand the terms as stated I am in hearty accord with all of them. I say this so that you may know if the question comes up in the Cabinet.[5]

Shortly after the Armistice was signed, Daniels, in discussing the proposed personnel of the peace commission with Wilson, dutifully mentioned his old friend's name, and soon thereafter he wrote the President a long letter in which he urged Bryan's selection, saying in part: "It is the crowning ambition of his life to have the opportunity of rendering this service and I trust you will feel that you can name him as one of the Commissioners. I know there are thousands . . . who would be gratified at his selection." [6] In a reply marked "Personal and Confidential" Wilson refused Daniel's request, writ-

3. Wilson to Tumulty, January 15, 1918, Wilson Papers, File VI, Box 491.
4. Wilson to WJB, January 22, 1918, ibid.
5. WJB to Daniels, October 14, 1918, Daniels Papers, Box 37. Bryan wrote a similar letter to Postmaster General Burleson, October 14, 1918, Burleson Papers, Vol. 21; and asked James Brown Scott, the Secretary of the Carnegie Endowment for International Peace, to recommend him to Secretary Lansing as one of the Peace Commissioners. See Scott to WJB, October 18, 1918, Bryan Papers.
6. Daniels to Wilson, November 14, 1918, Daniels Papers, Box 14.

ing that despite his own "cordial personal feeling towards Mr.
Bryan" he could not appoint him to the peace commission
"because it would be unjustly but certainly taken for granted
that he would be too easy and that he would pursue some
Eutopian [*sic*] scheme." [7]

This rebuff hurt Bryan deeply, but it did not cause him to
lose his temper or his perspective. He praised and defended
the President's widely debated decision to attend the peace
conference in person,[8] and acted as if he expected Wilson to
change his mind at the last moment and ask him to accompany
the American mission. Bryan simply refused to believe that
he, who had worked so diligently for peace, could be ex-
cluded from the very council chambers where peace would
become a reality. It was probably not until the *George Washington* sailed for Europe on December 4 carrying Wilson, his
peace commission, and an entourage of experts and corre-
spondents, that Bryan's last hopes faded. Thus while Wilson
was being applauded, honored, and feted in the streets of Europe, and frustrated and disillusioned in its council chambers,
Bryan remained at home continuing his fight for prohibition
and woman suffrage and eagerly devouring all the dispatches
emanating from the other side of the Atlantic.

(2)

During the early months of 1919 personal problems mo-
mentarily diverted Bryan's attention from the dramatic events
transpiring in his own country and the world. His wife, who
had been in poor health for several years, entered a Baltimore

7. Wilson to Daniels, November 16, 1918, ibid. The President later
told Daniels that because he could not have too many Democrats on
the commission, if he had appointed Bryan he would have had to
drop either House or Lansing, and this he refused to do. Daniels to
Ray Stannard Baker, October 24, 1938, R. S. Baker Papers, Box 28.
8. WJB to Wilson, November 20, 1918, Wilson Papers, File VI, Box
491.

hospital in February, and Bryan, who rushed to Baltimore to be with her, came down with what at first appeared to be a heavy cold. He immediately left for Washington and placed himself under the care of his former physician Dr. Kelly and his good friend Dan Bride at whose home he stayed. "I was very much alarmed," he wrote Mrs. Bryan a few days later. "I feared that my cold might develop into pneumonia—this, you know, has been my terror for thirty years, and I had an anxious night when we could not get the doctor, but his coming assured me. . . . He said I had no symptoms of pneumonia." Bryan's malady was diagnosed as facial erysipelas, an inflammation which left him prostrate and in pain for several weeks.[9]

For a man of Bryan's temperament and habits the worst thing about this interlude was not the pain but the inactivity and feeling of impotence. During his illness the first act of the dramatic battle over the League of Nations began to unfold. Wilson returned from the Peace Conference for a brief visit, was confronted by his Republican critics, defiantly announced that the League Covenant could not be dissected from the treaty without destroying the "whole vital structure," and then departed for Europe again. Senators Lodge and Brandegee proposed a Senatorial Round Robin, signed by thirty-five of their Republican colleagues in the Senate, which rejected the League in its present form, and the country as a whole began to stir with the first faint signs of an impending struggle.

Bryan, as weak as he was, squirmed with impatience. He eagerly questioned friends like Secretary Daniels and Senator Kenyon who came to visit, and he had a long chat with the correspondent David Lawrence who had just returned from Paris with the Wilson party. "I wish I could tell you on paper

9. WJB to Mary B. Bryan, February 27, 1919, WJB to Richard Hargreaves, March 1, 1919, Bryan Papers.

all that I learned from Dave Lawrence this morning," he wrote his brother on March 2. "He was in Paris and on the inside. We have not overestimated the trouble they have had. . . . My position is we should take the League as the best thing we can get but that we must make it as good as possible. . . . I have some improvements to suggest." [10] His physical condition, however, made it impossible for him to take any action. "I am lying here so weak that I can hardly think," he complained to his brother two days later. ". . . you can't imagine how helpless I am, but I must wait till God gives me strength before I undertake anything in the way of leadership. . . . Be patient with me. I have never felt so helpless before, so without strength . . ." [11]

Shortly after Wilson's second departure for Europe, rumors appeared in print that Bryan was going to oppose the League of Nations. Certainly there were sufficient reasons for Bryan's opposition. Had he fit neatly into any of the numerous molds fashioned for him by his host of detractors he would have sought revenge for Wilson's humiliating snub by opposing the peace plan which the President was to bring home for Senatorial approval. He could easily and consistently have joined forces with those opposed to the League of Nations, for he had already gone on record as an opponent of a similar plan advocated earlier by the League to Enforce Peace, and in 1917 had prophesied that "the proposed League, being a child . . . of the European war and being nourished by the spirit of preparedness . . . will find its final repose in the calm that will follow the restoration of peace." [12] Precisely when and why Bryan changed his mind is difficult to determine. The sight of the United States being led into a struggle with which it had no apparent concern could not

10. WJB to Charles W. Bryan, March 2, 1919, ibid.
11. WJB to Charles W. Bryan, March 4, 1919, ibid.
12. WJB and Taft, *World Peace*, p. 142.

have failed to have a sobering effect upon him and may well have impressed him with a fact which all too many of his countrymen were soon to forget: that whether we took an active part in world affairs or not, those affairs concerned us and had a direct effect upon us.

Bryan's desire to aid in bringing about a lasting and universal peace had proven stronger than his love for office, and it also proved stronger than any personal desire for revenge. Despite his illness, as soon as word of the newspaper rumors reached him he drafted a careful statement which was widely distributed and which inaugurated his long and heated battle in behalf of the League. The League of Nations, he announced, was "the greatest step towards peace in a thousand years." It substituted reason for force in the settlement of international disputes by providing for investigation of all disputes before hostilities began, just as his own treaties had, by requiring reductions in armaments, and by abolishing secret treaties. "If the League of Nations did nothing more than these three things," he proclaimed, "our nation would be justified in supporting it to the utmost." Bryan was ready to admit that the League was not perfect, and he called for "free and frank discussion to perfect the League." He himself felt that the League Charter should be more specific regarding the sanctity of the Monroe Doctrine, should present greater safeguards against interference by the League in the internal affairs of a member nation, and should make the obligation of members to accept a League mandate optional rather than obligatory. In addition, Bryan felt that the basis of representation in the League was not fair to the larger nations and that new members should be admitted by a majority rather than a two-thirds vote. On the whole, however, he was more than satisfied with the League, and he assured his readers that its imperfections were not great enough to lead to its rejection. "We must take risks, no matter whether we accept the League or reject it. The risks

that we take in accepting it are less than the risks we take if
we reject it and turn back to the old ways of blood and
slaughter." [13]

Throughout the President's stay in Europe, Bryan continued to display his faith in Wilson's ability to conclude a just
and lasting peace and refused to be stampeded into panic by
any of the rumors that were making their way across the
Atlantic. "The President has reason to be proud," he announced when the first copies of the treaty were published.
The terms accorded to Germany he applauded as "harsh but
just," and his applause extended to almost every other provision of the treaty.[14] If there were any iniquities in the settlement, such as the cession of Shantung to Japan, the way to
resolve them was not to defeat the treaty and invite chaos, but
to ratify it, bringing into existence the League of Nations
where such questions could be amicably settled.[15] Bryan's
unconcealed eagerness to see the League begin operating led
him to withhold criticism of a document which under other
circumstances probably would not have met with his unques-
tioned approval.

As Bryan's strength gradually returned he became increasingly active. By the end of March he was back in harness
making speeches with the same old fire and enthusiasm. In
addresses in Pennsylvania, Michigan, Missouri, and Washington, D.C., Bryan reiterated his faith in the ability of
the League to bring about lasting peace. The League, he as-

13. *New York Times*, March 12, 1919. Bryan asked Daniels to send
a copy of his statement to the President in Paris, and to assure him
that while Bryan favored some changes in the Covenant, the League
was so "transcendent and so necessary to the future of the world" that
he was prepared "to accept it without change rather than to lose the
benefits which can come in no other way than through the united
action of the free nations of the world." Daniels to Woodrow Wilson,
March 27, 1919, Daniels Papers, Box 14.

14. *The Commoner*, May 1919, pp. 1–2.

15. Ibid. October 1919, p. 1.

serted, was built upon a revolutionary idea, "that war is not necessary, that war is not desirable, that war can be prevented . . ." [16]

The only issue on which Bryan opposed the President during the spring and summer of 1919 was the proposed treaty with France in which the United States agreed to give immediate aid to that country in case of an "unprovoked" attack by Germany. To Bryan such an alliance seemed directly antithetical to the idea of a League of Nations. If the latter organization had any *raison d'être* it was to destroy petty jealousies by creating a community of interest between all nations and instilling a spirit of brotherhood among them. Private alliances were directly inimical to this purpose; they established "a league within a league" which could only serve to resuscitate all of the old barriers and suspicions between nations.[17] Interestingly enough, while Bryan opposed the alliance because it would hinder the spirit of cooperation among nations, he also opposed it because it would impair the sovereignty of the United States. "The proposed alliance treaty," he wrote, "should be rejected by a majority so decisive that Europe will understand that we reserve the right to decide war questions when wars come, and that we will not surrender the Constitutional right of Congress to declare war." [18]

In the early days of the debate on the League Bryan was understandably optimistic. The League gave the world something it never before possessed — machinery for peace — and it was inconceivable to Bryan that the most peaceful nation on earth could reject that machinery. As early as April 1919, he saw the possibility that the Republican majority in the Senate might succeed in blocking early ratification of the Treaty, but this prospect left him unperturbed. In that event,

16. *New York Times*, May 18, 1919.
17. *The Commoner*, July 1919, p. 1.
18. Ibid. May 1919, p. 1.

he wrote, the issue would be brought into the election of 1920 and the people could decide for themselves. And with the impending victory of the suffrage amendment, which would in all probability give women the vote by the election of 1920, there was no doubt in his mind as to how the people would decide. "Make no mistake," he warned the opponents of the League. "The American people will endorse the League of Nations." [19] When in May the first draft of the Covenant was revised so as to remove several American objections to it (including some of those Bryan himself had made), Bryan predicted that the Senate would now ratify it by an "overwhelming majority." [20]

There were many in Washington who did not share Bryan's optimism. Secretary Lansing expressed his conviction succinctly when he wrote in his diary: "No Compromise; No Ratification." [21] Hitchcock, the Minority Leader of the Senate, also advised compromise. "Let Lodge compromise, Senator," Wilson replied. "Well, we might hold out the olive branch," Hitchcock suggested again. "No," Wilson answered adamantly, "let Lodge hold out the olive branch." [22] "The situation," Hitchcock informed Bryan, "is unusually bad." [23] Still Bryan stood with Wilson and refused to counsel compromise: "Every change desired can be made afterwards, without the risk that is involved in an attempted change at this time." [24]

When, on November 19, 1919, the obstinacy of Wilson crashed head-on with that of the reservationists, resulting in the defeat of the Treaty, Bryan began to reconsider his posi-

19. Ibid. April 1919, p. 3.
20. Ibid. May 1919, p. 2.
21. August 11, 1919, Lansing Diaries.
22. Gilbert M. Hitchcock, "Wilson's Place in History," undated address in the Hitchcock Papers.
23. Hitchcock to WJB, October 4, 1919, Bryan Papers.
24. *The Commoner*, October 1919, p. 1.

tion. His willingness to see the League issue introduced into the 1920 election — an event made more likely by the failure of the Senate to ratify it — began to fade. It may be that Bryan began to mull over his own highly unsuccessful attempts to transform the elections of 1900 and 1916 into referenda on the issues of imperialism and peace respectively. In addition, he was fearful that should the League issue be postponed for another year it would be impossible for the country's progressives to focus attention upon important economic and social questions. Bryan and William Gibbs McAdoo, in an exchange of letters, agreed that "the Philistines are upon us" and that the "well-organized and confident forces of reaction" could be beaten only if the Democratic party asserted itself "militantly and enthusiastically." [25] It is clear that with Wilson's illness Bryan sensed a power vacuum developing in the party and he was determined to see it filled by progressives like himself. The struggle for control of the Democratic party would take place at its national convention in July and Bryan was fearful that if the League question was not settled before then it would becloud the issue and prevent the party from facing the clear-cut conflict between progressivism and conservatism.[26]

Five days after the treaty was rejected, Bryan made his conversion public in a letter he sent to every Democratic member of the Senate. The President, he began, had agreed to the treaty as it was drawn at Paris and therefore had an obligation to insist upon ratification without reservations. "But," he quickly added, "having made his fight and failed he should recognize the Senate's right to say the final word. . . . He can not ignore the Senate no matter how much its action may displease him." Neither the party nor the country could afford to make the League a campaign issue. "We have do-

25. McAdoo to WJB, December 29, 1919, Bryan Papers.
26. *The Commoner*, May 1920, p. 1.

mestic questions of vital importance which can not be ignored . . . while the Democrats are standing out against a few reservations the reactionary element will be securing a grip on the government." He would have preferred entering the League without reservation but the reservations were not important; the important thing was to take the United States into the League and make any necessary changes later.[27]

After a brief vacation the Senate reconvened in December and Bryan was on hand to plead for compromise. He spoke to Senators individually and in groups, addressed a dinner given in his honor at the Shoreham Hotel at which twenty Democratic members of the Senate were present, and consistently advised his fellow Democrats that the treaty had to be ratified, with mild reservations if possible, with the Lodge resolutions if necessary.[28] His activities led to a front page *New York Times* headline: "BRYAN INFLUENCE LOOMS ON PEACE TREATY," and prompted Senator Lodge to point him out as one of the forces behind a compromise.[29] Following the Christmas recess Bryan was back in Washington moving from Senator to Senator, using all of his powers of persuasion and his entire battery of arguments to obtain consensus for a practical compromise. He was thought to be the guiding force behind the attempt of a group of Democrats led by Senator Kendrick of Wyoming to by-pass both Senators Hitchcock and Lodge and win the support of the Republican mild-reservationists for a new set of compromise resolutions.[30] On the whole, however, Bryan concentrated on his fellow Democrats and found that, while many of them were perfectly willing to accept reservations of one sort or another,

27. WJB to "My Dear Senator," November 24, 1919, Bryan Papers.
28. *Washington Post*, December 19, 1919, clipping in ibid.; *New York Times*, January 7, 1920.
29. Ibid. December 24, 26, 1919.
30. Ibid. January 7, 1920.

they were either too fearful of the President or too loyal to him to do so without his consent. In the face of this apparent stalemate, Bryan, whose efforts to effect a compromise had thus far produced little controversy, decided to broaden his appeal.

The occasion came on January 8, 1920, at the annual Jackson Day dinner given by the Democratic National Committee. Until Bryan's speech the high point of the evening was the reading of a letter which Wilson had sent from his sickbed, in which he advised that if necessary the election of 1920 should be transformed into "a great and solemn referendum" on the League of Nations. "We must take it [the League Covenant] without changes which alter its meaning or leave it," he asserted.[31] It was well past one in the morning when Bryan arose to address a room full of tired and restless Democrats who had spent the past few hours lustily cheering the statements of the President and other Administration notables. Bryan began slowly, speaking humbly, almost obsequiously, by calling himself a "dead politician" and apologizing for the lateness of the hour. These were tactics designed to win the interest and sympathy of the audience and that they succeeded was demonstrated at a quarter of two when his assurance that he would soon conclude his remarks was greeted by cries of "Go on," "Go on." [32]

Thirty minutes later he repeated this performance and upon receiving the same response he suddenly grew serious and, as one newspaper put it the next day, "he thrust his knife home" by telling the assembled Democrats that they had an unparalleled opportunity to lead the world. "The Democratic Senators stood with the President for ratification without reservation, and I stood with them. . . . But our plan has been

31. Ibid. January 9, 1920.
32. "Bryan Wakes up the Sleepers Again," *Literary Digest*, LXIV (January 31, 1920), 47.

rejected and we must face the situation as it is. We must either secure such compromise as may be possible or present the issue to the country." This latter course, he maintained, was impractical, for it meant a delay of at least fourteen months and even then success was not likely, as it was mathematically impossible for the Democrats to capture two-thirds of the Senate seats in 1920. "We can not afford," he continued, "either as citizens or as members of the party, to share with the Republican party responsibility for further delay. . . . The Republicans have a majority in the Senate and therefore can by right dictate the Senate's course. Being in the minority, we cannot demand the right to decide the terms upon which the Senate will consent to ratification." [33]

When the full impact of what Bryan was saying reached the assembled Democrats there were mutterings of disapproval and one irate listener rose and shouted: "Stand by the President." This cry was met by a roar of approval which lasted several minutes. When the cheering subsided, Bryan met the ultimatum with one of his own:

> My friend, if you will guarantee that eight million voters will stand by the President, I will bow to their decision, but until you do that I prefer to appeal from the eight hundred here to the eight million in the country, and that appeal I am entirely ready to make if I must. I am talking to people who can pay six dollars to come to a place like this; but the real Democratic party is not made for social occasions. . . . I am willing to take the responsibility for what I believe is right and appeal to the plain men and women who are not present and cannot come to a place like this.[34]

"Bryan Splits the Democratic Party Wide Open," ran a headline in the *New York Sun* the next day. And a reporter

33. *The Commoner*, January 1920, p. 8; *New York Times*, January 9, 1920.
34. *Literary Digest*, LXIV (January 31, 1920), 47.

from the same paper picturesquely described the mood of Bryan's audience as it left the banquet: "There were men who came out into the fog and rain who cursed the very name of Bryan, calling him Belial or worse; but there were others — many, many others — who nodded their heads in satisfaction, saying that Bryan was right." [35] Bryan attempted to quell all talk of a party schism by repeating his well-worn phrase: "The President and I differ only in method and not in purpose." [36] But the fact remained that he had directly challenged Wilson's leadership and, if newspaper comment is any indication, many Democrats throughout the country approved of his stand.[37] "The party loyalists, particularly the Bryanites, are greatly distressed," Robert Lansing noted with undisguised amusement. "They want to applaud Bryan but they are equally anxious to support the President. They stand first on one foot and then on the other like turkeys on a hot stove." [38]

As the deadlock over the treaty continued, Bryan's demands for immediate ratification grew more insistent. He was in and out of Washington, contacting Democratic Senators personally and through the mails. He begged them not to hide behind the outmoded procedure which allowed only a majority of Congress to declare war but which required a two-thirds vote of the Senate to make peace. The delay in ratification, he proclaimed, was "a shame, an outrage and a disgrace on our type of Government and we can't allow it to last." [39]

On March 19, 1920 — Bryan's sixtieth birthday — 23 Democrats, following Wilson's instructions, joined 12 Republicans to defeat the treaty with the Lodge reservations. At his birthday dinner in New York's Aldine Club that evening,

35. Reprinted in ibid. (January 17, 1920), p. 11.
36. *The Commoner*, January 1920, p. 7.
37. See *Literary Digest*, LXIV (January 17, 1920), 11.
38. January 10, 1920, Lansing Diaries.
39. *New York Times*, January 10, 12, 16, 20, 1920; *New York Sun*, January 12, 1920.

Bryan was angrily denouncing the two-thirds rule when someone called out: "The treaty is dead." "I am not willing to believe that it is dead," Bryan shot back. "Read the morning newspaper," his antagonist replied. "The Treaty has been defeated — I know that," Bryan answered, "but I believe that the people of the United States are greater than the United States Senators and can make them ratify." Then, leaning slightly forward and surveying the diners around him, Bryan said solemnly: "I think the world needs us and that if we refuse to do our duty and enter the League of Nations and if we are foolish enough to permit conditions in Europe to continue there will be a new war over there." [40]

The following day, on a trip through New England, Bryan denounced the Senate's action as "a colossal crime against our country and the world," and told a thousand Harvard students in Cambridge: "The action of the Senate made my blood boil. . . . While 100,000 precious lives were given to make the world safe for democracy, a Senate minority keeps us out of the only means of safeguarding the nation against future wars." [41] He could understand how Wilson, who was broken in health and had been denied many essential facts, could have been guilty of such poor judgment, but he could not understand how twenty-three Democratic Senators could have followed the ailing leader.[42] Bryan had failed in his efforts to keep the League out of the Democrats' forthcoming convention, but there still remained a slim possibility of keeping the issue out of the campaign, and that was to convince the Democratic National Convention to override Wilson's wishes and demand immediate ratification with reservations. It was at best a highly improbable and thoroughly distasteful

40. *New York Times*, March 20, 1920.
41. *Nebraska State Journal*, March 21, 1920; *New York Times*, March 21, 1920.
42. Ibid. April 11, 1920; *The Commoner*, May 1920, p. 1.

task, and few men other than Bryan would have dreamt of undertaking it.

(3)

During the years between his resignation and the conventions of 1920, Bryan not only fought for peace, prohibition, and woman suffrage but characteristically made himself the champion of a host of other reforms.

From the beginning of his career Bryan had been the victim of an unfair press which delighted in distorting his views. For years he had attributed his poor political showing in the Northeast to this factor. The people of the West and South, he said shortly after those sections had elected Wilson to a second term, were not "at heart" any different than the people of the East; the difference was in their access to accurate information and in their environment. "In the east, the common man is overshadowed by concentrated wealth . . . and then, too, he is the victim of a press that publishes the truth by accident and falsehood by consistently cultivated habit." [43]

Following his departure from the State Department, with the scorn and ridicule of the nation's press ringing in his ears, Bryan began to urge the government to relieve the people of the necessity of obtaining their information solely from a highly partisan press. "The time has come," he wrote, "when Congress should consider the propriety of issuing a national bulletin for the information of the public . . ." Such a reform was not only desirable, it was necessary for the perpetuation of democratic government, for as long as the "great financial interests" controlled the press the people could not be expected to think for themselves or select their representatives wisely. In a democracy the fate of the nation depended upon the will of the people and that will could not be ex-

43. Ibid. January 1917, pp. 16–17.

pressed intelligently if the people were not given accurate and reliable information.[44]

A national bulletin issued periodically by the federal government for the dissemination of essential information and balanced editorial views, Bryan maintained, would eradicate the evils implicit in the nation's dependence upon a one-sided and self-interested press. The bulletin's policies would be formulated by a bipartisan editorial board selected jointly by both houses of Congress and the President, and editorial space would be provided to all parties represented in Congress in proportion to their voting strength. The bulletin would be furnished free of charge to all newspapers, educational institutions, and libraries, and would be sold at a nominal charge to any private citizen desiring to subscribe. Bryan pressed his idea upon Congress and the Administration, and tried to induce the states to issue their own state bulletins.[45] When by January 1919 his efforts had borne no fruit, he made the issue a partisan one by stating frankly: "The Democratic party's GREATEST need is NEWSPAPERS. It is greatly handicapped by the fact that the Republican party is much better supplied with the means of reaching the public." The party's sole hope lay in a well-distributed government publication which could print all the facts simply and without bias and give the Democrats an equal opportunity to answer their opponents.[46] This proved to be the first step in Bryan's attempt to have the reform included in the 1920 Democratic platform.

Another cause to which Bryan lent himself during these years was government ownership of the railroads. In promoting this reform Bryan had come a long way from the 1896 campaign in which he had ignored the Populist plank calling

44. Ibid. August 1915, p. 2, December 1915, p. 3, September 1919, p. 3, May 1920, p. 7.

45. Ibid. January 1917, p. 4; WJB to William G. McAdoo, June 27, 1916, McAdoo Paper, Box 161.

46. *The Commoner*, January 1919, p. 2.

for government ownership of railways and other utilities. Not until 1906 did he make his first plea for government owner-ship, and then the public furor his speech precipitated caused his political advisers to persuade him to quietly drop the sub-ject. Even at this early date Bryan had not advocated outright federal ownership, but, borrowing upon his European experi-ences, he evolved a plan which he christened "the dual plan of ownership," whereby the federal government would own and operate all interstate lines, and the state governments would own and operate all local lines.[47] This was, he maintained per-sistently, the only scheme which "has the advantages of gov-ernment ownership without the danger of centralization.[48]

His plan, however, lay dormant for more than ten years and was revived only when, in 1916, the Republicans at-tempted to establish exclusive federal control over the rail-roads, thereby relieving the states of all their regulatory powers. This attempt, which Bryan saw as an overt effort on the part of railroad magnates to take regulation of the rail-roads out of the hands of the people and put it where it could be more easily controlled, led him to revive his own plan of dual ownership. Testifying before a Senate committee in Jan-uary 1917, Bryan made it quite clear that he personally leaned toward the "individual idea" rather than to the "collective idea," but, he insisted, wherever free competition was impossi-ble, government ownership was the only alternative.[49] The successful management of the country's railroads by the gov-ernment during the war furnished Bryan with what he termed "a final and conclusive argument in favor of govern-ment ownership." "Government ownership and operation of

47. Bryan's address calling for government ownership of the rail-way system was delivered in New York City upon his return from Europe on August 30, 1906. See WJB, *Speeches*, II, 63 ff.

48. WJB to Louis F. Post, August 29, 1919, Post Papers.

49. For Bryan's testimony, see *The Commoner*, January 1917, pp. 6–11, 21–3.

railroads will be the natural outcome of the war," he declared.[50]

With the termination of the war, Bryan fought to make his prediction come true, extending his plan of government ownership to the telegraph and telephone systems as well. The issue between private monopoly and government ownership, he maintained, was "our greatest economic question today" and constituted "by far the largest of the reconstruction problems now confronting the nation." [51] The solutions recommended by Bryan were in line with the New Freedom philosophy upon which the Democratic party had campaigned in 1912 and from which Wilson had often deviated. A private monopoly, Bryan argued, "cannot be controlled — it must be prevented. . . . Our greatest task today is to protect the God-made man from the man-made giant. The God-made man has natural rights; the corporate giant has no rights except those conferred by the law." [52] If conditions required a monopoly, it had to be a government monopoly "so that the benefits may be enjoyed by all the people and not by a few." "Man," he added, "is still too selfish to be entrusted with the power a monopoly is able to exercise." [53] "If I had to choose between the concentration of all this power in New York in the hands of railway magnates and the centralization of all this power in the hands of Government officials," he told the House Committee on Interstate and Foreign Commerce in 1919, "I would without a moment's hesitation prefer to risk concentration in the hands of public officials . . ." [54]

50. Ibid. January 1918, p. 2; WJB to William G. McAdoo, December 29, 1917, Wilson Papers, File VI, Box 491.

51. *The Commoner*, January 1919, p. 3, May 1919, p. 12.

52. Ibid. May 1919, p. 12.

53. Ibid. December 1918, p. 1.

54. *Statement of Honorable William Jennings Bryan Before the Committee on Interstate and Foreign Commerce of the House of Representatives, Sixty-Sixth Congress, First Session, on H.R. 4378* (Washington, D.C.), p. 1687.

Bryan's fight for the adoption of these reforms was waged as a part of his concerted effort to prevent a postwar reaction from setting in. The fear of such a reaction was implicit in almost all his editorials following the Armistice. "Big Business," he wrote in the spring of 1920, "is attempting to transfer the burdens of the government from the shoulders of the rich to the backs of the poor. . . . private monopoly is massing for a combined attack upon the right of the people to use their own government for their own protection . . ." [55] Bryan viewed the renewed power, prestige, and resources with which the American business community had emerged from the war as a threat to the accomplishments which he and his fellow progressives had made during the years preceding the war. Employing the rhetoric of the past, he sought not merely to maintain but to extend progressive reform. In January 1919, he issued a fifteen-point program which included: construction of a comprehensive national highway system financed by the federal and state governments, government ownership of railways, telegraphs, telephones, and the merchant marine, extension of the power of the Federal Trade Commission and creation of state trade commissions, national and state amendments providing for initiative and referendum, government guarantee of bank deposits, restoration of freedom of speech and press, strict enforcement of prohibition laws, ratification of the suffrage amendment, establishment of a national bulletin, and maintenance of the rule of the people in every possible way.[56] He later added a plank calling for compulsory investigation of all labor disputes, and continued to champion the entire platform until the very eve of the Democratic convention.[57]

55. *The Commoner*, May 1920, p. 1.
56. Ibid. January 1919, p. 5.
57. See ibid. June 1920, p. 1; and WJB, "Democratic Policies at San Francisco," *Review of Reviews*, LXII (July 1920), 42.

His aim, he insisted, was not to socialize the economy but rather to prevent any single interest group, be it business, labor, or agriculture, from dominating it. ". . . this is a DEMOCRACY," he proclaimed, "not a one class government to be administered either by a plutocracy or by an industrial proletariat. . . . Our government is . . . and must be a PEOPLE'S government, in which each citizen is the equal before the law of every other citizen, a majority speaking for all." [58] The power of the government to protect its citizens, he told a Los Angeles audience, "is as unlimited as the greed of any citizen," and the government was delinquent unless "it provided the machinery necessary to protect every man from every arm uplifted for his injury." [59] The principle by which he was guided was one which he had laid down years before: "that respect for human rights is a condition precedent to the security of property rights." [60]

It was in this frame of mind and with these aims in view that Bryan entered the political turmoil of 1920.

(4)

By 1920 speculation concerning Bryan's Presidential chances had become almost as well established a quadrennial national tradition as leap year. Indeed, many of Bryan's friends and supporters could hardly restrain themselves until election year. As early as December 6, 1916, during an address at the Washington Banquet celebrating Wilson's victory over Hughes, Representative Warren Worth Bailey of Pennsylvania had intimated that Bryan would be the logical Democratic candidate in 1920.[61] Similar suggestions were made with increasing frequency in the following years, and by the

58. *The Commoner*, November 1919, p. 1.
59. "Pressing Domestic Problems," ibid. October 1920, p. 8.
60. Ibid. July 1915, p. 13, January 1920, p. 4.
61. Ibid. January 1917, p. 13.

beginning of 1920 a number of Bryan's supporters took concrete steps without Bryan's knowledge or approval. In New York, Harry W. Walker and Frank H. Warder resurrected the old Bryan League and toured the state in an attempt to revive interest in it, and in Washington, D.C., a Bryan Democracy Club was organized with the sole purpose of securing Bryan's fourth nomination for the Presidency.[62] Even such critics as the *Chicago Tribune* and *The Nation* grudgingly admitted that Bryan was a force to be reckoned with at the forthcoming Democratic convention.[63] Politicians throughout the country considered him a serious candidate. Every trip he made, every political address he delivered, every contact he had with party members, was interpreted as another step in his drive for the party's chief prize.[64]

As in the past, the most prolific and, to Bryan, probably the most satisfying source of support was the people themselves. Scores of letters urging Bryan to seek a fourth nomination were printed in *The Commoner* almost every month for the better part of a year, most of them containing sentiments of devotion and absolute loyalty: ". . . in the name of God I'll stand by you to the last ounce of my ability." [65] I am first for Mr. Bryan and next for whom he wants. He is the only man in the United States whom I would follow without question. . . . I want to live to see Mr. Bryan President . . ." [66] "It would fulfill the greatest desire of my life in a political

62. *New York Times,* December 31, 1919, January 2, 3, 7, March 17, 1920.

63. *Chicago Tribune,* January 8, 1920, quoted in *The Commoner,* January 1920, p. 10; *The Nation,* CXI (January 1920), 98–9.

64. For typical examples of this type of speculation, see *New York Times,* December 26, 29, 30, 1919, January 3, March 15, 1920; *New York Tribune,* December 19, 20, 29, 1919; *Christian Science Monitor,* December 20, 1919.

65. O. W. Newman to WJB, *The Commoner,* April 1919, p. 5.

66. C. E. Sugg to *The Commoner,* ibid. November 1919, p. 6.

way to see him in the White House where he ought to be now." [67] "I would rather see you elected than any man on earth." [68]

Though these appeals undoubtedly pleased Bryan they failed to spur him into taking any action. The sixty-year-old Nebraskan, despite his occasional impracticability, was still enough of a political realist to see the futility of attempting to secure a fourth nomination. Nor is there any evidence that he actually desired to run for the Presidency again. "I shall remain in politics for the rest of my life," he announced after resigning from the State Department, but, he added, "I have no political expectations whatever and no plans looking to the holding of any office in the future." [69] The Presidency no longer meant anything to him, he told Dan Bride in 1919. It could bring him no additional honor, fame, or power. He was, he argued, in a better position to aid the people as an individual free to travel among them and speak his mind honestly than he would be as a President surrounded by sycophants, office seekers, and possibly a hostile Congress.[70] By the spring of 1920, with the number of letters requesting his candidacy still mounting, he relented somewhat by promising that "if the situation became such that my nomination were actually demanded . . . I would feel it my duty to consider it," but "I hope no such situation will arise." He neither needed nor desired public office, he explained, for the party had already honored him as it had few men and he had been more than amply rewarded for his services "not with office, which is the least of rewards — but with the satisfaction of seeing nearly every reform I have advocated written into the unrepealable law of the land, and now I see my peace plan made the chief

67. T. H. Baum to *The Commoner*, ibid. December 1919, p. 14.
68. Harry Baxter to WJB, ibid. p. 8.
69. Ibid. August 1915, pp. 7, 14.
70. Dan Bride Memo, March 1921, in Bryan Papers.

cornerstone of the League of Nations. This is reward enough for any man." [71]

More than a year before the convention Bryan urged the party to seek a candidate who was "young enough to organize and lead the fight against private monopoly. He may not win in 1920 — it may take as long as it did to win the fight commenced in 1896, but we must begin now." [72] This statement indicated that Bryan was not overly optimistic about the chances for a Democratic victory, and in January 1920, he jokingly told a reporter that Democratic prospects were so poor it would be perfectly natural for the party to want to draft him.[73] Bryan himself had no single candidate to recommend. "There is no logical candidate this year," he wrote on the very eve of the convention.[74] Nevertheless, he did urge Josephus Daniels and Senator Owen of Oklahoma to throw their hats into the ring, and he spoke of Secretary of Agriculture Meredith as being "one hundred per-cent available." [75] As in previous years he also dug deeply into his bag of political unknowns and this time came up with Representative Henry T. Rainey of Illinois and Dean Walter Williams of the University of Missouri, both of whom, he announced, would make excellent Presidents.[76]

For the most part, his observations on the most widely mentioned candidates were in a negative vein. He vigorously opposed Governor Edwards of New Jersey who had promised to make his state "as wet as the Atlantic Ocean," and

71. *The Commoner*, March 1920, p. 1.
72. Ibid. April 1919, p. 1.
73. Ibid. January 1920, p. 10. See also WJB to Louis F. Post, April 1, 1920, Post Papers.
74. WJB, *Review of Reviews*, LXII (July 1920), 42.
75. WJB to Daniels, July 12, October 12, November 25, 1919, Daniels Papers; Robert L. Owen to WJB, December 1, 1919, Bryan Papers; *The Commoner*, June 1920, p. 6.
76. Henry T. Rainey to WJB, November 15, 1919, Walter Williams to WJB, December 3, 1919, Bryan Papers.

warned that "If Nebraska instructs for Edwards and I am a delegate I'll resign. I'll never vote to nominate a man like that." [77] He was unenthusiastic over the candidacies of Vice President Marshall, who he felt had little chance, Attorney General Palmer, who had done nothing about profiteering, or Secretary McAdoo, who he claimed had vacillated on the treaty issue and was too intimately connected with the President.[78] He treated the Presidential aspirations of Governor Cox of Ohio with contempt because of his failure to champion prohibition. In 1917 Bryan had viewed Cox as one of the most "available" men the Democrats had and urged the Ohio Governor to take a leading role in the prohibition campaign. "You have the chance of your life. A failure to act will, I think, be fatal to your ambition as well as harmful to the party." [79] Cox's refusal to heed this advice transformed Bryan from a warm admirer into a dangerous opponent. "I tried to keep him from committing suicide," he wrote a Cox supporter several months before the convention, "but even a friend can not help a man after his attempt at suicide has succeeded." [80] Cox's nomination, he predicted, "would make the Democratic party the leader of the lawless element of the country, and his election . . . would turn the White House over to those who defy the government and hold law in contempt." [81]

It was not who the candidate was but what he stood for that interested Bryan. "The platform is more important than the man," he declared in May. "Principles ought to control; policies ought to decide elections." The reactionary forces of the nation, he warned, "will try to control both parties, write both platforms and nominate both candidates, then they will

77. *New York Times*, January 22, 1920.
78. "The Democratic Presidential Candidates," *The Commoner*, June 1920, p. 3, July 1920, p. 4.
79. WJB to James Cox, December 26, 1917, Bryan Papers.
80. WJB to Harvey C. Garber, March 6, 1920, ibid.
81. *New York Times*, April 14, 1920.

be able to throw the Democratic Party on the ashpile and give the Republican Party a majority large enough to encourage it recklessly to obey the instructions from Wall Street." The only hope for victory was to adopt a progressive plat- form — presumably Bryan's own 1919 platform — in an attempt to attract the independent voter.[82]

It is evident that what Bryan hoped to attain at the 1920 convention of his party was not honors but power. He wanted and expected to play the same role that he had in the Baltimore convention of 1912 when he had been influential in both nominating the candidate and framing the platform. To accomplish his aims effectively it was, of course, necessary for him to attend the Democratic convention in San Francisco as a delegate. As in 1916 this proved to be no trifling task. Sena- tor Hitchcock still controlled the Nebraska Democracy and in the four years that had elapsed since the last election he and Bryan were driven even further apart by their antithetical positions on the Lodge reservations. Bryan might have avoided a bitter intra-party conflict and assured his own elec- tion had he given some small encouragement to Hitchcock's rapidly developing Presidential aspirations, but this he refused to do. The Senator's nomination, he stated emphatically, "would be a triumph for Wall Street . . ." Bryan then threw away all possibilities for a rapprochement by announc- ing that if the Nebraska delegation was instructed to vote for Hitchcock for the Presidential nomination and he was a dele- gate he would allow his alternate to vote, but he himself would never cast a ballot in favor of the Senator.[83]

In view of the opposition of the regular Democratic organ- ization, which included the only two state-wide daily papers in Nebraska, the *New York Times* predicted that Bryan's

82. *The Commoner*, May 1920, p. 6, June 1920, p. 6.
83. Ibid. April 1920, p. 2; *New York Times*, March 10, 1920; *Ne- braska State Journal*, March 20, 1920.

campaign for delegate at large was "likely to be the hardest fight of his career," and most political observers agreed.[84] Bryan inaugurated his campaign on April 7, and spent the next two weeks canvassing the state, basing his campaign upon his own political program, with particular emphasis on the need for enforcing prohibition and guaranteeing both farmers and wage-earners "just treatment" and "a fair share of the wealth they produce." [85]

In most respects the 1920 primary campaign resembled that of 1916. Hitchcock accused Bryan of disloyalty to the President and the party, dwelt at some length upon his "desertion" from duty in 1915, condemned his advocacy of government ownership, characterized him as the leader of a "wrecking crew" which had adopted a "rule or ruin" policy, and warned the voters that if they sent Bryan to San Francisco as a delegate he would "run amuck in the convention and raise a row over the terms of the platform." [86] Bryan countered by calling Hitchcock the representative of Wall Street and the liquor interests. He analyzed Hitchcock's voting record and concluded that the Senator was "a Western man with Eastern ideas." [87] The results of the election proved beyond a doubt that in Nebraska at least Bryan had regained much of his popularity and power. He and ten of the candidates running on the "Bryan ticket" were victorious, giving him control over eleven of Nebraska's sixteen delegates. "Nebraska is free," he cried triumphantly, ". . . the State's flag will not be lowered to either Wall Street or the liquor traffic." [88]

The Hitchcock-owned *Omaha World-Herald* admitted that Bryan had won "one of the most notable personal triumphs of his long public career." His election, it predicted,

84. *New York Times*, March 23, April 17, 1920.
85. *The Commoner*, April 1920, p. 1.
86. *Nebraska State Journal*, April 14, 1920.
87. *New York Times*, April 19, 1920.
88. *The Commoner*, May 1920, pp. 1, 3.

meant "that there will be 'hell a-popping' at San Francisco, with Mr. Bryan the chief fireman and troublemaker." [89] The *World-Herald*'s fears were shared by the Administration forces, none of whom took Bryan's victory casually. Pro-Wilson papers warned stridently of Bryan's "destructive" purposes, the *New York World* estimating that two hundred delegates at San Francisco would be Bryan men.[90] Democratic National Chairman Homer Cummings informed the President that Bryan controlled at least 100 to 125 votes and would probably be able to increase his strength significantly in his attempt to wrest control of the party from Wilson.[91] Similarly, Postmaster General Burleson wrote McAdoo that Bryan's first step in his bid for party leadership would be to control the Resolutions Committee and mold the platform to his own liking, and that he might well succeed if steps were not taken to stop him immediately.[92]

These fears were augmented by Bryan's performance in the Michigan Presidential preference primary in which, despite his efforts to have his name withdrawn, his refusal to lift a finger to aid his own cause, and the lack of any real organization on the part of his Michigan supporters, Bryan placed third behind Herbert Hoover and McAdoo and ahead of Governor Edwards and Attorney General Palmer.[93] The extensive *Literary Digest* poll was a further indication that

89. Quoted in the *New York Evening Post*, May 8, 1920.

90. *New York Times*, June 30, 1920; "The Bryan-Wilson Split," *Literary Digest*, LXV (May 15, 1920), 26–7; *New York World*, June 24, 1920, quoted in Wesley M. Bagby, "Progressivism's Debacle, the Election of 1920" (unpublished Ph.D. dissertation, Columbia University, 1954), p. 364.

91. May 31, 1920, Homer S. Cummings Diary, in R. S. Baker Papers, Box 3. Wilson, still smarting from Bryan's defection on the League, told Cummings that a Bryan bolt would "re-establish the reputation of the party more than anything else could." Ibid.

92. Burleson to McAdoo, May 22, 1920, McAdoo Papers, Box 235.

93. *New York Times*, April 23, 1920; James H. Lee to WJB, May 5, 1920, Bryan Papers.

whatever his actual political power might have been, Bryan's name continued to have appeal for many Democrats across the country. Once again without any effort on his own part and without any organization, he finished among the first five Democrats in the nation, behind McAdoo, Wilson, and Edwards, but more than 14,000 votes ahead of Cox.[94]

As convention time drew nearer Bryan's militancy increased. He exuded the confidence of a man who expected to control the convention, shape the platform, and select the candidate. In an editorial addressed to all prospective Presidential candidates he demanded that they publicly announce their platforms. "Do you stand for private monopoly, or with the people? Are you with the pirates of high finance, or with their bleeding victims? Speak out NOW." [95] In May he toured Alabama in an unsuccessful attempt to defeat Senator Oscar Underwood, whom he considered a reactionary, in his bid for renomination.[96] When Homer Cummings was selected to deliver the convention's keynote address, Bryan minced few words: "The selection of Chairman Cummings is worse than a comedy; it is a tragedy. It is a melancholy beginning. . . . If the Democratic party is to be wrapped in a 'wet' shroud, locked up in a Wall Street safe and buried at sea, Cummings is just the person to officiate . . ." [97]

Bryan was making it evident that he was going to act as the party's conscience regardless of the party's own wishes.

(5)

Before journeying to San Francisco for the Democratic convention, Bryan covered the Republican convention at Chicago for a syndicate of newspapers. He circulated among

94. The final figures of the poll were: McAdoo, 102,719; Wilson, 67,588; Edwards, 61,393; Bryan, 46,448; Cox, 32,343; *Literary Digest*, LXIV (June 12, 1920), 20.
95. *The Commoner*, May 1920, p. 1.
96. *New York Times*, May 9, 1920.
97. Ibid. April 14, 1920; *The Commoner*, May 1920, p. 1.

the delegates and candidates vainly trying to build up support for the adoption of a dry plank and promised that he would see to it that the Democrats adopted the identical plank.[98] "I have been attending national conventions for forty-four years," he wrote on the fifth day of the Republican proceedings, ". . . [but] this convention is the most reactionary that I have had the privilege of attending." When, later on the same day, Harding was nominated, Bryan's only comment was: "he fits the platform." The results of the convention left Bryan with a mixed feeling of optimism and consternation. The capitulation of the Republicans to the conservative element of their party greatly increased the Democrats' chances of attracting the independent voter. On the other hand, having captured the Republican machinery, the conservatives would intensify their efforts to win over the Democrats, and should they succeed the triumph of "reaction" in 1920 would be assured.[99] Thus, as Bryan left for the Coast, he was more convinced of the necessity of his mission than ever. "I shall see," he said confidently, "that the platform is exactly the opposite of that adopted by the Republican Party at Chicago." [100]

The Democratic National Convention opened in San Francisco's Civic Auditorium on June 28, and Bryan spent the first four days behind closed doors, where he and the other members of the Committee on Platforms and Resolutions labored to construct the Democratic platform for 1920. It was behind these doors that Bryan staged his first fight — and received his first defeat. It did not take him long to perceive that the committee was safely in the hands of the President's friends.[101] His impassioned plea to keep the League out of the cam-

98. *New York Times*, June 9, 1920.
99. WJB, syndicated newspaper report, June 12, 1920, reprinted in *The Commoner*, June 1920, p. 10.
100. *New York Times*, June 25, 1920.
101. See Homer Cummings to Woodrow Wilson, June 30, 1920, R. S. Baker Papers, Box 3.

paign by adopting a plank calling for immediate ratification
with whatever reservations were necessary to command a two-
thirds majority in the Senate, was ignored.[102] His attempts to
secure a prohibition enforcement plank were defeated by a
vote of 36 to 12; the majority, attempting to avoid the con-
troversial issue, insisted that prohibition was a closed issue.
His efforts to insert in the labor plank a provision calling for
compulsory investigation of labor disputes was also defeated,
as was his attempt to alter the plank on profiteering. His proposal for a national bulletin received the most favorable reception but fell one vote short of acceptance. His successes
were limited to persuading the committee to insert the word
"only" after the word "revenue" in the tariff plank and to
strike from the soldier's plank several words which in his
judgment would have been offensive to servicemen.[103] Except for these very minor achievements Bryan gained nothing
from the Resolutions Committee. Victory, if it was to be
achieved at all, would have to be won at the hands of the full
convention.

As usual Bryan was optimistic. He told an assembly of
women delegates that a delegate had asked him if he thought
he could win: "I replied that a Christian ought not to ask that
question. If you are on the side of a righteous cause you never
know what you can do until you try. The Bible says that one

102. However, Senator David Walsh of Massachusetts, who alongside Bryan led the fight aganst the Administration's League plank,
managed to add to Wilson's original plank which read: "We advocate
the immediate ratification of the treaty without reservations which
would impair its essential integrity," the clause: "but do not oppose
the acceptance of any reservations making clearer or more specific the
obligations of the United States to the league associates." Bagby,
"Progressivism's Debacle," pp. 377–8.

103. This account of Bryan's role in the Resolutions Committee is
taken from his syndicated news reports of the convention entitled
"San Francisco Letters," and reprinted in *The Commoner*, July 1920,
pp. 8 ff., August 1920, pp. 10 ff.

with God shall chase a thousand, there are about that many delegates in this convention. The Bible also says that two shall put ten thousand to flight. I am looking for the other man." [104] In spite of Bryan's almost total defeat in the committee, his opponents were unhappy at the prospect of a floor fight with Bryan as their chief adversary. "Bryan . . . is a watchful, tireless, vengeful enemy," Secretary of State Colby wired the President. "He does not wince under the adverse votes on his propositions that the Platform Committee has already taken and will go before Convention in same spirit." [105]

On the fifth day of the convention, after the chairman of the Resolutions Committee, Carter Glass, had spent two hours reading the longest platform in the party's history to the assembled delegates, Bryan rose to offer his amendments. He proposed three planks pledging the party to seek effective enforcement of prohibition, the establishment of a national bulletin, and the defeat of any attempt to institute universal compulsory military training in time of peace. He asked the delegates to put teeth into the innocuous plank on profiteering,[106] and he called for an amendment to the equivocal League plank which would pledge the party to seek an immediate reconvening of the Senate in order to secure ratification "with such reservations as a majority of the Senators may agree upon . . ."[107]

104. *New York Times*, July 1, 1920.
105. Colby to Wilson, July 2, 1920, R. S. Baker Papers, Box 3.
106. Specifically, Bryan called for legislation which would eliminate unnecessary middlemen, limit the profit of necessary middlemen, prohibit anyone engaged in interstate commerce from making the sale of one article dependent on the purchase of another, require interstate corporations to make public the difference between cost price and selling price, and encourage the creation of trade commissions in every state.
107. *Official Report of the Proceedings of the Democratic National Convention Held in San Francisco, California, June 28, 29, 30, July 1, 2, 3, 5, 6, 1920* (Indianapolis, 1920), pp. 200–203. Cited hereafter as *Official Proceedings . . . 1920.*

Bourke Cockran of New York, who had crossed swords with Bryan over the income tax in 1894 when both were young Congressmen, next rose to propose his own amendment to the prohibition plank. It provided for a federal law allowing the manufacture and sale, for home consumption only, of cider, light wines, and beer. The debate which followed these proposals was conducted principally by Bryan on one side and Cockran, Bainbridge Colby, and Carter Glass on the other.[108] Bryan's 45-minute address, which was easily one of his most stirring convention utterances, dealt eloquently with all of his proposals, but centered upon the League and prohibition. He denied the charges of disloyalty to the President by pointing out that "it was my treaty plan that he took to Paris; I have helped him to become immortal. If I could secure ratification without reservations and give to Woodrow Wilson the honor of securing it, I would walk to the scaffold today and die with a smile upon my face. But I cannot do it, my friends; nobody else can do it." Those who urged the injection of the League fight into the campaign were insuring its defeat, for they knew very well that neither party could win two-thirds of the Senate. And if the Treaty was defeated, the Democratic party would have to bear the chief responsibility. "We have a Democratic President who can reconvene the Senate; we have enough Democratic senators to convert a majority into the necessary two-thirds majority. . . . The issue lies with us, and we cannot shift the blame, however inexcusable the opposition of Republican senators has been." [109]

On the prohibition issue Bryan used every oratorical weapon in his repertoire. To those who ignored prohibition on the ground of political expediency, he pleaded: "Are you

108. For Cockran's address, see ibid. pp. 220 ff.; for Colby's and Glass's, see ibid. pp. 242 ff.
109. Ibid. pp. 214–15, 238–9.

afraid that we shall lose some votes! Oh, my countrymen, have more faith in the virtue of the people . . . Remember that it is better to have the gratitude of one soul saved from drink than the applause of a drunken world. (Great applause.)" Growing militant, he turned to the Eastern delegations and demanded: "Are you ashamed of what your party did? (Applause.) Are you ashamed that a Democratic Senate and House submitted prohibition, and that every Democratic state ratified?" When a delegate from the East cried out: "I voted for you," Bryan snapped back: "Yes, my friend, you voted for me. If you are sorry you did, if you go back on me because I stand for the home against the saloon, I will get two in your place. (Extended applause.)" [110]

As Bryan stepped back from the speaker's stand, "A great shout went surging up into the vaulted dome of the roof in an endless sea of sound." A Texas delegate jumped to his feet, snatched the state standard from the floor, and made his way down the aisle to the platform where he was joined by delegates from state after state. Bryan, tears streaming down his face, was called to the edge of the platform again and again. The Nebraska standard was pressed into his hands, and he stood quietly on the dais waving it to and fro, absorbing the sounds and sights upon which he had thrived for twenty-five years. For more than twenty minutes the spotlights played upon Bryan's figure, and then, under Chairman Robinson's firm gavel and threats to clear the gallery, the demonstration slowly petered out and was over.[111] Colby and Glass mounted the stand to defend the platform and the Administration.

In one respect at least the 1920 convention marked the end

110. Ibid. pp. 209, 211–12, 240–41.
111. New York Evening Post, July 3, 1920; Mrs. J. Borden Harriman, From Pinafores to Politics (New York, 1923), pp. 331–3; Bagby, "Progressivism's Debacle," p. 391.

of an era. For the first time in convention history a loud-speaker system was used, and although Bryan reputedly thrust it aside with contempt, others had more respect — and more use — for it. No longer could Bryan be assured that he would be one of the few speakers whose voice would reach every delegate in the hall. Now even Carter Glass's thin, wispy voice penetrated to all corners of the auditorium.[112] Mere audibility was, of course, no substitute for eloquence, and in this respect no one at San Francisco quite matched Bryan. And yet the delegates voted against his proposals with the same abandon with which they had cheered his oratory. Out of a total of 1,085 votes, only 155½ were cast in favor of his prohibition amendment. The defeat was made all the more humiliating when, a few minutes later, Cockran's amendment, which was also defeated, received more than twice as many votes. Bryan's four other proposals were then quickly defeated by a voice vote.[113] The same delegates who had lustily cheered Bryan had also succeeded in destroying the dreams he had nurtured for more than two years. He had staked everything on the fight for what he considered a truly progressive platform and received one of the most thorough defeats of his career. "It was evident that his party had left him," wrote William Allen White, "and he was a rather sad, lonely figure, surrounded by a new generation of Democratic politicians to whom 1896 was but a tale that is told." [114]

Bryan had again exhibited his almost uncanny ability to evoke emotion and admiration even from those who opposed him. Yet his experience at the 1920 convention cannot be explained quite this simply. The applause he won was not due solely to his personal qualities; many of the delegates who

112. James F. Byrnes, *All in One Lifetime* (New York, 1958), p. 48; Arthur F. Mullen, *Western Democrat* (New York, 1940), p. 185.

113. *Official Proceedings . . . 1920*, pp. 256 ff.

114. William Allen White, *Masks in a Pageant* (New York, 1930), p. 271-2.

voted against his proposals probably did so in spite of their own convictions. The party that was to come close to committing suicide in 1924 was not as united in 1920 as the vote on the platform made it appear. Southern and Western delegations, for instance, gave Bryan's attempt to insert a prohibition plank in the platform much less support than their attitude toward prohibition normally would have led them to do.[115] Without the Administration's overt hostility, some of Bryan's planks might well have received the approval of the convention. The hand of Woodrow Wilson, which had been powerful enough to hold a sufficient number of Democratic Senators in line on the League of Nations, remained strong enough in San Francisco to prevent the platform debate from turning into the ruinous sectional struggle that was to ensue in four years.

On the question of the Presidential nominee, however, Wilson's grip relaxed and the sectional stresses and schisms that were to dominate the party during the Twenties became more evident. The reasons behind Wilson's apparent lack of interest in his potential successor are not fully clear, although there is evidence that he desired the nomination himself. Secretary Colby, Wilson's chief liaison man at San Francisco, was, in fact, on the verge of putting his chief's name into nomination — with Wilson's knowledge, and presumably with his approval — when the idea was vetoed by other key Administration leaders.[116] With no effective pressure from the Administration, the battle for the nomination gradually nar-

115. Sixteen states below the Mason-Dixon line, including Oklahoma, Texas, and West Virginia, gave Bryan's plank only 33½ votes out of a possible 336. See the tables in *Official Proceedings . . . 1920* pp. 256–7, 259–60.

116. Colby to Wilson, July 2, 1920, July 4, 1920, R. S. Baker Papers, Box 3. See also Ray Stannard Baker interviews with Colby, June 19, 1930, and Stockton Axson, September 2, 1931, and Homer Cummings Memo, January 18, 1929, ibid. Boxes 26, 19, 3.

rowed down to one between James M. Cox, who drew most
of his support from the wet, urban-dominated delegations,
and William Gibbs McAdoo, who, because of his dry leanings
and his relationship to the Administration and the President,
became the *bête noire* of these same groups.[117] Thus while
the sectional and cultural division between the forces behind
each candidate never became so finely drawn as they were to
be at the New York convention four years later, San Francisco witnessed the prelude to that explosion.

During the days of stalemate that followed, Bryan poured
all of his deep frustration and disillusionment into the daily
reports he was writing for a nation-wide syndicate of newspapers. The day after the defeat of his platform proposals he
commented: "If those who control this Convention are to be
taken as the leaders of the party, Democrats will not be considered crusaders in this campaign. They are more likely to be
branded as evaders." "I have never known a convention in
which the spirit of intolerance was so dominant and unconcealed," he noted a few days later.[118] He persistently cast his
ballot for Senator Owen and carried a majority of his delegation with him from the fourth to the forty-fourth and final
ballot.[119] McAdoo, the one man capable of being nominated
against the wishes of the wet, city machines, was, ironically,
one of the men Bryan adamantly refused to support despite all
of the pressure which was exerted to change his mind.[120] He

117. Bagby, "Progressivism's Debacle," pp. 311, 341, 365, 367, 408.
118. "San Francisco Letters," July 3, 6, 1920, *The Commoner*, July
1920, pp. 11, 13.
119. On the first three ballots the entire Nebraska delegation voted
for Senator Hitchcock as it had been instructed to do. Bryan presumably let his alternate vote on these early ballots. See Arthur F.
Mullen to William G. McAdoo, July 30, 1920, McAdoo Papers, Box
239.
120. See John Skelton Williams to WJB, July 1, July 4, 1920, ibid.
Box 238; George Fort Milton to McAdoo, June 8, 11, 1920, ibid. Box
236. In a letter written after the convention, McAdoo made it clear

argued that McAdoo's candidacy would be fatally handicapped by his close relationship to the President. "I love my
country more than I love any man," he told a reporter after
the convention, "and I was not willing to share responsibility
for the defeat that would have followed his nomination." [121]

According to Robert Woolley, at the close of the twentieth
ballot Bryan circulated a list of ten names, any one of which,
he contended, would receive more votes than any candidate
currently before the convention.[122] If this is true, it was the
only time that Bryan seriously tried to alter the outcome of
the contest. By the twenty-fifth ballot he made it clear that he
was washing his hands of the entire affair, telling reporters
that the cause of the deadlock was the inability of the three
dominant groups in the convention — the White House,
Wall Street, and the liquor interests — to agree upon a candidate.[123] When, on the forty-fourth ballot, Governor Cox
was finally selected as the standard bearer, Bryan wrote sadly:
"The nomination of Govenor Cox signalizes the surrender
of the Democratic party into the hands of the reactionaries . . ." [124]

But it was not Cox, nor the delegates, nor even the "reactionaries" to whom Bryan ascribed the defeat of progressive
Democracy; it was the President. It was Wilson who prevented the convention from voicing its faith in prohibition; it

that Bryan's attitude disappointed and surprised him but added that it
was probably not an important factor in his defeat. McAdoo to John
Skelton Williams, July 9, 1920, ibid. Box 238. On this latter point,
several of his supporters disagreed maintaining that Bryan's active
support could have been decisive. George Fort Milton to McAdoo,
August 5, 1920, ibid. Box 239; Harriman, *From Pinafores to Politics*,
p. 377.

121. *The Commoner*, July 1920, p. 4.
122. Woolley, Memoirs MSS., Chapter XXX, Woolley Papers.
123. *New York Times*, July 6, 1920.
124. "San Francisco Letters," July 6, 1920, *The Commoner*, July
1920, p. 13.

was Wilson who prevented the adoption of an anti-compulsory military service plank and an effective plank on profiteering; it was Wilson who prevented the United States from taking its rightful place in the League of Nations:

> . . . having reached the highest pinnacle of fame to which a human being was ever lifted he [Wilson] has rewarded the confidence of his nation and the generosity of his party by an exhibition of egotism which would be pathetic if it were not tragic.[125]

These words, it should be remembered, were not buried in the pages of a private diary nor hidden in the lines of a letter to be perused by only a few select friends; they were conspicuously placed in a syndicated newspaper column to be pondered over by the nation at large. It is difficult to find a more accurate portent of Bryan's subsequent actions during the fall campaign.

(6)

On July 21, two weeks after the Democratic delegates departed from San Francisco, delegates of the Prohibition party assembled for their national convention in Lincoln, Nebraska. The site of the convention was particularly fitting in view of the determination of the majority of the delegates to make Lincoln's most famous son their Presidential candidate. Some time before the convention, a delicately worded inquiry was sent to Bryan to determine whether he would accept the nomination if it were tendered him. "I appreciate your confidence in me," responded Bryan and then, to the disappointment of his advocates, he added: "Please see my brother C. W. Bryan. He will fully explain why acceptance is impossible." [126]

125. Ibid. p. 14.
126. This and the subsequent facts pertaining to the Prohibition Convention of 1920 are taken from the account of that convention published in the *Nebraska State Journal* and reprinted in ibid. August

Upon arriving in Lincoln, the delegates duly sought out Charles Bryan who informed them that his brother had not changed his mind and still desired them to omit his name from consideration. The leaders of the party seemed willing to adhere to Bryan's wishes, but the delegates were determined to grace their party's ticket with the popular Nebraskan. Cries of "We want Bryan," "We'll win with Bryan," "Watch the prohibitionists sweep the country," filled the convention hall. When Clinton N. Howard tried to convince his fellow Prohibitionists that Bryan had made it quite clear that he would not accept the nomination, he was interrupted by a fervid delegate who sprang to his feet crying: "God Almighty will not let William Jennings Bryan decline this nomination." Following a prolonged demonstration, Bryan was nominated by acclamation.

The nomination was both a source of pleasure and embarrassment to Bryan. In a letter written from Norris, Montana, where he had been vacationing, he thanked the convention for the honor but politely refused to accept. "My connection with other reforms would make it impossible for me to focus attention on the prohibition question alone, and besides, I am not willing to sever my connection with the Democratic party . . . which has singularly honored me in the past . . . whatever I may feel it my duty to do in the campaign, I expect to continue a member of the Democratic party, and to serve my country through it." [127] In view of the Prohibition party's long-standing interest in the very economic and politi-

1920, pp. 4 ff. See also *New York Times*, July 22, 23, 1920 and the account in the Grace Bryan Hargreaves MSS., Bryan Papers.

127. WJB to Charles W. Bryan, July 22, 1920, *The Commoner*, August 1920, p. 4. This entire episode has been strangely neglected by historians. Not one of Bryan's biographers makes mention of the fact that Bryan was nominated by the Prohibition party in 1920. Similarly, the official historian of the party in his account of its 1920 convention has omitted all mention of Bryan's name. See Colvin, *Prohibition in the United States*, pp. 457–64.

cal reforms which Bryan had devoted himself to since the
1890's, and their willingness to incorporate into their 1920
platform not only his plank on liquor but his planks on the
League and profiteering as well, Bryan must have realized that
his acceptance of their nomination would not have precluded
his working for other reform measures. Rather, it was Bryan's
second reason — his refusal to sever his connection with the
Democratic party — which was the decisive one.

Bryan could not break irrevocably with the party partly
because he felt he owed it too much. It had lifted him out of
obscurity, thrice bestowed upon him its highest honor, and
for more than twenty years had given him the opportunity of
placing his beliefs before the country. These were things that
a man of Bryan's temperament could not easily forget. Besides
this factor of loyalty, there was that of faith. Since 1896 the
Democratic party had been "the party of the common people
and the champion of the rights of the masses." If it occasionally faltered and allowed itself to fall into the hands of reactionaries, as it had in 1904, it retained its capacity for self-
appraisal and reorganization. After its brief fling with the
conservatives in 1904, it had returned to the progressive camp
in 1908, and this was precisely what it would do in 1924. "The
Democratic Party is sound at heart," he declared in October,
". . . it is the best hope of those who believe in a people's
government administered in behalf of the people." [128] It was
this combination of loyalty and faith that kept Bryan within
the Democratic fold.

But if Bryan could not bring himself to leave his party, he
was equally unable to campaign in its behalf. In his first post-
convention press interview he refrained from discussing his
future plans, saying: "My heart is in the grave with our cause,
I must pause until it comes back to me." The pause was to last
virtually until the day after the election. For the first time in

128. *The Commoner*, October 1920, p. 2.

his adult life Bryan sat out a Presidential campaign. He could not, he explained, make speeches in harmony with those of the Democratic candidate. Specifically, he could not support Cox's evasion of the liquor question or his advocacy of a repeal of the excess profits tax, which Bryan termed "a gratuitous abandonment of the national platform in order to throw a sop to Wall Street." [129]

Bryan's defection became all the more important in the light of Wilson's inability to render effective aid, the defeatist attitude of a number of Administration leaders, and the party's generally low morale, poor organization, and disastrous financial condition. Bryan became the object of an intensive campaign put on by the Democratic National Committee, Cox's personal supporters, and a number of his own close friends to induce him to reconsider his decision. "FRIENDS AND FOLLOWERS AMONG DEMOCRATS CONVINCED A PUBLIC DECLARATION BY YOU FOR COX WILL INSURE VICTORY FOR THE LEAGUE. THEY KNOW THIS WOULD BE THE GREATEST OF YOUR MANY GREAT SERVICES TO HUMANITY. WONT YOU MAKE IT?" Robert Woolley wired him in September. Emissaries from the Cox camp were sent to plead personally with him, and Governor Cox himself journeyed to Lincoln, where he spoke of the support he had given Bryan in the latter's three campaigns for the Presidency and declared that he would have gladly supported him a fourth time had he been nominated at San Francisco.[130]

129. *New York Times*, July 7, 1920; *The Commoner*, July 1920, p. 1, November 1920, p. 2; WJB to Pat Harrison (undated), Bryan Papers.

130. Pat Harrison to WJB, August 5, 1920, Woolley to WJB, September 24, 1920, ibid.; Woolley to James Cox, October 22, 1920, Woolley Papers, Box 6; Thomas J. Walsh to J. C. W. Beckham, October 7, 1920, Walsh Papers, Box 372; *New York Times*, August 15, 16, September 28, 1920.

These appeals were of no avail. Not only did Bryan persist in his refusal to aid the Democratic ticket, but he openly criticized the candidates and the platforms of both parties. In his most widely delivered Chautauqua lecture during the summer of 1920, Bryan attacked both parties for adopting meaningless planks on profiteering and for making the League a partisan issue. He spoke of the failure of either party to adopt a plank safeguarding prohibition as "the most bitter disappointment of my life . . ." and then, to the amusement of his listeners, he stated: "Let no Republican boast that his candidate is wetter than ours; I will guarantee that, by any standard of moisture ever invented, they will both register one hundred percent wet, if not more." [131]

Such observations were not designed to enhance the chances of a Democratic victory. Nor was the suggestion he printed in *The Commoner* in September: "Let us elect just as many progressives to Senate and House as possible — a Republican progressive if the Democratic Candidate is reactionary, just as we should elect a Republican dry if the Democratic candidate is wet." [132] This was easily the most important concession to nonpartisanship he had ever made. It was not until just a few weeks before election day that Bryan finally announced his intention of traveling the almost 2,000 miles from Miami, Florida, where his wife was confined because of poor health, to his legal residence in Lincoln in order to vote for his party's Presidential candidate. He was going to do so, he explained, not because of Cox but in spite of him; because in the final analysis he believed that economic reforms and world peace would be best maintained by a Democratic executive working in conjunction with a progressive Congress.[133]

131. "But Where Are the Nine?" *The Commoner*, September 1920, pp. 8–10.
132. Ibid. p. 2.
133. Ibid. October 1920, p. 2, November 1920, p. 2.

The Republican victory in the 1920 election came as a surprise to few Democrats, least of all to Bryan, though the magnitude of the victory undoubtedly shocked even him. The temporary political alliance of the West and South which had proved decisive in 1916 had been shattered. Still, there is no indication that these events left Bryan particularly distraught. The defeat, in fact, fitted neatly into his plans for the future. The Democrats had refused to heed his advice and had run eagerly into the arms of the reactionaries. They had been rewarded for their pains by one of the most overwhelming defeats in their history. The way was now open for a progressive reorganization of the party. The Republican victory, he assured his fellow Democrats, did not connote a vote of confidence in the Republicans but rather was merely a protest against the Democrats' repudiation of the people. Let the party adopt "a program, an ideal, issues and leaders who represent the needs and ambitions of the people," and victory would be assured. "The day is past," he proclaimed, "when the liquor machines and Wall Street interests of the large cities can successfully dictate to the great moral majority of the nation. Make the Democratic party deserve to win, then organize for the coming struggle." [134]

It was a simple and thoroughly comforting analysis of the 1920 election, but, as the years that followed were to show, it was far more applicable to the Populist and Progressive eras of the past than to the new, puzzling decade that was now upon the nation.

134. Ibid. November 1920, p. 1.

V: The Lean Years

Do not let the chill of many destroy the ardor of the few. . . .
The germ of life lies in every truth. — WJB

(1)

"WHAT a God-damned world this is! . . . If anyone had told me ten years ago that our country would be what it is today . . . I should have questioned his reason." [1] Thus in a few brief sentences William Allen White summed up the mood of frustration and bewilderment common to so many of the old progressives during the Twenties. The same White who in 1919 had written confidently to the Chairman of the Republican National Committee: "don't ever think you can elect anybody who is an incrusted old reactionary. It cannot be done . . . no one who thinks in the terms of Lodge, Penrose, Lowden, Goodrich, Harding, and Watson is going to get anywhere in this country," was complaining to Herbert Croly just one year later: "I am low in my mind. . . . The Pharisees are running the temple and bossing the religion and handling the caucuses and the people are getting the worst of it. But so long as the folks think the worst of it is the best of it, there doesn't seem to be anything to do. We who feel like going in and making a roughhouse in the temple will only be crucified in the attempt." [2]

Croly himself listened painfully to Harding's plea for "not

1. William Allen White to Ray Stannard Baker, December 8, 1920, Walter Johnson, ed., *Selected Letters of William Allen White*, p. 213.
2. White to Will Hays, August 6, 1919, White to Herbert Croly, September 11, 1920, ibid. pp. 199, 207.

heroics but healing; not nostrums but normalcy; not revolution but restoration . . . not surgery but serenity," took a long look at the equally uninspiring Democratic standard bearer, and cast his vote for the new Farmer-Labor ticket.[3] Other liberals joined Bryan in sitting out the campaign, while still others voted unenthusiastically for one or the other of the major candidates. "I am wondering what progressive men are going to do," Senator Kenyon of Iowa lamented to Bryan. "Harding is a hopeless reactionary and Cox is worse . . . the 3rd party has blown up. . . . Under these circumstances I shall support Harding but not work very hard at it — what justice is there in all this?"[4]

Kenyon did well to bring his troubles to Bryan, for the latter still felt he had some concrete answers to the nation's problems. An increasing number of former progressives, especially among the intelligentsia, would have met the Iowa Senator's query with a bewildered shrug. At worst this group simply stopped caring; at best they retreated, as gracefully as possible, from the frustrating world of American politics. When Professor James Harvey Robinson of Columbia University was asked to comment on the political situation, he responded: "I have no reforms to recommend except the liberation of intelligence."[5] Ray Stannard Baker, who by the middle of the decade had buried himself in his multi-volume study of Woodrow Wilson, proclaimed himself a radical still, but a wiser and more contemplative radical. The error of his prewar days, Baker confessed, was the belief that reform could be achieved by the adoption of "certain easy devices of social invention." He had since learned that there were no

3. Herbert Croly, "The Eclipse of Progressivism," *New Republic*, XXVI (October 27, 1920), 205.
4. William S. Kenyon to WJB, July 21, 1920, Bryan Papers.
5. Morton White, *Social Thought in America*, p. 199. See Chapter XII for an excellent discussion of intellectuals and reform attitudes during the Twenties.

short cuts to reform, no miracles in progress: "there is only
the plodding but beautiful adventure of inquiry and education." Statutes, he now realized, were no substitute for personal conviction; goodness, efficiency, justice came not "from
without or above, but from within and deep down."

> Don't blame us then [he concluded] because we are no longer
> so sure as we were or so noisy; think of us as having gone back
> to get acquainted with life, of liking better for a while to ask
> questions than to answer them; of trying to understand. And
> don't worry; you will hear of us again later . . . we shall be
> coming up from the soil all muscular with new power.[6]

Baker, of course, was not speaking for all progressives.
Men like Bryan, Norris, and La Follette never heeded his call
for more introspection and less concreteness. They still had
specific solutions to specific problems and were far from reti-
cent in advocating them. Progressivism was by no means entirely moribund during the 1920's. Having said this, however,
we must be careful not to go too far. There were still many
progressives in the Twenties, but there was no organized progressive movement. Liberals in Congress might combine to
thwart the more blatant schemes of reactionary Republicans
and occasionally push across some limited legislation of their
own, but they lacked a coherent program, unity of purpose,
and viable leadership. In the Twenties the prewar progressive
coalition broke down, and progressives found themselves occupying a position on the periphery of power in both
parties.[7]

The prewar progressives had eloquently maintained that if
only the people were given the opportunity they would vote

6. "Where are the Pre-War Radicals?" *The Survey*, LV (February
1, 1926), 557–8.
7. Arthur S. Link, "What Happened to the Progressive Movement
in the 1920's?" *The American Historical Review*, LXIV (July 1959),
833–51.

into law the interests of the broad majority. By 1920 they had succeeded brilliantly in giving the masses the opportunity to be heard. The Seventeenth and Nineteenth Amendments, the widespread use of the primary system, and the initiative, referendum, and recall were marks of their success, yet they were rewarded by what appeared to be one of the most extensive displays of political apathy and indifference in American history. It was perhaps this fact more than any other that caused so many progressives to become disillusioned and lose interest in reform. "No appeal to idealism and altruism is today effective," Robert Lansing noted as early as 1919. "The time for such an appeal has long passed. The mood of the American people is no longer receptive." [8]

Many historians have long agreed with Lansing's description of what had taken place. Certainly much that was to occur in the decade following his statement seems to bear out its essential validity. Yet a closer scrutiny of the 1920's makes one wonder whether the Americans' capacity for idealism, for banding together to protect and further a set of beliefs, had really diminished. Robert La Follette, after all, was to poll close to five million votes in 1924; Al Smith was to become a symbol of the aspirations and needs of the urban-immigrant populace, not only of his own state but of the country as a whole; and William Jennings Bryan, on a number of issues such as religion and prohibition, was to evoke as much enthusiasm and response in the rural areas of the country as he had at any time in his career. What really seems to have taken place in the 1920's was not so much a diminution of the American urge to perfect society and protect its basic verities as a fractionalization and rechanneling of that urge.

The rural and urban components of the Progressive era could no longer co-operate and went their separate and conflicting ways. This was due less to a difference over specific

8. November 25, 1919, Lansing Diaries.

economic and political programs than to something far more
fundamental. The reform programs put forward by a Bryan
and a Smith in the Twenties differed more in emphasis than in
substance. Smith concentrated to a greater degree on urban
problems and Bryan on rural problems, but there were no
unbridgeable gaps in this realm. There was no economic or
political reason why the two men and their followers could
not have combined their programs into a new progressive
platform. There were, however, cultural reasons which prevented such an alliance. The America for which Al Smith
spoke was increasingly different from that for which Bryan
was a spokesman. They not only differed but threatened each
other. To speak of the 1920's as an era marked by those severe
tensions and contradictions characteristic of a time of transition may seem trite, for every age is an age of transition. But
some periods are happily unaware of this fact. The flow of
history seems smooth; the changes are not readily apparent;
life seems to be as it has always been. In other eras—and the
Twenties was one of these—the opposite is true. The old
beliefs and myths no longer come easily; many of the old
values and traditions seem less firmly based; the realities of a
rapidly changing world are omnipresent; life no longer seems
stable and certain.

If the economic and political struggles of the Progressive
era were not continued with the same force in the Twenties,
they were replaced or, more properly, supplemented, by new
struggles waged over prohibition, religion, immigration restriction, the rights of Catholics and Jews; struggles which
symbolized the cultural schism between rural and urban
America. To call an era marked by conflicts of this nature one
of apathy or complacence is inaccurate. To millions of Americans in the Twenties these were the conflicts and issues which
were of primary importance, and it was into these channels
that they poured their idealism and fervor and energy. The

rural-urban conflict, which had always threatened the unity of the progressive movement, now became a schism which the hardiest progressive had difficulty bridging.

For Bryan, as for so many Americans, the urges of the past and the realities of the present converged in the 1920's in a confusing and often paradoxical manner. Bryan's attempts to continue the political patterns of the past will be described in this chapter, and the effects upon him of the new forces at work in the postwar era will occupy the final chapters. It would be a serious mistake, however, to draw too wide a line between these two aspects of Bryan's final years. They are dealt with separately here only in order to describe them more sharply.

(2)

The Bryan of the Twenties has been pictured so often as a bitter, disillusioned old man wholly engaged in the crusade for a literal interpretation of the Bible, a strict enforcement of the Eighteenth Amendment, and little else that it is difficult to see him in a different light. Indeed, in view of the mood of postwar America, the despair and division prevailing among the progressive ranks, and Bryan's own rebuff by the Democratic party, the motives for his abandonment of the cause of political and economic reform are present, but, in fact, no such abandonment took place. The new forces abroad in the country during the Twenties narrowed Bryan's appeal even further and frequently impeded his struggle to extend the achievements of progressivism, but nevertheless that struggle was to continue throughout his final years. While the new decade saw Bryan lend his voice and prestige to the rising tide of fundamentalist fervor, he continued to espouse the reforms with which his name has become identified.

"I believe in optimism," Bryan said on the occasion of his sixtieth birthday in 1920, ". . . an optimism built upon confi-

dence in the virtue and intelligence of our people." [9] It was
this element in Bryan's nature that helps to explain his continued advocacy of various reforms despite the unreceptive atmosphere of the Twenties. The heart of the people, he believed, was still sound, their ideals still high, and if they failed
to rally to the standards of reformers immediately it was because of lack of information and prejudice. In the long run
they learned and they responded.[10] This fact he felt was
clearly illustrated in his own career, for although he had been
denied the Presidency, he had lived to see more of his causes
enacted into law than most of the men who reached that
pinnacle. "One can afford to be in a minority," he declared in
1922, "but he cannot afford to be in the wrong; if he is in the
minority and right he will someday be in the majority." [11]
This much at least he had learned from his own struggles. But
if his optimism and determination were important factors in
his refusal to abandon the cause of reform democracy, his lack
of perceptiveness was equally important. Continuing to think in
terms of the past, he did not realize fully for several years that
the old order was gone.

Acting upon the premise that progressivism was never
stronger and that "If the Democrats take a firm stand for the
rights of the common man . . . then they cannot help but go
back into power with a bigger landslide than they went out
with," [12] Bryan set about trying to reorganize his party. The
first step was to purge the party of "the representatives of the
special interests so that the people will believe in the party's
sincerity and trust it with the government." "If the Democratic party is not willing to champion the interests of the
plain people it has no reason for existence," he thundered in a

9. *The Commoner*, April 1920, p. 9.
10. Ibid. March 1921, p. 4.
11. WJB, *In His Image* (New York, 1922), p. 189.
12. *The Commoner*, November 1920, p. 2; *Philadelphia North
American*, May 24, 1921.

speech in which he urged the selection of progressive Democratic National Committeemen in all parts of the country.[13] Bryan's plans, of course, were greeted with little enthusiasm by the party's leaders. Even before he had made his intentions clear, Senator Hitchcock announced that if any reorganization was needed it would not be carried out by those outside the party. Bryan had given the Democracy little support in the last election and could not expect to have any voice in the party's councils. Claude Kitchin summed up his feelings even more pointedly: "If some of these near-leaders, would-be-leaders and self-appointed advisers would keep their mouths shut it would help a lot toward harmony in the party." [14]

Bryan's schemes were further hampered by the rapidly growing factional dispute within the inner circles of the party organization. The 1920 election returns were hardly in before the supporters of William McAdoo, led by Robert Woolley, began a drive to wrest control of the party machinery from Governor Cox's hand-picked national chairman George White.[15] Woolley, who tried desperately to enlist Bryan's aid in the fight, has recorded that Bryan turned up at his Washington offices one day in early January 1921, and announced that Woolley himself was his personal choice to succeed White.[16] Actually Bryan seems to have refused to take sides. "I want to stand neutral as between the Cox and McAdoo factions," he informed Louis Post in February, "in order

13. *The Commoner*, February 1921, pp. 2, 5.
14. *New York Times*, November 10, 1920. For additional comment by Democratic leaders on the subject of reorganization, see ibid. November 12, 1920.
15. For the details of their dispute see Robert Woolley Memoirs MSS., Chapter XXX, Woolley Papers.
16. "What interested me greatly," Woolley has written of this incident, "was that the elderly gentleman was apparently obsessed with the idea that he was still the head of the party. In any event his overture was a friendly gesture which I appreciated." Ibid. See also Woolley to WJB, December 4, December 13, 1920, Bryan Papers.

that I may be in a better position to persuade them both to
put policies above personalities." [17] Publicly he warned:
"The people are intensely in earnest, and the committee can
best serve the party not by burning incense before any particular idol, but by getting down to work for the protection of
the public against exploiters." [18]

Specifically, Bryan and his brother Charles called for the
drafting of "constructive" national, state, and municipal legislative programs representing the consensus of progressive
opinion in the country, and for intensive organization among
the "privates" in the party so that when the time came to
select members of the Democratic National Committee the
voters would understand the issues and be enabled to regain
control of the party's machinery. In February, Judge R. C.
Roper of Nebraska set up headquarters in New York's Hotel
Endicott in behalf of both Bryans. For twenty-five years,
Roper told interested reporters, Charles Bryan had kept a
card index of the "right kind of Democratic leaders." Now
that system was being put into action, and before long every
"pure" Democratic leader in the country would be contacted
and informed of Bryan's aims. Bryan had revealed earlier that
he planned a series of state and regional conventions of progressive Democrats to discuss issues and adopt platforms. The
first of these conventions was scheduled for Kansas City on
May 1. The slogan of the gathering was to be "Cast Tammany Out," and such urban politicos as Murphy, Taggart,
Brennan, Nugent, and Moore actually were to be read out of
the party. In addition, Roper announced that on March 19,
dinners in honor of Bryan's sixty-first birthday would be held
in all parts of the country.[19]

17. WJB to Louis F. Post, February 28, 1921, Post Papers.
18. *New York Times*, February 11, 1921.
19. Ibid. January 21, February 10, 11, 1921; *The Commoner*, February 1921, p. 5.

It is difficult to tell just what lay behind all of this intensive activity. It may be that Bryan really contemplated a whirl-wind assault upon the organization at the grass roots level, or he merely might have been attempting to win a larger voice in the party's councils by throwing a scare into its leaders. In either case he failed. Many of the Bryan birthday celebrations were held as planned, but few, if any, of the far more impor-tant conventions ever took place. Bryan's attempted reorgani-zation of the party won him nation-wide publicity and little else.[20] It became clear that if he was going to purify the party he would have to rely upon his old pattern of agitating for reforms until the people picked up the cry and forced the party leaders to acquiesce or retire from the picture.

With the failure of his attempt to win control of the Demo-cratic organization, Bryan inaugurated a campaign to deepen his hold over the party's members. The first step in this plan was made public in November 1921 when he announced a "Special Educational Campaign Contest" for the purpose of widening the circulation of his periodical, *The Commoner*. The objective of the contest was to win new *Commoner* readers in every county, village, and township in the United States.[21] Again Bryan showed his persistent faith in his ability to win over the voters if only he could get his message to them. And again he failed to do either. By February 1922, only three months after the contest had been inaugurated, all news of its progress ceased, never to be resurrected. Since the quan-tity of advertising in *The Commoner* remained great and even increased during the following year, it is evident that the hard core of faithful *Commoner* readers, many of whom had sub-scribed to the paper since its inception in 1901, remained stable. But the attempt to double or treble their number had

20. For a representative sampling of newspaper comment on Bryan's plans see ibid. pp. 5–7.
21. Ibid. November 1921, p. 4.

failed, and, in view of the brevity of the circulation drive, it evidently failed rather badly.

This failure, though it was disappointing, was not fatal. Bryan still had greater access to the public's ear than any other private citizen in the land, and more than the majority of public officials as well. His voice was heard through his newspaper, his magazine articles and books, and, most important of all, through his public addresses. The Nebraskan continued to be as indefatigable an orator as ever. During the summers he embarked upon his Chautauqua lectures, the winters found him speaking anywhere he was wanted: at political rallies, college commencements, religious gatherings, and even before business groups. Nor is there any evidence that the effectiveness of his oratory diminished to any great extent during the Twenties. "I shall never forget your speech at Ogden [Utah]," one of his followers wrote him in 1923.

> . . . A Republican sat by my side and made slighting remarks about you and your ideas before you began to speak. He was cold blooded and cynical. His slurs began to weaken after you had spoken five or ten minutes and inside of twenty minutes you had him cheering lustily and even stamping his feet. I have never heard anything so masterful as that speech.[22]

As he had done throughout his career, Bryan continued to maintain a close association with the people's representatives in Washington. Though his power to influence Congress had greatly diminished, his contacts within it remained surprisingly large, and his relations with its members were extremely cordial. Many Congressmen from both parties continued to treat Bryan with great deference. Representative Cordell Hull of Tennessee, who had replaced George White as Chairman of the Democratic National Committee, wrote Bryan in 1923: "I have circulated among the leaders at both ends of the Capi-

22. J. G. Burr to WJB, August 21, 1923, Bryan Papers.

tol and repeated to them the different statements, facts and arguments which you were kind enough to give me the benefit of in the course of our conversation at the Hotel. This I shall continue to do." [23] Congressmen from La Follette on down continued to seek his advice and send him proposed legislation for his opinion.[24] Bryan was never too busy to respond, even to the most uninfluential members of Congress.

> Your letter gave me a great deal of satisfaction [wrote a Representative from New York]. I confess I sent you my speech on the subject of "excess profits" with misgiving and imagined you would only do what so many others have done: acknowledge it courteously and throw it in the waste basket. It is now brought home to me why you have so many friends and admirers all over this union: you take pains and don't hesitate to send out a cheerful encouraging word to those whom you believe are struggling for the Right. Your letter to me was like a breath of fresh, rejuvenating air.[25]

A number of Congressmen continued to write Bryan letters which indicate that in their eyes at least his influence had not waned. "If you shall get in touch with Finis Garrett, democratic minority leader," wrote Representative Howard of Nebraska, "please tell him to put me on either the committee on agriculture or interstate commerce. That will satisfy me." [26] Finally, there were those members of Congress to whom the sight of Bryan traveling through the country thundering against Wall Street, in his old-fashioned alpaca coat and wide-brimmed hat, was refreshing in a world which was becoming

23. Hull to WJB, January 20, 1923, ibid.
24. For example see letters from the following to Bryan: William S. Kenyon, December 10, 1920, Arthur Capper, September 27, 1921, Claude Kitchin, April 29, 1921, February 22, 1922, Robert La Follette, January 11, 1924, ibid.
25. Repesentative Anthony J. Griffin to WJB, January 24, 1921, ibid.
26. Edgar Howard to WJB, April 10, 1923, ibid.

all too strange. "When I get discouraged," Senator Kenyon
confided, "I think 'Oh well Bryan is keeping up the fight —
there are some left to battle for the every day folks' and so I
get renewed inspiration and determine to fight on." [27]

(3)

Bryan had spent the greater part of his more than thirty
years in politics as a member of a minority party. Thus, when
the 1920 election cast him in that role once more, he was by
no means on unfamiliar grounds. He had, by now, learned
that perhaps one of the most efficient means of regaining political ascendancy was to allow the party in power to make its
own mistakes. It was a waiting game, and Bryan was in no
immediate hurry. Indeed, in the beginning he seemed as anxious
to aid the new Administration as any ardent Republican. In
the first issue of his periodical following the election, Bryan all
but congratulated the Republicans on their victory and "respectfully" suggested several "needed reforms" which he professed to believe the Administration would seriously consider.
These included three Constitutional amendments, the first of
which provided for ratification of treaties by a majority vote
of the Senate, or better yet, of both houses, a second one
designed to make the Constitution more easily amendable, and
finally, an amendment requiring a referendum on a declaration of war. In addition, Bryan urged the creation of two new
Executive departments dealing with health and education, and
suggested several statutory reforms which he had recommended without success to his own party just a few months
before.[28]

In a private letter of congratulations, Bryan urged the
President-elect to "purge your brain and heart of the silent
influence that blurs one's vision and misleads one's judgment,"

27. Kenyon to WJB, July 21, 1920, ibid.
28. *The Commoner*, November 1920, p. 2.

by announcing that he would not be a candidate for re-election. "None of us are so strong," Bryan advised in a fatherly tone, "that we can safely risk the temptations that come with the exercise of such tremendous power as is vested in the president so long as we harbor a selfish ambition." [29]

Most interesting of all was Bryan's announcement that the Republican victory authorized Harding to proceed with his "Association of Nations" scheme, and his recommendation that Wilson resign immediately, that Vice President Marshall, after becoming President, appoint Harding Secretary of State and then emulate Wilson's action thus elevating Harding to the Presidency four months before his scheduled inauguration. This plan, Bryan announced, would "hasten the beginning of our nation's participation in the association of nations." This rather fanciful proposal was born of a combination of Bryan's growing enmity toward Wilson, whom he considered the architect of the Democratic defeat, and his desire to put the Republicans on the spot with regard to the League. His suggestion, of course, had no effect whatever, save that it helped to open his own eyes to the absurdity of postponing the inauguration of the newly elected President until March, and led him to become one of the chief proponents of an amendment calling for the inauguration of the President and the convening of the new Congress in January.[30]

In December, at Harding's request, Bryan journeyed to Marion, Ohio, to advise the President-elect on international affairs. Afterward he told reporters that the conference confirmed his opinion that Harding "would stand for international cooperation in the interest of peace." [31] During the early months of 1921 Bryan continued his policy of accepting

29. WJB to Harding, November 3, 1920, Bryan Papers.
30. *The Commoner*, December 1920, p. 3, February 1921, p. 1.
31. Harding to WJB, November 12, 1920, Bryan Papers; *New York Times*, December 12, 18, 1920; *The Commoner*, January 1921, p. 2.

Harding's campaign promises at face value. In February he played host to Harding and his wife during their Miami vacation. In March he wrote an unusually saccharine editorial praising Harding's inaugural address and his choice of Hughes as Secretary of State. A month later he had a friendly visit with the President at the White House and lavishly bestowed his praise upon Secretary of the Navy Denby and Secretary of Labor Davis for various acts they had performed.[32] Throughout this entire period Bryan had hardly a harsh word for his political opponents. Never had his utterances been less partisan. Yet he had undergone no change; he was merely attempting to give the Republicans enough rope to hang themselves, and they in turn promptly obliged by acting precisely as he knew they would. But if neither Bryan nor the Republicans had changed, the mood of the country had, as Croly and White had perceived months before.

Bryan received his first intimation of the change during the controversy stirred up by the Administration's revenue bill in the fall of 1921. The bill as proposed provided for the repeal of the excess profits tax and the reduction of taxes on large incomes from a maximum of 65 per cent to a maximum of 40 per cent for 1921, and thereafter 33 per cent. This was exactly the type of issue Bryan had been waiting for. His friendly attitude toward the Republican Administration vanished as suddenly as it had first appeared. After studying the new law, he branded it "the most unblushing piece of piracy ever proposed in Congress." "If the people stand for such exploitation," he continued, "the plutocrats will bite still bigger next year, but it looks like the farmers, the laborers, and the small businessmen are about to revolt. It is time." [33]

32. Harding to WJB, February 19, 1921, Bryan Papers; *New York Times*, April 19, 1921; *The Commoner*, March 1921, p. 1, April 1921, p. 2.
   33. Ibid. September 1921, p. 1.

Senator Arthur Capper of Kansas, one of the founders and leaders of the Farm Bloc in Congress, agreed that farmers were dissatisfied with the pending tax bill, but branded Bryan's assertion that the farmers were on the verge of revolt an exaggeration.[34] Economic discontent was widespread enough in 1921 to justify Bryan's conviction that the people would not stand for the favoritism which the Republicans were bestowing upon the nation's higher income groups, and a number of observers echoed his predictions.[35] Capper, however, proved to be the more accurate prophet. No new revolt of the American conscience was to take place. Senate progressives, it is true, succeeded in modifying the revenue act, but even after their work was completed the excess profits tax remained repealed and the maximum surtax was reduced to 50 per cent. Secretary of the Treasury Mellon had taken an important first step in his ultimately successful drive to transfer as much of the tax burden as possible from the shoulders of the rich to those of the middle and lower income groups.[36]

Bryan had difficulty containing his anger. In his editorials

34. *New York Times,* September 24, 1921.
35. Mark Sullivan, for instance, wrote Bryan on January 25, 1921: "It is as apparent to me as any future thing can be to anybody that during the coming year or two there is going to be a situation in the country, and especially in the Middle West and West, which will be a duplicate of the conditions which brought about your own entrance into politics in the early nineties. . . . There is going to be a radical movement. . . ." Bryan Papers.
36. By 1926 the surtax had been reduced to 20 per cent; see John D. Hicks, *Republican Ascendancy, 1921–1933* (New York, 1960), pp. 53–4, 106. It should be mentioned that Professor Arthur Link views the struggle over the Revenue Act of 1921 in a wholly different manner. The ability of Senate insurgents to alter Mellon's original tax program, he writes, was a significant victory because it attested to the power of progressives in Congress and gave evidence of "the strong survival of advanced progressive tax theories." See *American Epoch: A History of the United States Since the 1890's* (New York, 1955), p. 262.

and his speeches he attacked the act as "utterly inexcusable," and argued that it constituted positive proof that the nation had fallen under "the rule of the rich." "Now we have a government," he announced in November 1922, "by the representatives of Big Business for the benefit of Big Business." [37] "The masses are in bad shape," he cried, and produced facts and figures designed to prove that the farmers were in worse condition than they had been for thirty years and that those laborers who were employed were working for reduced wages.[38] He railed against the Administration's refusal to grant a bonus to veterans while it lavishly bestowed hundreds of millions of dollars of relief upon millionaires and profiteers. He cried out against the government grant of a half billion dollars to guarantee the dividends of railroad corporations and asked when the government ever had guaranteed a fair income for farmers, laborers, or merchants.[39] He inveighed against the machinations of the Federal Reserve Bank, which he charged had become "the tool of Wall Street," and demanded that the Administration appoint to the Board a "farmer who farms," a "laborer who labors" and a "businessman who is not a banker." [40] He warned against the intention of the Administration to draft "a new tariff law which will still further oppress the farmers." [41] But even as he was thundering these pronouncements from the platform and printing them in bold type in *The Commoner*, Bryan could hardly have failed to realize that things were not what they once had been. His campaign against the revenue policies of the Republicans elicited little response; certainly it brought about no mass protests. Indeed, it was in the midst of this campaign that

37. *The Commoner*, October 1922, p. 7, November 1922, p. 1.
38. Ibid. February 1922, p. 2.
39. Ibid. October 1922, p. 1.
40. Ibid. August 1921, p. 1.
41. Ibid. January 1922, p. 1.

his attempt to increase the circulation of his periodical failed so badly.

Bryan had been correct in seeing discontent abroad in the land, but he had been mistaken in thinking that it would follow the old pattern of protest and reform. In the Northeast there was some organized protest in the form of industrial strikes, but these were fought mainly for limited ends, and they eventually petered out in the face of the "rushing revival" of 1923. In the main, the uneasiness of the populace was vented not upon Wall Street but upon "Bolsheviks" and "reds" and dissenters of every kind. In the agricultural South and West, where adverse economic conditions were more pervasive and permanent, there were rumblings of protest and cries for relief, but these the country largely ignored. Some, like La Follette, Norris, and Borah, tried, not entirely without success, to channel rural discontent into the political arena, but it seemed to flow more readily into nonpolitical areas and helped account for the growth of evangelical religion and the revival of racial and ethnic hatreds.

Despite his growing feeling of helplessness, Bryan rarely shared the paralyzing despair of so many of his fellow progressives. He occasionally gave evidence of varying degrees of disillusionment and frustration both in his religious addresses and activities, which we will examine in a later chapter, and in some of his political pronouncements. In the winter of 1922 he said almost wearily: "This is a people's government if the people will only take charge of it . . . so long as the farmer gives his exclusive attention to the old plow and leaves the producing of the laws to the non-producers he will not meet them at the summer resorts." [42] And a year later he complained: "If the plundered masses were half as vigorous in the protection of their rights as the monopolists are in overreach-

42. Ibid. February 1922, p. 2.

ing the public, it would not take long to restore justice." [43]

But such complaints were the exception rather than the rule. For the most part Bryan remained as optimistic and outspoken as ever. In the beginning of 1921 he had presented a twenty-two-point "National Legislative Program" which he hoped the Democrats might adopt as the core of their 1924 platform. This program included most of the planks contained in the fifteen-point program he had issued in 1919, and in addition called for the adoption of the amendments discussed earlier in this chapter, another amendment limiting the President to one term of not more than six years, legislation prohibiting speculation in foodstuffs, additional protection of debtors by reorganization of the Federal Reserve System and the Farm Loan Bank, legislation providing for voting by mail, adoption of a National Primary Law, and an American-sponsored disarmament conference. [44] Bryan not only issued this platform, he energetically championed most of its provisions during the following years.

As in the past, Bryan considered the establishment of a national bulletin the "gateway to all needed reforms." Without such a medium of free expression, he argued, the people could not be expected to overcome their indifference and act intelligently upon the major issues of the day. [45] "We are helpless," he complained to Louis Post in 1921, "we cannot get our side before the people and the condition is growing worse instead of better. A bulletin is our only hope." [46] In 1922, Representative Huddleston introduced Bryan's proposed bulletin into the House as H.R. 12604, but even as he was doing so the Alabama Congressman informed Bryan: "Of

43. Ibid. March 1923, p. 1.
44. Ibid. February 1921, p. 1.
45. WJB to Jonathan M. Davis, November 25, 1922, Bryan Papers; WJB, "A National Bulletin," *Forum*, LXV (April 1921), 455–8; see also Bryan's Statement dated April 1, 1924, in Bryan Papers.
46. WJB to Post, February 28, 1921, Post Papers.

course there is no prospect to get the present hard-boiled Congress to do anything along these lines." [47]

Bryan was no less persistent in his attempts to secure government ownership of private monopolies and the elimination of profiteering. In his address before the Nebraska Constitutional Convention on January 12, 1920, Bryan replied to the numerous charges of irresponsible radicalism which his fight for government ownership brought him by stating: "I am an individualist and yet I have often been called a socialist. Why? Because I believe in the government doing certain things that it can do better than individuals can." He urged the convention to adopt a constitution which would "authorize the state, the counties and the cities to take over and operate any industry they please. . . . The right of the community is superior to the right of any individual." [48] Later that year, in an address before the League of the Southwest in Los Angeles, he strongly recommended government ownership and development of the nation's water power.[49] In a speech before the Florida Legislature in the spring of 1921, he urged the state to establish state-owned and operated stock yards, slaughter houses, and sales agencies.[50] A few weeks later he shocked an assembly of Kansas City businessmen when, in the midst of an address before the real estate board of that city, he suddenly thundered: "Stop your stealing! Drive your profiteers out of business! They are the big, fat middlemen bearing down on the producer and crushing the life out of him. . . . Limit and restrain the profits of the middleman." [51]

Throughout his remaining years Bryan continued to reiterate his belief that "a private monopoly is indefensible and

---

47. Huddleston to WJB, December 8, 1922, Bryan Papers.
48. *The Commoner*, February 1920, pp. 8–9.
49. Ibid. October 1920, pp. 7–8.
50. Ibid. May 1921, p. 3.
51. *Kansas City Times*, May 14, 1921, clipping in Bryan Papers.

intolerable." In 1923 he directed a vitriolic attack against the "Standard Oil Monopoly" and demanded that the government take immediate steps to protect the people from "these conscienceless profiteers." [52] Although Bryan was a proponent of federally-owned and operated "natural" monopolies, his fear of too much centralization of power in Washington led him to favor having municipal and state governments do the job wherever possible. He warmly supported Mayor Hylan's plan to have New York City own and operate its own transit system, and he urged other local officials throughout the nation to take similar steps. [53] Just a few months before his death he was appealing to Governor Martin of Florida to combat high gasoline prices by threatening to establish non-profit government-owned filling stations throughout his state. [54]

What most disturbed Bryan was not the individual actions of specific corporations or government officials, but the entire philosophy underlying the relationship of government and industry during the Harding-Coolidge era. When, in 1923 and 1924, the scandals of the Harding Administration were exposed, Bryan appeared to be less shocked and outraged than most of his fellow Democrats. The amount stolen by corrupt officials, he maintained, was a pittance compared to the amounts voted out of the pockets of the people by respectable Republicans. The $100,000,000 which Doheny expected to make out of his oil leases should be compared to the $450,000,000 given to business by the repeal of the excess profits tax, the three or four billions put into the hands of protected interests by the Fordney-McCumber Tariff, and the untold

52. *The Commoner*, March 1923, p. 1.

53. WJB to John F. Hylan, August 30, 1922, Bryan Papers. See also WJB to Jonathan M. Davis, November 25, 1922, WJB to Pat M. Neff, August 14, 1923, WJB to Clayton S. Cooper, February 11, 1925, all in Bryan Papers.

54. WJB to John M. Martin, February 10, 1925, ibid.

relief given the wealthy by the Mellon tax plan. "The greatest value of the oil investigation," he wrote,

> will not be found in the punishment of a few criminals, but in awakening the mass of the people to the menace of the policy upon which the Republican leaders act. It is based upon the theory that society is suspended from the top and that the Government should legislate for the well-to-do and let the people wait until that prosperity leaks through on those below. . . . It is a vicious policy and should be repudiated at the polls, because it concentrates wealth and invites corruption of officials. [55]

(4)

During these years, as throughout his career, Bryan's reform efforts were closely oriented toward the needs and aspirations of the nation's agricultural population. It was from these rural folk that Bryan himself had sprung, and to the end of his life he remained their special champion and spokesman. If this was a bias, Bryan made no attempt to conceal it. In an address at New Orleans in 1921, he said, using phrases almost identical to those contained in his Cross of Gold speech: "The prosperity of the city rests upon the prosperity of the farm. . . . If the farms were abandoned the cities would soon decay." "For this reason," he continued, "there ought to be a clear understanding of the relationship between the city and the county — *but the country must be considered first for the protection of both.*" [56]

Accordingly, he spent much of his time and energy working for the establishment of government trade commissions in every state, legislation designed to eliminate unnecessary middlemen and limit the profits of necessary middlemen, dual

55. "Statement of Mr. William Jennings Bryan on the Oil Investigation" (undated), ibid.
56. "The Southern Farmer," *The Commoner*, October 1921, p. 3. Italics added.

ownership of the railroads, federal development of water resources, and the establishment of minimum prices for such
staple crops as cotton, corn, and wheat, all of which were
reforms of prime concern to farmers. He was outspoken in his
defense of the Farm Bloc in Congress. "I have never known a
time," he told the National Agricultural Congress in 1922,
"when there was not a Wall Street bloc or a big business bloc
in Congress. The only difference is that these blocs operate in
secret while the Agricultural bloc has the courage to do its
work in public." [57]

Nevertheless, Bryan did not overlook the interests of the urban workers. In 1916 he had told John Reed: "I believe that the
government may properly impose a minimum wage, regulate
hours of labor, pass usury laws, and enforce inspection of
food, sanitation and housing conditions." [58] All this he believed was consistent with individualism, its purpose being not
to overthrow free enterprise but to protect and perpetuate it.
During the post-war wave of strikes, Bryan defended the demands of labor with but one exception — the Boston police
strike of 1919. "No man can serve two masters," he wrote
during the course of that strike. "The policeman owes his first
allegiance to the government and he cannot subordinate the
government to any organization." Though he opposed the
strike, once it had been crushed he was one of the first to urge
Governor Coolidge to reinstate the strikers — a step which the
latter adamantly refused to take.[59] The widespread labor disputes of 1919, which at times threatened to paralyze the nation, led Bryan to advocate the creation of some means of
ascertaining the weekly or monthly fluctuations in the price
level of foodstuffs and other necessities so that wages could be

57. Ibid. pp. 3–4, December 1922, p. 1; *New York Times*, January
24, 1922.
58. Reed, *Collier's*, LVII (May 20, 1916), 41.
59. *The Commoner*, October 1919, p. 5.

immediately adjusted to increases in the cost of living without arousing antagonism between capital and labor.[60]

In 1920 Bryan urged the members of the Nebraska Constitutional Convention to adopt a constitution which would guarantee the right of labor to organize, encourage profit-sharing and co-operation, empower the legislature to fix minimum wages, recognize the right of collective bargaining, and erect a commission empowered to investigate all labor disputes. This latter idea, which Bryan had first advocated many years before, now became one of his favorite proposals.[61]

In his fight for the rights of the laboring man, Bryan was convinced that he was struggling for the preservation of the American system. If Bolshevism has a breeding place, he declared, it was in "conscienceless profits," and "unpatriotic plundering." [62] "I am simply trying to prevent wrong doing," he told a reporter in 1920, "and in this I believe I am stemming the tide of radicalism, because after me may come— the extremists." [63] The only weapon Bryan denied to labor was the right to employ physical force. "Those who resort to lawlessness are enemies of labor . . ." he declared during a violent labor outbreak in Chicago. "Force can be employed by the government and by the government alone." With this single exception he was willing to grant labor every means of achieving their rights. "All interested in progress and popular government," he wrote toward the close of 1922, "must . . .

60. Ibid. August 1919, p. 5.

61. Ibid. January 1920, p. 3, February 1920, p. 11, February 1922, p.3, December 1922, p. 1; *New York Times*, June 2, 1920.

62. *The Commoner*, December 1919, p. 4.

63. Ibid. June 1920, p. 11. On a trip through the West in 1922, Bryan said to a companion: "I told the nation in 1896 that they had better take me then or they would have to take a later man they did not want. In 1896 I simply said 'Thou shalt not steal.' A later man will surely come and say, 'Give it back.'" Recollections of Louis J. Alber in the *Cleveland Plain Dealer*, March 14, 1937, clipping in Daniels Papers, Box 761.

be interested in everything that materially affects the wage earner's standard of living and the conditions that surround him." [64]

When in 1922 the Supreme Court overthrew the National Child Labor Act of 1919, Bryan vigorously denied the claim that the decision was a victory for state rights, and called it instead "a victory for capitalism whose greed coins the blood of little children into larger dividends." [65] During the critical railroad strikes of 1922, Bryan strongly supported the employees' demand for seniority rights and castigated the employers for opposing it. He demanded that Harding "use a people's government for the people's welfare" and ask Congress for authority to seize and operate those roads which refused to deal fairly with labor. In August, he was in Washington urging Democratic Senators to support Senator Walsh's bill embodying this proposal.[66] He answered the charges that his demands were an assault upon industrial individualism by rejecting that philosophy entirely. "Is a man really attending to nothing but his own business when he attempts to fix the conditions under which thousands and tens of thousands shall live?" he asked. "Granted that a man has a right to decide things that affect HIMSELF ONLY, but what right has he to decide arbitrarily matters that affect the lives of a multitude?" He supported the railroad workers' demand for a minimum wage, but went them one better by asking: "Why not consider a minimum wage for all labor, and a minimum price for all farmers? And why not a maximum profit for the middleman?" [67]

In the very last issue of *The Commoner* — that of April 1923 [68] — Bryan continued his demands for justice to the

64. *The Commoner*, June 1922, p. 3, December 1922, p. 6.
65. Ibid. June 1922, p. 3.
66. Ibid. August 1922, p. 2; *New York Times*, August 29, 1922; WJB to David J. Walsh, August 26, 1922, Bryan Papers.
67. *The Commoner*, September 1922, p. 3, November 1922, p. 1.
68. Charles Bryan, who had operated *The Commoner* since its in-

worker by denouncing the Supreme Court's invalidation of a Federal law fixing minimum wages for women in Washington, D.C., as "another Dred Scott decision." " The 'sacredness of contract,' " he declared angrily, "becomes a cruel farce when the employee can be forced into labor that is devitalizing. . . . Humanity will react against the policy which the court has endorsed. . . . It is a return to barbarism." [69] "Something is fundamentally wrong," he told the 1924 convention of the Brotherhood of Locomotive Engineers, "when the most deserving people and those who work the hardest get the least, and those who work the least get the most out of the system." "In my opinion," he assured them, "if it were not for organization among the laboring men, the wage earners of this country would be reduced to the position of serfs. Capital is organized." [70]

(5)

During the early Twenties, Bryan's interest in the country's international obligations and in the maintenance of peace continued undiminished. By the fall of 1921, he somewhat belatedly came to the realization that Harding had no intention of leading America into the League and that his hazy proposal of forming an association of nations had been made for the benefit of credulous voters. Though the idea of American participation in the League died hard, Bryan finally accepted its defeat and proposed, as an alternative, universal disarmament and the implementation of his own thirty peace treaties. At the Democratic convention of 1920, Bryan had suggested that the United States cancel the war debts owed to it by European nations on the condition that those nations agree to disarm, and he continued to advocate this proposal

ception, was elected Governor of Nebraska in 1922. With his inauguration, publication of the journal ceased.

69. *The Commoner*, April 1923, p. 1.

70. WJB, "Labor and Good Government," *The Locomotive Engineers Journal*, July 1924, copy in Bryan Papers.

during the years that followed. The debt would never be paid anyway, he reasoned, so "Why not buy a PRICELESS peace with a WORTHLESS debt?" [71]

Bryan proved to be one of the foremost proponents of disarmament in the country. "We should stand for disarmament by agreement if possible and by example if necessary," he declared in a speech in which he proposed an immediate 10 per cent reduction in American armaments.[72] He steadfastly opposed all attempts to push any sort of complusory military training bill through Congress, and repeatedly urged the President to call for an international conference to discuss the question of arms reduction. He attended the Congress on Reduction of Armaments held in Chicago in the spring of 1921 and helped to secure the adoption of a resolution asking the President to invite England and Japan to participate in a conference for the reduction of naval forces. A week later he persuaded the Presbyterian General Assembly to adopt a similar resolution. "I have no doubt that a disarmament conference will be called," he told an audience of 12,000 in New York's Central Park in July.[73]

When Harding invited the leading nations of the world to assemble in Washington on November 11, 1921, to participate in just such a conference, Bryan praised him effusively and predicted hopefully: "The Disarmament Conference may become the most important gathering in centuries. IT MAY END WAR. . ." [74] Bryan himself attended the Washington Conference as a representative of the United Press.[75]

71. *The Commoner*, January 1921, p. 3, October 1921, p. 1, July 1922, p. 4.
72. "Democracy's Opportunity," ibid. June 1921, p. 10.
73. *New York Times*, May 20, May 26, July 10, 1921.
74. *The Commoner*, August 1921, p. 1.
75. From a letter of Mrs. Harding's in the Bryan Papers, it would appear that Mrs. Bryan had asked the First Lady to query her husband about the possibility of naming Bryan to the delegation which was to

When Secretary of State Hughes, in his inaugural address to the conference, made a dramatic proposal for the limitation of capital ships, Bryan was moved to tears. "I was never happier in my life than when I sat there and heard Secretary Hughes read his proposals for the scrapping of navies," he told an audience in Carnegie Hall two weeks later. "I am a sanguine man, and I had great hopes. But what Secretary Hughes proposed was more than I could have hoped for." [76] During the first two months of the negotiations Bryan remained optimistic, but by January he grew somewhat disillusioned and admitted that "many questions seem likely to be left unsettled." When the conference adjourned a month later, however, he was more enthusiastic than ever, writing: "The Arms Conference has passed into history after a session that may be regarded as the beginning of an epoch. . . . World peace is seemingly nearer than it has ever been before; the song of the shepherds of Bethlehem may soon become the international anthem." [77] After convincing himself that the Four Power Treaty allowed the United States to retain its freedom of action, Bryan returned to Washington in March to urge Democratic Senators to vote for it, and after the treaty's passage he publicly criticized the twenty-three Democrats who had failed to support it.[78]

represent the United States at the Conference. Mrs. Harding replied: "I will gladly convey your wishes to the President and second them, because I esteem your good husband most highly myself." Florence King Harding to Mary B. Bryan, July 28, 1921, Bryan Papers.

76. Sumner Welles, *The Time for Decision* (New York, 1944), p. 43; *New York Times*, November 26, 1921. See also WJB to Grace Bryan Hargreaves, November 15, 1921, Grace Bryan Hargreaves MSS., Bryan Papers.

77. WJB to Elihu Root, December 6, 1921, National Archives, Washington, D.C.; *The Commoner*, January 1922, p. 1, February 1922, p. 1.

78. WJB to Warren G. Harding, January 26, 1922, Bryan Papers; *New York Times*, March 7, 1922; *The Commoner*, March, 1922, pp. 1, 13, April 1922, p. 1.

In addition to his efforts to bring about disarmament, Bryan worked for a greater degree of American participation and co-operation in international affairs. In an open letter in May 1922, Bryan urged President Harding to appoint an American representative to the League without power to make binding agreements but with power to observe and advise.[79] In the years that followed Bryan called upon the United States to accept every invitation extended to it by foreign nations "for advice and for the exercise of our moral influence for promotion of peace." Specifically, he advocated the appointment of American representatives to the World Court and all other international tribunals and investigatory bodies, the calling of a second disarmament conference to deal with land forces, and an international agreement outlawing wars.[80]

When the French occupied the Ruhr in 1923, Bryan chided them for imperiling the peace of the world, but he had still harsher words for his own government whose indifferent attitude toward international affairs, he charged, helped bring the crisis into being. The election of 1920, he wrote in a national magazine, had committed Harding "to some sort of [international] co-operation. Two years have passed since Mr. Harding's election and . . . NO steps have been taken looking to any effective co-operation and the Administration has turned a deaf ear to the appeals that have come from Europe."[81]

In 1924 Bryan and his wife drew up a program for peace which they entered in the Bok Peace Plan Contest. Although the plan, which strongly resembled Bryan's peace treaties, won no prize, Bryan recommended its implementation to the

79. Ibid. May 1922, p. 1; *New York Times*, May 1, 1922.

80. WJB to William S. Woods, February 28, 1923, *The Commoner*, March 1923, p. 3; *New York Times*, April 9, July 28, 1923; WJB to Henry Goddard Leach, April 7, 1925, Bryan Papers.

81. WJB to Frank D. Pavey, February 24, 1923, ibid. WJB, "Our Responsibility for the Ruhr Invasion," *Current History*, XVII (March, 1923), 898–9.

President and the Secretary of State.[82] In the beginning of 1925 Bryan made one final attempt to induce the President to cancel our former allies' debts in return for their promise to reduce their armaments. "As long as we demand the money from our allies," he wrote, "they will feel justified in demanding the amount from Germany. This creates ill-feeling and is made an excuse for preparedness and may involve Europe in another war. Can we afford to take that responsibility?" Coolidge replied with his characteristically icy cordiality: "Your interesting letter received. It has not seemed moral to me to cancel obligations. If you are in town some time, I hope to see you." [83] Undaunted by the President's cold response, Bryan called on him at the White House three weeks later. For a while the two men amicably discussed the problem of world peace, but when Bryan tried to steer the conversation to the subject of cancellation, Coolidge cut him short by pointing out that the government's position was embodied in a Congressional act under which the Executive had to proceed.[84]

"The great question," Bryan had written in 1923, "is whether the United States . . . shall live up to its responsibilities as the greatest of the Christian nations and the only nation that can speak peace to the world." [85] By 1925 it must have been clear, even to him, that this was a question which he would not see resolved during his lifetime.

(6)

Perhaps one of the chief characteristics of the rural American ethos during the Twenties was its preoccupation with

82. A copy of the plan may be found in the Bryan Papers. See also WJB to Calvin Coolidge, May 1, 1925, and WJB to Frank B. Kellogg, May 1, 1925, ibid.
83. WJB to Coolidge, January 1, 1925, Coolidge to WJB, January 5, 1925, ibid.
84. *New York Times,* January 28, 1925.
85. WJB, *Current History,* XVII (March, 1923), 899.

questions of a moral nature. This fact is of prime importance in understanding Bryan's entry into the fundamentalist crusade. It is also important in evaluating his championship of several other moral reforms during the decade. Of these the most important was his crusade for prohibition enforcement. The overwhelming defeat of Bryan's prohibition plank in the 1920 Democratic convention made it increasingly clear that the fight for effective enforcement of the Eighteenth Amendment was going to be as difficult as the struggle for the adoption of the reform itself had been. Certainly the implementation of the Volstead Act was never so simple and straightforward as Bryan and his fellow prohibitionists had imagined. As one contemporary observer put it: "Enforcement, from the beginning, was generally inefficient, undignified, very costly, in some cases violent, in others corrupt." [86] "If you think this country ain't Dry," Will Rogers quipped, "you just watch 'em vote; and if you think this country ain't Wet, you just watch 'em drink." [87]

One of the chief difficulties was that for a large number of Americans temperance and morality had no readily visible connection. It was in this sphere that the prohibitionists had failed most markedly — and this failure was to cost dearly. Bryan himself recognized this fact in an address before the Alliance of Reformed Churches in 1921, when he admitted that: "Prohibition laws cannot live, except as they have back of them a sentiment in favor of total abstinence." [88] And again in a magazine article in 1923 he wrote: "It is necessary to instruct each new generation in the effect of alcohol . . . the only way to make prohibition secure is to keep the temperance sentiment at full tide. The bootlegger will cease to trouble us

86. Sullivan, *Our Times*, VI, 213.
87. Quoted in Oscar Handlin, *Al Smith and His America* (Boston, 1958), p. 125.
88. "World-wide Prohibition," *The Commoner*, October 1921, p. 7.

when people cease to patronize him . . ." [89] Bryan's recognition of this fundamental truth, coupled with his inordinate faith in the power of written agreements to do away with such evils as war and intemperance, led him to propose a plan whereby the entire faculty and student body of every educational institution in the land, together with all government officials from the President down, would sign total abstinence pledges.[90]

A campaign of education by precept and example, however, required time, and Bryan was equally interested in immediate results. Consequently, he carried on a campaign for "enforcement in earnest." Because the liquor question cut across party lines, the majority of politicians attempted to pay it as little attention as possible. Realizing this, Bryan attempted to organize the friends of temperance to fill the void thus created and, in addition, he appealed to his countrymen's sense of duty. "Respect for law," he declared, "should not depend upon the citizen's opinion of the law, it should rest on loyalty to government." Any man who takes a drink these days, he asserted, is a "philosophical anarchist." He advocated more effective methods of search and seizure in the campaign against bootlegging, more stringent laws against smuggling liquor in from abroad, and government ownership and distribution of the entire supply of alcohol being distilled for legal purposes.[91]

During the Congressional elections of 1922, Bryan cam-

89. WJB, "Prohibition," *Outlook,* CXXXIII (February 7, 1923), 264.

90. Ibid.; *The Commoner,* January 1923, p. 2. For a copy of Bryan's proposed pledge and copies of the letters he sent to the president of every state university in the land urging them to have their faculty and students sign it, see Bryan Papers.

91. *The Commoner,* April 1921, p. 1, September 1921, p. 3, October 1921, p. 10; WJB, *Outlook,* CXXXIII (February 7, 1923), 264; *New York Times,* April 11, 24, 25, 1921, March 21, 1922.

paigned vigorously for the election of a Congress which would bring such measures into being. "Let no man be nominated for Congress or the Senate," he declared months before the election itself, "who is not openly and unequivocally for the law as it now stands and for any additional laws that may be found necessary to make prohibition effective." [92] Bryan's open enmity toward Al Smith, which was to have important repercussions at the Democratic National Convention in 1924, dated from 1923 when the New York Governor signed a bill repealing New York State's prohibition enforcement act. "The Governor of the largest state in the Union," Bryan charged, "boldly raises the black flag and offers to lead the representatives of an outlawed traffic in their assault upon the nation's honor and the people's welfare. . . . Governor Smith has simply dishonored his office and disgraced himself; he cannot lead the nation back to wallow in the mire." [93]

Although Bryan's very campaign for effective enforcement of the Eighteenth Amendment was an admission that prohibition thus far had been something short of a success and had not yet ushered in the millennium its devotees had prophesied, he showed no signs of disillusionment or despair. He adamantly refused to admit that the prohibition experiment had been proven a dismal failure. Prohibition, he maintained, was unsuccessful only in those sections where the wets were strong enough to elect officials "pledged in advance to violate their oaths of office." In spite of this flagrant lawlessness great progress had been made. Had not Prohibition Commissioner Haynes shown that since the Eighteenth Amendment went into effect twelve million people had stopped drinking, that two billion dollars formerly spent for intoxicants were now available for better uses, and that arrests for drunkenness had decreased by 66 per cent? "And yet, we are told that prohibi-

92. *The Commoner*, February 1922, p. 1.
93. *New York Times*, June 10, 1923.

tion is a failure and . . . should be repealed. The law against murder has been on the statute books for thousands of years; must we repeal it also because it is frequently violated? Shall we repeal the law against theft because some commit larceny?" [94] Not only did he persist in maintaining that the country would never repudiate the Eighteenth Amendment, but he continued to predict that he would live to see prohibition adopted by every civilized nation on earth. "There is no turning back," he wrote in 1923. ". . . That intoxicating liquor . . . is destined to disappear throughout the civilized world is as sure as the rising of the morning sun. . . . Our nation will be saloonless for evermore and will lead the world in the great crusade which will drive intoxicating liquor from the globe." [95]

In conjunction with prohibition, Bryan attacked two other widespread vices during these years. In his address before the Nebraska Constitutional Convention in 1920, Bryan inaugurated his abbreviated campaign to secure the adoption of what he termed "the single standard of morality," by which he meant that whatever punishment was inflicted upon women for breaches of sexual morality should be inflicted upon men as well. The time has come, he insisted, when man "must live up to the standards of morality he had laid down for women." Although he publicized these views in *The Commoner* and two national magazines, his campaign proceeded little further than the planning stage.[96] A similar fate awaited his proposed crusade against gambling, which he also had introduced in 1920 and which lay more or less dormant until he attempted to revive it during the final year of his life, when he suggested

94. WJB to Earl Reeves, April 5, 1922, Bryan Papers.
95. WJB, *Outlook*, CXXXIII (February 7, 1923), 264–5.
96. *The Commoner*, April 1920, p. 10; *New York Tribune*, May 27, 1920; WJB "Single Moral Standard," *Collier's*, LXV (March 13, 1920), 7; WJB, "Morals for Men and Women," *Hearst's International* (June, 1923), 29–32.

to Representative Ayres of Kansas that he introduce a bill denying to the mails newspapers that published gambling data on horse races, elections, prize fights, and lotteries.[97]

No matter how deeply Bryan may have believed in these two reforms, he found the tasks of championing political and economic reform in a period of Republican conservatism, prohibition in an era of hedonism, and fundamentalism in an age of scientific advancement more than enough to keep him fully occupied.

(7)

The deep conservatism of the Harding Administration convinced Bryan that the elections of 1922 and 1924 would be "the most important in the entire history of our country." More than a year before the Congressional elections of 1922 he began to counsel the members of his party to cast about for "courageous, progressive" candidates for Congress. "Most of the Democrats now serving in the Senate and House," he wrote, "are doing well and should be reelected, but the records of all should be examined and unfaithful ones retired." Throughout the remainder of 1921 he continued his attempts to arouse the voters' interests in the forthcoming elections. He urged them to organize their forces, select their candidates, and get to work. "No district," he reminded them, "is hopeless next year." [98] During the early months of 1922 he continued these pleas, persistently maintaining that if only the Democrats would champion the cause of the people and nominate progressives they could easily win control of the House in November and open the way for a complete return to power in 1924.[99]

97. W. A. Ayres to WJB, January 21, 1925, Bryan Papers.

98. *The Commoner*, August 1921, p. 1, November 1921, p. 1, December 1921, p. 4.

99. Ibid. January 1922, p. 1, March 1922, p. 11, July 1922, p. 1.

As in previous years, Bryan's services in the campaign were in great demand.[100] After completing his seasonal Chautauqua lectures, Bryan campaigned through six Western states in which important senatorial contests were being held. The heart of his attack upon the Administration centered upon its policies of discriminatory taxation and tariff protection and was designed to prove that the nation was in the clutches of Big Business.[101] His efforts won the unqualified praise of almost every candidate in whose behalf he spoke. "If I am elected, I know that I will owe it almost exclusively to the speeches you made in my behalf," wrote Representative Ayres of Kansas. "The effect of your two days' work in the District was marvelous," wrote an Illinois candidate. "Your speeches were logical, eloquent and convincing and you are stronger than ever in Arizona," Senator Ashurst assured him. Democratic National Chairman Cordell Hull sent his "unmeasured thanks for your invaluable services to the Democratic party." "You were in the thickest of the fight everywhere and wonderful results attended your efforts." [102]

The results of the election, though failing to fulfill Bryan's optimistic predictions, were nonetheless encouraging. The Republican majority in the House and Senate was reduced substantially. Bryan was elated. The election, he announced,

100. J. V. McClintic to WJB, September 6, September 18, 1922, WJB to Representative Joe Sears, August 1, 1922, WJB to Senator Park Trammel, August 1, 1922, Bryan Papers.

101. *The Commoner*, October 1922, p. 7, November 1922, p. 1.

102. W. A. Ayres to WJB, October 19, 1922, Jesse Black, Jr., to WJB, November 28, 1922, Henry F. Ashurst to WJB, November 28, 1922, Cordell Hull to WJB, November 11, 1922, Bryan Papers. For other letters of thanks and tribute from candidates and state party leaders see the following letters to Bryan: D. C. Dunbar (Utah), November 14, 1922, Governor-elect Jonathan M. Davis (Kansas), November 18, 1922, O. K. Kvale (Minnesota), November 20, 1922, Senator A. A. Jones (New Mexico), December 4, 1922, Senator-elect Anna D. Oleson (Minnesota), December 8, 1922, ibid.

"was a revolt against the rule of the rich," and inspired him "with new hope and new confidence in our form of government." The fact that the election strengthened the hand of Republican progressives at the expense of the Old Guard seemed to please Bryan almost as much as the gains his own party had made.[103] "The Democrats have made great gains —remarkable gains," he wrote the editor of the International News Service, "but there is so much political independence now that neither party can hope to win by an appeal to partizanship. The fights of the future must be made for principles and policies. The party lash is no longer effective as a coercive influence. The word 'progressive' was written largely in the election returns — a fact that both parties should heed." [104]

Although Bryan was still able to speak of the Democratic party as "the only party of any size that represents the producing masses of the nation," [105] and although he made no attempt to further progressivism by cooperating with such nonpartisan groups as the Conference for Progressive Political Action, his own partisanship, while it continued to be a limiting factor, became less inflexible during the Twenties. Certainly his new attitude was probably more than casually related to his rebuff by the Democratic convention in 1920. He not only had seen it overwhelmingly defeat his reform platform, but he had had to sit idly by while a man whom he considered a conservative carried the party's banner in the campaign. "I used to think that all the good was in my party and all the bad was in the Republican party," he had remarked shortly before the 1920 election. "I am wiser now." [106] In an address which he delivered frequently during the

103. *The Commoner*, December 1922, pp. 1, 3; WJB to Louis F. Post, November 26, 1922, Post Papers.

104. WJB to Editor, International News Service, December 4, 1922, Bryan Papers.

105. *The Commoner*, January 1923, p. 1.

106. Ibid. October 1920, p. 9.

Twenties, he reiterated the same idea: "Well, I used to feel, when I was younger, that unless my party won that the world would go to ruin, but I am older now. I decided quite a while ago that no party could ruin this country even if any party wanted to do it." [107] Bryan supported his party to the end of his life, but he seemed a bit less certain that a Democratic victory was necessarily a victory for progressivism. "We seem to be very much at sea," he wrote to a fellow Democrat in 1923. ". . . we have the Wall Street element that is as bad as the reactionary Republicans. . . . We also have the wet contingent; they are far too much absorbed in their excitement to get a drink to think of their party's welfare." [108]

If the Republican Old Guard's losses at the polls in 1922 were to be converted into a victory for the forces of reform, there would have to be a coalition of progressives on both sides of the aisle in Congress. Bryan was more than willing to see this take place. In December he announced that now that the Democrats had a working minority in both houses they should enlist the aid of progressive Republicans in implementing a constructive program of reform, and Bryan himself, of course, had just such a program to recommend.[109] When Republican Senator La Follette and Democratic Representative Huddleston issued a call for a conference of progressives to meet in Washington, D.C., during the first week in December, Bryan applauded lustily, and while there is no evidence that he attended, he was in the Capital a week later assuring La Follette of his support.[110]

During the spring and summer of 1923 Bryan continued to

107. "Brother or Brute," copy in Bryan Papers.
108. WJB to Marvin J. Hutchins, July 5, 1923, ibid.
109. Bryan's new program embraced almost every plank of his earlier programs already discussed in this chapter. *The Commoner*, December 1922, p. 1.
110. Ibid.; *New York Times*, December 12, 1922.

keep in touch with progressives of both parties. In July he
wrote a number of Democrats in the House and Senate urging
them to lay the groundwork for a coalition of Democrats and
progressive Republicans which would be able to organize the
new Congress when it convened in December. The initial
response to his plan was not encouraging. Senator Dill of
Washington sounded out the Democratic leadership in the
Senate and reported that they doubted the wisdom of Bryan's
proposal.[111] In the House George Huddleston of Alabama
received a similar reception. Finis Garrett of Tennessee, the
Democratic Minority Leader, John N. Garner of Texas, and
others he spoke to felt that the best strategy for the Democrats was to avoid a coalition so that the divided Republican
majority would have all responsibility for the inaction and
deadlock they were sure would ensue. "I believe," he informed Bryan, "that a majority of Republican progressives in
the House will even allow the Democrats to name the Speaker
provided they are given recognition on the Committees . . .
the chief trouble seems to be with men like Garrett, Garner,
Pou and Crisp." [112] Still, Bryan did not abandon his hope of
seeing the new Congress begin with a progressive revolt. "I
hope that you will plan to be here some little time before the
Congress meets," La Follette wrote him, "as I believe it will
be a very important time in the life of the progressive movement." [113]

As members of the Sixty-eighth Congress began to gather
in Washington in December, Bryan was on hand to make one
final attempt to effect a progressive coalition. "I believe that
the Progressive Democrats and the Progressive Republicans
ought to organize both Houses, take control of committees
and proceed to enact remedial legislation," he told a reporter.

111. C. C. Dill to WJB, July 30, 1923, Bryan Papers.
112. Huddleston to WJB, July 30, 1923, ibid.
113. La Follette to WJB, July 29, 1923, ibid.

Since progressive Democrats outnumbered progressive Republicans, the latter ought to support the candidates of the former in the elections for officers of Congress. But if they refused to do so, then "the Democrats being in the minority and being unable to control either house by themselves, can better afford to support Progressive Republican candidates for Speaker and President pro tempore of the Senate than to compel a union of Progressive Republicans and reactionary Republicans." [114]

When Congress convened on December 3, the Senate, with La Follette out ill, organized promptly, but in the House of Representatives the division within the Republican ranks erupted into an open schism. Seventeen Republican insurgents refused to support Frederick H. Gillett, their party's nominee for Speaker, and voted instead for Representative Henry Allen Cooper of Wisconsin. With the Democrats voting in a solid bloc for their own leader, Finis Garrett, the House remained deadlocked throughout the day's four ballots. Needing 208 votes, Gillett never received more than 198, and on the third ballot he actually received one vote less than his Democratic counterpart. The next day saw four more fruitless ballots with Garrett leading Gillett three times and tying him once. On the last two ballots the Democratic leader came within ten votes of election. Yet the Democrats made no overtures to the insurgents who continued to vote for Representative Cooper. Garrett insisted that this was strictly a Republican affair. "We will stay here four days or forty days," he informed a correspondent, "we don't care." [115] The regular Republican leadership, however, did not seem to take Garrett's statement at face value; the longer the deadlock dragged

114. *New York Times,* December 4, 1923.
115. Ibid. December 4, 5, 1923. Of the seventeen Republican insurgents, nine came from Wisconsin, six from Minnesota, one from North Dakota, and one — Fiorello La Guardia — from New York.

on, they realized, the greater the possibilities of a coalition.
That evening they held out the olive branch to the insurgents
by promising them better committee assignments and an opportunity to liberalize the House rules. The following day the
seventeen progressives fell into line and Gillett was elected
Speaker.[116]

The conditions allowing for a Democratic-progressive Republican organization of the House of Representatives, which
Bryan had foreseen months earlier, had indeed been present,
but his own party had cautiously failed to take advantage of
them. "I don't know when I have been more disappointed in
anything than this," Representative Ayres wrote him:

> . . . We have thrown away the greatest opportunity we have
> ever had and in all probability ever will have, especially dur-
> ing this Congress, to get the progressive Republicans into
> the Democratic party, not only here in Congress but in the
> election this coming fall. I am not only disappointed but am
> disgusted and disheartened.[117]

In a similar frame of mind, Huddleston informed Bryan: "I
think we should recognize that the minority control in the
House is . . . further from harmony with the Republican
progressives than with the standpatters." [118] "American progressives seem unable either to dispense with party organizations or to control them in the interest of a liberal purpose,"
Herbert Croly had written in 1920, and his remark was to
ring truer still as the Twenties progressed.[119]

116. Ibid. December 5, 6, 1923. Mark Sullivan, writing in the *New
York Tribune*, attributed this outcome largely to Bryan: "It became
so apparent that Mr. Bryan's work might turn the Democrats from
neutrality to alliance with the La Follette insurgents that the regular
Republican leaders within a few hurried hours compromised with the
insurgents. . ." December 17, 1923, clipping in Bryan Papers.

117. Ayres to WJB, December 18, 1923, ibid.

118. Huddleston to WJB, December 24, 1923, ibid.

119. Croly, *New Republic*, XXIV (October 27, 1920), 211.

Except for a letter to Cordell Hull in which he noted how badly the House Democrats had reduced their power by refusing to join with the insurgent Republicans, Bryan kept his reactions to himself.[120] Though his interest in politics remained alive, Bryan in his last years showed an increasing tendency to advocate extra-political means towards the achievement of the reforms he cherished. The machinations of the leaders of the Democracy in 1923 could only have served to increase that tendency.

120. WJB to Hull, December 18, 1923, Bryan Papers.

VI: The Voice of God

*Have faith in mankind. . . . Mankind deserves to be trusted.
. . . If you speak to the multitude and they do not respond, do
not despise them, but rather examine what you have said. . . .
The heart of mankind is sound; the sense of justice is universal.
Trust it, appeal to it, do not violate it. . . . Link yourselves in
sympathy with your fellowmen; mingle with them; know them
and you will trust them and they will trust you. —* wjb

*"They love him because he first loved them" can be said of all
who have been loved by the people. —* wjb

(1)

THE USUALLY HOSTILE *Chicago Tribune* in 1920 called Bryan
"the expression of the normal American citizen," and commented: "He will be a leader so long as he lives, because he is
the expression of the normal habit, taste, moral thought, cus-
tom and habit of life." [1] Five years later, after Bryan's death,
another Chicago newspaper, the *Evening Post*, described him
as having been "a man of the people, understanding them
instinctively, thinking as they thought, and feeling as they
felt." [2] The relationship between Bryan and the populace
which these two Chicago journals so accurately divined was
easily the most salient feature of Bryan's life. If he had anything even remotely approaching a philosophy, it can be
found in his frequent discourses on the subject of popular
rule. To attempt to evaluate any period of Bryan's career, his
final years most especially, without taking this factor into

1. Reprinted in *The Commoner*, January 1920, p. 10.
2. Reprinted in *Literary Digest*, LXXVI (August 8, 1925), 6.

consideration is to risk a serious misunderstanding of the man and his actions.

When he died in 1880, Silas Bryan left his twenty-year-old son a legacy consisting primarily of a profound faith in the existence of an omnipotent and omniscient creator and an equally sincere belief in the innate wisdom and goodness of his fellow man. As Bryan himself expressed it: "My father taught me to believe in Democracy as well as in Christianity. He taught me to believe that every human being was entitled to the same rights that I claimed . . ." [3] Throughout his lifetime the younger Bryan was to cling to this heritage. In 1894, when his attempt to win election to the United States Senate ended in defeat, he sought to comfort his supporters and himself by paraphrasing the language of Job: "The people gave and the people have taken away, blessed be the name of the people." [4] Two years later, when his campaign for the Presidency had a similar outcome, he wired the victorious candidate: "We have submitted the issue to the American people and their will is law." [5] These words in themselves were not unusual, for untold numbers of unsuccessful politicians have uttered similar phrases. What was unusual was the complete sincerity with which they were spoken. Nothing, not even constant defeat, could alter Bryan's faith in the common man. After a lifetime of personal political disappointment and frustration, Bryan was still able to speak of the "virtuous masses" who are motivated by nothing "other than the noblest spirit." He was still able to maintain that "There is more virtue to be found in the people themselves than can be found anywhere else." He was still able to enjoin his listeners "to trust the people. Have faith in them because that faith is the foundation of free government." And, in the last year of

3. "Applied Christianity," *The Commoner*, May 1919, p. 12.
4. *Memoirs*, p. 240.
5. WJB to William McKinley, November 5, 1896, ibid. p. 270.

his life, he was still able to tell an audience: "the longer I live,
the more faith I have in the people. I am willing to trust the
people." [6]

We can, of course, put too much emphasis upon Bryan's
personal political defeats. Bryan himself became conditioned
to political reverses and evolved a rationale which enabled
him to accept them with a good will that elicited admiration
even from his heartiest detractors. "My place in history," he
was fond of saying in the years following his third and final
unsuccessful campaign for the Presidency, "will depend on
what I do for the people and not on what the people do for
me." [7] He was able to laugh at his own political misfortunes
and enjoyed telling the story of the mud-bespattered stranger
who approached him at the railroad station of a small town
where he was scheduled to speak. "Colonel Bryan," the man
said, "I have ridden fifty miles to hear you speak tonight. I
have always read every speech of yours that I could get hold
of. I would ride a hundred miles to hear you make a speech.
And, by gum, if I wasn't a Republican, I'd vote for you." [8]
He was impatient with those who continually told him how
sorry they were that he had never been rewarded with the
Presidency for what he had done. "I am no object of pity," he
said in a typical rejoinder in 1921.

> . . . I have advocated several things in my lifetime that
> would have cost my life two hundred years ago — not only ad-
> vocated them but I lived to see them written into the unrepeal-

6. Ibid. p. 203; WJB, *In His Image*, p. 243; *The Commoner*, February 1920, p. 7; WJB, "Labor and Good Government," *The Locomotive Engineers Journal*, July 1924, copy in Bryan Papers.

7. Wayne C. Williams, *William Jennings Bryan* (New York, 1936),
p. 502. During his last years Bryan frequently repeated this statement
or variations of it. See for example, *Nebraska State Journal*, March 20,
1920.

8. Daniel C. Roper, *Fifty Years of Public Life* (Durham, North
Carolina, 1941), pp. 87–8.

able law of the land,— despised and spit upon some years ago, and yet accepted now as not only not dangerous, but absolutely necessary to the country. There is nobody has as much reason to be grateful as I have. Nobody is happier than I. . . . I rejoice in the triumph of these things, and I thank God that I have lived to see so many of them triumphant.[9]

When, in the last five years of his lifetime, he finally sat down to begin his memoirs, he announced that he would entitle them "A Child of Fortune." [10]

The measure of a man's greatness, he convinced himself, was to be found in his service, not his rewards — in what he had given, not what he had received.[11] And on this score Bryan had few doubts. Standing on a railroad platform in a small rural community on a warm July day in 1916, Bryan surveyed the mass of farmers and their families pressing down upon him to shake his hand and exchange a few words of greeting; he observed some mothers raising their children into the air so they might get a glimpse of the great man, and he murmured to a nearby reporter: "These are the people who believe in me and stick by me." Then, after a moment's pause, he continued almost incredulously: "I often marvel how my causes have survived. Isn't it wonderful. I have had only the plain people to back me, and the rich interests have always been against me. I have never had money behind me." [12]

It was this survival, and eventual triumph, of so many of his causes that sustained and nourished Bryan's faith in the people. "As I look back over twenty-five years," he said in 1921, "I know that the people can be trusted for I have seen them weighed — and not found wanting." To the end of his days,

9. WJB, "Brother or Brute," address given at Shakespeare Lodge, Masonic Hall, New York, April 21, 1921, copy in Bryan Papers.

10. *San Francisco Call and Post*, June 18, 1924, clipping in ibid.

11. *The Commoner*, February 1919, p. 1.

12. This account is taken from an article in *Lyceum Magazine*, July 1916, reprinted in ibid. November 1916, pp. 28 ff.

Bryan refused to believe that the common man had been responsible for his political defeats. If the majority of the people had voted against him in his three bids for the Presidency, it was because they had been misled, misinformed, and coerced by the special interests. "For twenty years," he told a political rally in 1916, "there has not been an election but what a hundred men in Wall Street could, by the coercion they had in their power, change the results of the election." [13]

As a result of this sort of reasoning, constant political defeat, rather than warping and emasculating Bryan's principles, became a means of enforcing them; an additional bit of evidence that confirmed his original analysis of where the wrongs in American society were lodged and of how they could best be eradicated. And if he went about his mission with an even greater zeal, it was because of his unshakable faith that although Wall Street might keep him out of the White House it could not keep him out of history.

(2)

While Bryan's democratic faith stemmed in part from the teachings of his father and was kept alive by the triumph of so many of his causes, it was equally indebted, according to Bryan himself, to the writings of one man — Thomas Jefferson. To Bryan, Jefferson was "The greatest constructive statesman democracy has produced during all the world's history," and his speeches and writings were sprinkled more liberally with quotations from Jefferson than from any other single source save the Scriptures. [14] Throughout his career

13. Ibid. June 1916, p. 16.
14. *The Commoner*, April 1921, p. 1. Bryan drew up a list of ten books in "the order in which they have entered into my life, affected my thought and influenced my conduct." Directly after the Bible, which was, of course, first, he placed Jefferson's writings. The remaining eight entries, in the order listed, were: Tolstoy's Essays, Carnegie Simpson's *The Fact of Christ*, William Cullen Bryant's poetry, Plu-

Bryan pictured himself as the political heir of Thomas Jefferson, and in some respects this belief was justified. Both men paid homage to the principles of democracy, majority rule, the rights of man, self government, and both sang of America's mission and destiny. Yet, though many of their ideas were similar, the *way* in which they were held was often so different as to break the ostensible chain of compatibility. It is not necessary to review all of these differences, but one or two must be examined if the basis of Bryan's thought is to be understood.

Bryan could echo Jefferson's justification of "absolute acquiescence in the decisions of the majority" as "the vital principle of republics, from which there is no appeal but to force," while ignoring his warning that "though the will of the majority is in all cases to prevail, that will to be rightful must be reasonable . . ." [15] This was a distinction which Bryan was too often unable to perceive. This failure stemmed from still another difference in degree between Bryan and his political mentor. While Jefferson believed that the voice of the people was *generally* not *invariably* just, Bryan asserted that the voice of the people must be recognized "if not as the voice of God, at least as Bancroft defines it, as the best expression of the divine will to be found upon the earth." [16] And if the will of the majority was indeed "the best expression of the divine will to be found upon the earth," who would be so presumptuous as to assert that it could ever be anything but rightful and reasonable? Thus it was that two years before his death he continued to maintain that "No concession can be made to the minority in this country without a surrender of

tarch's *Lives*, Shakespeare, Demosthenes' "Oration on the Crown," Homer's *Iliad* and *Odyssey*, and the novels of Charles Dickens. Bryan Papers.

15. Paul L. Ford, ed., *The Works of Thomas Jefferson* (New York, 1904–1905), IX, 195, 198.

16. *Memoirs*, p. 320.

the fundamental principle of popular government. The people have a right to have what they want. . ." And so too was he able to define democracy as simply "the right of the people to rule — the right of the people to have what they want in government. That is all there is to democracy." [17] In this respect there is an element of validity in Edgar Lee Masters's assertion that to Bryan "The desideratum was not liberty but popular rule." [18]

William Allen White has written that ". . . Bryan was fooled by the ballot box. . . . Bryan never realized what nonsense and confusion can come out of the ballot box . . ." [19] Indeed, how could he when he interpreted the voice of the box as the voice of God? The people were supreme, and anything that stood in their way was blocking not merely the popular will but the divine will. It was this interpretation of majority rule that was partially or wholly responsible for many of the less fortunate aspects of Bryan's career: his opposition to civil service reform, which to his mind removed the government worker from the authority of the party and thus of the people; [20] his failure to defend the civil liberties of the Southern Negro and his silence throughout the entire anti-red hysteria that followed World War I; his conception of elected officials as mere automatons whose sole function was to echo the thoughts and desires of their constituents without ever thinking or speaking for themselves — a conception which resulted in one of Bryan's most dubious proposals, that "candidates for offices in which they can influence public policies should be compelled to file a statement of their position on issues before the public. . . . Statements on public

17. WJB, "Prohibition," *The Outlook*, CXXXIII (February 7, 1923), 263; "Applied Christianity," *The Commoner*, May 1919, p. 11.
18. Edgar Lee Masters, "The Christian Statesman," *The American Mercury*, III (December 1924), 391.
19. William Allen White, *Masks in a Pageant*, p. x.
20. See *The Commoner*, April 1917, p. 4.

policy should be regarded as a contract between the candidate and his constituents, and violations should be defined as an embezzlement of power and punished with imprisonment"; [21] and finally, the battles for fundamentalism and scientific obscurantism which marred his last years.

Still it was this same interpretation that led Bryan to struggle for so many economic and political reforms of lasting value. In the final years of his life Bryan championed the doctrine of majority rule with a vehemence. He continued to press for the extension of the initiative and referendum "in every municipality, in every state, and in the nation." He attacked the Senate rules concerning cloture as "the last bulwark of plutocracy" and advocated a rule permitting a majority to close debate. He actively supported the Borah Amendment requiring the assent of seven judges rather than a mere majority before the Supreme Court could declare a law unconstitutional. And he advocated the adoption of a series of amendments designed to render the amending process itself more responsive to the will of the majority, to permit a majority of the Senate to ratify treaties, and to require a national referendum before the nation could enter a war. [22]

The concept of majority rule was the source of both the most noble and least worthy aspects of Bryan's career simply because he accepted it more absolutely than analytically, because his idea of the popular ruler was too often that of a man who follows rather than leads. In his memoirs Bryan attributed the great impact of his "Cross of Gold" speech to the fact that it had "put into words the sentiments of a majority of the delegates to the Convention." He had met with success in the Convention of 1896, he asserted, because he had been

21. Bryan first made this proposal to the Nebraska Constitutional Convention in 1920. See *The Commoner*, February 1920, p. 11.

22. Ibid. May 1919, p. 8, March 1917, p. 2, March 1923, p. 2, April 1923, p. 6, February 1921, p. 1.

"the voice of a triumphant majority." [23] Similarly, in a speech delivered in the Twenties, Bryan explained that his long run of political leadership had materialized "not because of any personal reasons, but because I took the people's side and, because they knew me and regarded me as an exponent of their rights and interests, my influence continued." [24] He was convinced that "Moulders of public opinion do not create opinion; they simply put into effective form the opinion which exists." "My work," he wrote over and over again during these years, "is not the work of a pioneer." [25] When Louis Post criticized Bryan's reform program of 1921 on the ground that it dealt too exclusively with symptoms and ignored the real disease, the latter agreed, but defended his proposals as being the only practical ones. Reformers, he explained, ought

> to go as fast and as far as public sentiment will permit, leaving to the future the questions that are not now ripe for settlement. This is not the position of the pioneer but my environment has made it seem wise for me (not necessarily for others) to fight with the army for the things that can now be secured instead of being a scout.[26]

It was this side of Bryan that Jonathan Daniels had in mind when he observed: "Indeed, men . . . in small towns and some cities, too, across the West and South were not so much Bryan men as they had made Bryan their man and the voice of their determination." [27] This was still as true in 1925 when Bryan strode through the streets of Dayton, Tennessee, denouncing the doctrines of Darwin, as it had been in 1896 when a much younger Bryan stood on a platform in Chicago

23. *Memoirs*, p. 114.
24. *The Commoner*, June 1921, p. 10.
25. WJB to _____ (undated letter), WJB to S. C. Singleton, December 23, 1921, Bryan Papers.
26. WJB to Post, February 28, 1921, Post Papers.
27. Jonathan Daniels, *The End of Innocence*, p. 43.

denouncing the doctrines of Mammon. If the cause which he was espousing had become less worthy in the intervening years, the principles and faith from which it stemmed changed little, if at all.

(3)

Although Bryan constantly invoked the name and image of Jefferson, he would have been far more at home in the age of Andrew Jackson than in that of Jefferson. Bryan, of course, was no more a pure Jacksonian than a pure Jeffersonian, but in his antipathy toward civil service, his distrust of the expert, his reliance upon the average citizen to run the government, his notions about political parties, and the way in which he held many of his ideas about democracy, he was closer to the former than to the latter. Professor John William Ward has noted that the three main concepts underlying the ideology of the age of Jackson were Nature, Providence, and Will.[28] Insofar as he can be said to have had an ideology, Bryan adhered to all three concepts in much the way the Americans of the early nineteenth century did.

To the end of his days, Bryan believed that the heartland of the nation was rural America. The farmer, he told an audience in 1921, "is the basis of industry and the foundation of progress. Food and clothing are the first necessities and the farmer furnishes both." [29] Far more crucial than the farmer's material importance was his spiritual superiority. "The general average of morality is higher in the country than it is in the city," he wrote in 1917. There were three reasons for this:

1. The man in the country is in daily contact with nature and witnesses the miracle which every plant as well as every

28. John William Ward, *Andrew Jackson: Symbol for an Age* (New York, 1955), Chapter I and *passim*.
29. "To Southern Farmers," *The Commoner*, October 1921, p. 3.

animal exhibits. . . . It is not at all difficult for him to believe in God, for he constantly beholds the evidences of the intelligence, the omnipotence and the love of the creator. . . . It would be strange if the farmer did not breathe in with the free air of his domain a sense of responsibility to God, as well as a sense of dependence upon Him.

2. The fact that the farmer draws his wealth from the breast of Mother Earth, rather than from his fellow men, tends to strengthen his moral principles. The farmer adds to the wealth of the nation without subtracting from the wealth of any individual. He is neither a parasite nor a pilferer. . . .

3. . . . His hours of labor and his need of rest combine to shield him from the dissipations that find cover in urban darkness; he is out of the reach of those who, profiting by sin and vice, lay snares and set traps for the young men of the cities.[30]

Bryan celebrated Nature because under its influence man could develop naturally those instincts with which God endowed all men. In one of his most popular religious books he wrote: "I fear the plutocracy of wealth; I respect the aristocracy of learning; but I thank God for the democracy of the heart." [31] Wisdom was in the reach of all men, he believed, for it was not solely a product of the intellect but of the spirit as well. "I want to talk to your hearts," he told a Masonic lodge in 1921. "I found out a long while ago that talking to men's heads don't count. It is a poor head that can't find a reason for doing what the heart wants to do. You must talk to the hearts of men . . . for in human progress it is the heart that leads the way." [32]

This aspect of Bryan's thought as well as his reliance upon the second of Professor Ward's trinity of concepts — Providence or God — will be developed fully in the next chapter.

30. "Prohibition and the Farmer," ibid. September 1917, p. 8.
31. WJB, *In His Image*, p. 186.
32. Address at Shakespeare Lodge, Masonic Hall, New York, April 21, 1921, copy in Bryan Papers.

But though Bryan believed that "God keeps watch above His own; those who trust Him cannot fail. . . . He will lead us if we put our trust in Him," [33] he, no less than his nineteenth century forebears, believed in the importance of will. God demanded faith but He also required works; He gave man the opportunities, but man had to make the most of them, and if he failed he had no one to blame but himself. Bryan had progressed a number of steps beyond the Jacksonians in his thinking about the relations between the state and the economy, yet much of his effort was still directed toward preventing selfish cliques from blocking economic opportunity for the majority. Once the state had opened the road upward, it was up to each man to climb it for himself. "There is no reason why any boy should fail in life, you least of all," he wrote his grandson. "The way to Success is plain and easy if you will but follow it." He assured his grandson that if only he would be honest and industrious, eschew gambling, drinking, and swearing, and believe in God, he could not help but succeed.[34]

In spite of his understanding of the unequal economic relationships of his own age and his support of such combinations as labor unions and farm blocs, Bryan still could employ the conventions of the past and frequently spoke as if man made himself. "I do not agree with those who think that the fortunate child is in the home of the well-to-do," he wrote shortly before his death. "A child raised in a home where necessity is a spur to industry and to economy has a better chance in life than the child reared in an environment that saps energy and permits idleness." [35] The twentieth century made more than a small impact upon Bryan as his economic and political plat-

33. WJB, *Famous Figures of the Old Testament*, p. 24.
34. WJB to John Baird Bryan, April 13, 1917, February 27, 1919, Bryan Papers.
35. WJB to Mrs. R. L. Goss, April 15, 1925, ibid.

forms make clear. Still he continued to straddle two worlds with one foot firmly planted in the early nineteenth century.

(4)

In an interview with John Reed in 1916, Bryan revealed that in art and culture, as well as in politics and government, he was willing, even eager, to be guided by the tastes of the common man. He made it abundantly clear that he could not really appreciate beauty for its own sake. He continually spoke of art and music in terms of their "influence" and "message." His favorite painting, he told Reed, was the "Madonna and Child." When Reed asked: "Which one? Raphael's?" Bryan responded: "It doesn't make any difference which one. Raphael's is very good, but I prefer Bodenhausen's. The 'Madonna' is great because it deals with the tenderest human relationship." When Reed asked him if he cared for symphonic music, he replied in the negative and referred the correspondent to one of George Bancroft's essays in which that historian wrote: "The People are the final judges of music as of other things." In answering a whole series of questions, Bryan revealed that his favorite poems were those of Bryant and one entitled "Amen" whose author escaped him. His favorite musical compositions were three hymns and such popular pieces as "Silver Threads Among the Gold," and "La Paloma." His favorite play was "Ben Hur."

What is important here is not so much the fact of Bryan's cultural poverty as the cause of it. It resulted primarily neither from a lack of intelligence nor a lack of interest but from Bryan's conception of art itself. To Bryan the function of all culture was didactic and inspirational. The value of a painting or a poem or a piece of music was in direct proportion to its resemblance to a sermon. Speaking in the third person, Bryan told Reed that his interest in a picture is not because some famous painter painted it, but because of the idea it represents. And so with poetry. He defines poetry as the clothing of a beautiful idea in beautiful words. You might say: "He likes music." But as with pictures and poetry, it is music that embodies a sentiment. The tune is only interesting to him because it presents words impressively.[36]

"He cared little for art or music," Grace Bryan Hargreaves has written of her father,

> . . . The old melodies of his childhood days that his mother sang to him, hymns that "praised his Creator" he found pleasure in listening to, but other music he seldom enjoyed. . . . The only artistic expression besides the art of his oratory that he cared for was architecture. The home was a human need . . .[37]

In every aspect of human endeavor, then, Bryan cheerfully and complacently paid homage to the people. It was in this respect that he differed most fundamentally from Jefferson. Bryan did not have to identify with those whom he represented, he was one of them. He did not have to adopt their aspirations and hopes and fears, they were his inherently and he accepted them almost uncritically. He was more articulate than the masses and thus more outspoken; he was more ambitious and thus more bold; he was more educated and thus more self-assured; but he was never able to shed certain of their characteristics: the parochialism, the fears, the mistrust of what he could not understand, and the certainty, born perhaps more of resignation than egotism, that what he and they were represented the highest and the noblest.

36. Reed, *Collier's*, LVII (May 20, 1916), 45 ff.
37. Grace Bryan Hargreaves MSS., Bryan Papers.

(5)

Simply because this affection for his followers was actual and not theoretical, and also because of his own evangelical sense of mission, Bryan not only enjoyed but needed to go among those citizens of the rural West and South whom he always thought of as "the people." He needed to speak to them, mingle with them, listen to them. "He loved the freedom of the platform speaker; the ever changing scenes and crowds, for he loved people," his daughter has written. "Meeting them in all the little towns and hamlets as well as in the great cities, he could better understand their needs; he could better mirror the spirit of democracy which he so ardently expressed." [38] William Phillips, who served under Bryan in the State Department, has recalled that Bryan would return from his Chautauqua lectures "refreshed and stimulated from his contact with the masses. He loved crowds . . ." [39] "Upon the Chautauqua platform Mr. Bryan was always perfectly at home," his wife once noted.

> When Mr. Bryan stood in the Chautauqua tent at night under the electric lights and the starlight, with practically every adult and most of the children from miles around within sound of his voice, he could forget the hardships and weariness of travel. His voice would grow deep and solemn, for he knew he was speaking to the heart of America. [40]

Though he wrote a great deal, Bryan's medium was always the spoken word. He not only needed to speak "to the heart of America," he had to do so personally. In 1924 he estimated that since 1894 he had averaged about two hundred lectures a year for a total of some five thousand lectures and had

38. Ibid.
39. Phillips, *Ventures in Diplomacy*, p. 63.
40. *Memoirs*, pp. 286-7.

traveled the equivalent of once around the world each year.[41] At no time in his adult life was Bryan content for very long away from the lecture platform and the people.

During his final years his determination to continue the patterns of the past involved him in a conflict of loyalties. Throughout his career Bryan's wife had been his alter ego; she was his confidant, his secretary, his traveling companion. "The flame of love that the first sight of you kindled in my youthful heart glows on undiminished," he wrote her on their thirty-first anniversary. "You have been my only real companion for more than three decades — the sharer of every secret and the partner of every purpose. If I have found favor in the sight of God I pray that He may show it by allowing you to be my comfort while I live . . ." [42] Bryan's prayer was to be answered, though not completely. In the years following his resignation, Mary Bryan developed a severe case of arthritis which became progressively worse. It brought her long periods of intense pain and left her a semi-invalid. The tenderness and affection that had always characterized their relationship continued until the end. "I love you more than I did 32 years ago," Mrs. Bryan wrote her husband in 1916, ". . . and that is saying something too." [43] She continued to travel with him when she was up to it, and as always she followed his career with a devoted and at times critical interest. "About your speeches," she wrote him in 1920. "*Do not be too serious.* The tendency is, as we get older, to cut out the lighter parts. *People do love to laugh.* So give them some of your wit and sarcasm, even if you don't make every argument possible. *Be bright*, do you hear?" [44] She constantly worried about his health, especially the diabetic condition which he

41. WJB to Mark Sullivan, March 11, 1924, Bryan Papers.
42. October 1, 1915, ibid.
43. October 1, 1916, ibid.
44. September 17, 1920, ibid.

had developed in 1914, and her letters were filled with such admonitions as "eternal vigilance is the price of good health," *"don't catch cold," "be careful."* [45]

Yet her illness imposed an isolation on Mary Bryan which she found increasingly irksome. Her three children were all married and far away, and her husband was home for only brief periods. She seems to have made a desperate effort to find ways of filling up her day, and those few letters to her husband which have survived are filled with detailed accounts of her activities. "Wouldn't I be spending my time to advantage if I used two or three hours each day all summer in sending out speeches?" she asked at one point. "That would give me employment and might lay a foundation for future work — what do you think? I shall be consumed with loneliness if I do not keep busy." [46] More and more she lamented her husband's constant absence and their lack of a real home. "Am the house guest of the Dietrichs," she wrote in 1916. "When I get in a home like this I get anxious for our own home. Won't it be nice to see our poor, scattered belongings collected and our books in place? I do hope God will spare us for a few more years — to enjoy our home when we get it." [47] A year later she was complaining: "I do wish you could be here one time when I am moving. It makes me heart sick to think of it." [48]

At first there was hope for Mrs. Bryan's complete recovery, but the hope died, and by 1924 out of desperation she was consulting a faith healer.[49] "Poor mother is so weak that I am worried about her," Bryan wrote his daughter Grace in 1921, and four years later he informed one of his supporters:

45. For example see Mary B. Bryan to WJB, March 12, 1916, October 1, 1916, ibid.
46. March 12, 1916, ibid.
47. October 1, 1916, ibid.
48. May 27, 1917, ibid.
49. *New York World*, April 28, 1924.

"My wife . . . is entirely helpless, unable to stand or walk or to dress or undress herself." [50] Though he never seems to have craved the amenities of home life as his wife did, Bryan was lonely without her. "I long to be with you," he wrote over and over, "O, 'had I the wings of a dove.' " [51] He provided her with the servants necessary to make her life comfortable and in 1919 changed his will so as to insure her all the medical attention she needed before any of his other heirs received anything. [52] Still he felt conscience-stricken over leaving her alone as much as he did. "Mrs. Bryan improving so slowly that I would not feel safe in fixing a date before I know I can fill it," he informed a prohibitionist ally in 1919. "My first duty is to her and all engagements will be made subject to her. . . . I want a clear understanding that she comes first all the time . . . she is more than money and greater than any cause." [53]

Bryan was to make this resolve again and again, but he never lived up to it fully. During the Twenties he did spend long periods in the winters with Mrs. Bryan at their Miami home, and in 1923 he even attempted to spend the entire winter season from November to April with her, but it was a losing battle. During that one six-month period alone he made four extended trips North to champion his various causes and spent three weeks touring Florida on behalf of the state university. [54] Even when he was at home his time was not his own — or his wife's. "The public," Mrs. Bryan noted in a statement which came close to being a complaint, "were like the poor — we always had them with us . . ." [55] Between

50. WJB to Grace Bryan Hargreaves, October 17, 1921, WJB to Mrs. R. L. Goss, April 15, 1925, Bryan Papers.
51. March 3, 1916, January 20, 1918, February 24, 1919, ibid.
52. WJB to Mary B. Bryan, January 12, 1919, ibid.
53. WJB to Howard H. Russell, March 1, 1919, ibid.
54. WJB to J. Frank Norris, May 1, 1923, ibid.
55. *Memoirs*, p. 435.

his trips, speeches, and visitors, Bryan had little time for anything else. He was constantly behind in his correspondence, he tried for four years to write his memoirs but they were less than half finished when he died, and he had almost no time for contemplation or study. "I do not have the time to read the printed books relating to subjects that I am discussing. I have to run through them picking up a thought here and there." ". . . how large a portion of my time is given to others," he mused in 1923, "and how little I have for my own affairs." [56]

In his later years as in his earlier ones, Bryan's public life was virtually his entire life. The people were his family, the platform his study, crusading his relaxation.

(6)

While Bryan's dreams of progress and reform were being dealt some hard blows during the postwar era, and complications were developing in his previously untroubled personal life, his financial position was improving to a point which would have staggered the imagination of the struggling young politician who twenty-five years earlier had journeyed to the Democratic National Convention in Chicago with little more than his driving ambition, a magnificent voice, and an unwavering faith in his own destiny. In 1920 this same politician, now neither young nor struggling, valued his estate between $250,000 and $300,000. Five years later, after his death, he left an estate estimated to be worth $1,111,948.50.[57]

The five-year period between 1920 and 1925, then, was easily the most lucrative one of Bryan's career. In the past Bryan's earnings had been derived almost exclusively from his writings and his lectures. During the last five years of his life

56. WJB to James F. Johnson, January 9, 1922, WJB to John W. Hill, January 3, 1924, WJB to ———, November 25, 1923, Bryan Papers.

57. *The Commoner*, March 1920, p. 3; *New York Times*, October 25, 1927.

his income from these two sources increased. In 1920, for instance, the Central Press Association paid him $12,000 for covering the national political conventions, and in 1923 alone his syndicated Bible Talks brought him in over $21,000.[58] To these means of earning a living Bryan added two new sources during the Twenties. In 1921 he joined the law firm of Douglas, O'Bear and Douglas, which specialized in representing the interests of a number of Latin American nations in the United States. Bryan's activities seem to have been confined to arguing in behalf of the firm's clients before State Department officials.[59]

Far more lucrative than his new legal career, which never occupied much of his time, was Bryan's almost accidental ventures in real estate. In 1912, on the advice of doctors, Bryan took his ailing wife to Miami for the winter. Pleased with the mild climate they continued to make this journey during the following years, and Bryan, with the aid of his cousin, Governor Jennings of Florida, purchased some land on the outskirts of Miami, where he built his winter home "Villa Serena." At approximately the same time he built a summer home in Asheville, North Carolina, and, during the years which we have already reviewed, he divided most of his leisure time between the two locales. He continued to maintain his legal residence in Lincoln, however, although his visits there became more and more infrequent. He did manage to tour Nebraska at least once a year, usually in October, and in every important elec-

58. V. V. McNitt to WJB, July 27, 1920, Guy T. Viskniskki to WJB, March 1, 1924, Bryan Papers.

59. *New York Times*, May 26, 1921; Douglas, O'Bear and Douglas to WJB, April 1, 1921, WJB to Charles A. Douglas, April 20, 1921, Bryan Papers. Following the elections of 1922, Bryan and his wife traveled through Mexico and a number of Central American countries on a trip that appears to have been connected with his new affiliation. For details of this journey see *New York Times*, November 14, 1922; and material in the National Archives, Foreign Affairs Branch, Washington, D.C.

tion save that of 1918 he journeyed to Lincoln to vote. In 1917 he assured the citizens of Nebraska that "I want to be known in the future as I have been for more than a quarter of a century, as Mr. Bryan of Nebraska." [60]

Bryan's frequent trips to Florida exposed him to the virus of land speculation that had recently begun to sweep the southern tip of the state, and he did not prove immune. His greatest single financial killing, however, was due more to chance than to his own efforts. Between 1909 and 1924 property values in Miami increased 1,000 per cent, and less than a decade after Bryan built his home he was able to sell it for a profit of somewhere between $200,000 to $300,000. At the time of his death, his real estate holdings in Miami, Los Angles, and Lincoln, Nebraska, totaled more than $600,000.[61] In addition to investing in Miami's future, Bryan also loaned it his verbal support. In return for $250 a lecture, Bryan sang of Miami's climate, told of his "increasing faith" in its future, and hailed it as the "Magic City." [62]

Bryan never actually sold Florida real estate, as he has been accused of doing, but it is true that for the first time he used his oratorical abilities for something other than a public cause. Why he did so is not clear. The money was unquestionably an inducement, but Bryan had withstood many financially attractive offers in the past, and during these same years he engaged in a number of acts of financial generosity, such as donating his $50,000 home in Lincoln to the Methodist church.[63]

60. "Florida East Coast," undated fragment in Bryan Papers; *Nebraska State Journal*, October 6, 1917, reprinted in *The Commoner*, October 1917, p. 4; ibid. June 1920, p. 11.

61. Edward Dean Sullivan, *The Fabulous Wilson Mizner* (New York, 1935), p. 306; *New York Times*, August 11, 1925, October 25, 1927; *New York Post*, June 5, 1925.

62. For typical lectures on this subject see *The Commoner*, December 1920, p. 15, and "Bryan's Opinion of Miami," address delivered at Rotary Club, November 16, 1923, in Bryan Papers.

63. WJB to Mrs. W. A. Sunday, February 10, 1923, ibid.

His sheer need for activity while he was keeping his wife company in Miami and the fact that he was really very much attached to the "wonders" of his new state may also have played a role. Whatever the reasons, it is clear that Bryan was defensive about his activities and the fact that they were making him a wealthy man. In the last year of his life several newspapers publicized his financial ventures and scornfully contrasted his professed role as the Great Commoner with his new status as a millionaire. Bryan, who generally took newspaper criticism in his stride, was unable to do so in this case. In a widely publicized letter to a Florida editor, Bryan denied that he was a millionaire, claiming that at most he was worth $500,000. He stressed his annual donations of 10 per cent of his income to charity and his continued advocacy of the rights of those "who, though just as deserving as I am, are still in the clutches of those who prey upon society." [64] "If there is any sin in buying a home and have [sic] it rise in value because of the growth of the city, then I have sinned," he wrote another correspondent. "The exaggerated reports of my prosperity," he complained to a supporter, "has [sic] brought more distress than has ever come to me before except from sickness in my family." [65]

By 1921, Bryan's desire to maintain his legal residence in Nebraska was becoming increasingly impractical, since it prevented him from taking an active part in Florida's local politics and necessitated a long and costly journey each time he

64. WJB to E. D. Lambright, April 20, 1925, ibid. It is entirely possible that Bryan actually did not realize that he was a millionaire since shortly after his death his estate was estimated at $860,000 and a year later an appraisal filed in a Miami court valued it at only $688,-303.74. It was not until more than two years after he died that his estate was finally declared to be worth more than $1,000,000. See *New York Times*, August 9, 1925, March 6, 1926, October 26, 1927.

65. WJB to George W. Moore, May 13, 1925, WJB to Mrs. Eva F. Park, May 11, 1925, Bryan Papers.

wished to vote. On the thirty-first of May, 1921, Bryan made the inevitable announcement. He had decided, he told a group of reporters, to make Miami his legal as well as his actual home. He went on to say that his decision had been made reluctantly, for he owed Nebraska more than he could ever repay and was becoming a citizen of Florida only in order to share in determining its position on national questions. "This will require no change in my attitude on public questions," he continued, "because the South has been a loyal supporter of every reform in which I have been interested. . . . I shall find myself as much at home in Florida as in Nebraska." [66]

The South, indeed, went out of its way to make the Nebraskan feel at home. "Yes, welcome, thrice welcome, Mr. Bryan to our sunny southland," wrote the *Montgomery Journal* in a typical editorial. "A brave and chivalric people . . . all join in this welcome to the great Commoner, the first citizen of the world." [67] In Florida, where the leading citizens labored to add the names of distinguished personages to their state's roster with the avidity of an entomologist hunting down a rare butterfly, Bryan's announcement was met with widespread rejoicing. It was not long before the more perceptive realized that while "Mr. Bryan of Florida" had a nice ring to it, "Senator Bryan of Florida" sounded infinitely better and would bring the state far more free publicity. A large percentage of the state's citizenry, surmised the *Miami Herald*, "would consider it an honor for Florida to be represented in the Senate by a man of the international reputation of Mr. Bryan." [68] The *Jacksonville Observer*, after hailing Bryan as "one of the greatest men in the world," and predicting that "he would probably carry every county in Florida,"

66. *The Commoner*, June 1921, p. 1.
67. *Montgomery Journal*, undated clipping in Bryan Papers.
68. Reprinted in *The Commoner*, February 1922, p. 11.

stated candidly: "Bryan as a senator from Florida would place Florida on the map as no other state has ever enjoyed . . . he would directly be worth millions to it in advertising." [69] Other newspapers picked up the cry, and Bryan soon found himself deluged with petitions from every part of the state asking him to file as a candidate in the Democratic Senatorial primary to be held in the fall of 1922.[70] "It seems your stock for the Senate is going up all the time," his cousin May Jennings informed him. "It will not do to let any grass grow under our feet if you are going to run. I wish you would let me know right away so we can commence." [71]

The idea of ending his days in the Senate was not repugnant to Bryan, who had first dreamed of sitting in that body as a boy of twelve. Yet he consistently refused to campaign actively for the office. He would seriously consider running should the nomination be offered to him, "but I have no thought of entering into a contest for the office. . . . No friend will expect me at my period of life, when my political record is known to all, to solicit support . . ." [72] Bryan, at the age of sixty-two, with a wide range of activities to keep him busy, a desire to write his autobiography, an ailing wife to look after, and a serious case of diabetes, had more than a few doubts about the wisdom of further burdening himself with the cares of public office. But the most potent deterrent appears to have been his fear of defeat. "I have never been defeated for a nomination in my party — in fact, never had to make a fight for a nomination," he explained to a newspaperman. "If, in a Democratic state, and after my experience in public life, I was defeated for a nomination, my enemies

69. *Jacksonville Observer*, undated clipping in Bryan Papers.
70. *The Commoner*, May 1922, p. 2.
71. May M. Jennings to WJB, December 15, 1921, Bryan Papers.
72. *The Commoner*, February 1922, p. 4.

throughout the country would make effective use of it, and it might, by discrediting me, impair my usefulness as a private in the ranks." [73]

In the days that followed, the clamor for Bryan to run continued to be heard but it was not universal. Park Trammell, the incumbent, declared that he would defend his Senate seat and denounced Bryan as a "rank outsider." [74] Nevertheless, Bryan's chances still appeared to be excellent, but he refused to budge from his original position. "I cannot at my age turn . . . to personal politics," he declared in April, ". . . I shall not be a candidate." "I have had a very mixed feeling in regard to this contest," he confided to a friend. "I dreaded the thought of it and am greatly relieved to be out of it." [75]

It was to be some time before Bryan regretted this decision and attempted to rectify it. For the time being the Fates saw fit to allow him ample freedom and leisure to engage in the rising battle for a strict interpretation of the Scriptures, and he made full use of the opportunity.

73. WJB to J. Fred Essary, February 15, 1922, Bryan Papers.
74. *New York World*, February 5, 1922.
75. WJB to Frank Harris, April 13, 1922, Bryan Papers; *The Commoner*, May 1922, p. 2.

VII: Brother or Brute?

There are only two attitudes that man can assume in relation to his fellow man; . . . he is either restrained by the consciousness of the ties of kinship, and feels toward him as a brother ought to feel toward a brother, or he hunts for prey with the savage loathing of a beast. . . . I believe that the fundamental question that the people of the world have got to ask and answer is whether man is to be a brother or a brute . . . I believe that what the world needs today is to get back to a real belief in a real God. . . . Civilization is built upon it. And anything that weakens that belief in God endangers humanity and civilization. — WJB

(1)

WHILE DELIVERING several speeches in Norfolk, Nebraska, in 1920, Bryan stayed at the home of a local newspaper corre spondent. After Bryan's departure, the reporter, who admitted to having voted the Republican ticket in the past, wrote:

There is an indefinable something about the man that draws you to him. He is clean. He is fine. His very presence exalts you, edifies, inspires you to better things. To be with him is to see with him, to feel with him, to be just glad you are able to do whatever little you may do for him.

. . . Somehow, the little home seems more of a sanctuary, a sacred place because of his having been there; somehow there is a peace about him that calms, that blesses. Somehow he gives one the feeling that must have been that of Mary Magdalene when He appeared before her at the tomb.[1]

1. *Norfolk Press*, reprinted in *The Commoner*, May 1920, p. 14.

One might be tempted to dismiss this expression as the fervid outpouring of an incurable sentimentalist, if it were not so typical. Throughout his career Bryan was referred to as a "Saul come to lead the Israelites to Battle," as a "Moses come to lead the people from the Wilderness," as a "St. John," an "Elijah," a "second Saint Paul," even as a latter-day Christ. When in 1918, during Bryan's apparent political eclipse, a Minnesota newspaper asked facetiously: "By the way what has become of one William Jennings Bryan of whom we used to hear occasionally in times gone by . . . where is Bryan?" a neighboring journal angrily answered: "Where is Bryan? Bryan is here, there, everywhere. . . . 'Where is Bryan?' As well might one ask, where is the saviour of the world?" [2] "I stood by W. J. Bryan, sometimes far into the night," Dan Bride has written, "as I watched that earnest look in his face, it was as though I were looking into the face of our Heavenly Father in heaven." [3]

Such expressions were prompted by the fact that Bryan was never a politician pure and simple. Rather, he was, as one student has called him: "The great political evangelist of his day . . . the prophet and priest of millions." [4] Bryan not only acted like a prophet, it is probable that he felt like one. Throughout his career there is evidence that he frequently

2. *Red Wing Eagle, Fairmont Sentinel*, editorials reprinted in ibid. May 1918, p. 12.

3. Dan Bride, "Comment on the Colonel House Correspondence," manuscript in Bryan Papers. After Bryan's death, Bride comforted Mrs. Bryan with the thought that her husband had "now risen to a height in the minds and hearts of the Christian world equal to none since the time of the Saviour." Dan Bride to Mary B. Bryan, July 17, 1925, ibid.

4. Charles E. Merriam, *Four American Party Leaders* (New York, 1926), pp. 82–3. For a fuller exposition of this theme see Richard Hofstadter, *The American Political Tradition* (New York: Vintage Edition, 1954), Chapter VIII, "William Jennings Bryan: The Democrat as Revivalist."

expected and perhaps even desired martyrdom for the cause. Again and again he asked the people to judge his actions and destroy him if he proved unworthy. In 1910 he told his fellow Democrats in Nebraska that if he had fallen below the standards of statesmanship "I shall not ask you to deal leniently with me. . . . If I have not foreseen coming evils and told you of them, spare me not; if I have advocated that which is not good for this state, let me feel your wrath. . . . If you find that I have done anything that is not for the benefit of the Democratic party, I ask no mercy at your hands." [5] Almost immediately after resigning from the State Department he issued a message "To The American People" in which he invited them to judge the wisdom of his actions and stated: "If your verdict is against me, I ask no mercy." [6] These statements were not merely dramatic or rhetorical. "Mary," he told his wife more than once, "if my death is necessary to further this cause, I am ready to go." [7]

Bryan's charisma stemmed in large part from the deeply religious quality which pervaded almost all of his speeches, writings, and actions. It was this quality that led so many Americans to see in Bryan not just a politician but a kindred soul; that enabled them to write him countless letters in which they expressed not merely their political wishes but their everyday hopes and fears and dreams; that prompted them to refer to their desire to see him elected President as "the greatest desire" of their lives, and to refer to him as "the greatest all around man in the world," who had "done more for mankind than any other being except our Saviour." [8] It was this quality that caused a Kentucky lawyer to write haltingly: "Your

5. WJB, *A Defense of County Option* (1910), p. 3.
6. *The Commoner*, June 1915, p. 3.
7. *Memoirs*, p. 297.
8. For numerous examples of such letters see the correspondence columns of *The Commoner* and the correspondence in the Bryan Papers.

humble friend, the writer . . . for more than twenty years, has loved you; although . . . you have weightier matters in mind, may he beg you to read this love-letter." [9] Theodore Roosevelt, although in a vastly different manner, recognized this quality when in a discussion with Joel Chandler Harris he said of Bryan: "By George, he would make the greatest Baptist preacher on earth." [10]

(2)

To be a Baptist preacher, indeed, had been Bryan's earliest ambition; one which burned brightly within him until he witnessed his first immersion at the age of six. Due to what Bryan later described as a youthful fear of water, this experience not only altered Bryan's desire, it led him away from the church of his father and into the Presbyterian fold at the age of fourteen. But while Bryan may have lost the ambition to be a preacher he never lost the qualifications. Bryan's father, a stern, somewhat forbidding individual who raised his eyes to heaven three times a day to pray for salvation, and his mother, a quiet, unassuming woman whose simple devotion embodied all of the Christian virtues, lost no opportunity to impress upon their son the importance of dedicating his life to the service of God and of accepting the Bible not only as God's infallible word but as the fountain of all wisdom. Every day without fail his father would call him from whatever he might be doing, and together they would read passages from the Scriptures until they were committed to memory.[11]

The word of God, as presented to the young Bryan, was not something to be evaluated or reasoned through, but to be

9. Aubrey Moorman to WJB, *The Commoner*, April 1921, p. 10. Bryan's followers frequently used the word "love" to sum up their feelings for him. See, for example, Allen R. Carter to WJB, December 29, 1916, E. J. Merriman to WJB, October 22, 1919, Bryan Papers.

10. *The Commoner*, July 1916, p. 9.

11. *Memoirs*, pp. 17, 18, 43-4.

accepted. So well did he learn this lesson that throughout the eight years he spent away from home at academy, college, and law school, he never seems to have seriously questioned the faith of his boyhood. Though in later years Bryan was to refer to the period spent at college as the "critical age," his own college career was singularly uncritical. If Bryan ever investigated ideas and doctrines that differed from the Christian faith, they left him so unimpressed and disturbed his beliefs so little that many years later he could say in utter sincerity: "In my life I cannot find anything of moral principle I have added to my character since I was twenty-one. If I have anything of moral principle, I feel that I owe it to a Christian environment, and a Christian father and mother." [12] Upon graduating from college, Bryan wrote his future wife: ". . . full of gratitude for the blessings of the past, I turned, with some trembling, to contemplate the unknown future . . . I would dread to be compelled to set forth upon this sea with nothing but the light of my reason to aid me. What a blessing it is that we have that guide, the Bible. The future looks bright." [13]

The future was always to look bright to William Jennings Bryan, for he invariably viewed it from the standpoint of the faith so carefully inculcated in him by his parents and so closely nurtured and guarded by himself: the faith in an omnipotent God; the faith in an afterworld; the faith that virtue would not go unrewarded nor evil unpunished, if not in this world then in the next; the faith that mankind, with all its multifarious imperfections, was essentially good, and, with God's guidance, was capable of approaching perfection and of creating upon this earth a richer and more rewarding life; and, above all, the faith that if one would know God's word, if, indeed, one would know all that was worth knowing and

12. Reed, *Collier's*, LVII (May 20, 1916), 46.
13. WJB to Mary Baird, March 19, 1881, *Memoirs*, p. 450.

all that man had to know, one need only turn to the Bible, "the only Book that is good always and everywhere." [14]

It is not surprising that during the last decade of his life Bryan could tell his followers: "The Bible has been more to me than any party platform." [15] Throughout his career Bryan had found in the Scriptures strength, guidance, and support. During those final trying days between Germany's announcement of a resumption of unlimited submarine warfare and America's declaration of war, when Bryan found himself the object of nation-wide opprobrium, he took comfort in the words of Christ: "Blessed are the peace-makers. Blessed are ye when men shall revile you, and persecute you, and say all manner of evil against you falsely, for my sake." [16] In the last few years of his life, his unwavering belief in an afterlife cushioned him against the blow which he knew soon must befall him. "Old age would be unbearable if it brought an end to so intimate a relationship," he wrote to a lifelong friend in 1923, "but we have the satisfaction of believing that death is only a narrow-starlit strip between the companionships of yesterday and the reunions of tomorrow." [17]

Because of Bryan's emphasis upon religious precepts and his dependence upon the Bible as a source of inspiration, a guide, and at times a rationale, it is impossible to draw any arbitrary line between his purely religious and his purely political endeavors. In a sense, the latter never actually existed, for all of Bryan's political works were inextricably bound up with, and based upon, his religious faith. Bryan's interest in politics was antedated only by his interest in religion, and religious works always constituted one of his main concerns. His political speeches themselves were studded with Biblical allusions and

14. *The Commoner*, December 1916, p. 3.
15. Ibid.
16. *The Commoner*, February 1917, p. 4.
17. WJB to A. R. Talbot, November 5, 1923, Bryan Papers.

references, and even at the height of his political glory he found the time to deliver religious lectures. In the most famous of these, "The Prince of Peace," which he first gave in 1904 and continued to deliver from Chautauqua platforms for many years thereafter, Bryan made no secret of his interest in religion:

> I am interested in the science of government, but I am more interested in religion than in government. I enjoy making a political speech . . . but I would rather speak on religion than on politics. I commenced speaking on the stump when I was only twenty, but I commenced speaking in the church six years earlier — and I shall be in the church even after I am out of politics.[18]

The reason for this preference Bryan explained by his conviction that "the most important things in life lie outside the realm of government and . . . more depends upon what the individual does for himself than upon what the government does or can do for him. Men can be miserable under the best government and they can be happy under the worst government." [19]

Bryan, of course, did not immediately act upon the implications embodied in these principles. Rather, he continued to devote his time and energy to the field of politics, but it was politics with a strong religious orientation. Not only did he attempt to improve the government under which men lived, but he strove to improve the men themselves. "Law," he wrote in 1920, "is but the crystallization of conscience; moral sentiment must be created before it can express itself in the form of a statute." Thus before a politician could be effective

18. WJB, *The Prince of Peace* (New York, 1909), p. 5. Daniel Roper once asked Bryan which of his speeches he considered to be the greatest. Bryan replied: "My greatest speech, and the one I wish to be remembered by longest is the 'Prince of Peace.'" Roper, *Fifty Years of Public Life*, p. 88.

19. WJB, *The Prince of Peace*, p. 6.

he must inculcate broad moral principles in his constituents, and in order to do this he must turn to religion, for "religion is the basis of morality." [20] The politician no less than the minister must appeal to the spiritual in man, for that "is the only force that can give him a moral nature and preserve it from decay." [21] The one point Bryan was endeavoring to make clear was that "The teachings of Christ apply to the structure and administration of government as well as to the life and conduct of the individual." [22] This is what he meant by the term "applied Christianity," and this basic doctrine formed the heart of all of his political crusades from the very beginning. Toward the close of his life, Bryan pointed this out unmistakably:

> Whether I speak on politics, on social questions, or on religion, I find the foundation of my speech in the philosophy of Him who spake as man never spake; who gave us a philosophy that fits into every human need and furnishes the solution for every problem that can vex a human heart or perplex the world.[23]

While it is true that Bryan gave voice to many of these principles only during the last five years of his life, it is wrong to assume that they did not play a strong role in the earlier phases of his career as well. Those who have asserted that Bryan's pervading interest in religion came only with his decline in the political arena have seriously misread his entire career prior to 1920, and have mistaken a change in emphasis for a change in principle.[24] Certainly, it cannot be denied that

20. "But Where are the Nine?" *The Commoner*, September 1920, pp. 8–9.

21. WJB, *In His Image*, p. 67.

22. "Applied Christianity," *The Commoner*, May 1919, p. 12.

23. "The Bible and its Enemies," ibid. June 1922, p. 11.

24. See, for instance, Werner, *Bryan*, p. 280; T. V. Smith, "Bases of Bryanism," *Scientific Monthly*, XVI (May 1923), 506; Louis M. Sears, "The Presidency in 1924 — William Jennings Bryan?" *Forum*, LXX (August 1923), 1814-15.

Bryan's interest in religious causes was greatly augmented during the postwar era, but it had its roots in the strong emphasis which he had always placed upon religious principles and ideals. When Bryan wrote an acquaintance in 1920: "I beg to say that Christian men MUST take an interest in politics. . . . The Christian must live his religion in politics and in business as well as at home," he was merely announcing a doctrine which had always guided his actions.[25]

(3)

While a great deal of emphasis has been placed upon Bryan's preoccupation with religious matters during the 1920's, little attention has been focused upon his attempts to induce institutionalized religion to enter more fully into the world of politics. During the postwar era, Bryan placed increasing reliance upon the social gospel or what he preferred to call "applied Christianity."

In 1919, a year of severe labor unrest, Bryan addressed an open letter "to the churches of the United States," in which he pointed out the growing antagonism between capital and labor, and asked: "Can the churches be indifferent . . . or fail to exert their great influence to bring about a reconciliation? . . . Unless this is to be a war of extermination. . . . Capital and Labor MUST BE BROUGHT TOGETHER. . . . Can you neglect this great opportunity — Aye, this great duty?" In an editorial written during 1919, Bryan accused the church of "having too little sympathy for those who toil" and implored it to "cast its influence on the side of labor by supporting the demand for a half holiday on Saturday." In his address "Applied Christianity," delivered during

25. WJB to Bryan N. Railsback, December 20, 1920, *The Commoner*, January 1921, p. 2. The religious nature of Bryan's earlier political career is discussed in Paul W. Glad, *The Trumpet Soundeth: William Jennings Bryan and His Democracy, 1896–1912* (Lincoln, Nebraska, 1960), pp. 27–30 and *passim*.

the same year, Bryan directed the attention of the church to the issue between private monopoly and government ownership and asked: "Can the Christian church ignore the issue or its ministers be asleep upon the subject?" The greatest task of the church, he advised, "is to protect the God-made man from the man-made giant." At the Presbyterian General Assembly of 1919, Bryan suggested that the churches ought to take the lead "in arousing public sentiment against the crime of the profiteer," and declared that "we should drive all the profiteers out of the Presbyterian Church so that when they go to the penitentiary, they will not go as Presbyterians." [26]

After the conventions of 1920, when it became increasingly clear to Bryan that neither one of the major political parties was willing to champion the progressive program he had outlined, he increased his efforts to use the churches of America as a means of propagating social and political reforms. In one of the Chautauqua lectures he delivered during the Presidential campaign of 1920, Bryan announced his profound disappointment in the platforms and candidates adopted by both parties but refused to become overly discouraged, for he had learned that, although it sometimes took years, the people invariably informed themselves of the real issues and cast their influence on the side of right. "In the meantime," he declared, "the churches should be at work and lead in the creation of a sentiment that will coerce the parties into action — for parties act not from inclination but under compulsion." Accordingly, he outlined a three-point progressive program for the churches to implement and asked: "Does the church realize that God has given into its keeping . . . not only A solution but the ONLY solution of all problems?" [27]

A year later Bryan informed a gathering of the Council of

26. *The Commoner*, May 1919, p. 12, August 1919, p. 5, October 1919, p. 2, September 1920, p. 8.
27. "But Where are the Nine?" ibid. pp. 8–9.

the Alliance of the Reformed Churches at Pittsburgh that "The church is the hope of the world. . . . Every problem that . . . affects human welfare, human society, and human progress, must receive the attention of the Christian Church." [28] Throughout the Twenties Bryan continued to criticize American churches for their apparent indifference toward such issues as profiteering, monopoly, industrial injustices, tax exploitation, and international anarchy, and urged them to bind their members more closely to them by forming organizations that would issue low-cost loans, and "care for the sick and bury the dead." [29]

During this period Bryan began to act vigorously upon the principles he had first enunciated in his "Prince of Peace" address nearly twenty years earlier. The basis of these principles was that politics was a much less important sphere of action than religion, for even the most virtuous government enacting the most progressive legislation was impotent if the people themselves were not imbued with the spirit of morality: ". . . there is a zone between that which can be legally required and that which is morally desirable," he wrote in 1922. "When the government has done all in its power . . . there will be inequalities in success, based upon inequalities in merit. There must, therefore, be a spiritual law to govern when the statute law, based upon economic principles, has reached its limit." [30] This much needed spiritual law was embodied in what Bryan called "the divine law of rewards," which he had first spoken of in an article written in 1916, and which he now elaborated upon:

I beg to call attention to what I regard as the real disease that afflicts the world. It is the overthrow of God's law of rewards. When God gave us the earth . . . His voice proclaimed

28. "World-Wide Prohibition," ibid. October 1921, p. 7.
29. See, for example, WJB, *In His Image*, pp. 144 ff.
30. Ibid. p. 226.

. . . "Go to work, and in proportion to your industry or intelligence so shall be your reward." This is God's law and it must prevail. . . . The government has no more important work than the establishment of God's law on earth and this can only be done by legislation . . . the church . . . must endeavor to teach its members to know and respect God's law so that they will not desire to collect from society beyond what they earn by service to society. If every American citizen would resolve . . . not to collect from society one dollar without conscientiously endeavoring to give to society a dollar's worth of service in return, injustice would be eliminated . . .[31]

Thus justice was to be effected by a combination of political and clerical endeavor. This is what Bryan meant when he wrote in 1922: "I was never more interested in politics . . . and never more interested in religion. There is no conflict between them." [32]

But even as religious principles were becoming more explicitly established as the very basis of Bryan's political and social credo, he began to feel that those principles, and thus his entire program, were being endangered by the twin forces of modernism and evolution.

(4)

The Twenties were bewildering, frustrating years for rural America. During the postwar era the South and West continued to be what they had been for so many years: sections in revolt. If the earlier reform movements were, as Richard Hofstadter has maintained, "an effort to realize familiar and traditional ideals under novel circumstances," [33] the goals of the

31. WJB, "Citizenship in a Republic," *School and Society*, IV (July 15, 1916), 88; "The Southern Farmer," *The Commoner*, October 1921, p. 4.
32. Ibid. June 1922, p. 2.
33. Richard Hofstadter, *The Age of Reform* (New York, 1955), p. 213.

new revolt were not substantially different. What had changed was the nature of the stimuli. The forces that had given rise to Populism and to the agrarian wing of the Progressive movement had been activated by an economic and political threat to the independence and integrity of the rural way of life in the 1890's and early 1900's. Although this stimulus was still present in the Twenties, as the existence of the Agricultural Bloc attests, the overshadowing threat was no longer economic but social and cultural. This "was the age of 'the revolt against the village,' the attack on the country mind . . ." [34] Mass society was impinging upon rural life in all areas. The census of 1920 revealed that for the first time in American history the majority of the population were living in urban centers. The Eighteenth Amendment, which had nationalized a rural code of conduct, was being flouted openly, as were traditional standards of morality in general. Science had emerged after World War I as the leading intellectual force in the country, and in the educational institutions of the South and West, as well as the North and East, there was an increasing tendency on the part of the young to inquire into all things and submit them to the test of reason. Everywhere, it seemed, the sanctions and prohibitions of religion were being weakened.[35] The Yankee-Protestant inhabitants of rural America felt increasingly isolated and envisioned themselves as beleaguered islands in an alien sea. Since the danger was no longer primarily economic and political, the responses it elicited took new and in many ways more futile forms.

The anxieties which the forces rampant in postwar America

34. Ibid. p. 285.
35. Excellent accounts of these changes may be found in Allen, *Only Yesterday*, and William E. Leuchtenburg, *The Perils of Prosperity, 1914–1932* (Chicago, 1958). For the response of the religious press to some of these changes see Sister Mary Patrice Thaman, *Manners and Morality of the 1920's, A Survey of the Religious Press* (New York, 1954).

produced throughout the West and South were manifest in the resurgence of the Ku Klux Klan and the growth of the fundamentalist controversy. Although these were distinct movements with their greatest strength in different sections of the country, they had common roots and shared a number of characteristics. Both movements warned stridently of a grave threat to America's heritage and destiny, praised education and feared intellectuals, placed greater faith in instinct than in reason, deified the common man, defended the Scriptures as established truth which needed no amplification, appealed to the rural and small-town American, were built upon the Yankee-Protestant ethos, and, above all, both movements were attempts to preserve a way of life which was being eroded rapidly by the "acids of modernity." [36]

This last factor was perhaps the most vital in explaining the rise of the Klan and fundamentalism at this particular juncture in American history. In the addresses and writings of the leaders of both movements, one senses a strong feeling of loss or impending loss: ". . . the Nordic American today is a stranger in large parts of the land his fathers gave him," lamented Hiram Wesley Evans, Imperial Wizard and Emperor of the Klan, and a fundamentalist. "Old-stock Americans," he insisted, had been betrayed by the liberalism in which they had placed their faith.

> It has undermined their constitution and their national customs and institutions, it has corrupted the morals of their children, it has vitiated their thought, it has degenerated and perverted their education, it has tried to destroy their God. They want

36. There are a number of studies of the Klan and fundamentalism. The most insightful and useful are: John Moffatt Mecklin, *The Ku Klux Klan: A Study of the American Mind* (New York, 1924); H. Richard Niebuhr, "Fundamentalism," *Encyclopedia of the Social Sciences* (New York, 1931), V, 526–7; Norman F. Furniss, *The Fundamentalist Controversy, 1918–1931* (New Haven, 1954).

no more of it. They are trying to get back to decency and common sense.

The Klan literally is once more the embattled American farmer and artisan . . . demanding . . . a return of power . . .[37]

In spite of the similarities between the Klan and the fundamentalist movement, Bryan had almost nothing to do with the former. Although Bryan refrained from openly repudiating the Klan — probably because too many of his old followers belonged to it — he had little sympathy for most of its program. The one exception was Bryan's attitude toward the Southern Negro, which, though he rarely made it public, was worthy of any Klan member. In 1922 Bryan was reported as feeling that the passage of the anti-lynching bill then before the House of Representatives would be a "grave mistake." The following year in a speech before the Southern Society in Washington, D.C., in an article in the *New York Times*, and in his personal correspondence, Bryan defended white supremacy as "a doctrine absolutely essential to the welfare of the south," and argued that "The black people in the south have the advantage of living under a government that the white people make for themselves. The laws apply to everyone and are better laws than the black man would make for himself." [38]

At no time, however, did Bryan share the Klan's extreme xenophobia or its militant anti-Jewish and anti-Catholic feelings. During these years Bryan served on the General Committee of the American Committee on the Rights of Religious

37. Hiram Wesley Evans, "The Klan's Fight for Americanism," *The North American Review*, CCXXIII (March-April-May, 1926), 39, 43, 49.
38. *Christian Science Monitor*, January 24, 1922, February 24, 1923; *New York Times*, March 18, 1923, Section VIII; WJB to Thomas Walsh, December 30, 1922, WJB to Kenneth B. Griffin, February 24, 1923, Bryan Papers.

Minorities, and he frequently spoke out in behalf of Catholics and Jews. In 1916 he lent warm support to Wilson's appointment of Louis Brandeis to the Supreme Court.[39] During the war he urged Secretary Baker to appoint Catholic and Jewish Chaplains.[40] In 1920 he denounced the Protocols of the Elders of Zion as a "libel" upon "one of the greatest races in history," and subsequently refused to support Henry Ford's Presidential aspirations because of his anti-Semitic sentiments.[41] He protested against the indiscriminate application of Sunday Blue Laws, maintaining that "those who worship any other day as a matter of conscience and religion should not be compelled to observe our Sabbath . . ."[42] Long a friend of the Catholic Church and a defender of its right to maintain its own schools, Bryan, in a speech before the Marquette Club in 1920, hailed it as "the greatest branch of the Christian Church."[43] Resisting the attempts of the Klan and of a number of fundamentalist leaders to make fundamentalism an exclusively Anglo-Saxon, white Protestant movement, Bryan made a number of attempts to enlist the aid of Catholics and Jews in the crusade to bar the teaching of evolution from the schools.[44]

It was, then, the second of these two movements — fundamentalism, with its literal belief in the infallibility of the Bible, the Virgin Birth and Deity of Christ, His Resurrection and

39. *The Commoner*, February 1916, p. 3.

40. WJB to Newton D. Baker, April 20, 1917, Bryan Papers.

41. *The Commoner*, December 1920, p. 2; *New York Times*, December 14, 1920. See below, p. 300.

42. WJB to C. S. Longacre, September 28, 1921, Bryan Papers.

43. *The Commoner*, August 1915, p. 4; *New York Times*, March 22, 1920.

44. WJB to P. H. Callahan, July 17, 1925, Bryan Papers; WJB, *Orthodox Christianity vs. Modernism* (New York, 1923), p. 6; WJB to editor, the *Talmud Magazine*, March 23, 1922, *The Commoner*, May 1922, p. 10.

substitutionary atonement for the sins of the world, and His second coming, and its program calling for the ouster of the modernists from the church and the teaching of evolution from the schools — that won Bryan's wholehearted sympathy and support. It would be a mistake to see fundamentalism as a product of America's lunatic fringe. Whatever one may think of the fundamentalists' faith and prescriptions, their plight was far from illusory. Something *was* wrong with religion in the Twenties: its absolute truths were being taken with a grain of salt; its prestige and appeal were declining; certainty was being replaced by uncertainty, faith by doubt, security by insecurity.[45]

Revivalism had by the Twenties "failed most miserably in its attempts to reenthrone in the minds of Americans the nineteenth-century small-town code of beliefs and behavior which was the basis of fundamentalism," and was on the wane.[46] Fundamentalists found that within their own churches and schools control was slowly passing into the hands of modernists. Throughout America, as church attendance declined, churches were adopting a more worldly vernacular and appeal and incorporating a host of secular activities.[47] More and more people were beginning to echo the plea of a New York Protestant minister for "the substitution of sociology for theology, of a program of social life for a system of theological dogma." [48] For two consecutive years the

45. Walter Lippmann has written a remarkably perceptive account of these changes in his *A Preface to Morals* (New York, 1929).

46. William G. McLoughlin, Jr., *Modern Revivalism, Charles Grandison Finney to Billy Graham* (New York, 1959), p. 445.

47. Herbert W. Schneider, *Religion in 20th Century America* (Cambridge, 1952), p. 12; Luther C. Fry, "Changes in Religious Organization," *Recent Social Trends in the United States* (New York, 1933), II, 1058.

48. John Haynes Holmes, *New Churches for Old* (New York, 1922), p. 155.

nation's best seller lists were headed by a work that spoke of Christ not as the son of God who was sent to earth to atone for men's sins, but as the most successful executive in history, "the founder of modern business." [49] Harry Emerson Fosdick, one of the nation's leading modernists during the Twenties, admitted in 1935 that modernists had

> watered down the thoughts of the Divine, and, may we be forgiven for this, left souls standing like the Ancient Athenians, before an altar to an unknown God. . . . We have been all things to all men . . . We have adapted and adjusted and accommodated and conceded . . . we have at times gotten so low down that we talked as though the highest compliment that could be paid to Almighty God was that a few scientists believed in him.[50]

Fundamentalism, for all of its aggressiveness, was basically a movement on the run; a movement that was attempting to defend not only its theology but a complete social and cultural framework which rested squarely upon the foundation of that theology.

(5)

Although the fundamentalist controversy ostensibly broke "like a summer thunderstorm" after World War I, it was, as the most recent historian of the movement has noted, merely a continuance of the conflict first precipitated within theological circles after the appearance of Darwin's theory in the last half of the nineteenth century.[51] But whereas the earlier conflict was largely confined to the educated clergy, the increasing dissemination of the evolutionary theory, as well as the appearance of other forces already alluded to, greatly en-

49. See Bruce Barton, *The Man Nobody Knows* (Indianapolis, 1924), Introduction and pp. 104. 106, 143, 156, 159.
50. Quoted in Schneider, *Religion in 20th Century America*, pp. 107–8.
51. Furniss, *The Fundamental Controversy*, pp. 10 ff.

larged the scope of the later controversy and made its effects far more devastating.

During the years that preceded the struggle of the Twenties, Bryan gave frequent indications that he was by no means oblivious to the teachings of Darwin, and his recognition of the dangers implicit in those teachings actually antedated that of most of the later leaders of the fundamentalist crusade. As early as 1904, in his widely delivered "Prince of Peace" address, Bryan stated that he was not yet convinced that man was a lineal descendant of the lower animals, since he knew of no argument that could be used to prove that man was an improved monkey that could not also be used to substantiate the far more plausible theory that the monkey was a degenerate man. "It is true," he admitted, "that man in some physical characteristics resembles the beast, but . . . The mind is greater than the body and the soul is greater than the mind, and I object to having man's pedigree traced on one-third of him only — and that the lowest third." He objected to Darwin's theory, too, because he believed that it would cause man to lose "the consciousness of God's presence" in his daily life and because it depicted man as having reached his present state "by the operation of the law of hate — the merciless law by which the strong crowd out and kill off the weak," while he preferred to believe that "love rather than hatred is the law of development." But while he personally could not accept the Darwinian theory he stated emphatically: "I do not mean to find fault with you if you want to accept the theory. . . . I shall not quarrel with you about it." [52]

Bryan, of course, had seen Darwin's teachings used to bolster political and economic conservatism in the form of Social Darwinism, and he objected to them on this ground as well. In 1905, after reading Darwin's *Descent of Man*, Bryan told the sociologist E. A. Ross that "such a conception of man's

52. WJB, *The Prince of Peace*, pp. 13, 15, 16.

origin would weaken the cause of democracy and strengthen class pride and the power of wealth." [53] In spite of these religious and political reservations, Bryan made little mention of evolution until the outbreak of the World War. The spectacle of Christians slaughtering rather than loving their neighbors, and Christian nations piously engaging in an international blood bath, affected Bryan profoundly. But at no time did he allow himself to see in the war a bankruptcy of Christian ideals. Rather, the war began because some force had led man to stray from the teachings of Christ. In 1916 he made his first tentative attempt to explain this when he told an audience that Darwin's theory of the survival of the fittest had produced such philosophers as Nietzsche who maintained that the world belongs to the strong. "We must be careful how we apply this doctrine of the strongest," he warned, "for I have found . . . that the evolutionary theory has been consciously or unconsciously absorbed in a way which has a tendency to paralyze the conscience. Whether men know it or not, they have permitted it to become antagonistic to the principles of Christianity which make the strongest the servants of humanity, not its oppressors." [54]

Bryan's convictions about the cause of the world's plight were solidified during the years following America's entry into the war. Two books which he read in this period — the first an American war relief worker's account of his conversations with German officers, which showed the positive influence of Darwin upon their thinking, and the second an elaborate attempt to trace a straight line from Darwin through Nietzsche to the growth of German nationalism, militarism, and materialism [55] — convinced Bryan that his original analy-

53. Edward Alsworth Ross, *Seventy Years of It* (New York, 1936), p. 88.
54. *The Commoner*, March 1916, p. 18.
55. Vernon Kellogg, *Headquarters Nights* (Boston, 1917); Benjamin Kidd, *The Science of Power* (New York, 1918).

sis had been correct. Darwinism, he assured a meeting of the
World Brotherhood Congress in 1920, "is the most paralyzing
influence with which civilization has had to contend during
the last century." Nietzsche, in promulgating a philosophy
"that condemned democracy . . . denounced Christianity . . . denied the existence of God, overturned all standards of morality, eulogized war . . . praised hatred . . .
and endeavored to substitute the worship of the superman for
the worship of Jehovah," had merely carried the Darwinian
theory to its natural conclusions.[56]

Although Bryan's attacks on evolution were slowly growing in intensity, they remained relatively infrequent during
this period and were not to emerge in their final militant form
until he fused them with his growing conviction that something was wrong with religion in America. Bryan gave voice
to this feeling in 1916 when he called for a reinstitution of the
revival meeting on a mass scale and the emergence of more
preachers like Billy Sunday. "There is nothing which the
world so much needs today," he wrote, "as the baptism of the
Holy Spirit, a great revival of spiritual religion." [57] Bryan
took the first step toward linking evolution and religion when
he charged that in many schools throughout the country "irreligion is being taught under the guise of philosophy." He
returned to this theme during his address to the Constitutional
Convention of Nebraska in 1920. "The greatest menace to the
public school system today," he asserted, "is . . . its Godlessness. We have allowed the moral influences to be crowded
out. . . . We do not ask public school teachers to teach religion in the schools, and teachers, paid by taxation, should not
be permitted to attack our Bible in the schools. . . . We can-

56. *The Commoner*, November 1920, p. 11.
57. Ibid. March 1916, p. 18, December 1916, p. 1. For a fuller exposition of this theme, see WJB, *The First Commandment* (New York,
1917).

not afford to have the faith of our children undermined." [58]
All that remained for Bryan was to discover that the theory
of evolution was in and of itself an attack on the Bible and the
faith.

Toward the end of 1920 the World's Christian Fundamentals Association invited Bryan to head a "Layman's Movement" against modernism and evolution, but he was not yet
prepared to accept such an offer.[59] It was not until the spring
of 1921 that Bryan's former toleration of the evolutionary
theory, which had been wearing thin gradually, finally came
to an end, and he issued a series of attacks upon the doctrine
which instantly placed him in the forefront of the fundamentalist forces.

The most important of these was Bryan's lecture, "The
Menace of Darwinism," which was the lengthiest, the most
effective, and, as its title indicates, the most hostile attack
Bryan had yet delivered. Though it makes for rather tedious
reading today, "The Menace of Darwinism" won Bryan immediate acclaim in fundamentalist circles throughout the nation and, reprinted in pamphlet form, it was widely distributed and eagerly read. Written before the controversy over
evolution had reached the peak of bitterness it soon attained
and before Bryan himself had won the enmity of innumerable
educators, journalists, and liberal clergymen, this address is
restrained and free from the vituperativeness of many of his
later writings on the subject.

All morality and virtue, Bryan said in opening, was dependent upon religion and a belief in God, and therefore anything
that weakens belief in God weakens man and makes him impotent to do good. He then proceeded to show in detail that
the evolutionary theory achieved just this end not by denying
the existence of God but, more subtly and more dangerously,

58. *The Commoner*, August 1916, p. 5, February 1920, p. 11.
59. Furniss, *The Fundamentalist Controversy*, p. 50.

by "putting the creative act so far away that reverence for the creator is likely to be lost"; by promulgating the idea of the survival of the fittest which was the very antithesis of all Christian values; by putting man on a brute basis and ignoring all spiritual values; by directly contradicting the word of the Scriptures thus reducing them to "a scrap of paper"; by destroying man's belief in immortality, thereby robbing him of his major stimulus to righteous living and his only source of hope. Evolution was not only dangerous but unscientific. Darwin had adduced not one substantial fact which proved his theory; his entire case was founded upon nothing but conclusions drawn from similarities; his books were studded with such words as "apparently" and "probably," and the phrase "we may well suppose" alone occurred more than eight hundred times in his two principal works. "The eminent scientist," Bryan concluded triumphantly, "is guessing. . . . Darwinism is not science at all; it is a string of guesses strung together. There is more science in the twenty-fourth verse of the first chapter of Genesis . . . than in all that Darwin wrote." Indeed, to accept Darwin's theory of natural selection "requires more faith in CHANCE than a Christian is required to have in God." The evolutionists were asking man to make too great a sacrifice — to give up a faith that offered him a beneficent and omnipotent father, a reason for existence, and a philosophy of life for a scientific theory that had to be revised every few years. It was on this note that Bryan closed with his characteristically stirring peroration:

> Man was made in the Father's image; he enters upon the stage, the climax of Jehovah's plan. He is . . . greater than any other created thing — but a little lower than the angels. God made him for a purpose, placed before him infinite possibilities. . . . God beckons man upward and the Bible points the way. . . . Looking heaven-ward man can find inspiration in his lineage. . . . Mighty problems demand his attention; a

world's destiny is to be determined by him. What time has he
to waste in hunting for "missing links" or in searching for
resemblances between his forefathers and the ape? In His
Image — in this sign we conquer. We are not the progeny of
the brute. . . . We are the handiwork of the Almighty. . . .[60]

(6)

Bryan's decision to enter the ranks of the anti-evolutionists
was accompanied by numerous charges of personal ambition,
demagoguery, opportunism, apostasy, and even senility. It is
true that Bryan's advanced age, his political decline, his many
disappointments and frustrations all undoubtedly figured in his
decision, yet by themselves they offer no satisfactory explanation of his final years. Bryan's entry into the fundamentalist
crusade was neither sudden nor surprising. Bryan was raised
with the common fundamentalist belief that all religious verities rested upon an infallible Bible, and if this were shaken
nothing else could stand. He had objected to the theory of
evolution as early as 1904, and while his later objections were
more developed and specific they were substantially the same
as his earlier statements. What had changed was not Bryan's
conception of evolution but his toleration of it. By 1921 he
had become convinced that the evolutionary thesis was no
longer a potential danger but an immediate threat.

By the 1920's the extension of higher and secondary school
education to larger numbers of students and the growing popularity and availability of science courses, on both levels, provided a vastly increased audience for Darwin's theories.[61]
Bryan was made aware of this development both by his frequent visits to colleges and high schools throughout the country and by a book written in 1916 by James H. Leuba, a

60. "The Menace of Darwinism," *The Commoner*, April 1921, pp.
5–8.
61. Charles H. Judd, "Education," *Recent Social Trends in the
United States*, I, 331, 339.

professor of psychology at Bryn Mawr, which contained a statistical study of the adverse effects of college education upon belief in God and immortality.[62]

During the postwar era Bryan's attention was drawn to these effects in a more personal way. His wife tells us that "his soul arose in righteous indignation when he found from the many letters he received from parents all over the country that state schools were being used to undermine the religious faith of their children." [63] A Baptist preacher informed Bryan that at Columbia University a professor of geology made it a practice to begin his classes by telling his students to throw away all they had learned in Sunday school; a Methodist minister told him that a professor at the University of Wisconsin was teaching his students that the Bible was a collection of myths; a student at the University of Wisconsin complained to him of his professor of German who asserted that all thinking men were agnostics; he heard that in one of the classrooms at Bryn Mawr a vote was taken to determine the existence of God — and God lost, 43 to 23; a Congressman told him that when his daughter returned from Wellesley she remarked glibly: "Nobody believes in Bible stories now"; another Congressman and three ministers informed him that their sons, after studying evolution at divinity school, had lost their faith; in Southern Ohio he came across a Methodist preacher who taught his classes that Christ was a bastard; he received a letter from a resident of Iowa who claimed that

62. James H. Leuba, *The Belief in God and Immortality* (Boston, 1916). Chapters VII–VIII. Bryan made frequent use of Leuba's study which showed that while "young people enter college possessed of the beliefs still accepted . . . in the average home of the land. . . . It seems probable that on leaving college, from 40 to 45 percent. . . deny or doubt the fundamental dogmas of the Christian religion." Ibid. p. 280. Leuba also concluded that among academicians and scientists non-believers were preponderant. Ibid. Chapter IX.

63. *Memoirs*, p. 459.

three-quarters of the student body and nine-tenths of the faculty at the state university were free-thinkers.[64]

All this not only disturbed Bryan profoundly but presented him with an explanation of the postwar decline in progressivism and the unmistakable apathy of the people toward his own attempt to lead a new reform movement. The growing conservatism of both political parties had led Bryan to turn more and more to the church as an instrument of reform, but even here he had met with indifference. It became increasingly clear to Bryan that something had happened to the people — some devitalizing force was causing them to forsake their spirituality for crass materialism, their soberness for hedonism, their worship of Christ for worship of the dollar. To one who had always been so thoroughly committed to the conspiracy thesis, who had always attempted to personalize impersonal forces, it was neither uncharacteristic nor even illogical to point a finger toward the new scientific attitude to which the young were being subjected. Bryan had fought plutocracy and imperialism, war and liquor because they dehumanized man; because they were more worthy of the brute. Now he found in the quiet, unhurried atmosphere of the classroom a group of teachers promulgating the thesis that man after all *was* a brute! Now he could better understand the apathy and indifference of the younger generation. How could they be expected to see anything noble or fine or godly in the progeny of wild beasts? They were indifferent not because they did not care, but because the doctrines taught to them in their schools caused them to lose faith in man's ability ever to become anything other than he was. No longer could

64. Long, *Bryan the Great Commoner*, pp. 350–52; Werner, *Bryan*, p. 304; *The Commoner*, November 1921, p. 3; *New York Times*, July 10, 1921; George Murphy to WJB, May 6, 1921, WJB to E. W. Blakeman, October 4, 1921, WJB to Edward S. Worcester, October 7, 1921, WJB to the President, Wellesley College, July 16, 1925, Bryan Papers.

they believe in the ultimate triumph of righteousness or in a life after death where their virtue and patience would be rewarded.

In one of the addresses he delivered in the spring of 1921, Bryan painted a picture of a child reared in a pious home going to college and learning that man came from the beasts below, that his development was not part of God's plan, and that even his morality was man-made, "no God, no church, no conscience, — none of these things mentioned; just materialism."

> And the child goes out with its faith in God shaken, and its faith in the Bible shaken, and its faith in immortality shaken, and its faith in prayer shaken.
>
> Oh, are you surprised that men become brutish as they deal with each other?
>
> . . . That is the sentiment today. "There is no God; there is no future; we will do as we please." And doing as we please is bringing the world into dangerous ground.[65]

There was always a pragmatic note to Bryan's objection to Darwin's teachings. Bryan was arguing not only for the fact of God but for the need of God. "If one actually thinks that man dies as the brute dies, he will yield more easily to the temptation to do injustice to his neighbour when the circumstances are such as to promise security from detection," he warned as early as 1904.[66] "The world *does not need* a purely human Christ," he wrote in 1925. "It has had philosophers enough. If Christ is to save the world, He *must be* a supernatural Christ, the only begotten Son of God . . ."[67] Bryan was convinced that without a belief in God man could

65. WJB, "Brother or Brute," address delivered at Shakespeare Lodge, Masonic Hall, New York, April 21, 1921, copy in ibid.
66. WJB, *The Prince of Peace*, p. 37.
67. WJB to Mrs. Graham Patterson, January 31, 1925, Bryan Papers. Italics added.

have no courage to do the work of life. "How can one fight for a principle unless he believes in the triumph of right? How can he believe in the triumph of right if he does not believe that God stands back of the truth and that God is able to bring victory to His side?" [68] Darwinian evolution, by diminishing the power and presence of God, indefinitely prolonged the time needed for reforms and thus discouraged altruistic effort. Evolution led man back into the dim past to search for his heritage; Christianity spurred him forward into the future to work for his destiny.[69]

The service a man rendered to his fellow men, he was convinced, was determined not merely by his capacity but by his disposition as well. "All of our training is intended to increase our capacity but only religion can furnish the disposition. Nothing less than a sense of responsibility to God can give the coercive power necessary to insure the consecration of all our energy and time to that which is the highest and best." [70] A belief in evolution enabled man to accommodate to the world as it exists; a belief in the teachings of Christ — a surrender to the power of Christian love — made man a reformer: "Love makes money-grabbing contemptible; love makes class prejudices impossible; love makes selfish ambition a thing to be despised. . ." [71]

We have seen that Bryan continued to struggle for political, social, and economic reforms even after he entered the fundamentalist movement. It should be added that Bryan joined the anti-evolutionists not in order to retreat from politics but in order to combat a force which he held responsible for sapping American politics of its idealism and progressive spirit.

W. J. Cash has called the anti-evolution crusade "an au-

68. WJB, *In His Image*, pp. 8, 264.
69. "The Menace of Darwinism," *The Commoner*, April 1921, p. 8; *New York Times*, June 14, 1922.
70. WJB to Martha Hughes, February 7, 1923, Bryan Papers.
71. WJB, *In His Image*, p. 235.

thentic folk movement," and has written of it: "Having observed it at close range, I have no doubt at all that it had the active support and sympathy of the overwhelming majority of the Southern people. And not only among the masses." [72] Other observers have placed the strength of fundamentalists in the various churches of the South at as high as 99 per cent and never lower than 50 per cent.[73] These facts constituted still another crucial reason for Bryan's entry into the movement. From the very beginning Bryan was convinced that the preponderance of the Southern and Western populace were opposed to having their children subjected to evolutionary theories. Less than a month before he died, Bryan wrote to a friend: "In this controversy, I have a larger majority on my side than in any previous controversy, and I have more intolerant opponents than I have ever had in politics." [74]

This intolerance of which Bryan spoke made him even more determined to champion the fundamentalist cause. The bigotry and parochialism of rural America in the Twenties had its counterpart in an attitude which might be termed urban fundamentalism; an attitude that reached its apogee in the supercilious mockery of an H. L. Mencken. Bryan could not see rural America, and especially the South, derided with equanimity. It had not only warmly supported him in the past but was the one section of the country that remained most congenial to him. Bryan embraced the South so heartily in his final years not because he had changed but because to his mind it had not. Industry was being introduced, but agriculture was still its backbone. Its faith was still the fundamentalism of his father; its politics, still the Democracy of his past; its ethics, still those of the agrarian America he so warmly

72. W. J. Cash, *The Mind of the South* (Garden City, New York: Anchor Edition, 1954), p. 338.

73. Edwin Mims, *The Advancing South* (Garden City, New York, 1927), p. 338.

74. WJB to Charles S. Thomas, July 1, 1925, Bryan Papers.

loved. Its people were the simple, shirt-sleeved farmers and workers who read their Bible and attended church and Chautauqua regularly; people whom he could understand and who could understand him; people who could and did accept the basic, elemental truths which Bryan himself had accepted so long without question.

If there were a number of reasons for Bryan's entry into the fundamentalist crusade, the most important ones centered on his determination to preserve and strengthen the values and faith of that portion of the American people with whom he had always been most closely identified.

(7)

Bryan's entry into the fundamentalist crusade gave that movement what it had previously lacked: a spokesman with a national reputation, immense prestige, and a loyal following. Traversing the country several times in behalf of the movement, Bryan delivered innumerable speeches, penned scores of pamphlets and articles, and wrote four books which received wide circulation. In addition to all this, Bryan soon became a syndicated columnist. Starting in 1917 Bryan had held a regular Sunday Bible class in Miami which was attended by from two to six thousand people each week. In 1921, Guy Viskniskki of the Republic Syndicate wrote Bryan and suggested that his weekly talks be published in the nation's press. Beginning that same year with sixty-eight papers in every section of the country, Bryan's Sunday lectures were, by 1923, reprinted in one hundred ten newspapers with a combined reading public of twenty to twenty-five million people.[75]

Despite Bryan's considerable influence — an influence so great that more than one scholar has seen in Bryan's death one of the main causes of the decline of the fundamentalist move-

75. *Memoirs*, p. 452; *The Commoner*, November 1921, p. 3; Hartt, *World's Work*, XLVI (September 1923), 473.

ment after 1925 [76] — it would be a mistake to feel, as a contemporary observer did, that "Mr. Bryan *is* Fundamentalism. If we can understand him we can understand Fundamentalism." [77] On a number of points Bryan found himself in sharp disagreement with many of his most influential colleagues. Fundamentalists as a group attempted to meet the challenge of technological change and scientific skepticism by retreating from the world, convinced that the function of religion was to save individual souls not society at large. The belief of liberal churchmen that religion must be judged, in part, by its success or failure in making the world a more ideal place in which to live was attacked vigorously. "We are sent to preach Salvation, not Society," wrote one fundamentalist, "Evangelism, not Economics; Redemption, not Reform; . . . Pardon, not Progress, a New Birth, not a new Social Order; . . . the Gospel, not Democracy; Christ, not Civilization." [78] Persuaded that the social gospel had deluded men into emphasizing this world instead of the next and had opened the way for the threat which secularism posed to the churches, many fundamentalists reacted against liberalism wherever they found it, in politics as well as in theology.[79]

76. See Furniss, *The Fundamentalist Controversy*, p. 179; Carter, *The Decline and Revival of the Social Gospel*, p. 52.

77. Glenn Frank, "William Jennings Bryan: A Mind Divided Against Itself," *Century*, CVI (September 1923), 794.

78. Ralph Lord Roy, *Apostles of Discord* (Boston, 1953), p. 214.

79. Paul Carter in his unusually perceptive study of religion during this period has shown that there was no necessary correlation between theological and political conservatism; that, in fact, the social gospel was often preached most vigorously from conservative pulpits. It was, Carter feels, the fact that fundamentalism was so extremely past-oriented and came under such sharp criticism, that primarily explains its conservative tendency in all areas, though he also offers an economic explanation. See *The Decline and Revival of the Social Gospel*, pp. 12, 47–56. See also H. Richard Niebuhr, "Fundamentalism," *Encyclopedia of the Social Sciences*, V, 527; Schneider, *Religion in the 20th Century*, pp. 14–15.

Bryan never shared militant fundamentalism's political conservatism, its other-worldliness, or its pessimistic view of
man. "I present my appeal to the young to accept Christ and
to enter upon the life He prescribes, not because they may *die*
soon but because they may *live*," he wrote.[80] He continued
to see Christianity as both a body of infallible beliefs leading
to eternal salvation and a social movement leading to the political and economic reformation of society; he saw no conflict
between the two. His excoriation of liberals was always confined to the theological variety. When a cartoonist named
Brown portrayed Bryan abandoning his hunt for the Republican elephant to pursue the Darwinian monkey into the
jungle, Bryan wrote him a friendly letter defending the right
of cartoonists to exaggerate. "However," he added, "if you
would be entirely accurate you should represent me as using a
double-barreled shotgun, firing one barrel at the elephant as
he tries to enter the treasury and another at Darwinism — the
monkey — as he tries to enter the school room." [81] If Bryan's
position differed from that of most of his fundamentalist colleagues and baffled many of his fellow reformers, he saw it as
a completely natural one. "People often ask me why I can be
a progressive in politics and a fundamentalist in religion," he
told a journalist in 1925. "The answer is easy. Government is
man made and therefore imperfect. It can always be improved. But religion is not a man made affair. If Christ is the
word, how can anyone be a progressive in religion? I am
satisfied with the God we have, with the Bible and with
Christ." [82]

Bryan's attempt to straddle the worlds of religious conservatism and political liberalism may have been natural enough
throughout most of his career, but by the Twenties it had

80. WJB, *In His Image*, p. 136.
81. News clipping in Bryan Papers.
82. *Chicago Daily Tribune*, May 28, 1925, clipping in ibid.

become a difficult, almost self-defeating, position. The fundamentalism of Billy Sunday or the Reverends J. Frank Norris and John Roach Straton was more extreme and less appealing than Bryan's, but it was also more consistent. In asking the church to enter the political arena, to take greater interest in the solution of grave social and economic problems, to establish itself as an institution which would heal the body as well as the soul, and help man with this world as well as the next, Bryan was leading it away from traditional religion. He never understood that by urging the church to open its eyes to the world around it in one area he was, in effect, forcing it to take in the *whole* world. If religion was to be plastic enough to accommodate itself to the new social and economic movements of the age, it could not shelter itself for long against the new intellectual developments.

Bryan's political position was only slightly less paradoxical. In aligning himself with the fundamentalists he found himself fighting alongside such strange bedfellows as Billy Sunday, who damned the social gospel and all its advocates; the Reverend Dr. Brooks, who taught that "Man has no inalienable right except the right to be damned"; and the fundamentalist geologist, Professor George M. Price, who exclaimed: "When Christ himself was here, though surrounded by crying abuses, oppression, and tyranny, he attempted no civil reforms; nor has he left his Church any commission to purify the governments of the earth." [83] Bryan not only refrained from condemning these views, but, in his desperate search for arguments to prove the need of Christ and the fallacies of evolution, he occasionally voiced sentiments no less inimical to reform. "Is

83. For interesting accounts of Sunday and his attitudes toward reform see McLoughlin, *Modern Revivalism*, Chapter VIII, and Bernard A. Weisberger, *They Gathered at the River* (Boston, 1958), Chapter VIII. Brooks is quoted in Hartt, *World's Work*, XLVI (September 1923), 474; Price is quoted in Furniss, *The Fundamentalist Controversy*, p. 27.

man's natural tendency downward or upward?" he asked
in one of his Bible lessons. "Who, if he examines himself
and understands others can doubt that it is downward?" [84]
After reading Edwin E. Slosson's volume, *Creative Chemistry*, in 1923, he became convinced that he could use the
"exact science" of chemistry to refute the "doctrine" of evolution: ". . . there is not a single fact brought out by chemistry that supports an evolutionary hypothesis," he wrote the
author. ". . . If there is any force at all, it is, as you point
out, destructive rather than constructive. . . . *Disintegration
and not advance would seem to be the law in nature.*" [85]

These statements are merely an indication of the difficulty
of Bryan's position rather than a sign of any radical change in
his views. Bryan continued to espouse a socially liberal brand
of fundamentalism which, among that movement's leadership
at least, was a minority position.[86] What Bryan did have in
common with all the other fundamentalist leaders was an unshakable belief in the infallible word of the Bible and a determination to eliminate the teaching of evolution from the nation's public schools.

The thirty-seven anti-evolution bills that were introduced
into twenty state legislatures between 1921 and 1929 were
products of the American faith that legislative action can
bring into being pure morals, right thinking, and patriotic

84. *The Commoner*, December 1922, p. 8.
85. WJB to Edwin Slosson, February 27, 1923, Bryan Papers. Italics
added. See also WJB to Dr. R. R. Snowden, March 5, 1923, ibid.
86. It is, of course, difficult to determine the position of the mass of
fundamentalist followers. It is interesting to speculate, however, that
since Bryan's entry into the movement increased its popularity and his
death dealt it a blow from which it never recovered, and in view of
the fact that he was easily the most potent fundamentalist preacher in
the land (even the popular Billy Sunday was experiencing something
of a decline during the Twenties), his species of fundamentalism may
well have had more appeal among the people than that of his more
extremist colleagues.

action. They were drawn up by a generation that ratified the Eighteenth Amendment, legislated against vivisection, passed the Lusk laws to root out political heresy, and attempted to purge textbooks in all disciplines of anything even remotely smacking of dissent from the established order.[87] As early as 1917 the Kentucky Legislature heard demands that it take action against the teaching of evolution in the schools, and in 1921 a rider was attached to an appropriation bill in the South Carolina Legislature providing that no moneys appropriated for public education should go to any school which taught "the cult known as 'Darwinism.' "[88]

Bryan's interest in such legislation was aroused in the beginning of 1922 when he heard of the success of Dr. J. W. Porter of Kentucky in having the Baptist State Board of Missions pass an anti-Darwinism resolution. He immediately wrote Porter: "The movement will sweep the country, and we will drive Darwinism from our schools. . . . We have all the Elijahs on our side. Strength to your arms."[89] On January 19, he addressed a joint session of the Kentucky General Assembly at their invitation. After devoting the first half of his speech to an appeal for the adoption of state trade commissions, Bryan turned to the subject of the "teaching of irreligion in our public schools and universities," and pleaded for a law which would bar the teaching of Darwinism in any institution supported by state funds.[90] Several days later Representative George Ellis presented such a bill to the Kentucky

87. See Howard K. Beale, *Are American Teachers Free?* (New York, 1936), and Besse L. Pierce, *Public Opinion and the Teaching of History in the United States* (New York, 1926).

88. Furniss, *The Fundamentalist Controversy*, p. 81; Maynard Shipley, *The War on Modern Science* (New York, 1927), p. 115.

89. Alonzo W. Fortune, "The Kentucky Campaign Against the Teaching of Evolution," *Journal of Religion*, II (May 1922), 227.

90. *Lexington Herald*, January 19, 1922, reprinted in *The Commoner*, February 1922, p. 5.

House of Representatives, and Bryan spent the rest of the
month touring the state in its behalf. After a long campaign of
almost unprecedented bitterness, Ellis's bill was defeated by a
single vote.[91]

Although the Kentucky crusade ended unsuccessfully, it
aroused widespread interest, and Bryan soon found himself
the recipient of invitations to speak before the legislatures of
Tennessee, Arkansas, Georgia, Mississippi, Ohio, Wisconsin,
West Virginia, and Florida. Bryan's entire campaign for anti-
evolution legislation was based upon his lifelong belief that
the majority must rule in everything. He denied that the legislation he was recommending was a violation of the rights
guaranteed in the first ten amendments. "It is no infringement
on their [the scientists] freedom of conscience or freedom of
speech," he told the West Virginia lawmakers in 1923, "to
say that, while as individuals they are at liberty to think as
they please and to say what they like, they have no right to
demand pay for teaching that which the parents and the tax-
payers do not want taught. The hand that writes the pay check
rules the school." [92] "Christians," he wrote in one of his most
persuasive articles, "do not ask that the teachers in the public
schools, colleges and universities become exponents of orthodox Christianity . . . but Christians have a right to protest
against teaching that weakens faith in God, undermines belief
in the Bible and reduces Christ to the stature of a man." If the
majority of the people who believed in Christianity did not
demand that their views be taught at public expense, by what
right did the minority who believed in atheism, agnosticism,
and evolution demand this privilege? No one, he protested,
was trying to abrogate the inherent rights of anyone else. All
the fundamentalists wanted was that the rights of all in matters of conscience and religious belief be equally protected.

91. Ellis to WJB, March 13, 1922, Bryan Papers; *New York Times*,
February 2, 1922.
92. WJB, *Orthodox Christianity vs. Modernism*, p. 29.

"When Christians want to teach Christianity, they build their own schools and colleges and employ their own teachers . . . why should not those who worship brute ancestry build their own colleges and employ their own teachers for the training of their own children in the brute doctrine?" [93]

An important factor in determining Bryan's attitude toward the teaching of evolution was his conception of education itself. Always a staunch advocate of education, Bryan nevertheless considered it a means not an end; and a means that had to be controlled carefully. It was the soul and not the brain that primarily concerned Bryan. "A trained mind," he wrote, "can add largely to the usefulness of life when it is under the control of the spiritual in man, but it can wreck any human being, even civilization itself, if it is allowed to exercise authority." [94] This was so because the mind was no more than a mental machine: "The brain will plot a murder or plan a burglary as willingly as it will labor for the welfare of mankind. All, therefore, depends upon the *heart* behind the brain. . ." [95] There was no necessary conflict between the two; every human being, he believed, was capable of a good heart and a trained mind, "but if I were compelled to choose between the two, I would rather that one should have a good heart than a trained mind." [96] "The sin of this generation," he wrote in 1921, "is mind worship — a worship as destructive as any other form of idolatry." What this country needed was "not more brains but more heart — not more intellect but more conscience." [97]

Bryan insisted that he was neither anti-science nor anti-

93. "Darwinism in Public Schools," *The Commoner*, January 1923, p. 2.
94. WJB, *Famous Figures of the Old Testament* (New York, 1923), p. 195.
95. WJB to James R. Anthony, February 10, 1923, Bryan Papers.
96. "But Where are the Nine?" *The Commoner*, September 1920, p. 8.
97. Ibid. August 1921, p. 3, November 1922, p. 3.

intellectual. "There should be no conflict between the discoverers of REAL truths, because real truths do not conflict." [98] But he had seen the learned misuse their powers too often for him to ever completely trust them. He enjoyed quoting the following observation, which he attributed to Theodore Roosevelt: "There is scarcely a conspiracy against the national welfare that does not have the brains of Harvard behind it"; and Bryan himself told his Chautauqua audiences in 1920: "It would not take long to correct the abuses of which the people complain but for the fact that back of every abuse are the hired brains of scholars who turn against society and use for society's harm the very strength which society has bestowed upon them." [99] The science that was demanding absolute freedom in the classroom was "The same science that manufactured poisonous gases to suffocate soldiers . . ." [100] "Science has no morality," he told a Brooklyn audience, "science gives us weapons and means for escape but not the means for control." [101] And control could come only from a morality based upon belief in the infinite intelligence and power of God. "It is better to trust in the Rock of Ages than to know the ages of the rocks; it is better for one to know that he is close to the Heavenly Father than to know how far the stars in the heavens are apart." "Man," he urged his audiences to remember, "is infinitely more than science; science, as well as the Sabbath, was made for man." [102]

Whether evolution was right or wrong, then, was not Bryan's concern. Whether it would hurt the spirit and bruise the faith was, and since he felt it did both of these things it should not be taught. Bryan himself admitted this when he wrote:

98. "The Menace of Darwinism," ibid. April 1921, p. 5.
99. *New York Times*, June 1, 1922; "But Where are the Nine?" *The Commoner*, September 1920, p. 7.
100. WJB to Johnnie Baldwin, March 27, 1923, Bryan Papers.
101. *New York Times*, May 19, 1925.
102. "The Menace of Darwinism," *The Commoner*, April 1921, p. 5.

"The objection to evolution, however . . . is not, primarily, that it is not true. . . . The principal objection to evolution is that it is highly harmful to those who accept it. . ." [103]

(8)

Bryan did not confine his crusade to the political arena. If it was important to stop the dilution of religious beliefs in the schools, it was no less important to stop it in the pulpit. To Bryan the real danger was not atheism or agnosticism which were "open enemies" but the subversive element within the churches which was attempting to reconcile Christianity and evolution. Modernism, he wrote, "permits one to believe in a God, but puts the creative act so far away that reverence for the creator is likely to be lost." [104] "Give the modernist three words, 'allegorical,' 'poetical,' and 'symbolical,' and he can suck the meaning out of every vital doctrine of the Christian Church and every passage in the Bible to which he objects." [105] Theistic evolution was an anesthetic: "it deadens the pain while the Christian religion is being removed." [106] Ministers had no more right to preach a doctrine which the majority of their congregation did not subscribe to than teachers had to spread beliefs antithetical to the convictions of a majority of the parents. "The modernists, though conscious that they are in the minority in all the evangelical churches, are seeking to take charge of all the church organizations," he charged. ". . . They denounce as intolerance every effort made by the conservatives to enforce majority rule, and they are more intolerant towards orthodox Christians than any orthodox church has been toward them. They question the intelligence

103. WJB, *Seven Questions in Dispute*, p. 144.
104. "The Menace of Darwinism," *The Commoner*, April 1921, p. 5; WJB, *In His Image*, p. 40.
105. WJB, *Seven Questions in Dispute*, p. 106.
106. WJB, "The Fundamentals," *The Forum*, LXX (July 1923), 1678.

of any one who accepts the Bible as the inspired word of God and would, if they had power, exclude all believers from positions of influence in church and school." [107]

"A church divided against itself cannot stand any more than a house," he wrote a liberal Presbyterian minister in 1921, "and I recognize as clearly as you do that you and I have no right to belong to the same church. One of us is out of place and I am just as sure that you have mistaken your place as you are that I have." To end the division Bryan suggested that the majority within each church draw up a confession of faith. Those who could not subscribe to it would then be free to join a church whose doctrines were more akin to their own beliefs. But in no instance should a minister be allowed to substitute his own conscience for the conscience of his church.[108] In 1923 he decided that the time was ripe for the application of this solution to his own church. In March he wrote to a number of Presbyterian ministers and asked them to express their opinion as to the wisdom of his seeking election to the Moderatorship of the church at the forthcoming Presbyterian General Assembly. The response was almost completely favorable, though a few ministers warned him that his candidacy would precipitate a hard struggle.[109]

When the General Assembly convened in Indianapolis in the middle of May, Bryan had not yet announced his plans publicly. "This is not like a political campaign where a man announces his candidacy and then goes out to secure dele-

107. WJB, "The Menace of Modernism," *Miami Tribune*, February 17, 1925, clipping in Bryan Papers.

108. WJB to Paul Moore Strayer, December 19, 1921, ibid.

109. WJB to Henry Chapman Swearingen, March 22, 1923, ibid. See letters to Bryan from the following: John A. Marquis, March 28, 1923, William McKibben, April 3, 1923, Joseph Taylor Britan, March 30, 1923, Rudolph Caughey, April 4, 1923, Henry B. Master, April 2, 1923, H. L. Bowlby, April 9, 1923, ibid.

gates," he told reporters. "The position of Moderator is the highest in our church and a man should be called to it by the voice of the Assembly."[110] By his own account, Bryan did not definitely decide to let his name be presented until the night before the election, when his supporters convinced him of the contribution he could make as Moderator.[111] Bryan was one of four candidates when the voting began on May 17. Needing 439 votes for election, he led on the first two ballots, with 391 votes on the first and 421 on the second. By the close of the second ballot two of the candidates withdrew, and the candidate of the liberals, Dr. Charles F. Wishart, the president of Wooster College in Ohio, where evolution was taught as a fact, apparently picked up most of their support, for on the third ballot he defeated Bryan 451 to 427.[112]

If Bryan's opponents thought that this setback would chasten him, they failed to understand the Nebraskan. On the afternoon of May 20, his resolution requiring that all Presbyterian preachers, church officials, and teachers in Presbyterian colleges "should be total abstainers and should urge upon their respective congregations and students the signing of total abstinence pledges," passed unanimously. Tasting victory for the first time since the proceedings had begun, Bryan promised the delegates "that the business of this assembly is beginning — just beginning."[113]

Two days later Bryan almost disrupted the assembly entirely by introducing a resolution designed to cut off all financial support to any Presbyterian school "that teaches, or permits to be taught, as a proven fact either Darwinism or any

110. *New York Times*, May 17, 1923.
111. WJB, "Report on General Assembly," privately circulated memorandum in Bryan Papers.
112. "The Vote of the General Assembly for Moderator by Sections," in ibid.; *New York Times*, May 18, 1923.
113. WJB, "Report on General Assembly," Bryan Papers; *New York Times*, May 21, 1923.

other evolutionary hypothesis that links man in blood relationship with any other form of life." [114] The three-hour debate which ensued became so tumultuous at times that the Moderator was forced to make frequent pleas for decorum and remind the delegates that they were "a court of Jesus Christ." "There has not been a reform for twenty-five years that I did not support," Bryan told the delegates in his hour-long address, "and I am now engaged in the biggest reform of my life. I am trying to save the Christian church from those who are trying to destroy her faith." "We have preachers in this audience," he thundered, "who don't believe in the virgin birth . . . who don't believe in the resurrection of Christ's body . . . who don't believe in the miracles." "I recognize that many regard the introduction of this resolution as a disturber of harmony. . . . I answer the charge. . . . We who favor this resolution are not the troublers of Israel. We stand upon the time honored doctrines of the church. . . . We believe in God. . . . We believe in Jesus Christ." [115]

Once again Bryan's eloquence proved to be no guarantee of victory. On a rising vote the Assembly discarded Bryan's resolution in favor of a more moderate and less specific proposal. Though he was disappointed, Bryan was not finished yet. The next day he helped to induce the Assembly to reaffirm, for the first time in thirteen years, the five Articles of Faith basic to fundamentalist theology. When the committee investigating the pulpit utterances of Dr. Harry Emerson Fosdick recommended leaving the matter in the hands of the New York Presbytery, Bryan spoke in support of a minority proposal calling upon the General Assembly to condemn Fosdick's teachings and require him to conform to the doctrines of the

114. Copy of resolution in Bryan Papers.
115. "Mr. Bryan's Speech on the Darwin Resolution," ibid.; *New York Times*, May 23, 1923.

church. On a roll call, which Bryan insisted upon, the Assembly voted 439 to 359 to condemn Fosdick.[116]

Characteristically, Bryan attempted to assure himself that his failures at the General Assembly were in reality a triumph. "I think my defeat for Moderator was providential," he wrote his daughter Grace. "I did far more on the floor than I could have done in the chair. . . . I got through four resolutions besides helping to secure a statement of the Church position on five important doctrines. It was a great victory for orthodox Christianity — other churches will follow. It means a new awakening of the Church. It was much better than being Moderator." [117]

While Bryan was experiencing some difficulty in convincing the leaders of his church of the dangers of evolution, the leaders of his adopted state proved far more attentive. In February and March 1923, the Oklahoma Legislature had passed a textbook bill barring the use of all texts teaching the Darwinian theory.[118] Encouraged by this development Bryan urged members of the Florida Legislature to take action against evolution. Bryan reiterated two points to the Florida legislators which were characteristic of every address he gave on the subject: first, that the law contain no penalties: "We are not dealing with a criminal class and a mere declaration of the state's policy is sufficient"; second, that the law only prohibit the teaching of evolution as a fact — "a book which

116. Ibid. May 23, 24, 1923; WJB, "Report on General Assembly," Bryan Papers.
117. WJB to Grace Bryan Hargreaves, June 3, 1923, Grace Bryan Hargreaves MSS., Bryan Papers.
118. Furniss, *The Fundamentalist Controversy*, p. 83. In December 1922, a member of the Oklahoma Senate informed Bryan that he was going to introduce anti-evolution legislation and asked for suggestions. There is no record that Bryan complied with the request, but it is probable that he did. See G. W. Moothart to WJB, December 5, 1922, Bryan Papers.

merely contains it as an hypothesis can be considered as giving
information as to views held, which is very different from
teaching it as a fact." [119] On May 14, the Florida Legislature
adopted a joint resolution, drafted by Bryan, which made it
"improper and subversive" for any teacher in a state-sup-
ported school or college to teach "as true" any theory linking
man to any other form of life.[120]

In the months that followed, Bryan's anti-evolution campaign continued in the same pattern. He addressed state legislatures on the subject; he worked closely with their members
in framing bills; he urged the mayors of New York and Chicago to ban the teaching of evolution from their city's
schools. In addition he took action wherever else he saw religion threatened. In the fall of 1923 he appeared at the Constitutional Convention of the Y.M.C.A. in Cleveland and opposed
the proposed elimination of membership in an evangelical
church as a prerequisite for membership. "The issue is a
simple one," he told the delegates, "whether the Y.M.C.A. is
to continue to be a spiritual force, such as it has been from the
beginning, or become merely a social club where young men
can secure physical training and a bath. . ." [121] The following spring he was again one of the leading figures at the Presbyterian General Assembly. He nominated the fundamentalist
Dr. Clarence E. MacCartney for Moderator and when the
latter defeated the liberals' candidate by eighteen votes, he appointed Bryan Vice-Moderator.[122]

The progress of the fundamentalist movement shook the
defenders of evolution out of their earlier complacency. The
prominent scientist and president of New York's Museum of
Natural History, Henry Fairfield Osborn, was a perfect ex-

119. WJB to Senator W. J. Singleterry, April 11, 1923, ibid.
120. House Concurrent Resolution No. F, copy in ibid.
121. *New York Times*, October 20, 1923.
122. "Mr. Bryan's Nominating Speech," Bryan Papers; *New York
Times*, May 23, 1924.

ample. "Early in the year of 1922," he wrote, "I was suddenly aroused from my reposeful researches in paleontology by an article in the New York *Times* . . . by William Jennings Bryan. . . . It struck me immediately that Bryan's article was far more able and convincing than any previous utterance of his or any other fundamentalist, and that there should not be a moment's delay in replying to it." [123] So began a long debate in the periodicals and on the platforms of the nation with scientists and liberal clergymen like Osborn, John Maynard Shipley, and Harry Emerson Fosdick on the one side and Bryan on the other. The very nature of the debate, perhaps, prevented it from being conducted on a very high level. In any case it unfortunately generated as much heat as light. Professor E. G. Conklin, for instance, in an article in the *New York Times*, stated: "Apparently Mr. Bryan demands to see a monkey or an ass transformed into a man, though he must be familiar enough with the reverse process." [124] In a reply printed in the same paper, Bryan thanked the editor for publicizing the views of professors Conklin and Osborn. "You have rendered a distinct service to your readers in bringing two distinguished 'tree men' down from their arborial lodging to terra firma. . . . The answers of the professors whom you selected have exhibited all the characteristics of their class. They misrepresent their opponents, look with contempt upon those who do not exhaust the alphabet in setting forth their

123. Henry Fairfield Osborn, *Evolution and Religion in Education* (New York, 1925), p. 3. Osborn's activities in the Twenties illustrate the dangers inherent in judging a man wholly by his actions in any one area. This leading advocate of scientific freedom and reason was the same man who wrote the preface to Madison Grant's racist tract in 1916, warned the Second International Congress of Eugenics of the peril of race crossing in 1921, and seriously maintained that Christopher Columbus was descended from Nordic stock. See John Higham, *Strangers in the Land* (New Brunswick, New Jersey, 1955), pp. 274, 277.

124. *New York Times*, March 5, 1922.

degrees, and evade the issue which they pretend to discuss . . . it is evident that they regard the discovery of the bones of a five-toed horse as a greater event than the birth of Christ." [125]

However militant Bryan was in his crusade against evolution he was not, as he has often been pictured, wholly vindictive and intolerant. "However wide apart we are in our convictions as to what shall be done," he wrote a liberal minister in 1921, "I hope that we are in agreement on this, that God over-rules in the affairs of men and will bring victory to which ever side is right. . . . I am more anxious that the right shall triumph than that my views shall, if I am mistaken." [126] The following year he wrote to a professor at the University of Michigan: "I am aware that men who think as you do are just as sure that I am doing harm to Christianity by insisting on the truth of the Mosaic account of creation as I think you are in substituting the guesses of scientists for the 'Thus saith the Lord' of the Scriptures." [127] In the last month of his life when an old friend broke his ties with Bryan over the evolution issue, the latter replied: "I am not able to terminate our long friendship as cheerfully as you do, and I shall not allow a difference of opinion on religion to blot out the pleasant memory of earlier days." [128]

The net effect of the counterattack of the scientific and intellectual community upon Bryan was to solidify his preconceptions and make him as adamant as he had ever been in his career. "The evolutionary hypothesis," he proclaimed in 1923, "is the only thing that has seriously menaced religion

125. WJB to Editor, *New York Times*, March 9, 1922, ibid. March 14, 1922. For Bryan's article in this debate see ibid. February 26, 1922; for Osborn's and Fosdick's, see ibid. March 5, 12, 1922.

126. WJB to Paul Moore Strayer, December 19, 1921, Bryan Papers.

127. WJB to J. B. Steere, August 28, 1922, ibid; see also WJB to Norman Hapgood, August 10, 1923, ibid.

128. WJB to Charles S. Thomas, July 1, 1925, ibid.

since the birth of Christ and it menaces . . . civilization as well as religion." [129] "A scientific soviet," he warned, "is attempting to dictate what shall be taught in our schools and, in so doing, is attempting to mould the religion of the nation. It is the smallest, the most impudent, and the most tyrannical oligarchy that ever attempted to exercise arbitrary power." [130]

Intolerance, of course, was not monopolized by either side. In 1922 Bryan's opposition to the modernists resulted in his being asked to withdraw as principal speaker before the International Sunday School Convention.[131] In 1923, Guy T. Viskniskki of the Republic Syndicate, which handled Bryan's "Bible Talks," complained of "a somewhat concerted movement on the part of the so-called liberal element in certain cities to get the papers to stop the Talks. . . . they sure are kicking and stirring up trouble and they have made not a few editors restless thereby." In subsequent letters he informed Bryan of papers that were canceling the articles and begged him to keep controversy out of the Talks.[132] Bryan's response was always the same: "The objection of the liberals is to me personally. They know that the fight is on and that I am the one conservative leader who can reach the public. . . . I would rather lose income than become a pensioner upon our opponents and allow them to blue pencil my comments upon the lessons." [133]

Even more troubling to Bryan were the frequent attacks upon his intellectual capacity. "Mr. Bryan is an honored friend of mine," Luther Burbank reputedly informed a Cali-

129. WJB, "The Fundamentals," *Forum*, LXX (July 1923), 1679.
130. WJB, *Seven Questions in Dispute*, p. 154.
131. *New York Times*, April 13, 1922. Widespread protest led to a reissuance of the invitation. Ibid. April 27, 1922.
132. Guy T. Viskniskki to WJB, June 9, 13, 14, 1923, December 3, 31, 1924, Bryan Papers.
133. WJB to the Republic Syndicate, June 15, 1923, ibid.

fornia audience, "yet this need not prevent the observation that the skull with which nature endowed him visibly approaches the Neanderthal type." [134] References like this disturbed Bryan more deeply than he was ever willing to admit. In lecture after lecture he would tell his audiences that if his opponents did not stop calling him an ignoramus he would list his two earned and eight honorary degrees on his personal cards, "and then I will challenge any son of an ape to match cards with me." [135]

134. The *New York World* printed its account of this speech under two pictures, one of the head of the Neanderthal Man and the other of Bryan. *New York World*, December 23, 1924.

135. WJB, "Is the Bible True," Grace Bryan Hargreaves MSS., Bryan Papers. See also *New York Times*, April 25, 1923; *New York Post*, May 15, 1925. Bryan's wife and other members of his family were equally concerned by the numerous attacks upon the Commoner's intellectual capacities. In 1926, while she was preparing her husband's papers for transmission to the Library of Congress, Mrs. Bryan wrote Josephus Daniels:

"I want to get your judgement upon this point: Some members of the family hold that the thousands of letters which Mr. Bryan received after the defeat of 1896 — letters which are crudely written and badly spelled but which are full of genuine devotion and love — should be kept intact so that future students in research will find there abundant proof of his great popularity among the common people. Other members of the family feel that the mere keeping of such quantities of illiterate correspondence might be taken as proof that Mr. Bryan belonged to the illiterate classes. Many reviews of Mr. Bryan's life speak of his great heartedness but say he was poorly educated and a man of no mentality. The members of the family who take this side claim that the mere keeping of these letters might show to future generations that he was illiterate and that we should keep comparatively few letters and those only from the well educated. The thing I want to do, naturally, is to do the things which will defend and help his memory in the best way. I can see reason in both these positions and would like to know what you think about it. I want to proceed to go over all his mail and weed out everything that can in any way be misunderstood."

January 12, 1926, Daniels Papers, Box 669. Daniels responded immediately: "I am strongly of the opinion . . . that you ought to send everything. . . . By all means send all the letters." January 19, 1926, ibid. From the number of letters contained in the Bryan Papers, it would appear that Mrs. Bryan followed Daniels's advice.

The attacks upon Bryan's intelligence were often extreme and unfair, but Bryan gave more than a little provocation for them. Although Bryan owned and probably read the works of Darwin, he understood, or, more properly, wanted to understand, very little of Darwinian evolution. No matter how much the scientists might protest, no matter how clearly they might explain, evolution to Bryan and most of his followers simply meant that man had descended directly from the ape and that every living organism was related to every other living organism. How, he asked, could anyone support a proposition that linked "the rose to the onion, the lily-of-the-valley to the hog-weed, the eagle to the mosquito, the mocking bird to the rattlesnake, the wolf to the lamb, the royal palm to the scrub oak, and man to all?" [136] Even more interesting was Bryan's own version of the evolution of the leg:

> The leg, according to evolutionists, developed also by chance. One guess is that a little animal without legs one day discovered a wart on the belly, it had come without notice or premonitory symptoms; if it had come on the back instead of the belly the whole history of the world might have been different. But fortunately this wart came on the belly, and the little animal finding that it could use the wart to work itself along, used it until it developed into a leg. And then another wart and another leg. Why did man stop at two legs while the centipede kept on until it got a hundred? [137]

Reinhold Niebuhr has observed that "It is no easy task to build up the faith of one generation and not destroy the supports of the religion of the other." [138] This perhaps was the crux of the religious difficulties of the Twenties, for neither the modernists nor the fundamentalists were able to accomplish

136. WJB, "Mr. Bryan Speaks to Darwin," *Forum*, LXXIV (July 1925), 102.
137. WJB, *Seven Questions in Dispute*, pp. 141–2.
138. Reinhold Niebuhr, *Leaves From the Notebook of a Tamed Cynic* (Chicago, 1929), p. 36.

the task. By setting up the Bible as an arbiter of scientific knowledge in an age which abounded with the fruits of scientific discovery, Bryan and his colleagues were giving impetus to the very forces they wished to halt. More tragic still was the fact that by defending every word of the Bible, Bryan was forced to admit that if any one part of the Scriptures could be proven false the whole would be valueless. "When the miracles of the supernatural are taken from the Bible," he wrote in 1923, "its inspiration denied, and its Christ robbed of the glory of a virgin birth, of the majesty of Deity, and of the triumph of a resurrection, *there is little left in the Bible to make it worth reading. . .*" Or, again: "When Christ is reduced to the stature of a man — to the stature of an 'unlettered' man — He has only a man's influence *and even becomes an object of pity, if not contempt.*" [139]

In a real sense the chief victims of fundamentalism were the fundamentalists themselves. Their insistence upon the literal truth of the Bible denied them not only the benefits of modern science but much of the beauty and spirit of the very religion they were attempting to preserve.

139. WJB, *Seven Questions in Dispute*, pp. 24, 102. Italics added.

VIII : The Enemy's Country

*Nineteen hundred years ago the wise men came from the East
— and New York editors think they are still coming. No reform ever started in New York and they can have no faith in
reform of any kind.* — WJB

(1)

"I RISE to let you know there are other streets and other
attitudes in New York besides Wall Street. I speak for Ave-
nue A and 116th Street instead of Broad and Wall." [1] These
words, spoken by Fiorello La Guardia to the Conference for
Progressive Political Action in 1924, embodied a truth which
Bryan grasped only partially if at all. Bryan may have been a
political supporter of the urban laborer, he may have backed
his struggles to achieve a better life, but he never was able to
understand him fully. Bryan, to the end of his days, continued
to be the spokesman of the rural ethos, the champion of the
agrarian ideal. To him New York remained the "enemy's
country," the lair of the Robber Baron and the industrial
exploiter. He was to stand before the New York convention
in 1924 pleading with his fellow Democrats not to offend
those from whom progressivism had drawn its major support
in the past, never comprehending that by so doing he himself
was offending those from whom progressivism, in a rapidly
changing America, would have to draw its main support in
the future.

Fixing his gaze stolidly upon the financial center of New
York City and the other urban areas of the North, Bryan

1. Arthur Mann, *La Guardia, A Fighter Against His Times, 1882–
1933* (Philadelphia, 1959), p. 171.

never allowed it to drift to those parts of the city of which La
Guardia spoke. Even if he had it is doubtful that he would
have understood what he saw. "The only time I ever knew
him defeated in religious work was one night when we went
to a mission along the water front in New York City," his
wife has written. ". . . When asked to speak, he did not
know what to say, and told me afterwards, 'It takes a man who
has been saved from the depths to reach men like these. I
cannot do it. I lack the necessary past.' " [2] Nor did he possess
the past or experience necessary for an understanding of the
urban immigrant culture of the Twenties. He did claim to
understand that there was no inherent difference between the
inhabitants of rural and urban America. "It is not a difference
in people, it is a difference in their means of information and
their environment." [3] But though he could verbalize such sentiments and though he might sympathize with the plight of
the urban populace, he was confused and even a bit repelled
by their cultural differences. To Bryan, "exploited masses"
meant primarily Yankee-Protestant rural Americans, and "reform" meant agrarian radicalism.

This lack of understanding, of course, penetrated both sides
of the geographical boundary. The frustration that Fiorello
La Guardia felt when he watched almost every one of his
fellow progressives in Congress vote in favor of immigration
restriction in 1924 was paralleled by the anger of the rural
progressives when they saw their urban counterparts attempting to nullify the Eighteenth Amendment. The inability
of Bryan and the agrarians to understand Al Smith's dual role
as machine politician and urban reformer was duplicated by
the inability of the urban politicos to understand Bryan's dual
role as fundamentalist and agrarian reformer. It was this wid-

2. *Memoirs*, p. 456.
3. *The Commoner*, January 1917, pp. 16–17.

ening cultural chasm rather than fundamental economic and political differences which prevented the establishment of a common meeting ground between those desiring reform, helped to produce the progressive stalemate of the 1920's, and came close to destroying completely the effectiveness of the Democratic party.

(2)

In 1923, when Bryan was maneuvering for the moderatorship of the Presbyterian Church, a New York minister warned him that should he be elected to that position his chances of attaining high political office would be ruined. Bryan's answer to this argument is important, for it has set the tone of many of the interpretations of his last years: ". . . my power in politics," he wrote the clergyman, "is not what it used to be and, therefore, my responsibility is not so great." "While my power in politics has waned," he continued, "I think it has increased in religious matters. . . . My interest is deeper in religious subjects . . ." [4]

Bryan made a number of such statements after 1920, and there was an element of truth in them. Historians, however, have tended to take them much too seriously, and have ignored the context in which they were made. Bryan used such statements to justify his increased activity in the religious sphere rather than to indicate any diminution of his interest in politics. His attitude was more accurately stated just after his resignation from the State Department when, in answer to a reporter's question about how long he intended to remain in politics, he told the story of the city dweller lost in the woods who came upon an old man sitting in front of a cabin. "The tenderfoot said: 'Hello!' The old man said: 'Hello!' The ten-

4. John A. Marquis to WJB, March 28, 1923, WJB to Marquis, May 4, 1923, Bryan Papers.

derfoot said: 'Have you lived here all your life?' The old man replied: 'Not yet!' " [5]

"I am not out of politics," he told six thousand New Yorkers in 1922,[6] and he meant it as his numerous political activities in the Twenties showed. If any doubts remained, Bryan's actions before, during, and after the 1924 Presidential election should have been sufficient to erase them. Bryan may have realized that he was no longer a political power, but this did not prevent him from behaving like one. Until his death Bryan continued to act out the role he had established for himself in the days of his political glory. He expended so much time and energy upon the Presidential contest of 1924 and engaged in such intricate and confusing political machinations, that his activities can only be touched upon here.

As before every Presidential election since 1896, Bryan once more found himself being urged to wage an active campaign for the party's nomination. As early as December 1920, he received letters from his supporters assuring him that he was the nation's only hope.[7] In the spring of 1923 his brother Charles, who had been elected Governor of Nebraska the previous November, added his voice to these pleas: "I feel you could be nominated and elected. . . . You would naturally have the dry vote, the woman vote and the vote of the moral element of the country . . . and the other factions would support you because you was [sic] fighting their battles on economic lines . . ." [8] Ten months later Representative Huddleston wrote Bryan that unless the liberals found a suitable candidate soon the Eastern reactionaries would walk away with the nomination. "As I see the situation, you are the

5. *Lincoln State Journal,* July 1, 1915, clipping in ibid.
6. *New York Times,* April 3, 1922.
7. *The Commoner,* December 1920, pp. 9–10, January 1921, pp. 8–9, March 1921, pp. 8–11. See also numerous letters in Bryan Papers.
8. Charles W. Bryan to WJB, May 19, 1923, ibid.

only available man. Circumstances point to you as our candidate. Won't you give this matter consideration with the view to a public statement that you will accept the nomination?" [9] On the eve of the convention the journalist John Temple Graves informed him in urgent tones: *"you yourself are the solution — the only solution"* to the division prevailing within the party. *"Make no enemies on the floor of the convention,"* Graves advised him. "That wrangling, tired, faction weary convention is waiting for you. They will rise to the one master voice . . . The second great psychological moment of your life will have come. They will recall 1896 — they will repeat Chicago!" [10]

If these familiar appeals rekindled the fires of Presidential ambition within Bryan, the cold voice of reality and his own fear of defeat soon quenched them. "I do not want the nomination and I have no ambitions to be President," he wrote in a typical letter to his backers. ". . . I have accumulated a great many enemies who would vote against me as a matter of habit, whereas they might vote for a new man even though he held the same views I do. It is so important for the party and for the country that we win this election that the personal ambitions should be entirely overlooked." [11] Should there be an attempt to unite all the Democrats and progressive forces behind one candidate and should the convention fail to find a candidate capable of bringing these forces together, Bryan felt that he might receive the nomination. "But, as I say," he wrote his brother, "this is only a remote contingency, depend-

9. George Huddleston to WJB, March 1, 1924, ibid.

10. Graves to WJB, June 16, 1924, ibid.

11. WJB to Arthur Brisbane, March 15, 1924, ibid. For other letters in a similar vein, see WJB to the following: W. H. Thompson, February 6, 1923, A. L. Fales, September 8, 1923, John Lentz, March 15, 1923, T. D. Judy, February 11, 1924, H. E. Newbranch, March 28, 1924, George Huddleston, March 30, 1923, March 6, 1924, ibid.

ing on so many 'ifs' that it is not worth while to build any calculations on it." [12]

As in 1920, Bryan did not assist those who desired to make him President. He refused to allow his name to be entered in the Arkansas Presidential primary. "I have neither the disposition, the time or the money to make a campaign for the nomination," he informed the secretary of the Bryan-for-President movement in that state, "and I would feel greatly humiliated to be put in the attitude of a candidate and then fail to secure a nomination. It would be an unfortunate ending of my political career." [13] He declined similar invitations from several states and would not support the formation of a Bryan-for-President Club in Florida.[14] When he was informed that the Oklahoma Legislature passed a resolution endorsing him for the Democratic nomination for President, he expressed his gratitude but stated emphatically: "I am not a candidate, and I am anxious to see a younger man nominated, who can do what I did in 1896, namely, take up the leadership of the party and continue the fight until victory is won." [15]

"I think the Democratic situation has gotten to where the eastern Democrats will either have to consent to a radical, progressive as a candidate or see the party annihilated in the coming election," Charles Bryan wrote his brother from the West.[16] The latter agreed completely. The great weakness of the party, he told Huddleston, was the ability of its reactionary element to prevent it from taking advantage of its opportunities. "I feel it is my duty," he added some months later, "to help make it impossible to select a reactionary and make

12. WJB to Charles W. Bryan, March 3, 1924, ibid.

13. WJB to George Wyman, March 5, 1924, ibid. See also, *New York Times*, March 11, 1924.

14. WJB to Arthur Brisbane, March 15, 1924; WJB to Charles W. Bryan, March 3, 1924, WJB to W. T. Brooks, March 6, 1924, Bryan Papers.

15. *New York Post*, March 19, 1924.

16. Charles W. Bryan to WJB, July 19, 1923, Bryan Papers.

more certain the nomination of a progressive." [17] The Democratic candidate, he announced more than a year before the convention, "must be dry and in favor of enforcement of the Eighteenth Amendment . . . Our candidate must be with the people as against Wall Street." Democrats could not expect to win "without a straightforward, unequivocal declaration in favor of the disinherited masses . . ." [18]

These criteria immediately ruled out a number of leading candidates, and Bryan was not reluctant to identify them. He, of course, opposed the candidacy of Al Smith, who "is both wet and for Wall Street, and has the Tamany [sic] millstone besides." [19] He was even more hostile to the aspirations of Senator Oscar W. Underwood of Alabama, whom he denounced as a wet, an opponent of woman suffrage, and a captive of Wall Street. "He is not a Southern candidate; he is a New York candidate living in the South . . ." [20] In February 1924, with the Birmingham News denouncing him as a "meddlesome old marplot," he entered Underwood's own state to oppose his candidacy.[21] While Bryan actively opposed Underwood he was convinced that the wets and Wall Street were merely using him as a "stalking horse" to line up votes which could eventually be switched to John W. Davis of West Virginia, "whose record is not known and upon whom they can rely." [22] Davis's position as an attorney for J.

17. WJB to Huddleston, August 30, 1923, March 6, 1924, ibid.
18. The Commoner, April 1923, p. 2.
19. WJB to C. E. Jones, June 18, 1923, Bryan Papers. See also, New York Times, June 19, 1924.
20. WJB to Frank Webb, February 9, 1924, Bryan Papers; WJB, "The Presidential Candidates in 1924," The Observer, November 24, 1923, p. 2, clipping in ibid.
21. Birmingham News, February 9, 1924, clipping in ibid.; New York Times, February 22, 27, 1924.
22. WJB to George Huddleston, March 30, 1923, Bryan Papers. As early as 1922, Bryan was warned against Davis's candidacy by Representative Neely of West Virginia. See M. M. Neely to WJB, October 24, November 29, 1922, ibid.

Pierpont Morgan, Bryan asserted, "sufficiently describes his connections and his political views." "I have no personal objection of any kind to Mr. Davis," he told reporters during the convention. "He is a man of high character. So is Mr. Coolidge. There is no difference between them." [23]

He lightly dismissed the boom for Henry Ford, writing one of the latter's supporters: "I do not like his attacks upon the Jews. It does not indicate the breadth of view that we need in those who are to speak for the entire country." [24] As in 1920 Bryan refused to align himself with his former colleague in Wilson's Cabinet, William G. McAdoo. In the intervening years McAdoo had swung to the left, definitely associated himself with the agrarian wing of the party, and agreed with Bryan on every important issue. Still, Bryan would not speak out in his behalf though he publicly refrained from opposing his candidacy. Privately he let it be known that he felt McAdoo's business association with E. L. Doheny, who was implicated in the oil scandals, had "seriously, if not fatally" impaired his chances. "I have entire confidence in his honesty," he wrote his brother, "but the fees received give the Republicans a point of attack and enable them to turn attention away from the guilty Republicans." [25]

Bryan's refusal to put himself in the camp of the one progressive Democrat with a chance of winning the nomination might have made some sense if he had set about finding another candidate of equal stature and progressivism. Instead he reverted to his traditional practice of muddying the waters by recommending a series of political unknowns who had no

23. WJB, "Wall Street's Second Choice," typed news release dated February 11, 1924, ibid.; *Tampa Morning Tribune*, July 2, 1924, clipping in ibid.

24. WJB to [Daniel Cruice?], undated, ibid. See also, Daniel Cruice to WJB, March 10, 1923, ibid.

25. WJB to George E. White, March 15, 1924, WJB to Charles W. Bryan, March 3, 1924, ibid.

chance to be considered seriously. In the past, Bryan had mentioned as potential Presidential candidates such men as Jethro W. Smith and Judge Walter Clark, both of North Carolina, Peleg Z. Jones of Oklahoma, and a Tennessee mayor named Head.[26] Bryan probably employed this practice not merely as a means of confusing his political opponents, but also to emphasize his own stature and availability and to indicate his faith in the Jacksonian doctrine that any average citizen could perform the duties of governing if he was on the people's side.

Never, however, had he used it with more gusto than in the pre-convention days of 1924. Of all the men he named as possible candidates only Josephus Daniels had anything approaching a national reputation. Bryan's dark horses included: Representative W. A. Ayres of Kansas, an Ohio Democrat with the unlikely name of Doheny, Braxton Bragg Comer of Alabama (a 76-year-old former Governor and Senator), Governor Walker of Georgia, Governor Trinkle of Virginia, and his own brother Charles.[27]

The two "candidates" upon whom Bryan finally concentrated were Governor Pat M. Neff of Texas and Dr. A. A. Murphree, President of the University of Florida. Bryan first seems to have hit upon Neff in an attempt to attract Underwood's Southern support.[28] During the summer of 1923 he broached the subject to the Texan, and finding him ready and

26. *New York Times*, July 9, 1923; Charles Willis Thompson, *Presidents I've Known and Two Near Presidents* (Indianapolis, 1929), p. 41.

27. WJB to W. H. Thompson, February 26, 1923, W. A. Ayres to WJB, March 24, 1923, WJB to W. A. Ayres, March 30, 1923, WJB to International News Service, August 1, 1923, WJB to T. D. Judy, February 11, 1924, WJB, "The Presidential Candidates in 1924," *The Observer*, November 24, 1923, all in Bryan Papers.

28. "I think the best way to combat Underwood in the South is to get a southern candidate." WJB to the Anti-Saloon League of Westerville, Ohio, undated, ibid.

willing to run he invited him to join the Bryan train as it passed through Texas in August. "I met Neff and was very much pleased with him," he wrote after the interview.[29]

But even while Bryan was courting Neff and was mentioning him favorably to fellow Democrats and newspapermen, he began to sound out Dr. Murphree.[30] Finding the Florida educator no less willing to be President than the Texas statesman, Bryan told reporters in December 1923, that if he were elected a delegate from Florida he would present to the convention the name of a Southern Democrat for President.[31] The following month, on the very eve of his departure for Texas to go duck hunting with Neff, he announced his support of Murphree: "He is a rare combination of intellect and heart. . . . He is dry and progressive and sound on economic questions. His popularity will grow as he becomes known." [32] "In presenting him," he declared in an address delivered some days later, "I shall have an opportunity to pay a debt that I owe to the South. It has supported me in three campaigns and the policies which I have advocated and I hope that in this convention — probably the last in which I shall sit as a delegate, for I am now nearly sixty-four — I may assist in removing the ban that has for sixty years rested upon Southern statesmen." [33]

Not only was Bryan's endorsement of an obscure Floridian unlikely to result in the nomination of a Southerner, but, iron-

29. WJB to Pat M. Neff, August 14, 1923, Pat M. Neff to WJB, August 25, 1923, WJB to Ira Champion, August 31, 1923, ibid.

30. WJB to A. A. Murphree, November 28, 1923, Murphree to WJB, December 10, 1923, ibid.

31. A number of Congressmen immediately predicted that Bryan had Josephus Daniels in mind. *New York Times*, December 16, 17, 1923.

32. News Statement, January 14, 1924, Bryan Papers; *New York Times*, January 14, 1924.

33. WJB, "The Campaign of 1924," abstract of an address delivered January 25, 1924, Bryan Papers.

ically, because Murphree's position legally prevented him from entering a political primary or election, Bryan had no candidate to oppose McAdoo and Underwood in the Florida Presidential primary, and as a result of that contest he found himself pledged to cast his vote at the convention for McAdoo.[34]

While it is unquestionably true that Bryan's political power was only a shadow of what it once had been, his preconvention activities — which took him through most sections of the country — were not dismissed lightly by either the nation's press or the aspirants for the Democratic nomination. Even a politician as widely divorced from Bryan's usual following as Franklin D. Roosevelt saw fit to court his favor. Early in 1923 Roosevelt visited Bryan at his home in Miami and urged him to support a national referendum on prohibition, intimating that it would result in a landslide victory for the drys. A few months later the future President, who was to nominate the soaking wet Governor of New York at the convention, informed Bryan that the drive to have the convention held in New York was being backed "by the hopeful idiots who think the democratic platform will advocate a repeal of the Eighteenth Amendment." Reactionary forces, he warned, "are working more or less together with the idea that even if they cannot nominate their own candidate and write their own platform they will have enough votes in the convention to prevent the nomination of a real progressive democrat or an outspoken dry candidate." In February 1924, Roosevelt's boat, the *Larooco*, docked in Miami long enough to allow its owner to have a "nice talk" with Bryan.[35]

34. A. A. Murphree to WJB, February 25, 1924, WJB to Charles W. Bryan, March 3, 1924, ibid.; William G. McAdoo to Gavin McNab, June 5, 1924, McAdoo Papers, Box 305.

35. Frank Freidel, *Franklin D. Roosevelt: The Ordeal* (Boston 1954), p. 161; Roosevelt to WJB, June 20, 1923, Bryan Papers; Elliott Roosevelt, ed., *F. D. R.: His Personal Letters*, II, 543.

As usual Bryan allowed few of the innumerable details which preceded a national convention to escape his attention. As early as January 1923, he was in Washington conferring with Democratic leaders about party policies and the political outlook for 1924. He contributed his money and his time to the effort to erase the party's financial deficit. He strongly opposed New York City as the site for the convention and urged Cordell Hull to hold it in a Southern city.[36] His opposition to New York led him to make a futile stab at inducing several prominent New York Democrats to combine with Senator Royal Copeland in an anti-Smith faction of the New York Democracy.[37] "I have been very much interested in you because of the opportunity that your position gives you," Bryan wrote Copeland. "I am sure your heart is with the masses but I am not sure to what extent your environment will permit you to become the champion of their cause. Big Business has its center in New York City and I know how heartless they are, as well as how influential." [38]

Failing in this, Bryan offered to trade Smith to the Republicans for Governor Gifford Pinchot of Pennsylvania, and should the Republicans prove reluctant he was willing to throw in a few more Democratic officials to boot.[39] More seriously, he took part in the debate over the abolition of the two-thirds rule then still in force at Democratic conventions. He favored the move only if the unit rule was abolished simultaneously; otherwise "the four big states, New York, Pennsylvania, Ohio and Illinois, could exercise an unfair in-

36. *New York Times,* January 16, February 21, 1923; W. W. March to WJB, July 12, 1921, WJB to W. E. Chilton, November 1, 1923, WJB to Hull, November 15, 1923, December 18, 1923, Bryan Papers.
37. WJB to William Schuyler Jackson, July 27, 1923, ibid.
38. WJB to Copeland, November 14, 1923, ibid.
39. *New York Times,* October 15, 1923.

fluence." [40] He also urged the adoption of a law requiring all candidates for the Presidential nomination and for the Presidency itself to publish a statement of the amount and sources of their expenditures. He was convinced, however, that the only permanent means of freeing candidates from "obliging themselves to the predatory interests" was to have the government pay the expenses of candidates for public offices.[41]

In response to a question from the Sunday editor of the *New York Times*, Bryan predicted that the main issues in 1924 would be the economic distress of the farmer, the increasing antagonism between capital and labor, the curbing of the profiteer, the inequitable burden of taxation, and government regulation of railroads and mines.[42] Bryan paid particular attention to the issue of taxation and concentrated his attacks upon the Secretary of the Treasury. He labeled Mellon "the foremost reactionary in the United States," and charged that his fiscal policy "concentrates wealth and increases the number of the disinherited. It multiplies the number of tenants, diminishes the number of home owners and drives the farmers from the farms." [43]

Although the Republicans had been more than generous in handing the Democrats issues which Bryan was convinced could win them the election, an uncharacteristic note of pessimism crept into his correspondence throughout most of 1923. "We are so helpless without newspapers," he complained in March, "that we may not find it possible to awaken the public to the real danger or to nominate anybody who has a chance

40. WJB to John H. Parry, July 26, 1923, Bryan Papers; *New York Times*, June 20, 1924.

41. WJB to Thomas J. Walsh, May 14, 1924, Walsh Papers, Box 373; *New York Times*, April 2, 1924. For a more detailed article by Bryan on this subject, see ibid. May 25, 1924, Section VIII.

42. WJB to Lester Markel, April 11, 1923, Bryan Papers.

43. WJB, "Secretary Mellon — Dictator," News Release, April 18, 1924, ibid.

to win." [44] "There is strong opposition to the Republicans," he wrote four months later, "but I am not sure we are going to be able to concentrate it by united action on our own part." [45] The off-year elections in the fall plus several speaking trips through the country seem to have revived Bryan's usual optimism and in February he informed his brother: "Everything is coming our way . . . things are growing more progressive all the time. . . . I never had more cordial receptions than I have had recently all through the South. . . . Everywhere there is the old-time friendliness." [46] "It looks now as if the Democrats have a good chance of winning the election," he wrote less than two months before the convention. [47]

Bryan's final step before the convention met was to campaign for election as delegate-at-large from his newly adopted state. Unlike 1916 and 1920, his election was never in doubt, but Bryan was cautious. "I have visited sixteen counties in the last ten days and the outlook is very encouraging," he informed one of his law partners in April. "I feel quite sure of election as a delegate, but it is so important that I do not want to take any chances." [48] Actually Bryan had inaugurated his campaign almost a year before the primaries by informing leading Democrats in Florida of his desire to be a member of the delegation. [49] He seems to have thoroughly enjoyed the experience of being a candidate once again. "I had a delightful time," he told reporters, and his wife noted that after each of his campaign trips, which eventually took him through all of Florida's sixty-six counties, he returned home "tanned by the sun and bright-eyed, full of happiness because he was begin-

44. WJB to John Lentz, March 21, 1923, ibid.
45. WJB to Marvin J. Hutchins, July 5, 1923, ibid.
46. WJB to Charles W. Bryan, February 9, 1924, ibid.
47. WJB to Charles A. Douglas, April 18, 1924, ibid.
48. Ibid.
49. WJB to C. E. Jones, June 18, 1923, WJB to John A. Taylor, July 17, 1923, ibid.

ning to know people all over the state . . ." [50] Bryan's candidacy was supported by McAdoo, who urged the voters to send him to the convention.[51] The latter responded more favorably than even Bryan had anticipated. He received over 42,000 votes more than any other candidate for delegate and a higher total of votes than any of the candidates in the Presidential primary.[52]

"FLORIDA VICTORY SENDS WILLIAM J. BYRAN AS INSTRUCTED DELEGATE FOR ME TO NEW YORK," McAdoo jubilantly wired one of his supporters.[53]

(3)

In the last week of June, Bryan journeyed to New York City to attend his final and most trying Democratic National Convention. Almost immediately upon arriving he announced that he had brought with him a complete platform which he intended to submit for approval. He then conferred with McAdoo for an hour and a half. Precisely what transpired at the conference is not known but upon emerging Bryan told the assembled crowd of reporters: "I am for him. McAdoo has all the qualifications for a candidate. The same forces that antagonized me are lined up against McAdoo." [54]

The convention opened at noon on June 24 before 15,000

50. *Johnstown* (Florida) *News*, May 22, 1924, clipping in ibid.; *Memoirs, p. 474.*

51. William G. McAdoo to WJB, May 28, 1924, Bryan Papers; William G. McAdoo to the *Jacksonville* (Florida) *Journal*, May 20, 1920, McAdoo Papers, Box 303.

52. Bryan received 85,462 votes. McAdoo, who won the Presidential primary, polled 82,523 votes. "Official Vote — Democratic Primary Elections, 1924, Tabulated by Counties," Bryan Papers.

53. William G. McAdoo to Gavin McNab, June 5, 1924, McAdoo Papers, Box 305. McAdoo wrote to Josephus Daniels the next day: "I am very glad to see that Mr. Bryan has been elected a delegate from Florida. Perhaps you will recall that I came out for him publicly and asking [sic] my friends in Florida to support him." Ibid.

54. *New York American*, June 23, 1924.

spectators who filled every available seat in Madison Square
Garden, with millions more following the proceedings over
radio. While the convention proper was listening to a variety
of speakers place prominent Democrats in nomination, the
Committee on Platforms and Resolutions, to which Bryan as
usual had been appointed, struggled to work out a satisfactory
platform. William Allen White, who has left us the most
complete eye-witness account of the convention, felt that
Bryan dominated the platform committee.[55] While this is de-
batable, the very length and nature of the platform finally
adopted do indicate Bryan's influence. Though the committee
failed to work out many satisfactory solutions to the various
problems it faced, it cannot be accused of neglecting anything. After five days of wrangling behind closed doors it
finally emerged with what was probably the most extensive
platform in the party's history. Many of the reforms which
Bryan was most interested in, if not championed as vigorously
as he might have wished, were at least mentioned: government aid to the farmer, government regulation of railroads,
mining industries, and "corporations controlling the necessar-
ies of life," government aid to education and development of
highways and waterways, tax reform, prohibition enforcement, elimination of the Lame Duck Congress, limitation of
campaign contributions and publicly financed publicity for
candidates running for federal office, an American sponsored
disarmament conference and, most pleasing of all, a provision
calling for a national referendum before a declaration of
war.[56]

As a member of the eleven-man subcommittee which
drafted the platform, Bryan was responsible for the inclusion

55. William Allen White, *Politics: The Citizen's Business* (New
York, 1924), p. 69.
56. For the Democratic platform see *Official Report of the Proceedings of the Democratic National Convention . . . 1924*, pp. 228-45.

of a number of these planks, particularly those dealing with election expenses, disarmament, and a war referendum.[57] At the behest of Eleanor Roosevelt and Robert Woolley he also fought for a strong plank on child labor, but here he was unable to convince his Southern colleagues.[58]

The two issues which divided the committee most seriously were those concerning the League of Nations and the Ku Klux Klan. The planks embracing these two questions were the only ones which the committee failed to adopt unanimously. The majority plank on the League, as finally presented to the convention, affirmed the party's faith in the world organization and called for a popular referendum to ascertain whether a majority of the American people desired to join it. Newton D. Baker led an abortive attempt to substitute a plank calling for immediate American participation in the Court of International Justice and explicitly pledging the Democratic party to work for American entry into the League. Bryan took no part in the League debate. His faith in popular referendums led him to favor the majority plank despite the absence of any Constitutional sanction for holding such a referendum.[59]

The issue that engendered the greatest degree of acrimonious debate, however, was what position the party should assume with regard to the Ku Klux Klan. In 1922 Senator Thomas Walsh of Montana had warned Bryan that the Klan was the rock upon which the entire party could founder. If the Southern wing of the party did not repudiate "this harpy

57. For Bryan's comments on the platform as well as other aspects of the convention, see the daily articles he wrote in the *New York American*, June 23–July 10, 1924.

58. Robert Woolley, Memoirs, MSS., Chapter XXXII, Woolley Papers.

59. For the League debate see *Official . . . Proceedings . . . 1924*, pp. 246, 249–79. For Bryan's attitude see *New York American*, June 29, 1924.

organization," Walsh predicted, "there will not be votes enough north of the Mason and Dixon line two years hence to justify obsequies over the Democratic Party." Bryan was quick to agree that it was "superlatively unfortunate" to have an organization built upon all the prejudices in the country. But prejudice was based upon ignorance, and ignorance could best be combated by enlightenment not by force. Any other course would make martyrs out of a group which would, in any case, soon perish due to the venality of its own leadership.[60] This was still Bryan's position in 1924, and it appeared to be the position of McAdoo as well. Although the California candidate had taken a comparatively enlightened position on race relations in the days before the 1920 convention, four years later he disregarded the pleas of those of his lieutenants who urged him to denounce the Klan.[61]

Every member of the platform committee agreed that the religious bigotry and intolerance fostered by the Ku Klux Klan should be condemned. The question was whether the Klan itself should be specifically mentioned. Those who came from sections of the country in which the Klan was powerful joined Bryan in favoring an anonymous rebuke. Commanding a majority, this group had its way, and the plank adopted by the committee merely reaffirmed the principle of religious freedom and condemned "any effort to arouse religious or racial dissensions." So heated had the committee's debate on this plank become, that at the close of its final session at six in the morning, Bryan as acting chairman asked Judge John H. McCann, a Catholic, to join him in leading the committee in prayer. After McCann recited the Lord's prayer, Bryan rose

60. Walsh to WJB, December 20, 1922, WJB to Walsh, December 30, 1922, Bryan Papers.
61. Mullen, *Western Democrat*, p. 242. For McAdoo's earlier position see: McAdoo to Thomas B. Love, June 24, 1920, McAdoo to P. C. Thomas, June 25, 1920, McAdoo Papers, Box 237.

and asked for "the wisdom to see the right and the courage to do the right." "Calm our passions!" he prayed. "Free us of our prejudices! Restore harmony in our councils!" [62]

As soon as the League question was settled, the convention took up the question of whether to amend the majority plank on religious freedom so as to condemn all secret political societies and pledge the party to oppose any effort on the part of the Ku Klux Klan "to limit the civil rights of any citizen or body of citizens because of religion, birthplace, or racial origin." It was late evening of the fifth day when the debate began. The galleries were packed with vociferous opponents of the Klan. "It was a queer crowd for a Westerner to see," recorded White, "the foreign-born were there, in a considerable majority, in the upper galleries. One understood, seeing the gallery crowd, why the signs admonishing against smoking or spitting on the floor were printed in Italian as well as English. Those bilingual signs told a real story." [63] It was well past midnight when Bryan arose to close the debate, and still the energy of the great crowd was not spent. "He stepped upon the platform," wrote White, "a fine, upstanding man, but middle-aged; no longer the boy orator, yet aflame with the ardor of his quenchless youth. . . . His agile movements, his almost buoyant step, his clear, soft resonant voice filling the entire hall with its electric power, cast him perfectly as the central figure of the second act." [64] Central figure or not, it was clear that on this issue and in these surroundings Bryan was in as difficult a position as he had ever been. The jeers and catcalls that greeted his opening remarks were as numerous as the applause. He had not spoken for five minutes before the

62. The version of Bryan's prayer printed in the newspapers the next day differs somewhat from the version later printed. Compare the *New York American*, June 29, 1924, with *Memoirs* p. 477.
63. White, *Politics: The Citizen's Business*, p. 79.
64. Ibid. p. 82.

Chairman had to rap for order three times and threaten to clear the galleries.[65]

Bryan's speech was a plea for unity.[66] The Democratic platform, he said, contained "the noblest principles that have been written into a platform." The majority plank was strong enough as it was, and specific condemnation of the Klan was superfluous and harmful. The Catholics and Jews did not need any such protection. "It is not necessary, and, my friends, the Ku Klux Klan does not deserve the advertisement that you give them. (Cheers and applause.)" The issue raised by the minority tended to divide the party and, more important, to plant seeds of dissension within the ranks of Christianity itself. It tended also to divert the party from the real issues of the day. The farmers were suffering, the laborers were crying for relief, monopoly and privilege were spreading:

> And while we have distress in this country that cries aloud for relief, and while we have a war-worn world across the Atlantic that needs our help and needs our guidance, these minority men say that we lack courage if we do a big work instead of starting out on a little hunt for something which is nearly dead and which will soon pass away. (Applause.) . . . Anybody can fight the Ku Klux Klan, but only the Democratic Party can stand between the common people and their oppressors in this land. (Applause.)

After reciting a long plea for Democratic and Christian solidarity in the war upon materialism and injustice, Bryan closed by crying: "It was Christ on the Cross who said, 'Father, forgive them for they know not what they do!' And, my friends, we can exterminate Ku Kluxism better by recognizing their honesty and teaching them that they are wrong. (Boos and hisses, followed by applause.)"

For two hours after Bryan ended, the delegates, amid much

65. *Official . . . Proceedings . . . 1924,* pp. 303–4.
66. For Bryan's speech see ibid. pp. 303–9.

wrangling and confusion, cast their ballots for and against the proposed minority plank. Out of 1,083-6/20 votes, the minority mustered 541-3/20 ayes against 542-3/20 nays.[67] Before the final vote was tabulated, Bryan retired to his hotel room convinced that his side had lost. He was awakened by his brother and Dan Bride who told him the good news. When his friends assured him that his speech had turned the tide, he replied: "No, it must have been the Lord's work; I would not have been willing to risk so small a margin." [68] The victory was narrower — and more futile — than Bryan imagined.

With the platform chosen, the convention settled down to the difficult chore of selecting a candidate. During the course of the balloting the sectional animosities, which had first been manifest during the platform debate, solidified, with the rural states largely supporting William Gibbs McAdoo, and the urban states backing Al Smith. The deadlock continued day after day and ballot after ballot. When Florida was called on the thirty-eighth ballot Bryan, who had been voting solidly for McAdoo, rose and asked permission to explain his vote. Permission was granted and Bryan strode to the platform amid an accompaniment of "cheers and applause mingled with hisses and boos." [69] Bryan had spoken to hostile conventions before but never one which was as determined to drown him out. During the thirty minutes allotted to him it is doubtful if Bryan was able to speak for fifteen. His pleas for McAdoo were constantly interrupted by cries of "Smith, Smith." Dele-

67. Ibid. p. 333.
68. WJB, "The Democratic National Convention, 1924," Bryan Papers. Later that same day Bryan wrote of his speech on the Klan: "In effectiveness I think it possibly surpasses any other speech I have ever made. I do not know of any greater service I have rendered to the party."
69. For Bryan's speech and the reaction to it see *Official . . . Proceedings . . . 1924*, pp. 527-37.

gates arose to demand that he be silenced. The galleries became so unruly that the chairman ordered them cleared.

Though Bryan rose to speak for McAdoo, he also intended to fulfill his promise to plead for the right of the South to be considered as the home of the Democratic candidate.

> We have a man in Florida. He is the President of our State University. (Laughter.) His name is Dr. A. A. Murphree. (Voices: "We want Smith." "We want Smith." Laughter, applause and cheers.) He is a Democratic scholar. (Hisses and boos.) He is a scholarly Democrat. (Voice: "Never heard of one.") Those who have not informed themselves upon the Nation's great men ought to be silent until they have had a chance to inform themselves. (Cheers and applause.)

Bryan then named two other Southerners, Josephus Daniels and Senator Robinson of Arkansas, and attempted to get nostalgic for a moment: "This is probably the last convention of my party in which I shall be a delegate. (Applause.) Don't applaud; I may change my mind. (Laughter, applause and cheers.)"

After naming several potential candidates from the West,[70] he began to urge the nomination of McAdoo, only to be met by cries of "oil," "oil," "oil," from the galleries and frenzied questions from the floor. The delegates would neither allow him to defend McAdoo's actions with regard to the oil scandals nor to veer away from the touchy subject altogether. For ten minutes they demonstrated, screamed, and prevented him from being heard. Order was finally restored, and Bryan closed his address with an attack upon the Republicans and an encomium to the Democrats. "We want to make this Government so good," he cried, "that to be a private citizen of the United States — (A voice: 'Stop speaking.') — will be better

70. Samuel Ralston of Indiana, E. T. Meredith of Iowa, his brother Charles, Senator Walsh of Montana.

than to be a king in any other country in the world. I thank you for your attention. (Applause and boos.)"

Bryan by his stand on the Klan issue had helped to draw the sectional lines of the convention taut, had helped to intensify the intolerance of the delegates and spectators, and had paid for it. As he made his way back to his seat he heard the voice of Charles O'Brien of New Jersey crying: "The same old Dollar Bill, the same old Dollar Bill." "I saw Bryan at Madison Square Garden in 1924," wrote Edgar Lee Masters, "not applauded but hissed; not carried on shoulders, but in danger of being booted. . . ." [71]

For the remainder of the convention Bryan, clad in his palm beach suit and carrying a cardboard fan, was a familiar figure on the floor as he moved from delegation to delegation pleading McAdoo's cause. As the strife-torn convention proceeded from one inconclusive ballot to another, Bryan formulated a plan for a general expense fund to pay the expenses of those delegates in financial distress, and he appears to have been a member of the group which favored moving the convention to Washington, D.C. He also increased the intensity of his attacks upon John W. Davis, whose nomination as a compromise candidate was made more likely by the deadlock. "The convention began with a fight against one 'invisible government,'" Bryan wrote in his daily newspaper column, "it seems likely to end in a fight against a government still more invisible and more powerful. The Klan claims to control only about a million men but the invisible government that resides in Wall Street extends its sway over a considerable portion of the membership of the two great parties." [72]

Bryan's efforts were to no avail. On an unprecedented 103rd ballot, the weary delegates finally settled upon Davis

71. Masters, *The American Mercury*, III (December 1924), 387.
72. *New York Times*, July 2, 3, 4, 1924; *New York American*, July 4, 6, 1924.

and then made Bryan's younger brother the Vice Presidential candidate. "The convention was remarkable in many ways," Bryan wrote a friend. "Its conclusion beat anything that I have ever known. To have a man whose nomination I opposed pick out my brother for his running mate demonstrates that this is a queer world." [73]

(4)

Lying on his death bed, Samuel Gompers listened to the Democratic proceedings over the radio. When the platform was read he commented to some friends: "It looks as if we are forced to turn to La Follette." After the nomination of Davis he declared: "There is no other way." [74] There was no other way for many of the nation's progressives. "Democrats have finally nominated a ticket that not even a brother can support," Fiorello La Guardia wired the chairman of the La Follette campaign. "No, not even William Jennings can make it progressive, and how will he explain its impossible political biology?" [75] La Guardia was mistaken. Bryan may not have been able to make the ticket progressive, but he was able to support it.

"Though my choice would have been otherwise," Bryan wrote in his final convention report, "I decide without hesitation that I can best serve my country as well as my party by supporting John W. Davis . . . and the one who may be named as his running mate." [76] Whether these words were written before or after he learned of Davis's choice of Charles Bryan to complete the ticket is impossible to determine, though it is improbable that his brother's nomination was the

73. WJB to John E. Osborne, July 29, 1924, Bryan Papers.
74. Quoted in Florence Calvert Thorne, "His Last Year," in Samuel Gompers, *Seventy Years of Life and Labor* (New York, 1925), II, 537.
75. Quoted in Mann, *La Guardia*, p. 170.
76. *New York American*, July 10, 1924.

decisive factor in Bryan's decision.[77] Ideologically, Bryan belonged in the ranks of Senator La Follette's new Progressive party.[78] Emotionally, he was unable to make the move. Despite the concessions he had made to the spirit of nonpartisanship during his final years, he was still too closely bound by a sense of obligation to desert his party completely. He might sit out a campaign, as he had in 1920, but he could not bring himself to champion the cause of an opposition candidate. In addition, Bryan still clung to the notion that the surest road to reform was through the Democratic party. The delegates at the convention of 1920 had cheered him lustily but defeated his platform planks one by one. Those at the convention of 1924 had assaulted him brutally but adopted a platform which, for all of its failings, contained enough of the elements of Bryan's own program to insure his support.

His brother's candidacy and his strong pre-nomination criticisms of Davis placed Bryan in the unaccustomed position of being on the defensive. Throughout the campaign he was forced to insist that his brother's nomination had nothing to

77. "I told the West Virginia delegation that I would support the candidate whom Mr. Davis procured, and I would have done so even if it had been necessary to oppose my brother Charles," Bryan insisted. *New York Times*, July 12, 1924. Charles Bryan was not Davis's initial choice. He first offered the nomination to Senator Walsh of Montana who declined the dubious honor and then probably offered it to E. T. Meredith of Iowa. Nevertheless, Robert Woolley has insisted that Davis's selection was determined by his desire to keep the elder Bryan from bolting the ticket. Robert Woolley Memoirs MSS., Chapter XXXII, Woolley Papers. Senator Walsh, on the other hand, felt that Bryan was not influential in the naming of his brother. Thomas J. Walsh to George Fort Milton, December 23, 1924, Walsh Papers, Box 375. See also Alfred E. Smith, *Up to Now* (Garden City, New York, 1929), p. 290, and *New York Times*, July 10, 1924.

78. Before the Democrats met Bryan had encouraged La Follette's moves toward the creation of a third party in the hope that this threat would strengthen the position of the progressives in the Democratic convention. WJB to Robert M. La Follette, June 2, 1924, cited in Fola and Bella La Follette, *Robert M. La Follette*, II, 1104.

do with his support of the ticket. "My brother Charles," he
declared again and again, was nominated on his own merits
"because he met the three requirements": that the Vice Presidential candidate be a Westerner, a progressive, and a dry.[79]
His defense of his brother was intensified by the campaign
tactics of the Republicans, who concentrated their artillery
upon Charles Bryan rather than Davis. A large vote for La
Follette, the Republicans reasoned, would deadlock the Electoral College and throw the election into the House of Representatives. The progressives in that body would prevent the
selection of a President, while their colleagues in the Senate
would combine with the Democrats to elect Bryan Vice President. With no President chosen, the younger Bryan would
become the nation's Chief Executive. "It is therefore up to the
voters," Secretary of War Weeks proclaimed in a radio
broadcast, "to make their choice between President Coolidge
and Charles W. Bryan." Safety with Coolidge or chaos with a
Bryan in the White House was the nation's only choice, according to Republican propagandists.[80]

Bryan also was compelled to give endless explanations of his
attitude toward Davis. He had opposed Davis, he maintained,
not because of anything he had done but because his professional affiliations made him vulnerable to attack. "Was he cor-
rupted? I never said he was. I had no knowledge of his views.
I know them now . . . I talked to him and I knew he was a
progressive when I came away. At heart he is with the people
and can be trusted by the people." He even went so far as to
assert that "Mr. Davis is as well qualified for the presidency as
any man who ever ran. . . . He is a better candidate than I

79. WJB, "My Brother Charles," *World's Work*, XLVIII (September 1924), 553.

80. For Weeks's remarks see *New York Times*, October 22, 1924.
John W. Davis felt that these tactics cost the Democrats and Progressives many votes. Kenneth C. MacKay, *The Progressive Movement of
1924* (New York, 1947), p. 169.

ever was." [81] Bryan's loyalty to Davis was tested very early in the campaign when the latter issued a statement condemning the Ku Klux Klan or any other organization which challenged the doctrine of religious tolerance. "I hope you approve of my action," Davis wrote Bryan almost immediately. "I read a copy of your speech," Bryan replied, ". . . It was admirable." Though he was quick to add: "Now that your position has been so emphatically stated, they will not expect you to divert attention from other issues by continuously mentioning it . . ." [82]

In spite of the embarrassment that his support of the ticket caused him, Bryan waged an active and vigorous campaign. Beginning in Fresno, California, on September 8, he toured California, Oregon, Washington, Idaho, Utah, Nevada, Arizona, and New Mexico. Returning to Florida for a few days in early October, he then traveled to his old stamping grounds in Nebraska, where he inaugurated a tour of the Midwest which lasted until election day. In all, he made over a hundred speeches in fifteen states. "The meetings were large and the audiences appreciative," he informed his daughter, "and I was never more highly complimented on the effectiveness of my speeches." [83] In his syndicated column, David Lawrence corroborated Bryan's judgment: "Mr. Bryan is speaking to enormous crowds. His powerful voice, his eloquence, his dynamic personality are still as fascinating as they were years ago. . . . It is not denied even by the Republicans that he

81. News clipping, October 1, 1924, Bryan Papers.
82. Davis to WJB, August 24, 1924, WJB to Davis, August 25, 1924, Bryan Papers. When reporters questioned Bryan about Davis's speech he told them it had his "hearty approval . . . I am with him in what he said about the Klan." *New York Times*, August 30, 1924.
83. WJB to John W. Davis, September 29, 1924, WJB, "To the Democrats of Florida," news release dated October 10, 1924, WJB to Grace Bryan Hargreaves, November 13, 1924, Grace Bryan Hargreaves MSS., Bryan Papers.

has made votes for Davis. At least he has kept many wavering ones from going to La Follette." [84] The Democratic Speakers' Bureau issued similar reports and its chairman wired Bryan congratulations on the "splendid campaign you have conducted wherever you have spoken." [85]

Bryan's campaign speech was typical of those he had delivered in previous battles. Coolidge and Dawes were fine men, but they were reactionaries representing "All the predatory interests, all the trusts, all the favor-seeking, privilege hunting corporations. . ." The Democratic party, he asserted, "burns the bridges behind it, while the Republican party . . . burns the bridges before it. The Democrats will not turn backward; the Coolidge Republicans will not go forward." He had only kind words for La Follette, but he begged his Western audiences to remember that the only way to advance the progressive cause was to vote for Davis since La Follette had no chance of winning.[86]

As he was stumping through the West, Bryan did not allow the personal warmth he met from those he addressed to blind him to the unpleasant truth that the Democratic crusade, hampered by inadequate finances, lack of friendly newspapers, and the existence of a third party, was making little progress. "I have found great apathy among Democratic voters everywhere," he complained to Davis.[87] The apathy lasted until election day when only 50 per cent of the eligible voters marched to the polls to send Coolidge back to the White House for another four years. "We have suffered a very severe defeat — much greater than I had any idea was possible,"

84. David Lawrence's column dated October 1, 1924, clipping in ibid.

85. *New York Times*, September 22, 1924; Claude A. Swanson to WJB, October 28, 1924, Bryan Papers.

86. *New York Times*, October 5, 1924; *Morning Democrat* (Baker, Oregon), September 20, 1924, *Boise Sunday Capital News*, September 21, 1924, clippings in Bryan Papers.

87. WJB to Davis, September 29, 1924, Ibid.

Bryan admitted. "But," he added with his usual optimism, "it is not as bad as 1920 when the Republicans elected an overwhelming majority in both the Senate and the House. If we make as great gains two years from now as we did in 1922, we can control the next Congress and lay the foundation for a successful Presidential campaign." Viewing the eclipse of the sun a few months later he told newsmen: "It's just like a Democrat defeat. The sun will shine again." [88]

(5)

Before the nation could feel the warmth of the Democratic sun again, the clouds of factionalism and discord had to be made to disappear. Bryan had hoped that the long, torturous New York convention would give "everything bad in the party . . . a chance to boil out." [89] His hope proved to be in vain. Even before the election returns were in, the party's leaders began to snipe at one another. "I am appalled at the state of the Democrats of the country," the Chairman of the Democratic National Committee wrote Bryan. "Our party seems to have been a varied number of groups and most of these full of intoleration [sic]." [90]

Al Smith, Robert Woolley, and a number of Congressional leaders attributed the overwhelming defeat to the voters' fear of Charles Bryan's Western radicalism. The latter was convinced that Davis's Wall Street connections had driven large numbers of progressive voters into La Follette's camp.[91] Mc-Adoo and Walsh believed that the party's "certain victory" was wrecked by the attempt of the urban Democrats to control the ticket. "The Democratic Party had a cancer in its

88. WJB to H. E. Newbranch, November 15, 1924, ibid.; *New York Times*, November 7, 9, 1924, January 25, 1925.

89. *New York American*, July 5, 1924.

90. Clement L. Shaver to WJB, November 8, 1924, Bryan Papers.

91. Smith, *Up to Now*, p. 291; Robert Woolley Memoirs MSS., Chapter XXXII, Woolley Papers; *New York Times*, November 10, 1924; Charles W. Bryan to WJB, December 5, 1924, Bryan Papers.

head and a cancer in its stomach," McAdoo wrote during the
campaign, " — the one, Tammany in New York and the
other, George Brennan and the Cook County machine in Illinois. We have got to perform a major operation and get rid of
these cancers before we can ever make anything of the Democratic Party." [92]

Bryan not only was in accord with McAdoo's diagnosis, he
was willing to wield the scalpel personally. "The only hope of
national success for the Democratic Party lies in a union between the producers of the South and West against the predatory corporations that dominate the politics of the Northeast," he announced in December. ". . . In 1916 we won
without the aid of the East, and we must win without its aid
in 1928 . . ." [93] The party's harmonizers could not be
brushed aside so easily however. Early in 1925, Franklin D.
Roosevelt went from one Democratic leader to another proposing a party conference to iron out differences and adopt a
united program. Roosevelt took his proposal to Bryan in Miami and found him dubious about the possibility of integrat-
ing the urban Democrats into a truly progressive party. Bryan
also felt that the party should concentrate upon the Congressional elections of 1926 before it thought in terms of the next
Presidential contest, for the issues of that campaign would be
determined in Congress and not in party conclaves. Although
Roosevelt announced that he finally had brought Bryan
around to his way of thinking, the latter did not seem particularly dismayed when the plans for a Democratic conference
fell through.[94]

92. McAdoo to Gavin McNab, July 17, 1924, McAdoo Papers, Box
306. See also Thomas J. Walsh to McAdoo, December 4, 1924, Walsh
Papers, Box 375.

93. News release, December 4, 1924, Bryan Papers.

94. Roosevelt to William A. Oldfield, April 11, 1925, quoted in
Freidel, *Franklin D. Roosevelt: The Ordeal*, pp. 211-13; WJB to
Edward F. Britton, April 1, 1925, Bryan Papers; *New York Times*,
April 9, 14, 1925.

Shortly after his conversation with Roosevelt, Bryan told a cheering audience in Brooklyn that he would be in politics until he died.[95] Almost as if to give his pronouncement added meaning, Bryan decided to campaign for election to the United States Senate in 1926. Bryan's decision evidently was prompted by his strong showing in the Florida primaries of 1924, by his desire to reduce his itinerant crusading so as to spend more time at the side of his ailing wife, and by his conviction that a Senate seat would provide a suitable platform from which to champion his principles during his declining years. "I dread the idea of taking on any additional load of care," he wrote the editor of the *Sanford* (Florida) *Herald*, "but I feel that this is my last opportunity to render a service to the party which has made me what I am and given me all I have. I regard a union of the South and West as the only hope of the party. Being a resident of the South and acquainted with the West, and having an influence, . . . I believe I can render the party more service than any other man now in the Senate or likely to be there during the next few years." [96] In a subsequent letter to a Washington editor he wrote: "The term in the Senate would enable me to help lay the foundations for the next Presidential campaign and for the Presidential campaign following. By that time I would be seventy-two and I dare not look much beyond that time." [97]

Bryan's determination to spend his last days in the dignified surroundings of the United States Senate came too late. The career that had begun so impulsively amidst the turmoil of the 1896 Chicago Democratic convention was to end no less suddenly in the frenzied evangelical atmosphere of a small Southern town.

95. Ibid. May 19, 1925.
96. WJB to R. L. Dean, March 11, 1925, Bryan Papers.
97. WJB to Edward Keating, April 10, 1925, ibid.

IX: The Last Battle

I have all the information I want to live by and to die by. — WJB

(1)

As HE DEPARTED from the convention of 1924, Bryan, with tears in his eyes, is reputed to have told Senator Heflin that he had never been so humiliated in his life.[1] During his final year he was to experience even greater humiliation. Yet that year dawned hopefully enough. By the beginning of 1925 neither Bryan nor any of his fellow fundamentalists could feel that their efforts had been in vain. Although no other state immediately followed Florida in declaring officially against the teaching of evolution, fundamentalist pressure in a number of states caused officials to ban textbooks which included Darwinian theories; the number of college professors and secondary school teachers who were forced to resign because of their belief in evolution was steadily increasing; and throughout the South and Midwest local school boards were ordering their teachers to ignore the new biological theories.[2]

This type of pressure and intimidation, because it was so difficult to isolate and combat openly, was unquestionably the most effective tactic the fundamentalists could have employed. Yet the leaders of that movement were not satisfied; they thirsted for statutes which would settle for all time the question of how man was created. Early in 1925 the lower house of the North Carolina Legislature defeated an anti-

1. Werner, *Bryan*, p. 280.
2. Furniss, *The Fundamentalist Controversy*, pp. 3, 85, 87; Shipley, *The War on Modern Science*, pp. 188-90; Beale, *Are American Teachers Free?*, Chapter X.

evolution measure by a vote of 67 to 46. During the struggle the presidents of the state university and of Wake Forest College had taken the lead in combating the proposed legislation.[3] This kind of opposition was lacking in the neighboring state of Tennessee, where the fundamentalists now focused their attention.

In 1924, W. B. Marr, a Nashville attorney, had invited Bryan to speak in Nashville. Impressed by his lecture "Is the Bible True?" Marr and his associates had several thousand copies printed and distributed throughout the state.[4] Shortly after the 1925 session of the Tennessee General Assembly opened, Senator John A. Shelton introduced an anti-evolution statute. Marr quickly sent five hundred copies of Bryan's speech to members of both houses in order to "guide" them during the deliberations.[5] The Senate Judiciary Committee, however, recommended rejection of Shelton's bill on the ground that "it would not be the part of wisdom for the legislature to make laws that even remotely affected the question of religious belief." [6] It was not Shelton but John Washington Butler, an obscure member of the Tennessee House of Representatives, who was destined to make his name immortal by attaching it to a statute prohibiting the teaching of evolution. Butler, a farmer from highly rural Macon County and a member of the Primitive Baptist Church, had first been elected to the House in 1922 on a platform stressing his belief in the literal Bible and his opposition to the teaching of evolution in the schools.

It was not until his second term that Butler decided to em-

3. Ibid. pp. 238, 241–2.
4. Kenneth M. Bailey, "The Enactment of Tennessee's Anti-evolution Law," *Journal of Southern History*, XVI (November 1950), 475.
5. Marr to WJB, July 6, 1925, Grace Bryan Hargreaves MSS., Bryan Papers.
6. Bailey, *Journal of Southern History*, XVI (November 1950), 477.

body his convictions in a bill. Once his decision was made, he did not consult Bryan or anyone else. On his forty-ninth birthday he sat down and drafted a bill which made it unlawful for a teacher in any school supported in whole or part by state funds "to teach any theory that denies the story of the divine creation of man as taught in the Bible, and to teach instead that man has descended from a lower order of animals." Butler's bill, which was submitted to the House on January 21, 1925, one day after Shelton's was introduced in the Senate, was accorded a happier reception. Two days after its introduction the House Committee on Education recommended its passage, and four days later the House adopted it overwhelmingly by a vote of 71 to 5.[7]

The Butler bill was then sent on to the Senate, where Senator Shelton threw his support behind it. He quickly solicited Bryan's suggestions for improving the measure, writing: "If necessary we can defer final action for a few days longer in order to have the benefit of your advice." "The special thing I want to suggest," Bryan responded immediately, "is that it is better not to have a penalty."[8] Upon first consideration the Senate Judiciary Committee recommended rejection of the statute but following a month's recess, during which public opinion made itself felt, the committee reversed itself and by a vote of 7 to 4 reported the law favorably. The debate in the Senate produced slightly more opposition to the proposed statute than it had faced in the House. One Senator tried to laugh it out of the legislature, as similar bills had been in other states, by proposing an amendment to "prohibit the teaching

7. Shipley, *The War Against Science*, p. 193; Bailey, *Journal of Southern History*, XVI (November 1950), 476. Although Butler's bill received overwhelming support from those legislators representing areas much like his own — intensely rural with a high rate of illiteracy — it should be noted that the majority of lawmakers from every urban county but one also voted for the bill. Ibid. pp. 488–9.

8. Shelton to WJB, February 5, 1925, WJB to Shelton, February 9, 1925, Bryan Papers.

that the earth is round." But all such attempts — and there were relatively few of them — failed, and the Senate approved the measure 24 to 6.[9] The bill now found its way to the desk of the state's able governor, Austin Peay. Peay's dilemma was a real one. Although he was reputed to have privately felt it to be an absurd bill, Peay found no groundswell of opposition to which he could appeal. During the debate in the legislature not one word of protest was heard from any of the state's leading citizens, from the State Department of Education, from the University of Tennessee, or from any other major educational institution in the state.[10] No aspirant to martyrdom, Peay signed the bill and defended his action by writing: "Right or wrong, there is a widespread belief that something is shaking the fundamentals of the country, both in religion and in morals. It is the opinion of many that an abandonment of the old-fashioned faith and belief in the Bible is our trouble in large degree. It is my own belief." [11]

Although Bryan was not pleased at the inclusion of fines from $100 to $500 for offenders of the statute, he hailed its enactment. "The Christian parents of the State owe you a debt of gratitude for saving their children from the poisonous influence of an unproven hypothesis," he wired the Governor. ". . . The South is now leading the Nation in the defense of Bible Christianity. Other states North and South will follow the example of Tennessee." [12] It was precisely this expectation that prompted the American Civil Liberties Union to make a *cause célèbre* out of a statute which was, in

9. Bailey, *Journal of Southern History*, XVI (November 1950), 479–82.

10. Shipley, *The War on Modern Science*, pp. 197, 199; Joseph Wood Krutch, "Tennessee: Where Cowards Rule," *The Nation*, CXXI (July 15, 1925), 88–9.

11. Bailey, *Journal of Southern History*, XVI (November 1950), 484.

12. WJB to Peay, undated, Bryan Papers.

reality, merely one more small ripple in the wave of prohibitory legislation that engulfed the nation during the Twenties.

As far as the Governor of Tennessee was concerned, the law to which he had just appended his signature was not intended to be an active statute. "After a careful examination," he wrote in a message to the legislature, "I can find nothing of consequence in the books now being taught in our schools with which this bill will interfere in the slightest manner. Therefore, it will not put our teachers in any jeopardy. Probably the law will never be applied." All that the framers of the legislation intended, Peay insisted, was to lodge "a distinct protest against an irreligious tendency to exalt so-called science, and deny the Bible in some schools and quarters. . ." [13] Peay, of course, was attempting to justify his own action, yet there is a certain validity in his interpretation of the law. During the period between its enactment and the beginning of the Scopes Trial, no attempt was made on the part of state officials to translate it into action. The contents of science courses and texts were not investigated, and students continued to learn biology from teachers and texts that accepted Darwin and his theories. [14]

The sole attempt to enforce the Tennessee "monkey-bill" was due not to the actions of its friends but of its foes. Shortly after the law was passed, the officers of the American Civil Liberties Union deliberated and decided to sponsor a test case. In the closing days of April the organization began its search for a plaintiff by informing Tennessee newspapers of its willingness to guarantee legal and financial assistance to any teacher who would test the anti-evolution law. [15]

13. Shipley, *The War on Modern Science*, p. 200.
14. Ray Ginger, *Six Days or Forever? Tennessee v. John Thomas Scopes* (Boston, 1958), pp. 7, 18.
15. Ibid. pp. 18–19; Pearl Kluger, "New Light on the Scopes' Trial," (unpublished Master's essay, Columbia University, 1957), pp. 17–18, 21.

One of those who read of the Union's offer was George Rappelyea, a young mining engineer in Dayton, Tennessee, who had opposed the law since its passage and who now decided that Dayton was the very place to test it. Calling in the town's 24-year-old science teacher, John Thomas Scopes, Rappelyea asked him if he could teach biology without teaching evolution. When Scopes answered in the negative, F. E. Robinson, the head of the county board of education, in whose drug store the interview was being held, accused him of violating the law. "So has every other teacher," Scopes replied and then explained that Hunter's *Civic Biology*, the state-approved textbook, taught from an evolutionary standpoint. "Let's take this thing to court and test the legality of it," Rappelyea suggested almost casually.[16] It took some doing to overcome Scopes's understandable reluctance, but the glib-tongued engineer, appealing to Scopes's duty as an American and as an educator, finally prevailed. "He therefore consented to the arrest and the plans were drafted," Rappelyea has recorded. "I wired the American Civil Liberties Union that the stage was set and that if they could defray the expenses of production the play could open at once. They agreed." [17]

All that remained was the selection of the principal actors. On May 7, Scopes was arrested. Five days later, Bryan, who was in Pittsburgh delivering a series of lectures, received a wire from the executive committee of the World's Christian Fundamentals Association informing him of his selection as their attorney at the trial. "I shall be pleased to act for your great religious organizations and without compensation assist in the enforcement of the Tennessee law provided of course it is agreeable to the Law Department of the State," Bryan re-

16. John T. Scopes, "The Trial That Rocked the Nation," *Reader's Digest* (March 1961), 137.
17. Rappelyea interview in a Mobile newspaper dated January 24, 1926, cited in Kluger, "New Light on the Scopes' Trial," p. 20.

plied.[18] It was more than agreeable, as Bryan learned a few days later when he received the following letter from Sue Hicks, one of the prosecuting attorneys:

> We have been trying to get in touch with you by wire to ask you to become associated with us in the prosecution of the case of the State against J. T. Scopes . . . but our wires did not reach you.
>
> We will consider it a great honor to have you with us in this prosecution.[19]

Almost immediately Clarence Darrow and Dudley Field Malone offered their services to John Randolph Neal, Scopes's local attorney. Scopes and Neal, acting on their own, accepted the offer, and the American Civil Liberties Union, which had planned to secure politically conservative and religiously orthodox attorneys to defend Scopes, found itself saddled with an outspoken skeptic and a prominent divorce lawyer.[20]

William Jennings Bryan, Jr., a Los Angeles attorney who had long been desirous of assuming an active role in the fundamentalist crusade and who, after his father's death, was to become president of the Anti-Evolution League of America, took his place alongside the elder Bryan as a member of the prosecution. The appearance of the two Bryans for the state

18. L. M. Aldridge to WJB, May 12, 1925, WJB to Aldridge, undated, Bryan Papers.

19. Hicks to WJB, May 14, 1925, ibid.

20. Scopes's refusal to ask Darrow and Malone to step out of the case forced the American Civil Liberties Union to accept them though its leadership continued to oppose their presence and tried to attract more conservative-minded counsel. Overtures were made to John W. Davis and Charles Evans Hughes, but both men declined. For the details of this situation see the correspondence in Vol. 274 of the American Civil Liberties Union Archives, Princeton University, Princeton, New Jersey, especially Forrest Bailey to Charles H. Strong, August 17, 1925, and Roger N. Baldwin to Raymond Fosdick, October 21, 1925.

and of Darrow, Malone, and the American Civil Liberties Union's attorney, Arthur Garfield Hays, for the defense, converted the trial into a free-for-all in which the fundamental issues at stake were often in danger of being forgotten. The Scopes Trial, occupying the center of national attention, offered the friends of academic freedom a rare opportunity to proclaim the essentials of their creed and to point out that while local communities had the unquestionable legal authority to regulate education, there were moral as well as legal limitations to the curb that could be placed upon free speech and thought in the classroom. This point, of course, was made more than once, but its applicability to other parts of the nation and to issues other than evolution was blurred by the cultural and sectional struggle which was being waged simultaneously.

At the very outset Bryan seemed to have a clear idea of what the trial was all about. "I have been explaining the case to audiences," he reported to Sue Hicks in May. "It is the *easiest* case to explain I have ever found. While I am perfectly willing to go into the question of evolution, I am not sure that it is involved. The *right* of the *people* speaking through the legislature, to control the schools which they *create* and *support* is the real issue as I see it." [21] "The first question to be decided," he announced in June, "is who shall control our public schools?" If not the people speaking through their legislatures, then who? The scientists? But there was only one scientist for every ten thousand people, "a pretty little oligarchy to put in control of the education of all the children." The teachers themselves? That proposition, Bryan felt, needed only to be stated to be rejected as absurd. "The teacher is an employee and receives a salary; employees take directions from their employers, and the teacher is no excep-

21. WJB to Hicks, May 28, 1925, Grace Bryan Hargreaves MSS. Bryan Papers.

tion to the rule. No teacher would be permitted to teach the students that a monarchy is the only good government and kings the only good chief executives." [22]

While on the one hand Bryan spoke as if he was willing to see the trial waged on the issue of how far the community could go in imposing limitations upon learning, on the other he acted as if the trial was to be a "duel to the death" between religion and evolution. "I greatly appreciate the opportunity the Fundamentalists have given me to defend the faith," he wrote one of his colleagues in the beginning of June.[23] Some days later he informed a supporter that "The American people do not know what a menace evolution is — I am expecting a tremendous reaction as the result of the information which will go out from Dayton . . ." [24]

During that brief period when he controlled the defense strategy, John Randolph Neal echoed Bryan's initial statements. "The question is not whether evolution is true or untrue," he asserted, "but involves the freedom of teaching, or what is more important, the freedom of learning." [25] His new associates, however, did not share his opinion. Their attitude was best summed up by their scientific ally Henry Fairfield Osborn, who observed on the eve of the trial: "The facts in this great case are that William Jennings Bryan is the man on trial; John Thomas Scopes is not the man on trial. If the case is properly set before the jury, Scopes will be the real plaintiff, Bryan will be the real defendant." [26] This was precisely what Darrow himself had in mind. In explaining his courtroom strategy, years after the trial, Darrow wrote: "My ob-

22. WJB, "The Tennessee Case," news release dated June 2, 1925, ibid.

23. WJB to W. B. Riley, June 7, 1925, ibid.

24. WJB to Dr. Howard A. Kelly, June 17, 1925, ibid.

25. Ginger, *Six Days or Forever?*, p. 45.

26. Henry Fairfield Osborn, *The Earth Speaks to Bryan* (New York, 1925), p. 2.

ject, and my only object, was to focus the attention of the country on the programme of Mr. Bryan and the other fundamentalists in America." [27] To Arthur Garfield Hays the issue was even more clear-cut. The trial, he wrote, "was a battle between two types of mind — the rigid, orthodox, accepting, unyielding, narrow, conventional mind, and the broad liberal, critical, cynical, skeptical and tolerant mind." [28]

(2)

The days before the trial were busy ones for Bryan.[29] In May he was in Columbus, Ohio, attending the 1925 General Assembly of his church. The situation at the Presbyterian conclave was confused since all of the leading candidates were fundamentalists. Bryan tried to ply the middle of the road by refusing to support either Dr. L. E. MacAfee, the candidate of the extreme fundamentalists or Dr. Charles R. Erdman a moderate fundamentalist whose candidacy was being advanced by the liberals. Instead Bryan backed Dr. W. O. Thompson, the retiring president of Ohio State University. On the day of the balloting Dr. Thompson withdrew from the race and Bryan, who had helped to break the ranks of the extreme fundamentalists, had to sit unhappily by and watch Dr. Erdman's election.[30]

During this period Bryan began to modify his earlier stand on religion and the schools. If the spiritual foundations of the

27. Clarence Darrow, *The Story of My Life* (New York, 1932), p. 249.

28. Arthur Garfield Hays, *Let Freedom Ring* (New York, 1928), pp. 27–8.

29. In the following pages only those aspects of the trial with which Bryan was intimately connected will be treated. No attempt will be made to recreate the trial in its entirety. Ginger, *Six Days or Forever?*, is a detailed account of the trial. The single most valuable printed source for the trial is Leslie H. Allen's excellent abridgment of the trial transcript, *Bryan and Darrow at Dayton* (New York, 1925).

30. *New York Times*, May 21, 22, 1925.

nation were being undermined by the teaching of evolution, were they not being weakened equally by the absence of any religious teachings in the schools? As early as 1914 he had suggested to Rabbi Wise and Cardinal Gibbons that "there should be some way of utilizing a part of the school time in the teaching of morals, and believing that morals rest upon religion, I know of no way of teaching them except under religious supervision." [31]

More than ten years later, in April 1925, Bryan wrote to Representative Taylor of the Florida lower house, proposing a law making the reading of the Bible compulsory in the public schools with a provision allowing parents to have their children excused if they so desired. "But I would go farther than this," he added. "We are interested in the religious development of young Jews and of young Catholics as well as young Protestants, and the law could, and in my judgment should, provide that any religious denomination or group of denominations shall have the privilege of using the school rooms on equal terms . . . for religious teaching.[32]

When the Florida Legislature passed a law providing for the reading of the Scriptures in the public schools, Bryan congratulated it but made it clear that he was not satisfied: ". . . the reading of the Bible a few minutes each day is not sufficient. The Bible needs to be taught, as school lessons are taught, by teachers who are free to interpret, explain and illustrate them." [33] This is as far as Bryan was prepared to go up to the time of his death, though his opponents charged that his plans were far more grandiose. During the Scopes Trial a *New York Times* correspondent informed the public that

31. WJB to James Gibbons, December 5, 1914, WJB to Stephen S. Wise, December 15, 1914, Bryan Papers.

32. WJB to John A. Taylor, April 17, 1925, ibid.

33. *Miami Tribune*, May 1, 1925, clipping in ibid. For more details relating to Bryan's scheme see WJB, "Plan for Religious Exercises in the Public Schools," manuscript in ibid.

Bryan was planning to "put God in the Constitution," an assertion which Bryan angrily denied.[34] And eight months after Bryan's death, Augustus Thomas, the playwright, who had nominated Bryan for President in 1908, claimed that he saw the actual wording of an amendment drawn up by Bryan which would have established the United States as a Christian nation.[35] Though it is possible that Bryan might have been driven to make such proposals had he lived, there is no evidence that he did so before his death.

In the beginning of June Bryan stopped at Nashville on his way home to Florida to confer with three fellow members of the prosecution, Wallace C. Haggard and the Hicks brothers. At the end of the conference the four men announced that they had come to a "clear understanding of the lines of the prosecution." [36] Nonetheless, Bryan continued to keep in close touch with the Tennessee prosecution. The one point upon which Bryan was adamant from the beginning of his association with the prosecution was the question of punishment. ". . . I don't think we should insist on more [than] the minimum fine," he informed Sue Hicks, "and I will let the defendant have the money to pay if he needs it. It is a test case and will end all controversy." [37]

"The unbelievers are evidently very much worried about the case," Bryan wrote Hicks on June 10. The defense, he noted, was frantically searching for big-name attorneys. "They seem to realize they are in for a real fight." Bryan himself, however, seemed a bit nervous. While he assured

34. WJB to *New York Times*, July 14, 1925, ibid. Bryan's letter to the *Times* was less than candid. He not only refuted the reporter's charge but also denied that he advocated teaching the Bible in the public schools.

35. *New York Times*, March 4, 1926.

36. *New York Post*, June 5, 1925.

37. WJB to Hicks, May 28, 1925, Grace Bryan Hargreaves MSS., Bryan Papers.

Hicks of his confidence that the prosecution as it was presently constituted could "meet their attack without any outside aid," he felt that the case was too important to take any chances, and he suggested that they too invite some prominent attorneys to join them. "The biggest lawyer I know of is Samuel Untermyer of New York. He has had large experience in big cases and is a match for any of the men on the other side. Being a Jew, he ought to be interested in defending Moses from the Darwinites. He has been my personal and political friend for twenty-five years and I am sure he will be glad to join us." Anxious to have as united a religious front as possible, Bryan also felt it might be useful to seek the aid of a prominent Catholic such as Senator Thomas Walsh of Montana or Senator David Walsh of Massachusetts.[38]

Without waiting to hear from Hicks, Bryan invited Untermyer to assist in the prosecution.[39] Hicks's first response was not encouraging. He had talked over Bryan's suggestion with Attorney General Stewart, Ben McKenzie, and other members of the prosecution, and they were of the opinion that the prosecution should stand pat. Stewart felt that it would be a greater victory to convict Scopes in spite of the talent he had representing him. "Knowing the sentiment of the court (who by the way is somewhat indiscreet in discussing the merits of the case with the Attorney General), General Stewart is confident their motion to quash the indictment will be over-ruled and all evidence will be admitted at the trial." [40]

The very next day Hicks and his associates had a change of heart and agreed that it might be useful to have additional counsel, "although, we some what doubt the advisability of having a Jew in the case for the reason that they reject part of the Bible and do not believe in the Divinity of Christ. How-

38. WJB to Hicks, June 10, 1925, ibid.
39. WJB to Samuel Untermyer, June 11, 1925, ibid.
40. Hicks to WJB, June 12, 1925, ibid.

ever we are willing to leave this matter to your judgment and accept the attorneys you advise." It was now Bryan's turn to be inconstant. Untermyer had gone to Europe and probably would not be able to help in any case, he informed Hicks. "I recognize the force of the objection you make to him and Walsh. . . . After reading your letter, I am inclined to think we shall not need any additional attorneys." "It is interesting to note the growing interest in the case," he added. "Am preparing myself on all imaginable points." [41]

When Bryan finally did hear from Untermyer, his suspicions were confirmed. The New York attorney would be in Europe throughout the month of July and thus could not aid in the prosecution of Scopes. He did, however, have some prophetic advice to give Bryan. He urged him to confine the issue strictly. "I would seek to exclude all discussions by experts or otherwise on the subject of Evolution (which to my mind has nothing whatever to do with the case . . .), and rest squarely on the proposition that the plain letter and spirit of the law have been violated, and that the burden rests upon the Defence to establish the unconstitutionality of that law not by introduction of evidence, but by discussion of the legal problem involved." "I am fearful however that there is so much of 'grand-stand play' involved in this prosecution and so great a desire on the part of the local influences to convert it into a sensational controversy instead of adhering closely to the issues involved, that it will not be easy to keep the trial within the legal limits." [42]

Toward the end of June, Darrow, Malone, and Bainbridge Colby, who was then associated with the defense, traveled to Dayton to look over the scene of the impending trial. Hicks and Wallace Haggard were quick to report the event to

41. Hicks to WJB, June 13, 1925, WJB to Hicks, June 16, 1925, ibid.

42. Samuel Untermyer to WJB, June 25, 1925, ibid.

Bryan. Both men found Darrow an impressive figure, and both thought he was surprised at the cordiality of his reception. "Darrow at one time said that some of the Northern people had the idea that they would be in bodily danger if they came down here among the fundamentalists," Hicks wrote.[43] The Progressive Club of Dayton held a banquet in Darrow's honor, at which the Chicago lawyer spoke for over an hour. Haggard described the reaction of the audience for Bryan: "Those in attendance seemed to shudder and even abhor the woe and despair that crept through his various thoughts and was even written on his countenance. . . . there can be no doubt, despite his intelligence and his magnetism, he cannot prevail upon our people." [44]

Bryan read these letters with interest. Darrow, he agreed, "is an able man, and, I think, an honest man." [45] As the opening day of the trial approached, Bryan seemed more convinced than ever that it would serve a great purpose. "There is no reason why the Scopes Trial should not be conducted on a high plane without the least personal feeling," he wrote one of his neighbors. ". . . The trial will be a success in proportion as it enables the public to understand the two sides and the reasons on both sides. Every question has to be settled at last by the public and the sooner it is understood the sooner it can be settled." [46]

(3)

The environment in which the Scopes Trial took place has been described too often to require repetition here. The little town of Dayton in the Tennessee hill country, the meetings of the Holy Rollers from surrounding areas, the sudden inva-

43. Hicks to WJB, June 23, 1925, ibid.
44. Haggard to WJB, June 23, 1925, ibid.
45. WJB to Hicks, June 25, 1925, Grace Bryan Hargreaves MSS., ibid.
46. WJB to Ed Howe, June 30, 1925, ibid.

sion of cranks of all sorts vying with one another to attract attention, the garish exhibits and banners enjoining the people to read their Bible and avoid damnation, the fundamentalist judge from Gizzard's Cove, Tennessee, who was to rule over the proceedings — all provided an unusually rich feast for the army of journalists, few of whom were able to restrain themselves. "The thing is genuinely fabulous," exulted H. L. Mencken. "I have stored up enough material to last me twenty years." [47]

Bryan left his home in Miami on Monday, July 6, and arrived in Dayton the next day. As he descended from his train he was cheered by three hundred residents. After an automobile procession down the main street, Bryan, in his shirt sleeves and with a pith helmet protecting him from the blazing sun, spent the afternoon strolling through the town getting acquainted. He really did not have to, of course. He had been in hundreds of towns like it before, and he knew it and its people well. In a speech before the Dayton Progressive Club that night Bryan threw down the gauntlet to his opponents. "The contest between evolution and Christianity is a duel to the death. . . . If evolution wins in Dayton Christianity goes — not suddenly of course, but gradually — for the two cannot stand together. . . . The atheists, agnostics and all other opponents of Christianity understand the character of the struggle, hence this interest in this case. From this time forth the Christians will understand the character of the struggle also. In an open fight the truth will triumph." [48]

The following night Bryan and his party drove six miles straight up into the mountains to keep a speaking engagement at the Morgan Springs Hotel. After dinner Bryan stepped out onto the veranda overlooking the Tennessee valley, and began

47. Edgar Kemler, *The Irreverent Mr. Mencken* (Boston, 1950), p. 185.
48. *New York Times,* July 8, 1925.

to speak to the two hundred hill folk sitting on the railings and steps around him. Directly in front of him sat an old man in a wheelchair who looked up at Bryan "with the rapt countenance of one who listens to someone inspired." Next to him stood a tall mountaineer who remained immobile throughout the speech, one hand grasping a glass of water if Bryan should want it. As he stood in the darkness, his figure silhouetted by a thin ray of light from the hotel door, an occasional flash of lightning and rumble of thunder made the scene seem almost contrived. Bryan spoke softly of his pride in the South and predicted the coming of a great religious revival which would begin in the South and sweep across the nation. His final words were met with a reverential hush.[49] "His voice, always a beautiful instrument, vibrated with feeling," wrote the *Times* correspondent, "his whole being was synchronized into a graceful machine for driving home his word . . ." This night convinced the journalist that Bryan "is more than a great politician, more than a lawyer in a trial, more even than one of our greatest orators, he is a symbol of their simple religious faith." [50]

The trial opened on Friday, July 10, 1925, and after a jury was selected court adjourned until Monday. Bryan found himself in great demand as a speaker during that first weekend. In these talks he explained the reasons for his participation in the trial. "The people of Tennessee," he said on Saturday, "have a right to protect the Bible as they understand it. They are not compelled to consider the interpretations placed upon it by people from other states." Speaking from the pulpit of the Methodist Episcopal Church the next morning he declared: "While God does not despise the learned, he does not give them a monopoly of His attention. The unlearned in

49. This account is based upon the picturesque report printed in ibid. July 10, 1925.
50. Ibid. July 9, 10, 1925.

this country are much more numerous than the learned.
. . . Thank God I am going to spend the latter years of my
life in a locality where there is a belief in God, and in the Son of
God, and in a civilization to be based on salvation through
blood." Speaking to a large gathering on the courthouse lawn
in the afternoon, Bryan denied the widely circulated statement which quoted him as having said that he intended to
"put God into the Constitution." "Our purpose and our only
purpose," he assured his listeners, "is to vindicate the right of
parents to guard the religion of their children against efforts
made in the name of science to undermine faith in supernatural religion. There is no attack on free speech, or freedom of
the press, or freedom of thought, or freedom of knowledge,
but surely parents have a right to guard the religious welfare
of their children." [51]

The opening days of the trial were glorious days for Bryan.
Everywhere he went he was met by throngs of devoted and
admiring followers. H. L. Mencken in his characteristically
hyperbolic style remarked: "There were many . . . who believed that Bryan was no longer merely human, but had lifted
himself up to some level or other of the celestial angels.
. . . It would have surprised no one if he had suddenly begun to perform miracles. . . . I saw plenty of his customers
approach him stealthily to touch his garments. . . . Those
with whom he shook hands were made men." [52] When the
court reconvened on Monday morning most of the one thousand spectators who crowded into the Dayton courtroom had
hopes of hearing their champion rise and defend the faith, but
Bryan was in no hurry. During the first four days of the trial
he sat in the stifling courthouse in his shirt sleeves waving a
large fan, and except for one or two brief statements he remained silent as the defense made a futile attempt to quash the

51. Allen, *Bryan and Darrow at Dayton*, pp. 7–9.
52. Mencken, *Heathen Days*, pp. 230–31.

indictment against Scopes on legal grounds. Nor did he break his silence as his fellow attorneys for the prosecution opened and closed their exceptionally brief case which consisted merely of calling four witnesses all of whom testified to the fact that Scopes had based his lectures in biology upon Darwin's teachings.[53]

As soon as the prosecution rested its case the defense announced that it would introduce fifteen scientists and clergymen who had journeyed to Dayton from all sections of the country and who would endeavor to show that there was no conflict between the Biblical and scientific accounts of creation. As Darrow was examining the first of these fifteen, Dr. Maynard M. Metcalf, a zoologist from Johns Hopkins University, Attorney General A. T. Stewart, and former Attorney General McKenzie objected to the introduction of such testimony.[54] The ensuing debate over the admissibility of scientific evidence, which consumed the entire fifth day of the proceedings, was the occasion of Bryan's first and last major speech of the trial.[55] "We do not need any expert to tell us what the law means," he said in opening, "an expert cannot be permitted to come in here and try to defeat the enforcement of a law . . . This is not the place to try to prove that the law ought never to have been passed. The place to prove that was at the legislature."

As Bryan spoke, the eyes of all the spectators were upon him. The residents of Dayton had been waiting for precisely this moment. They leaned forward expectantly to hear their champion demolish the opponents of their faith with words of derision and scorn, and Bryan, forgetting Untermyer's advice, did not disappoint them. Holding up a copy of Hunter's *Civic Biology*, the text from which Scopes had taught, Bryan

53. Allen, *Bryan and Darrow at Dayton,* pp. 10 ff.
54. Ibid. pp. 56 ff.
55. For Bryan's speech see ibid. pp. 63 ff.

turned to a diagram on page 194 which classified all the animal species:

> Of course it [the diagram] is only a guess, and I don't suppose it is carried to a one or even to ten. I see they are in round numbers, and I don't think all the animals breed in round numbers, and so I think it must be a generalization of them. (Laughter.)
>
> 8,000 protozoa, 35,000 sponges. I am satisfied from some I have seen there must be more than 35,000 sponges. (Laughter.)
>
> . . . Then there are the amphibia. I don't know whether they have not yet decided to come out, or have almost decided to go back. (Laughter.)
>
> . . . And then we have mammals, 3,500, and there is a little circle, and a man is in the circle. Find him; find man.
>
> There is the book. There is the book they were teaching your children; teaching that man was a mammal and so indistinguishable among the mammals that they leave him there with other mammals. (Laughter and applause.) Including elephants. (Laughter.)
>
> Talk about putting Daniel in the lion's den! How dare those scientists put man in a little ring like that with lions and tigers and everything that is bad?
>
> Tell me that the parents of this day have not any right to declare that children are not to be taught this doctrine — shall not be taken down from the high plane upon which God put man? Shall we be detached from the throne of God and be compelled to link our ancestors with the jungle — tell that to these children?

Bryan next picked up a copy of Darwin's *Descent of Man* and began to quote from it, after first apologizing "if I have to use some of these long words — I have been trying all my life to use short words, and it is kind of hard to turn scientist for a moment (Laughter) and try to express myself in their language." Drawing more laughter still by taking Darwin to task for having man descend "Not even from American monkeys but from Old World monkeys," Bryan grew more serious and militant. Pointing to Dr. Metcalf, he thundered: "I suppose this distinguished scholar who came here shamed them all by his number of degrees. He did not shame me, for I have more than he has. . . . Did he tell you where life began? Did he tell you that back of all there was a God? Not a word about it. Did he tell you how life began? Not a word and not one of them can tell you how life began. . . . They want to come in with their little padded-up evolution that commences with nothing and ends nowhere." He held up Nietzsche and the young Chicago murderers, Leopold and Loeb, as products of evolutionary teachings, and pointed out that in his defense of Leopold and Loeb, Darrow had argued that the professors who taught Nietzsche's doctrines to the young, impressionable Leopold were just as responsible for the murder as Leopold himself. When Darrow denied this, Bryan read verbatim extracts from Darrow's argument to prove his point.

Bryan ended as he had begun, by defending the right of a state to enforce its own statutes without outside interference. ". . . I think we ought to confine ourselves to the law and to the evidence that can be admitted in accordance with the law," he said in closing. ". . . The facts are simple, the case is plain, and if these gentlemen want to enter upon a larger field of educational work on the subject of evolution, let us get through with this case and then convene a mock court. . . . (Prolonged applause.)" "Papa spoke," Mrs. Bryan wrote her daughter Grace, "and I never saw him quite so agitated. He trembled when he stood up, and it has alarmed William and me very much. His speech was very well received." [56]

The differences — and similarities — between the two sides were perhaps brought out most forcibly in the speeches delivered by Darrow and Attorney General Stewart. Both men

56. Mary B. Bryan to Grace Bryan Hargreaves, July 20, 1925, Grace Bryan Hargreaves MSS., Bryan Papers.

spoke with deep fervor, both used similar arguments to bolster their case, and both tried to convince their audience that even one concession to their opponents would open wide the floodgates of disaster. The banning of evolution was only the first step, Darrow warned on the second day of the trial. Next "you may ban books and the newspapers. Soon you may set Catholic against Protestant, and Protestant against Protestant, and try to foist your own religion on the minds of men. . . . Today it is the public school teachers, tomorrow the private, the next day the preachers and the lecturers, the magazines, the books, the newspapers." [57] Stewart, in his speech a few days later, hailed Darrow as one of the greatest lawyers in America and remarked: "Great God! the good that a man of his ability could have done if he had aligned himself with the forces of right instead of aligning himself with that which strikes its poisonous fangs at the very bosom of Christianity." If evolution won this battle the next step would be to deprive Christians of their right to believe in the Virgin Birth, then in the Resurrection, "until finally that precious Book and its glorious teachings upon which this civilization has been built will be taken from us." [58]

It was not Bryan or Darrow or Stewart, but Dudley Field Malone who delivered the most eloquent speech of the trial. Malone had served under Bryan in the State Department and still referred to him as "my old chief and friend." Malone reminded his "old chief," however, that whether he knew it or not "he is a mammal, he is an animal, and he is a man." "Mr. Bryan," he thundered, "is not the only one who has spoken for the Bible. . . . There are other people in this country who have given their whole lives to God." "There is never a duel with truth," he said in his stirring peroration, "the truth always wins. . . . The truth does not need the forces

57. Allen, *Bryan and Darrow at Dayton*, p. 30.
58. Ibid. p. 88.

of Government. The truth does not need Mr. Bryan. . . . We feel we stand with progress. . . . We feel we stand with fundamental freedom in America. We are not afraid. Where is the fear? We defy it!" [59]

"Dayton thundered her verdict at the end of the speech of Malone," wrote the correspondent for the Memphis *Commercial-Appeal*, ". . . Women shrieked their approval. Men, unmoved even by Darrow, could not restrain their cheers. . . . People climbed over the rails to greet the New Yorker. Crowds surged into the aisle. It was a quarter of an hour before the room could be quieted." [60] The Daytonians showed unmistakably that despite their faith they could appreciate eloquence for its own sake. The reception accorded Malone was doubtless disquieting to Bryan, but it failed to make him more cautious. It failed also to move the Judge. When court opened on Friday morning, Judge Raulston read his ruling barring scientific testimony, though he dismissed the jury in order to allow the testimony to be read into the record in the event that the case was appealed to a higher court.[61] The court then adjourned until Monday.

Though the court was not in session the opposing attorneys continued to hammer away at one another throughout the weekend. On Saturday morning Darrow stated that although Bryan had been instrumental in precipitating the Scopes Trial and had called for a "battle to the death," his unwillingness to allow scientific testimony betrayed a lack of confidence in his own position and a fear of testing his views against those of eminent educators and scientists. Bryan, Darrow announced, "has fled from the field, his forces disorganized and his pretensions exposed." [62] On Sunday evening,

59. For Malone's speech see ibid. pp. 82 ff.
60. *Literary Digest*, LXXXVI (August 8, 1925), 46.
61. Allen, *Bryan and Darrow at Dayton*, pp. 91 ff.
62. *Chattanooga Daily Times*, July 18, 1925, clipping in Bryan Papers.

addressing an outdoor meeting in nearby Pikesville, Bryan spoke of "a gigantic conspiracy among atheists and agnostics against the Christian religion." He also took this occasion to strike back at the reporters who throughout the trial had been vilifying him and his followers. "These men," he told his listeners, "who come from another state to call you yokels and bigots, I wish I had them here to set them face to face with a humanity they cannot imitate. But in the end every critic you have will be rotted and forgotten." [63]

With the ruling out of scientific testimony it seemed that the trial was at an end. Darrow and his colleagues had based their entire case upon the testimony of the fifteen experts they had brought to Dayton, and there was apparently no one else they could call. H. L. Mencken was so positive that the trial was over that he packed his bags during the weekend and left the torrid Tennessee climate behind him, remarking that nothing remained to be done except "the formal business of bumping off the defendant." [64] With the end of the trial in sight the unusually large crowds that had been packing the courtroom grew larger still, for with such eloquent lawyers on both sides no one in or around Dayton wanted to miss the final arguments. Bryan had been waiting for this moment. For weeks he had been working on his final speech; a speech which he described as "the mountain peak of my life's effort." [65]

When the court reconvened on Monday morning Judge Raulston allowed the scientific experts to finish reading their testimony into the record, and then ordered the court to adjourn to the courthouse lawn for the danger of the building collapsing had increased with the crowd. This move was an

63. Allen, *Bryan and Darrow at Dayton*, pp. 108–9; Kemler, *The Irreverent Mr. Mencken*, p. 108.
64. Ginger, *Six Days or Forever?*, p. 146.
65. WJB, *The Last Message of William Jennings Bryan* (New York, 1925), pp. 7–8.

extremely popular one, since it allowed almost anyone who so desired to view the proceedings. The scene could not have been more propitious for the delivery of Bryan's final summation had he arranged it himself, but the defense had other ideas. As soon as the court was settled in its new surroundings Arthur Garfield Hays rose and asked Bryan to take the stand. This request, which according to Hays took even Darrow and Malone by surprise,[66] was vigorously opposed by Attorney General Stewart. Convinced as always of the righteousness of his cause, Bryan consented to testify despite Stewart's objections.

As Bryan took the stand, Darrow, clad in a blue shirt and blue suspenders, moved forward to examine him. Darrow, who had been an active supporter of Bryan in his earlier political battles, was nonetheless the perfect antithesis of Bryan in temperament and training. Raised on a diet of Darwin, Lyell, Buckle, Tyndall, and Spencer,[67] Darrow was an iconoclast, an agnostic, and in many respects a cynic, whose active, searching mind, unlike Bryan's, conceived of truth not as merely a possession to be defended but as a prize to be discovered. For the next two hours Darrow pursued Bryan relentlessly.[68]

Darrow began by questioning Bryan on his literal acceptance of the Scriptures. Did Bryan believe that the whale swallowed Jonah, that Joshua made the sun stand still, that the

66. Hays, *Let Freedom Ring*, p. 71. Ray Ginger disputes Hays's assertion and feels that Darrow's examination was premeditated and even rehearsed with Professor Kirtley Mather of Harvard acting as Bryan. See *Six Days or Forever?*, p. 148.

67. Darrow, *The Story of My Life*, p. 250.

68. For Darrow's examination of Bryan see Allen, *Bryan and Darrow at Dayton*, pp. 133 ff. The questions Darrow asked were first put to Bryan in 1923 through the newspapers. Bryan had refused to even look at them. "I know Mr. Darrow's attitude toward religion and I can give you an interview before reading the specific questions as well as I can after reading them." *New York Times*, July 5, 1923.

flood actually took place, that the different languages of the world really dated from the Tower of Babel, that Adam and Eve were the first people? To all of these questions Bryan answered in the affirmative, stating at one point that he would believe that Jonah swallowed the whale if the Bible said so for "one miracle is just as easy to believe as another." Darrow also endeavored to show Bryan's extremely narrow fund of knowledge. Bryan admitted that he knew little or nothing about ancient civilization, that he had never read a book on philology, that he never thought about how long man had been inhabiting the earth, or how old the earth itself was, that he knew nothing about Buddha or Confucius or Zoroaster, and that the entire subject of comparative religion was a vast wasteland to him.

Paradoxically, it was Bryan's more enlightened views rather than his narrower ones that probably led to his diminished popularity during the course of the trial. During their discussion of Joshua, Darrow forced Bryan to state reluctantly that he believed the earth moved around the sun and that in describing Joshua as having made the sun stand still the Bible was merely using language which the people of that time with their limited knowledge could understand. Similarly, in discussing the creation, Bryan admitted that the six days described in the Bible were probably not literal days but periods which might have encompassed millions of years. For the first time it became evident to many of Bryan's followers that their leader did not accept the Bible literally at all times. As we have seen, Bryan did not enter the fundamentalist movement primarily to defend the literal word of the Bible; his motives were far more complex than that. Bryan, in fact, seems to have been concerned about an absolutely literal reading of the Scriptures only in those areas where such an interpretation could help close the door upon a theory which he felt would have pernicious results for mankind. His literal acceptance of the Bible did not lead to his rejection of evolution so much as his rejection of evolution led to his willingness to accept literally certain portions of the Bible in the face of the educated portion of the community. Nevertheless, Bryan unquestionably committed a serious blunder in revealing his actual attitudes toward the creation and the story of Joshua on the stand, and it is probable that he regretted having done so.

During the examination Attorney General Stewart rose time and again to point out the irrelevancy of the proceedings and to demand that they be halted, but each time Bryan indicated his willingness to continue. "These gentlemen," he told Stewart at one point, "have not had much chance. They did not come here to try this case. They came here to try revealed religion. I am here to defend it, and they can ask me any questions they please." The nature of most of this much-heralded examination is illustrated by the following example:

> DARROW: Mr. Bryan, do you believe that the first woman was Eve?
> BRYAN: Yes.
> DARROW: Do you believe she was literally made out of Adam's rib?
> BRYAN: I do.
> DARROW: Did you ever discover where Cain got his wife?
> BRYAN: No, sir; I leave the agnostics to hunt for her.
> DARROW: . . . The Bible says he got one, doesn't it? Were there other people on the earth at that time?
> BRYAN: I cannot say.
> DARROW: You cannot say? Did that ever enter into your consideration?
> BRYAN: Never bothered me.

As questioning of this sort continued, the tempers of both men began to wear thin, and when Darrow returned to the question of Adam and Eve and demanded to know how the snake moved before God commanded him to crawl on his belly, Bryan grew angry and the following exchange took place:

> BRYAN: Your Honor, I think I can shorten this testimony. The only purpose Mr. Darrow has is to slur at the Bible, but I will answer his questions . . . and I have no objection in the world. I want the world to know that this man, who does not believe in God, is trying to use a court in Tennessee —
> DARROW: I object to that.
> BRYAN: to slur at it, and, while it will require time I am willing to take it.
> DARROW: I object to your statement. I am examining you on your fool ideas that no intelligent Christian on earth believes.

At this point both men were on their feet shaking their fists at one another. Judge Raulston banging his gavel promptly adjourned court until the next morning.[69]

Bryan had hoped to put Darrow on the stand the next day, but that night Stewart, who had opposed the cross-examination from the start and who had spoken to Judge Raulston immediately after court had adjourned, informed him that there would be no further examination of counsel on either side. When the court reconvened on Tuesday morning Judge Raulston ordered Bryan's testimony of the previous day expunged from the records. The time had now come for the final arguments, but the defense in declining to sum up their case dealt Bryan a final blow by depriving him · of the opportunity of delivering the speech which he had labored on for so long. In later years Darrow admitted that the defense had feared the effect that Bryan's oratory might have on the "assembled multitudes" and had felt that "by not making a closing argument on our side we could cut him down." [70]

The jury's verdict of guilty, which was arrived at after eight minutes of deliberation, surprised no one. Nor did it

69. Allen, *Bryan and Darrow at Dayton*, pp. 155–6.
70. Darrow, *The Story of My Life*, p. 260.

really disappoint anyone since Darrow and his colleagues had
desired such a verdict so that they might appeal the case to a
higher court.[71] Bryan in his few words of thanks to the court
said: "This case will stimulate investigation and investigation
will bring out information. The facts will be known, and
upon the facts as ascertained the decision will be rendered. I
think, my friends and your Honor, that if we are actuated by
the spirit that should actuate every one of us, no matter what
our views may be, we ought not only desire but pray that that
which is right will prevail, whether it be our way or some-
body else's."[72]

It was obvious that the Scopes Trial had done neither
Bryan nor his cause any good, but it is doubtful if Bryan ever
realized just how much harm it had done. He could not have
been unaware that the fundamentalists had received an enormous amount of bad publicity, that in the eight days of the
trial he and and his followers had been the objects of more scorn
and derision than the supporters of most causes generally receive in a lifetime. He also must have been aware that while
Darrow, Malone, and their colleagues had converted few
Daytonians to evolution, the force of their personalities and
eloquence had won the respect and even the friendship of
many of the local residents.[73] Nonetheless, Bryan took com-

71. Allen, *Bryan and Darrow at Dayton*, pp. 160–61.
72. Ibid. p. 163.
73. It has been too easily assumed that the increased esteem in
which Darrow and Malone were held at the end of the trial was the
result of the impact of their ideas. In reality, theirs was largely a
personal victory. They won friends but not followers. There is no
evidence to substantiate the view that the cause of scientific freedom
won many adherents in Dayton and the surrounding area at the close
of the Scopes Trial. The Tennessee anti-evolution statute has remained in force to this day. Several years ago when Senator Z. Carter
Patten of that state tried to have the law repealed he found only four
supporters of his repeal bill in both houses of the state legislature and
could not even get the bill out of committee. If Bryan lost popularity

fort in the knowledge that the anti-evolution statute had been upheld.

Nor was the trial a complete victory for the defense. In 1933, eight years after the Scopes Trial, Professor Howard K. Beale submitted a questionnaire to a cross-sampling of American teachers. One-third to one-half of them revealed that they were still afraid to express acceptance of the theory of evolution. But their inhibitions did not end here. One-fourth of the teachers polled felt it was unsafe to favor the abandonment of the Monroe Doctrine, criticize American actions in the Mexican War, or defend Britain's position in the American Revolution. One-third feared to disturb the aura of sanctity surrounding the heroes of American history. Large numbers felt it was dangerous to question the profit system or express disapproval of local businessmen. One-third were afraid to criticize President Hoover for using force to dispel the Bonus Army. Between one-third and one-half thought it the better part of discretion to avoid criticism of the Ku Klux Klan, the Daughters of the American Revolution, the American Legion, or the Confederate Veterans. Hardly any teachers felt it was safe to admit disbelief in God.[74]

Beale's study pointed out what should have been clear in 1925, but what, in fact, is still not entirely clear today — that the Scopes Trial was not unique; it was not merely an aberration of a backward part of the populace. "Try teaching communism in the schools of a community that denounced Tennesseean intolerance," Beale suggested.[75] The fact was that every American community had its sacred beliefs which no

among some of Dayton's residents due to the trial, it was not because they had been converted to Darrow's side, but because they were deeply disappointed at the concessions Bryan made under Darrow's questioning.

74. Howard K. Beale, *A History of Freedom of Teaching in American Schools* (New York, 1941), pp. 237–43.

75. Beale, *Are American Teachers Free?*, p. 258.

teacher could question with impunity. The "hired-man" theory for teachers was not restricted to any one section of the
country. When Bryan proclaimed: "The hand that writes the
pay check rules the school," he was not speaking for the fundamentalist South alone. The community whose teachers
were not governed by this dictum was a rare one. Men, however, are always reluctant to look too closely at their own
back yards. To view the Scopes Trial as symptomatic of the
evils in American education as a whole would have been too
painful an experience. The American people wanted to be
amused not perplexed by the trial, and they were not disappointed. They read with incredulity the lurid accounts of the
primitive hill folk of Tennessee; they chuckled with self-
satisfaction at the biting comments Mencken made at the expense of the "Babbitts," "morons," "peasants," "hill-billies,"
and "yokels" of Dayton; they shuddered with righteous indignation at the shameful lack of tolerance exhibited by the
people of the South; and they conveniently and comfortably
forgot that the teachers in their own communities wore muz-
zles hardly less restraining than the one placed on John
Thomas Scopes by the state of Tennessee.

To say this is not to deny the importance of the trial. The
prosecution, by dealing Bryan and his fellow fundamentalists
some heavy blows and by helping to check the spread of the
anti-evolution movement, unquestionably aided the cause of
academic freedom. Unfortunately, for too many Americans
the Scopes Trial was an end in itself. If Bryan and his followers were being simplistic in pointing to evolution as the root
cause of Christianity's ills, what can be said of their fellow
Americans who fastened upon fundamentalism as the only
real threat to education in the nation? It was important that
the battle in Dayton should have been waged, but it was no
less important to continue the struggle in the hundreds of
communities throughout the country where academic freedom still rested upon the shaky foundation of local prejudice

and whim. This simple fact was forgotten in the wave of jubilation that followed Bryan's humiliation in the Tennessee courtroom.

(4)

If Bryan left the Scopes Trial "an exhausted and broken man," as one writer has recently maintained,[76] he did a masterly job of concealing it during the five days of life remaining to him. The trial ended on Tuesday. Bryan spent Wednesday and Thursday in Dayton dictating his undelivered speech to his secretary, who typed it. Friday he traveled to Chattanooga to confer with George Fort Milton and arrange for the publication of his speech. The manuscript was taken to the Chattanooga Printing Company, and that evening Bryan began to read the first proof sheets. Early Saturday morning Mrs. Bryan drove down from Dayton, and she and her husband traveled to Winchester, Tennessee, the home of Judge Raulston and Attorney General Stewart, where Bryan was scheduled to speak.[77]

Before the Scopes Trial Bryan had announced his intention of retiring from the platform to devote his time to completing his memoirs and caring for his wife.[78] Subsequently, however, he made plans to lead a pilgrimage to Palestine during the coming winter,[79] and on his trip to Winchester he apparently indicated to his wife that he was going to carry on his fundamentalist crusade in the United States. Mrs. Bryan reminded him that care must be taken to prevent "the perfectly legitimate work" of protecting religion from degenerating into an encroachment upon individual religious belief; religious zeal must not become intolerance. Bryan responded: " 'Well,

76. Ginger, *Six Days or Forever?*, p. 175.
77. George Fort Milton, "Introduction," in WJB, *The Last Message*, p. 8; Grace Bryan Hargreaves MSS., Bryan Papers.
78. *New York Times*, June 4, 1925; WJB to W. B. Riley, March 27, 1925, Bryan Papers.
79. WJB to Charles F. Horner, June 30, 1925, ibid.

Mama, I have not made that mistake yet, have I.' And I replied, 'You are all right so far, but will you be able to keep to
this narrow path?' With a happy smile, he said, 'I think I can.'
'But,' said I, 'can you control your followers?' and more
gravely he said, 'I think I can.' And I knew he was adding
mentally, 'by the help of God.' " [80]

After his address in Winchester,[81] Bryan returned to
Chattanooga, where he spent the night reading proof. Sunday
morning at 9 a.m. he was back in Dayton and according to his
wife he was in an ebullient mood. He was pleased with the
progress the printers were making with his speech, he praised
his son's performance at the recent trial, he read a letter from
his oldest grandson that touched him, he was thankful for the
kindness of the people in Dayton. At eleven o'clock he went
to church and, asked to offer the prayer, he spoke for the last
time in public. At Sunday dinner he informed his wife of a
recent physical examination which indicated that he had at
least several more years to live.[82]

After dinner he made a few telephone calls to arrange for a
vacation in the Smoky Mountains for himself and his wife. At
three o'clock he phoned Milton in Chattanooga to discuss
his speech. "I want you to study this speech," he told the
editor. "I think it answers all the arguments of the evolutionists. . . . I am particularly hopeful that my speech will
be printed in full and distributed all over the country." [83] He
then lay down to take a nap from which he never arose. [84]

80. *Memoirs*, pp. 485-6.
81. For Bryan's Winchester address, see "The Last Speech of William Jennings Bryan," recorded and edited by Frank A. Pattie, *Tennessee Historical Quarterly*, VI (September 1947), 265-3.
82. *Memoirs*, pp. 486-7.
83. Bryan was to get his wish in this respect. The Associated Press
and the United Press sent every word of the 15,000 word address to all
of their clients, and the International News Service used almost one-
half of the text. Milton, "Introduction," in WJB, *The Last Message*,
pp. 9, 11.
84. The precise cause of Bryan's death is still a bit obscure. The

If Bryan's soul was, as his wife believed, still marching on "just beyond our mortal vision," it unquestionably enjoyed the final scenes — the thousands of letters of sympathy that poured in upon the widow; the funeral train speeding through the countryside on its way to Washington, D.C.; the crowds of farmers and their wives and children gathering at every little junction and station, even in the dead of night, to catch a glimpse of the train; the long lines of silent mourners who filed past the still body in Dayton, Chattanooga, Nashville, and Washington; the simple Christian eulogy spoken by a minister who as a young man had decided for the ministry after hearing Bryan lecture on religion. In death, as in life, William Jennings Bryan was tugging at the heartstrings of the people he loved so well.

newspapers reported that he died of apoplexy. See *New York Times,* July 27, 1925. Even his death, however, became the object of an attack by his enemies. Throughout most of his life Bryan had had a voracious appetite and his critics immediately accused him of having eaten himself to death. Clarence Darrow, for instance, upon being told that Bryan died of a broken heart is supposed to have mumbled: "Broken heart nothing; he died of a busted belly." Stone, *Clarence Darrow,* p. 64. In 1931, Bryan's daughter Grace, apparently still unsure of the nature of her father's death, wrote a letter of inquiry to his personal physician, Dr. J. Thomas Kelly. Although Kelly was not present when Bryan died and did not examine the body, his reply is the closest thing we have to a first-hand medical report. "In March 1914," he wrote, "at Mrs. Bryan's solicitation I examined the urine of Mr. Bryan and found it loaded with sugar, in other words, he had diabetes. He was immediately put on an anti-diabetic diet *and continued on the diet up to the time of his death.* I saw Mr. Bryan at frequent intervals, examined his urine and changed his diet as seen fit. . . . I saw many newspaper pictures of Mr. Bryan while he was in Tennessee and felt very apprehensive for him. You will remember it was very warm and *he was looking very thin.* Mr. Bryan died of diabetes melitis, the immediate cause being the fatigue incident to the heat and his extraordinary exertions due to the Scopes Trial." J. Thomas Kelly to Grace Bryan Hargreaves, June 25, 1931, Bryan Papers. Italics added.

Epilogue

(1)

AT THE OUTSET of this study I mentioned Bryan's caveat against evaluating a man on the basis of one segment of his life. I have tried to keep this in mind throughout this work. And yet, at its conclusion, it is difficult to refrain from pointing to his last years as a finely structured microcosm of his entire career. The impulses which drove him to act, the goals toward which his actions were directed, the characteristics which he exhibited, were not peculiar to his final years but were threads which stretched from the beginning of his life in Illinois through his Nebraska-based political career to his last few years in the South. Those last years may have witnessed the development of a number of variations in Bryan's life, but these are of less importance than the old drives which continued to exert a dominating influence.

The basis of Bryan's actions was Christian morality. His was not the shifting, often doubting mind of the pragmatic element within progressivism. Never did he echo the lament of J. Allen Smith: "The real trouble with us reformers is that we made reform a crusade against standards. Well, we smashed them all and now neither we nor anybody else have anything left." [1] Bryan's sense of Christian ethics and standards was not altered; it remained supreme. And always it was *social* Christianity. The message of Christ was not merely preparation for the future world but a mandate for this world as well. It was not a purely individual message but a corporate one. Man's

1. Eric F. Goldman, *Rendezvous with Destiny* (New York, 1956, Vintage edition), p. 240.

358

task was not merely to remake himself and await salvation but to remake society and create an earthly salvation. The Cross of Gold was not simply a temptation to be resisted; it was one that had to be destroyed in all of its varying forms — war, alcohol, greed, godlessness.

This devotion to Christian ideals did not mean that Bryan was not capable of compromise — he was, but not as Mencken believed because he was a charlatan or as others believed because he was primarily a politician, but rather because he remained a democrat. His democracy was the formative force behind all his compromises and all his putative opportunism: his role in passing the treaty ending the Spanish-American War, his late entry into the prohibition movement, his acceptance of American entry into World War I, his crusade against evolution. Never could Bryan entertain any objections to the sanctity of the will of the majority. His democracy was based upon the Jacksonian model. Collective wisdom was superior to individual wisdom; *every* man was capable of and worthy of directly participating in the governmental process, for what was important was not a man's training but his spirit.

In this latter respect Bryan's democracy and his Christianity complemented one another. But there were certain tensions as well. Bryan's doctrine, "The hand that writes the paycheck rules the school," was a dangerous one which he never fully explored. What if the majority of people in a school district were Catholic or Jewish or pagan? This of course was always an implicit danger in the democratic method, but Bryan had learned to live with it, comforted by his unwavering belief that the majority would usually or at least ultimately be on the side of righteousness — that, in short, the majority shared his own tenets. This belief was the rock upon which Bryan's compulsive optimism — still another of his enduring characteristics — was founded. I have alluded to this optimism frequently throughout this work, but perhaps an even more accurate word for it would be faith: faith that Americans were fundamentally pacific and dry and progressive and godly. Thus he could see the Gore-McLemore Resolutions defeated and preparedness adopted and go on working for the former and against the latter as if nothing had changed; thus he could see his country enter a war and go on believing in ultimate peace; thus he could see the Eighteenth Amendment widely flouted and go on stating that prohibition would sweep over the world in his own lifetime; thus he could see his people turn their backs on reform and go on proclaiming them progressives; thus he could see the growing materialism of the nation in the Twenties and go on calling its people religious. Each one of these changes was classified in his mind as an aberration, the work of a small clique or interest. His picture of the American, first formed in the nineteenth century, remained intact and no amount of change could alter it. It was, of course, a picture that still fit many millions of Americans, but its application was rapidly narrowing and with it Bryan's influence. Had Bryan ever truly grasped this, he might indeed have become the embittered and frustrated old man that has so often been pictured. The fact is that he did not or would not or could not see it. Thus his optimism continued. But he paid a fearful price for the luxury of his faith — a constantly diminishing understanding of the realities of a changing America.

The fact that must be constantly borne in mind is that at no stage of his career was Bryan a national leader. To Bryan the "majority" meant always the majority of those who came from those sections of the country which he represented and who fundamentally accepted the values he felt were essential. Bryan himself never understood his own ethnocentrism or the increasing narrowness of his following. That he could so easily confuse the majority of a section or a type with the

majority of the nation is an important clue to his whole orientation toward his nation and his people. For not the least
important of Bryan's enduring characteristics was his sec-
tionalism. Until his death Bryan remained the spokesman for
Western and Southern agrarian and small town America, and
at no time was he able to really adjust to the changes brought
about by industrialization, urbanization, and the new immigration, all of which seemed to be shaping an America alien to
his experience and expectations.

Bryan not only felt that he had to win his struggles without
the aid of the urban Northeast, *he preferred to win without
it*. As long as the urban sections of the nation remained dominated by political and financial conservatism there was little
noticeable tension between the reformist and anti-urban tend-
encies in agrarian progressivism. But as the history of the
Democratic party in the Twenties and the career of a number
of rural progressives in the Thirties illustrate, this tension was
always implicit in the rural reform tradition. The agrarians
were not anti-urban solely because the urban elements tended
to be dominated by economic and political conservatism. The
antipathy to urbanism was cultural as surely as it was anything else. This fact is central in understanding the actions of
Bryan and his followers in the Twenties and especially their
relationship to such new urban reformers as Al Smith. For
those who prefer to keep their reformism pure, it is pleasant to
dismiss the Bryan of the Twenties as an apostate, as an ex-
progressive, but we can do this only at the price of neglecting
the complex and ambiguous nature of much of the American
reform tradition. It was based upon a set of values and aspirations which included economic and political reform but also
included the maintenance of a way of life based upon a familiar and traditional model. The two did not merely live side by
side, they were inextricably bound together. Bryan had become interested in certain aspects of Populism and later Pro-

gressivism because he felt the reforms espoused by their followers were necessary for the integrity of the rural way of
life in a changing world. He became interested in prohibition
and anti-evolution for precisely the same reasons. In the
1890's he had waged war upon such leaders of the New York
Democracy as Grover Cleveland and David B. Hill, because
he saw them at the head of a movement destined to disrupt
and obscure the life of that part of the nation with which he
was identified. In the 1920's he fought Al Smith for identical
reasons.

Bryan's career, of course, was not quite so simple as this; it
did include paradox. Throughout his career, and especially in
the 1920's, Bryan was an outspoken champion of the urban
laborer. This was due both to political considerations and to
his deep humanitarianism and sense of justice. But just as
Bryan never recognized the full implications of his fundamentalist crusade for the future of the reform tradition, so too
he was unable to see the implications of his attempts to elevate
the urban masses for the future of agrarianism in the United
States. No less paradoxical was Bryan's attempt, through his
consistent emphasis upon the social gospel, to focus the attention of the church on the problems of a modern society and
his attempt, through the fundamentalist movement, to make it
hew the line of traditional theology. Ultimately, the paradox
of Bryan's final years was in a sense the paradox of American
history itself: a faith in the inevitability of progress coupled
with a desire to see America remain unchanged. Americans
have never been able to resist the lure of change but neither
have they been able to quell in themselves a certain dread of
it. Jefferson could speak of America's destined growth and
power and influence at the same time he urged it to remain a
nation of agrarians. Bryan helped to perpetuate this ambivalence; an ambivalence which colored so many of his earlier

reform efforts and continued to shape the character of his last years.

(2)

The enduring threads which run throughout Bryan's career have been obscured by the misguided effort to characterize him at various stages of his career as *either* a progressive or a reactionary, without understanding that a liberal in one area may be a conservative in another not only at the same time but also for the same reasons. Bryan has been taken to task for his tendency to view the world in terms of blacks and whites by men who have committed this very error in their own estimates of Bryan himself. It is entirely possible to applaud certain of Bryan's actions and to deplore others, but it is not accurate to separate them by a fixed chronological line or to ignore the fact that in all of his acts Bryan was attempting to achieve the same ends, and that more often than not he continued to espouse eloquently and accurately the hopes and the fears of the people he represented. Bryan remained to the very end of his life the creature and not the creator of his environment.

This is not to say that Bryan was exactly the same man in 1925 that he had been in 1896. Bryan, like most men, was subject to certain subtle changes in outlook. During the Twenties he began to put more faith in such non-governmental agencies as the church, and despite his continued and even expanded advocacy of governmental intervention in the economy he began to place more reliance upon individual action in bringing about the good society. It was becoming increasingly important in his scheme of things to have the individual American remain theologically and morally pure. This, in part, explains his participation in the prohibition and fundamentalist crusades and his desire to launch a battle against gambling and the "social evil." But none of this warrants calling him a changed man. The apparent transition in Bryan from the herald of reform to the guardian of tradition was due to a change in the age rather than a change in the man.

To represent the latter-day Bryan as a reactionary pure and simple is not only to oversimplify the complexities of the entire Progressive Era but also to do violence to the facts. During the very years when Bryan stood before religious gatherings denouncing evolution he also went before political rallies to plead for progressive labor legislation, liberal tax laws, government aid to farmers, public ownership of railroads, telegraphs, and telephones, federal development of water resources, minimum wages for labor, minimum prices for agriculture, maximum profits for middlemen, and government guarantee of bank deposits. Bryan's "apostasy" did not take place in those areas in which his progressivism had long been manifest, and in any case, as I have tried to show, there is far more consistency throughout all of his work than has generally been recognized. Bryan represented the agrarian wing of the progressive movement whose roots were deeply embedded in Populism. This populist-progressive mind which he so well exemplified was neither a particularly open or tolerant one. It did not seek, it knew. Its weapons were not pragmatic but moral. Its outlook was not relative but absolute. When viewed in this light there is little difference in essence between the political and religious Bryan. In both spheres he was a moral crusader; a petitioner for, not a seeker after, truth. In both spheres he was attempting to protect the common man from what he conceived to be selfish and irresponsible forces. In neither area was he willing to bear fundamental dissent, for one who *knows* the truth is morally culpable if he tolerates error. In the economic realm Bryan had been a consistent advocate of limiting individual freedom when it reached the point of becoming harmful to others. He saw no difference between intellectual man and economic man; both could be dangerous, and both must be controlled. Above all, Bryan, in his political and religious struggles, was attempting to maintain the basic, fundamental order which he had been taught to believe in and which he saw threatened by the emerging forces of industrialism and science. The Bryan of the Scopes Trial, for all his dismal obscurantism, was after all merely struggling in behalf of the three great faiths of his life — majority rule, the sanctity of the Bible, and the primacy of the rural way of life.

When the Bryan Memorial was unveiled in Washington, D.C., on May 3, 1934, President Franklin D. Roosevelt, during the course of his dedicatory speech, aptly quoted the following remarks which Bryan had spoken at the Democratic convention of 1904:

> You may dispute over whether I have fought a good fight; you may dispute over whether I have finished my course; but you cannot deny that I have kept the faith.[2]

And so he had. And if his final years ended in tragedy, it was not the tragedy of a good man gone bad, but the tragedy of a good faith too blindly held and too uncritically applied.

2. *William Jennings Bryan Memorial: Ceremonies Attending the Dedication of the Memorial to William Jennings Bryan* (Washington, D.C., 1934), p. 60.

Bibliographical Note

THE SOURCES used for this reconstruction of Bryan's final years are cited in full in the footnotes and no attempt will be made here to list them again. This note will be restricted to those sources most directly related to Bryan himself.

The Bryan Papers in the Library of Congress, though fuller for his final years than for most other periods of his life, are unfortunately incomplete. Nevertheless, they contain important materials available nowhere else. These include Bryan's correspondence, drafts of Bryan's speeches, copies of press releases, newspaper clippings, various personal data, such as an inventory of Bryan's library, and copies of memoranda and statements of a number of Bryan's friends and relatives, the most important of which is Grace Bryan Hargreaves's unfinished manuscript biography of her father. Equally indispensible are the files of Bryan's periodical, *The Commoner*. This was a totally Bryan-centered journal and contains not only Bryan's views on almost every conceivable subject but also news of Bryan's travels and activities, the texts of his important addresses, newspaper stories and editorials relating to Bryan from papers in every part of the country, and extremely valuable correspondence columns in which the views of Bryan's readers and followers are presented. *The Memoirs of William Jennings Bryan* (Philadelphia: The United Publishers of America, 1925), which was completed by Mrs. Bryan, characteristically lacks any introspective quality but is important for Bryan's own views concerning his career and for Mrs. Bryan's all too seldom recorded attitudes.

Bryan was a prolific author throughout his career and his final years were no exception. The following writings are all valuable for a study of his last years:

A. BOOKS AND PAMPHLETS

The Prince of Peace (Chicago: The Reilly & Britton Co., 1909).
A Defense of County Option: Speech (in part) of Hon. William Jennings Bryan Before the Democratic State Convention at Grand Island, Nebraska, July 26, 1910 (no publisher or date).
The Forces That Make for Peace: Addresses at the Mohonk Conferences on International Arbitration (Boston: World Peace Foundation, 1912).

Speeches of William Jennings Bryan. 2 vols. (New York: Funk & Wagnalls Co., 1913).

Two Addresses Delivered by William Jennings Bryan at Peace Meetings Held in New York June 19 and 24, 1915 (no publisher or date).

Prohibition: Address by Hon. William Jennings Bryan Presenting in Substance the Line of Argumentatiton by Him in the Sixty Speeches Made in Ohio during the Week of October 25 to 30, 1915 (Washington, D.C.: United States Government Printing Office, 1916).

Temperance Lecture Delivered Before the 128th General Assembly of the Presbyterian Church at Atlantic City, New Jersey, Sunday, May 21, 1916 (J. J. Hamilton Co., 1916).

Address of Hon. William Jennings Bryan to the Forty-Ninth General Assembly of the State of Missouri, January 24, 1917 (Jefferson City, Missouri: Hugh Stephens Co., 1917).

America and the European War: Address by William Jennings Bryan at Madison Square Garden, New York City, February 2, 1917 (New York: Emergency Peace Federation, 1917).

World Peace: A Written Debate Between William Howard Taft and William Jennings Bryan (New York: George H. Doran Co., 1917).

The First Commandment (New York: Fleming H. Revell Co., 1917).

Heart to Heart Appeals (New York: Fleming H. Revell Co., 1917).

In His Image (New York: Fleming H. Revell Co., 1922).

Famous Figures of the Old Testament (New York: Fleming H. Revell Co., 1922).

Orthodox Christianity versus Modernism (New York: Fleming H. Revell Co., 1923).

Seven Questions in Dispute (New York: Fleming H. Revell Co., 1924).

Christ and His Companions: Famous Figures of the New Testament (New York: Fleming H. Revell Co., 1925).

The Last Message of William Jennings Bryan (New York: Fleming H. Revell Co., 1925).

"The Last Speech of William Jennings Bryan," recorded and edited by Frank A. Pattie, *Tennessee Historical Quarterly* VI (September 1947), 265–83.

B. ARTICLES AND EDITORIALS

The Commoner, 1904, 1905, 1915–23.

"Why I Lecture," *Ladies Home Journal,* XXXII (April 1915), 9.

"The Democrats Should Win," *The Independent,* LXXXVI (April 3, 1916), 13–14.

"Citizenship in a Republic," *School and Society,* IV (July 15, 1916), 86–8.

"Why I am for Prohibition," *The Independent*, LXXXVII(July 17,
1916), 88–9.

"Prohibition's Progress," *The Independent*, XC (May 19, 1917), 332.

"The Rights of Residents," *The Independent*, XCVIII (April 5, 1919),
12–13.

"Single Moral Standard," *Collier's* LXV (March 13, 1920), 7.

"Democratic Policies at San Francisco," *Review of Reviews*, LXII
(July 1920), 42–5.

"A National Bulletin," *Forum*, LXV (April 1921), 455–8.

"God and Evolution," *New York Times*, February 26, 1922, Section VII.

"Prohibition," *The Outlook*, CXXXIII (February 7, 1923), 262–5.

"Our Responsibility for the Ruhr Invasion," *Current History*, XVII
(March 1923), 898–9.

"Morals for Men and Women," *Hearst's International* (June 1923),
29–32.

"The Fundamentals," *Forum*, LXX (July 1923), 1665–80.

"My Brother Charles," *World's Work*, XLVIII (September 1924),
548.

"Mr. Bryan Speaks to Darwin," *Forum*, LXXIV (July 1925), 101–7.

THE BRYAN-WILSON CORRESPONDENCE and other Bryan materials in the
National Archives contain information relating to his resignation and
some of his later activities. Because of the incompleteness of Bryan's
own papers, the manuscripts of his contemporaries constitute an im-
portant body of sources for his resignation, his peace crusade, and his
subsequent political actions. Especially valuable are the Ray Stannard
Baker Papers, the Albert S. Burleson Papers, the Josephus Daniels
Diary and Papers, the Gilbert M. Hitchcock Papers, the Robert Lan-
sing Diary and Papers, the William G. McAdoo Papers, the Louis F.
Post Papers, the Thomas J. Walsh Papers, the Woodrow Wilson
Papers, and the Robert W. Woolley Memoirs and Papers — all in the
Library of Congress — and the Warren Worth Bailey Papers in the
Princeton University Library. The Chandler P. Anderson Diary and
Papers, the Charles S. Hamlin Diary and Papers, the James Hay col-
lection, the Richmond P. Hobson Papers, and the John Sharp Wil-
liams Papers — all in the Library of Congress — are less valuable but
contain materials relating to Bryan's career between his resignation
and 1920. The George Fort Milton Scrapbooks and Papers in the
Library of Congress contain some interesting materials on Bryan's
post-1920 career, but the W. Bourke Cockran Papers in the New
York Public Library are thin for this period. On the Scopes Trial, the
American Civil Liberties Union Archives in the Princeton University

Library are valuable, while the Clarence Darrow Papers in the Library of Congress are primarily a collection of secondary materials available elsewhere.

In addition to these collections, Bryan figured prominently in the published autobiographies, memoirs, reminiscences, eye-witness accounts, correspondence, and addresses of his contemporaries. Of the many such sources listed in the footnotes, those by Josephus Daniels, Clarence Darrow, Mrs. J. Borden Harriman, Arthur Garfield Hays, David F. Houston, Robert Lansing, William G. McAdoo, H. L. Mencken, Arthur F. Mullen, George W. Norris, Daniel C. Roper, Alfred E. Smith, Charles Willis Thompson, Joseph P. Tumulty, and William Allen White, are particularly important for his final years, as are the published letters of Franklin D. Roosevelt, edited by Elliott Roosevelt, of Theodore Roosevelt, edited by Elting E. Morison, of William Allen White, edited by Walter Johnson, and the published papers of Colonel House, edited by Charles Seymour.

Bryan's activities were well covered in the newspapers and magazines of the period. The files of the *New York Times, New York World, New York American, Nebraska State Journal,* and *Omaha World-Herald,* were particularly helpful, as was the clippings collection in the Library of the School of Journalism, Columbia University. In addition to the magazines used for the many specific articles cited in the footnotes, the following periodicals provided useful materials and insights relating to Bryan and his causes: *The American Mercury, Literary Digest, The Nation, New Republic, The Outlook, Review of Reviews, World's Work.*

Paul W. Glad, *The Trumpet Soundeth: William Jennings Bryan and his Democracy, 1896–1912* (Lincoln: University of Nebraska Press, 1960), is the most successful study of Bryan yet published, though it is not concerned with the period covered in this work. Of the biographies published to date, Paxton Hibben, *The Peerless Leader: William Jennings Bryan* (New York: Farrar and Rinehart, 1929), which was completed after Hibben's death by C. Hartley Grattan, is probably the best, though it is unsympathetic and often harsh in its judgments. M. R. Werner, *Bryan* (New York: Harcourt, Brace and Co., 1929), is also extremely hostile. J. C. Long, *Bryan, the Great Commoner* (New York: D. Appleton & Co., 1928), is the best of the sympathetic biographies. Genevieve F. and John D. Herrick, *The Life of William Jennings Bryan* (Grover C. Buxton, 1925), and Wayne C. Williams, *William Jennings Bryan* (New York: G. P. Putnam's Sons, 1936), are appreciations written by supporters of Bryan. Charles McDaniel Rosser, *The Crusading Commoner: A Close-up of William Jennings Bryan and His Times* (Dallas: Mathis, Van Nort & Co., 1937), is an uncritical account written by a long-time friend of Bryan's but is valuable for the correspondence and personal recollections it contains. Merle E. Curti, *Bryan and World Peace* (Northampton, Massachusetts: "Smith College Studies in History," Vol. XVI, Nos. 3–4, April–July 1931), is an excellent study of Bryan's peace crusade. Provocative essays which relate to Bryan's last years, may be found in Richard Hofstadter, *The American Political Tradition* (New York: Vintage Book Edition, 1954), Walter Lippmann, *Men of Destiny* (New York: The Macmillan Co., 1927), Charles E. Merriam, *Four American Party Leaders* (New York: The Macmillan Co., 1926), and William Allen White, *Masks in a Pageant* (New York: The Macmillan Co., 1930).

In his final years, as before, Bryan was a favorite subject for magazine articles. The following provide useful information and interpretations:

Brooks, Sydney. "Mr. Bryan," *The Living Age*, CCLXXXVI (August 7, 1915), 323–32.

Creel, George. "The Commoner," *Harper's Weekly*, LX (June 26, 1915), 604–6.

Daniels, Josephus. "Wilson and Bryan," *Saturday Evening Post*, CXCVIII (September 5, 1925), 6–7.

DeCasseres, Benjamin. "The Complete American," *The American Mercury*, X (February 1927), 143–7.

Frank, Glenn. "William Jennings Bryan: a Mind Divided Against Itself," *Century*, CVI (September 1923), 793–800.

Hall, Frederick. "Bryan, Radio, and Religion," *The Outlook*, CXXXVII (July 30, 1924), 510–12.

Hard, William. "What about Bryan?" *Everybody's*, XXXIV (April 1916), 453–66.

Harvey, George. "The Revolt of Bryan," *North American Review*, CCII (July 1915), 1–6.

Kitson Arthur. "William Jennings Bryan," *Fortnightly Review*, CXXIV (October 1925), 558–67.

Krutch, Joseph Wood. "Darrow vs. Bryan," *The Nation*, CXXI (July 29, 1925), 136–7.

Masters, Edgar Lee. "The Christian Statesman," *The American Mercury*, III (December 1924), 385–98.

Merritt, Dixon. "Bryan at Sixty-Five," *The Outlook*, CXL (June 3, 1925), 181–2.

Milton, George Fort. "Mr. Bryan's Position," *Review of Reviews*, LII (August 1915), 213–16.

Norris, George W. "Bryan As a Political Leader," *Current History*, XXII (September 25, 1925), 859–67.

Osborn, Henry Fairfield. "The Earth Speaks to Bryan," *Forum*, LXXIII (June 1925), 796–803.

Reed, John. "Bryan on Tour," *Collier's* LVII (May 20, 1916), 11–12.

Sears, Louis Martin. "The Presidency in 1924—William Jennings Bryan?" *Forum*, LXX (August 1923), 1809–16.

Shaw, Albert. "William Jennings Bryan," *Review of Reviews*, LXXII (August 1925), 259–63.

Smith, T. V. "Bases of Bryanism," *Scientific Monthly*, XVI (May 1923), 505–13.

Ward, Henshaw. "Uncle Jasper and Mr. Bryan: Fundamentalism and Absurdity," *The Independent*, CXIV (May 2, 1925), 494–6.

Williams, Wayne C. "Democracy's Law Giver," *The Commoner* (May 1920), 13.

1968

While my book was in press, Paolo E. Coletta published the first volume of his biography, *William Jennings Bryan—Political Evangelist, 1860-1908* (Lincoln: University of Nebraska Press, 1964). If the second volume lives up to the standards set by the first, this will rank as the most scholarly, detailed, and balanced full-length biography of Bryan.

L.W.L.

Index